Oliver Heywood

The Nonconformist Register, of Baptisms, Marriages, and Deaths

Oliver Heywood

The Nonconformist Register, of Baptisms, Marriages, and Deaths

ISBN/EAN: 9783337403423

Printed in Europe, USA, Canada, Australia, Japan

Cover: Foto ©Suzi / pixelio.de

More available books at **www.hansebooks.com**

THE
Nonconformist Register.

Of Baptisms, Marriages, and Deaths,

Compiled by the

REVS OLIVER HEYWOOD & T. DICKENSON,

1644-1702, -1702-1752,

Generally known as the

am or Coley Register,

merous notices of Puritans and Anti-

rkshire, Lancashire, Cheshire,

London, &c.

ish Recusants, Quakers, &c.

—◆—

HORSFALL TURNER.

—◆—

LUSTRATIONS.

—◆—

BRIGHOUSE:

T, PRINTER, "NEWS" OFFICE.

—

MDCCCLXXXI.

CONTENTS.

ILLUSTRATIONS :

INTRODUCTION.

The " Nonconformist Register," more frequently styled the
" Northowram Register," being now in the hands of the Subscribers, the Editor has confidence in reprinting his description
of it:—

" No idea can be conveyed by such words as Register or
" Obituary of the multitudinous and multifarious Entries in this
" valuable MS. of 300 pages, which is often referred to by such
" writers as the Rev. Joseph Hunter, F.S.A.

" The words ' Puritan ' and ' Northowram ' equally fail to
" describe its character and scope. It is a supplement to many
" of the West Riding Registers, particularly those of Halifax and
" Bradford, and exceeds in details of incidents anything I have
" seen. Popes, Kings, Princes, Peers, Judges, Justices,
" Parsons, Peasants, Doctors, Lawyers, Schoolmasters, Soldiers,
" Conformist and Nonconformist Ministers, Quakers and Centen-
" arians find equal admission to these pages.

" Some hundreds of sudden deaths are recorded, and, which
" is very exceptional, the ages of deceased persons are generally
" given. The whole is spiced with remarks on character or pos-
" sessions, notices of runaway weddings, and incidents ' too
" numerous to mention.' "

I am sorry that so long time has elapsed since the publication of the Register was announced. The delay has occurred in
connection with the printer's arrangements. The Indexes have
cost an incredible amount of labour, but having done the
work alone, (probably 35,000 references,) I believe there will be
found but few errors. There is a tendency in indexing to put the
number of the page one too little, as 78 for 79.

As only a limited Subscription List can be expected for such
books, economy has been a great feature in the get-up, but the
accuracy has not suffered. It is an individual effort, backed by
no public Society, at a third the cost of Society prices, and
done by an Amateur *pro bono publico*.

The MS. has had a remarkable career for 240 years. It
would seem to have been the property of Coley Chapel six years
before Mr. Heywood became Curate there, and at the Ejection in

1662, he took the book with him. It was almost a blank book
in 1650 when he became Custodian, and, as the names would be
annually sent to the Registrar at Halifax Parish Church, there
was little in it which would be thought of any interest. Mr.
Heywood also kept a private Register in his Vellum Book with
one Clasp. On page 109, I have stated that these Vellum-Book
records have been copied into the Northowram Register in a
slightly more modern hand. There is little doubt that the copy-
ist was Mr. Dickenson, not Mr Heywood as I thought at first.
The perusal of some of Mr. Dickenson's MSS., at Mr. Swaine's,
near Guildford, confirms this, and I am surprised how I should
have mistaken Mr. Heywood's familiar handwriting. Just as the
printer was drawing to a close, this identical " Vellum Book with
One Clasp " came into my hands, along with several other volumes
of Mr. Heywood's MSS. (Diaries, &c.), and I find that the addi-
tions to Mr. Heywood's portion of the Northowram Register will
make about sixty pages. These, with his Diaries and Note Books,
referring to his wonderful journeys and numerous acquaintances,
will form a companion volume to the " Register " now in the
Reader's hands, and will be issued speedily.

Mr. Dickenson (and this is very remarkable) continued the
work his worthy predecessor had begun, for nearly another half
century. Members of the Dickenson family seem to have made
occasional entries afterwards. According to Mr. Slate, the " Register " became the property of the late Rev. Dr. Ryland. The
late Joshua Wilson, Esq., of Tunbridge Wells, became the owner,
rumour says, (though I cannot see any reason for it,) in return
for a subscription to Northowram Chapel. He lent it to several
gentlemen at Halifax, who made copious notes from it, and I had
the promise of it, but as Mrs. Wilson could not find it again, I
wrote (in my anxiety for its safety) to the Rev. Professor Newth,
Librarian *pro tem.* for the Congregational Memorial Hall Library,
to which Mr. Wilson had offered a large contribution of books.
Prof. Newth found the MS., and for further favours I gladly
return thanks to the Rev. Dr. Wilson and Mr. Knox Wilson.

The MS. is a small 4to, now inlaid in a firmly bound large
4to, bearing, on a fly leaf, the inscription :—" This Register hav-
" ing come into the possession of the late Joshua Wilson, Esq.,
" of Tunbridge Wells, is presented by Mrs. Wilson to the Con-
" gregational Library Memorial Hall. The MS. being in a dela-
" pidated state and the leaves too closely written to admit of

"binding, the whole has been inlaid in the present volume by my "daughter, under my direction.—SAMUEL NEWTH, November, "1877."

On the first fly leaf of the original Register are the following names (query—their purport):

Jan. 10. 1660	Samuel Spencer	Mary Burkhead
James Tetlaw	Abraham Brigge	Sarah Burkhead
Mary Tetlaw	Judith Brigge	Anne Rushworth
Mary Roides	Susanna Brigge	Sarah Rushworth
Susanna Earnshaw	Mary Smith	Susanna Rushworth
Sarah Bland	Richard Murgatroyd	John Aked
John Kershaw	Abraham Nickol	Nathaniel Aked
John Wilson	Isaac Nickol	Joshua Bartle
Mary Kershaw	John Nickol	John Askwith
Sarah Pollard	Abigail Nickol	Mary Aked
John Mitchell	Nehemiah Burkhead	Hanna Aked
Will. Mitchell	Grace Burkhead	Sarah Thomas.

Some of Mr. Heywood's entries of funerals are erroneously numbered, it will be seen; and it may be useful to state that the abbreviation *minr.* indicates minister, not minor.

Coley is one of the twelve ancient chapelries of Halifax Parish. It has no township, but the district comprises part of Hipperholme, Northowram, and Shelf, the Church being erected in the first-named township, on a bleak hill, hence its *cold* and *wintry* name. From boyhood, Mr Oliver Heywood has been more than human to me. I do not wonder that Mr Dickenson left a blank leaf in the Register, and yet no record of Mr Heywood's death, for, years before I saw the Northowram Register, in a series of articles on Coley Church, I acted similarly, merely giving his name and a promise of future notice. Good Dr. Fawcett had only two of his MS. volumes, and even those two he could not read as he confesses, and as will be seen on comparing the volume of Mr. Heywood's Diaries, now in the press, with the Doctor's *Life of Heywood.* Mr Slate copies these blunders, yet reveals more of the inner life of the venerable Puritan. Mr. Hunter, as an accomplished antiquary, is thoroughly accurate. Yet all three fail to some extent; the old man tells his own tale best. And tell it he shall, for by a singular and unexpected concurrence of events many of the original MS. volumes have been handed to me, and I have found that I could talk to and travel with my old friend, and find the half had not been told me. Ono hundred and eighty years have fled since his remains were deposited in the south chapel at Halifax Church, and nearly forty since Mr. Hunter's *Life* appeared, and I for one shall not be satisfied till every line of his MS. be printed, a worthy and useful memorial of one of Nature's noblemen.

I have compared most of Mr. Heywood's references to Bradford, Calverley and Bingley people, and many Halifax people, with the entries in the parish registers of those places, and am highly gratifred, almost astonished, at his accuracy.

My Notes to the Register, alphabetically arranged according to Families, would without an effort take as many pages as the Register itself. An idea of this may be formed by consulting one article, that on the Rooks family, in the *Bradford Antiquary*. Similar articles can be compiled on scores of families mentioned in this Register. Indeed, I have come to the conclusion that this Register will have to be a local book of reference.

Calamy's Lives of the Ejected will be well known to most readers. Autobiographies of Capt. Hodgson, Joseph Lister, Thomas Wright, are only a little less known. Halley's *Lancashire*, Mr. Abram's *Blackburn*, and numerous other Lancashire publications may be consulted with advantage. *Congregationalism in Yorkshire*, particularly Mr. Scale's Notes in the Appendix, *The Manchester Socinian Controversy*, Whitaker's *Funeral Sermons*, and other similar books occur to the mind as rendering help in many cases. Indeed, of writing notes to this Register there is no end.

I rejoice greatly that there is a growing desire to publish Parish Registers. Those affording special help to this book are : *Bradford Parish Register* from 1596, in the *Bradford Antiquary; Halifax Parish Register* from 1538, a noble undertaking, and *Calverley Parish Register* from 1574, edited by my friend Mr. S. Margerison.

The publication of these Registers, and especially of the Diaries and other MSS. of Mr. Heywood render it advisable to postpone the notes to a future local work.

I gladly acknowledge my obligations to the Rev. B. Dale, M.A., of Halifax, for valuable hints ; the Rev. C. B. Norcliffe, M.A., of York, for several notes from his vast collection; to Mr. W. J. Vint, for the loan of two plates ; to Mr. W. Scruton, for artistic work on Northowram Chapel ; to the Rev. W. H. Wawn, for the sketch of Coley Church ; to Mr. A. B. Sewell, for permission to compare Heywood's Register with the Bradford Parish Register.

In common with all the members of the Yorkshire Archæological Association I have to deplore the sad loss by death of Fairless Barber, Esq., F.S.A. To him I was indebted for pointing out the treasures hid away in the Sessions' Rolls at Wakefield, and for preparing the way for their consultation. The fifty pages added to Heywood's Register is but a tithe of this subject. He commenced to publish notes on other topics in the *Yorkshire Archæological Journal*. Numerous favours, days of congenial intercourse, added to his special interest in the Life of the Rev. Oliver Heywood, and his desire to see the Heywood MSS. placed in a permanent form, render it obligatory that I should pay this slight tribute to the memory of a generous Christian friend.

I have some original notes respecting Mr. Dickenson and Northowram Chapel, culled from papers during a visit to Brabœuf Manor, Guildford.

Mr. Jonathan Priestley, of Winteredge, (Mr. Oliver Heywood's executor,) surrendered Northowram Meeting-house to Nathaniel Priestley, of Ovenden, on the 15th of August, 1710. On the 21st of June, 1711, the Meeting House was enlarged. The Subscribers were :—Jos. Wright £6, Nath. Lea, £2, Jere. Clay £2, Jere. Baxter £1, Joseph Wilkinson £2, John Priestley £2, Jno. Simpson £1, and Edwd. Hanson £1.

Mr. Swaine has also a manuscript of 44 pages, on Job 1. 21, " A Funeral Sermon preached at Northouram, March ye 4th, oc- " casion'd by the Death of three Daughters of John Priestley of " Westercroft, viz., Judith, who died Jan. ye 21st, in the 15th year " of her age ; Mary, who died Feb. ye 4th, in the 10th year of her " age, and Hannah, who died Feb. ye 22d, in the 13th year of her " age, A.D. 1710." The author, I presume, was Mr. Dickenson.

Another MS. of 61 pages is entitled " Exemption from Condem- " nation, Or the Privilege and Happiness of all True Believers in and " by Christ Jesus, considered and improved in A Funeral Sermon " on Rom. 8. 1, preached in Northouram, November 17, occasioned " by the death of Mrs. Mary Priestley, widow, who departed this " life November the 5th, 1734, aged 65, by Thomas Dickenson."

In 1717 Mr. Dickenson preached at the opening of a preaching room at Ossett. He had been one of Mr. Frankland's students.

On the 22nd January, 1722, Mr. Jonathan Priestley, of Winteredge, yeoman, made his will. He directed his body to be buried " in Mr. Heywood's grave, next to my dear wife's grave."

Winteredge he bequeathed to his nephew Jonathan Priestley, then living with him ; Dodge Holme in Ovenden, which he purchased of *Timothy Heywood*, deceased, late of Sheffield, apothecary [son of John and grandson of Oliver], he gave to his nephew Nathaniel, son of his brother John Priestley, of Westercroft, deceased ; his lands in Shelf, purchased of Mr. Wm. Walker, of Crow Nest, he left to his nephew Jonathan, &c.

In 1734 John Speight sold the double stall or pew in the middle row of seats, "late my father-in-law's, Abraham Milner," for 5s. to Thomas Dickenson, John Clay and Nathaniel Priestley, three feofees.

Mr Nathaniel Priestley, in 1749, gave ground and stones for a minister's house at Northourum. The original receipt, dated 1750, giving the amount of cost at £189 14s. 8d. is preserved at Guildford. For repairs to the chapel house at Northowram, Nov. 15, 1767, the following subscriptions were paid: Nathaniel Priestley and John Priestley, ten guineas each ; Benj. Dickenson, John Ramsden and James Pollard, five guineas.

The name of the Rev. Thomas Drake, D.D., of Lambeth Palace, in 1786, appears as a Trustee for Northowram School. About the same time the following persons were proposed Trustees for the Chapel: Mr. John Priestley, Mr. Benj. Dickenson, Mr. Wm. Dickenson, Mr. James Pearson, Mr. Wm. Prescott, Mr. Benj. Irvin, Mr. David Asquith, Rev. Mr. S. Walker, Mr. Tho. Clark, Mr. W. Mitchell, and Mr. Richard Fawcett.

"Whereas Mr. Jonathan Priestley the elder, of Winteredge, "did by his last will bequeath an annuity to the minister at "Northowram, and Mr Jonathan Priestley his representative "proposes to pay £20 in lieu, we acknowledge the receipt of the "said sum: Samuel Walker, minister, Nathaniel Priestley, "Timothy Bentley, Jos. Wilkinson, Jno. Ramsden, Benj. Dicken-"son, John Priestley."

The Rev. Robert Hesketh was minister of Woodkirk, or Topcliffe, in 1736, Eastwood in 1739, and Northowram in the spring of 1744. He was educated at Glasgow, and was also minister at Bolton-le-Moors some time. At Northowram he records that he received 10s. 6d. for a funeral sermon for Mrs. Wilkinson, and £8 from London during the first quarter. "Since May 30, 1744, (he writes,) the day when my family "fixed at Northowram, received in presents—Joshua Robertshaw, "5s., Mrs. Priestley, chinay, 7s. 6d., Mrs. Ingham, two chinay

" basins 2s., Mrs Ramsden, of Warlers, a Table Cloth 10s. 6d."
By his marriage he was related to Capt. Pickering, of Tingley,
and the Lords Eure. Mr. Joseph Swaine (of an ancient Bradford family,) married Mr Hesketh's daughter Bathshua, in 1744,
and their eldest son Robert Swaine married Hannah, daughter of
Nathaniel Priestley, of Northowram, in 1769. To follow up the
Priestley and their allied families would require a little volume to
itself. Mr. Hesketh was interred at Northowram Jan. 23rd, when
Mr. Haggerston, of Ossett, preached, and on the following
Sunday, Jan. 30th, Mr. Walker preached. The stone in the
yard records :—" H. M. C. M. S. Reverendi Roberti Hesketh,
" olim in Academia Glasguensi Instuti qui Evanglii 52 et hujus
" Ecclesiæ 29 Annis concionator Præclarus Eruditus non
" mediocriter ac Moribus Inculpatis habebatur in Christo excessit
" e Vita Jan. 19. die, A.D. 1774, Æ. 77. Necnon Helenæ
" uxoris charissimæ ejusdem " &c [the rest covered with soil.]
A sundial bearing the inscription—1780, Tempus Fugit,
Ingruit Mors,—is *throwing about* (to use a Yorkshireism) in the
grave-yard.   I may be excused giving these few memorabilia
when I state there is not the slightest vestige of deeds or manu-
scripts referring to the old chapel, and very little indeed concern-
ing the modern " Heywood Chapel " though erected solately as
1837, preserved at Northowram, or known of by the Trustees.
Only two or three relics of the old chapel can be identified.
It stood nearer the highway as may be traced by the old
gravestones.   Reared against the adjoinining cottages is one
that claims special attention : " Under this monument lieth the
" Body of the Revd. Mr. Thomas Dickenson, a worthy Minister of
" the Gospel, who was eminent and exemplary for piety and useful-
" ness, behaved well in all stations of life, with meekness and
" universal charity. He was continued a shining light in this
" place 42 years and died comfortably and much lamented the
" 26th December, 1743, aged 74. " Also two of his sons who
" died in their minority. Also Thomas his son who died Nov.
" 24. 1754, aged 51. Also John his son who died June 25, 1764,
" aged 51. Also Hannah his wife died at London July 28, 1765,"
[the rest is below the soil.]   A stone near records :   " Ann
" widow of late Rev. Mr. Pendlebury of Leeds, died 2 July, 1755,
" aged 59.   Also Hannah, Thomas and Ann, children of Benjamin
" and Ann Dickenson."

SUBSCRIBERS.

Nelson D. Adams, Washington, U. S.

W. Adlam, F.S.A., Chew Magna, Somerset

W. A. Abram, Blackburn

W. Aldam, J.P., Frickley Hall, Doncaster

J. Amphlett, Clent, Stourbridge

W. Anderton, J.P., Cleckheaton

G. Ackroyd, Bradford

W. Andrews, F.R.H.S., Hull

Rev. W. E. Anderton, M.A., Morley

Rev. Alex. Anderson, Radcliffe, Manchester

Robert Arthington, Leeds

R. Arundel, Tanshelf Lodge, Pontefract

G. J. Armytage, F.S.A., Kirklees

Richd. Ashworth, Gt. Lever, Bolton

F. M. T. Attree, Springfield Ho., Worthing

Dr. Alexander, J.P., Halifax

Col. E. Akroyd, F.S.A., Halifax

Sir J. Bernard Burke, C.B., LL.D., *Ulster King of Arms*, Dublin

J. Bairstow, Mayor, Halifax

R. C. Bostock, L. Camden, Chislehurst

W. Beecroft, E. Grove, Keighley

Isaac Binns, F.R.H.S., Batley

A. Briggs, Rawdon

J. Barraclough, Stafford Lawn, Hx.

J. H. Bell, M.D., Bradford

J. W. Burnley, Gomersall

E. B. Wheatley Balme, Mirfield

J. L. Bailey, F.S.A., Stretford

F. A. Blaydes, Hockliffe, Leighton Buzzard, Beds.

J. G. Berry, Fixby

J. A. Bottomley, Huddersfield

J. B. Bilbrough, Leeds (2)

Messrs. Burnley, Heckmondwike

A. Beanlands, jr., Palace Green, Durham

I. Briggs, Wakefield

W. Brierley, Bond Street, Leeds

Rev. R. Balgarnie, Scarborough

Most Hon. The Marquis of Bute, London

Sir E. Baines, Knt., J.P., Leeds

W. H. Brayshaw, Malham

Rev. B. H. Blacker, M.A., Stroud

Rev. W. T. Blathwayt, Dyrham Rectory, Chipping Sodbury, Bath

T. Brayshaw, Settle

Col. Lytton Bulwer, E. Dereham

W. Berry, Gomersall

J. E. Burrow, Headingley

B. H. Beedham, Kimbolton

J. W. Berry, Charles St., Bradford

J. A. Busfeild, J.P., Upwood, Bingley

J. M. Barber, Heckmondwike

W. E. Bools, 7, Cornhill, E.C.

Miss J. Boyd, Leamside, Durham

J. F. Brigg, J.P., Greenhead, Huddersfield

Matthew Balm, Idle

J. Botterill, Cottingham, E. Riding

Mrs. Bulmer, Blenheim Lodge, Leeds

J. Boothroyd, Bradford

A. Barraclough, Halifax

Rev. Robert Collyer, D.D., New York

Col. J. L. Chester, LL.D., London

G. E. Cokayne, F.S.A., *Lancaster Herald*, College of Arms, (2)

W. F. Carter, Hazelwood, Bmnghm.

J. W. Clay, Rastrick, Brighouse

R. F. Crosland, Cleckheaton

Rev. T. Cox, M.A., Halifax

G. T. Clark, F.S.A., Dowlais

R. Creyke, M.P., Rawcliffe, Selby

Rev. J. R. Campbell, D.D., Bdfd.

W. Cudworth, Bradford

F. T. Cansick, F.R.H.S., London

W. H. Conyers, Ben Rhydding, Lds.

S. J. Chadwick, Mirfield

J.J. Cartwright, M.A.,Rolls House, London

Jas. Crossley, F.S.A., Stocks Ho., Cheetham Hill

J. D. Craven, Thornton, Bradford

E. Crossley, J.P., Halifax

R. Haughton, Subscription Library, York
Leonard Hartley, Middleton Lodge
Alfred Illingworth, M.P., Daisy Bank, Bradford
Booth Illingworth, St. Jude's Place, Bradford
C. Jackson, F.S.A., Doncaster
J. Jubb, J.P., Batley
A. J. Jewers, F.S.A., Mutley, Plymouth
W. F. Marsh Jackson, Smethwick
Rev. J. Julian, M.A., Wincobank Vicarage, Sheffield
Rev. F. W. Jackson, Bolton Percy
W. H. M. Jackson, Hills Place, Oxford Circus, W.
H. M. Jackson, Hull
J. Jowitt, Leeds
J. Kaye, J.P., Clayton West, Hdfd.
A. J. Knapp, Clifton, Bristol
Miss Rosa M. Kettle, Parkstone, Dorset
R. Kershaw, Crow Nest, Lightcliffe (2)
J. E. Knowles, Gomersall
Sir John Lawson, Bt., Brough Hall
J. T. Leather, F.S.A., Leventhorpe Hall, Leeds
W. H. Lee, Mayor, Wakefield
W. Lee, Hanover Sq., Bradford
J. Lister, M.A., Shibden Hall (2)
J. Lever, Bowdon, Cheshire
J. D. Leader, F.S.A., Oakburn, Sheffield
W. H. Leatham, M.P., Hemsworth, Pontefract
B. Langley, Sheffield
Leeds Free Library, (J. Yates.)
B. Lockwood, J.P., Storthes, Huddersfield
S. Margerison, Calverley, (2)
Rev. F. E. Millson, M.A., Halifax
R. B. Mackie, M.P., Wakefield
S. Milne Milne, Calverley
G. Marshall, Frith Bank, Boston, Lincolnshire
Col. Moore, F.S.A., Frampton Hall, Boston
J. Massey, J.P., Burnley
J. W. Mitchell, *Rothesay Herald*, Sidmouth
H. J. Morehouse, M.D., F.S.A., Kirkburton
A. W. Morant, C.E., F.S.A., Leeds
C. H. Marriott, Dewsbury

G. W. Marshall, LL.D., F.S.A. London
W. Mallinson, Leeds
W. Milnes, Addingham, Ilkley
Samuel Morley, M.P., London
Rev. A. R. Maddison, Lincoln
T. P. Muff, Ilkley
Rev. E. Mellor, D.D., Halifax
New England Hist. & Gen. Soc., Boston. Mass.
Rev. C. B. Norcliffe, M.A., York (2)
Major W. Newsome, R.E., Newcastle
Messrs Needham, Bros., Sheffield
J. H. Oxley, Masbro', Rotherham
W. H. Oxley, Batley
J. Peel, Knowlmere Manor, Blkbn.
John Parker, 19th Regt., The Barracks, Birmingham, (3)
W. Duncombe Pink, Leigh
B. Priestley, J.P., Calverley
Pudsey Mech. Inst. (S. Rayner)
Geo. Pearson, 223, Hall Lane, Bdfd.
Rev. T. Parkinson, North Otterington
F. S. Powell, J.P., Horton, Bradford
Ellison Powell, 44, Coleman St., City
J. Pye-Smith, Sheffield
Bernard Quaritch, Piccadilly, Lndn.
Most Noble The Marquis of Ripon, K.G.
Sir C. Reed, M.P., F.S.A., Earlsmead
J. S. Rowntree, Lord Mayor, York
Sir H. W. Ripley, Bart., Rawdon
W. U. S. Glanville-Richards, Windlesham, Surrey
J. Rawson, J.P., Halifax
J. R. Raines, Burton Pidsea, Hull
R. Reynolds Rowe, Park House, Cambridge
T. Stamford Raffles, J.P., Liverpool
S. Rayner, Pudsey
T. W. N. Robinson, F.S.A., Houghton-le-Spring, Fencehouses
J. Rusby, F.R.H.S., Regent's Park
T. Milville Raven, M.A., Crakehall, Bedale
S. T. Rigge, Halifax
Rev. C. Rogers, D.D., LL.D., Lndn.
J. P. Rylands, F.S.A., Warrington
Josiah Rose, Leigh
J. B. Reyner, J.P., Ashton-under-Lyne
Rev. David S. Ross, Edhell, Brechin
T. H. Rushforth, Coley Lodge,

Ald. T. Denham, Mayor, Huddsfd.
J. Dodgshun, Leeds (2)
Dean Clough Inst., Halifax (T. Dickenson)
Stanley Dickenson, Halifax
Rev. J. H. Deex, Northowram
J. Denham, Huddersfield
W. Downing, Acock's Green, Birmingham
W. Dunlop, J.P., Bingley
R. Dowman, Ardwick, Manchester
Rev. Dr. Dickenson, Bridlington
Rev. J. Ingle Dredge, Buckland Brewer Vicarage, Bideford
J. H. Duncan, Otley
Rev. Bryan Dale, M.A., Halifax
J. Dodgson, Briggate, Leeds
W. C. Dyson, F.S.A.S., Wilton Pk., Batley
J. H. Dewhirst, Skipton
Dudley G. Cary Elwes, F.S.A., Bedford
J. P. Earwaker, M.A., F.S.A., Withington, Manchester
W. M. Egglestone, Stanhope
T. T. Empsall, Bradford
F. Eastwood, Huddersfield
Cap. Fawcett, Wainsford, Lymington, Hants.
Osgood Field, F.S.A., Grosvenor Mansions, S.W.
J. L. Ffytche, F.S.A., Thorpe Hall, Elkington, Lincolnshire
T. Fairbank, Windhill
F. Royston Fairbank, M.D., Doncaster
J. F. Fuller, F.S.A., Dublin
T. F. Firth, Heckmondwike
John Foster, J.P., Lightcliffe
W. Foster, J.P., Queensbury
E. Fraser, F.R.C.S., Hull
C. A. Federer, Bradford
Lt. Col. Fishwick, F.S.A., Carr Hill, Rochdale
Rev. W. T. Garrett, M.A., Crakehall, Bedale
J. G. Goodwin, Eccleston Sq., London
R. H. J. Gurney, Norwich
L. Gaunt, Farsley
H. Gray, Cathedral Yard, Manchr. (3)
W. Gregson, Baldersby, Thirsk
J. J. Green, Stansted, Essex
A. Gatty, F.S.A., Rouge Croix, Ecclesfield

J. Gourlay, Bradford
Rev. A. B. Grosart, LL.D., F.S.A., Blackburn
Lady Heathcote, Winchester
Rt. Hon. Lord Houghton, D.C.L., Fryston
J. D. Hutchinson, M.P., Halifax
T. Rowley Hill, M.P., Worcester
I. Holden, J.P., Oakworth, Keighley
W. A. Hoyle, Newcastle-on-Tyne
John O'Hart, F.R.A.H.S., Dublin
J. J. Howard, LL.D., F.S.A., Blackheath
J. Habershon, Masbro', (2)
Robert Hovenden, Croydon
Thomas Hughes, F.S.A., Chester
Angus Holden, J.P., Mayor, Bradford
L. Hainsworth, Bowling, Bradford (2)
R. Holmes, Pontefract
E. Hailstone, F.S.A., Walton Hall
Ald. J. Hill, Apsley Crescent, Bradford
R. Hanby, Cheetham's Library, Manchester (2)
Ald. T. Hill, Manor St., Bradford
Rev. H. Harrison, Idel, Leeds
J. Hutton, Eccleshill
S. Edgar Hirst, Crow Trees, Rastrick
J. Hirst, Ladcastle, Dobcross, Saddleworth
Heywood Sunday School, Nthowm.
G. Higgin, 3, Gt. Geo. St., Westminster
Rev. R. Poole Hooper, 31, Cambridge Rd., Brighton
G. Hanson, Rochdale Free Library
W. Harrison, F.S.A., Samlesbury Hall, Blackburn
Rev. T. Hunter, Dr. William's Library, London
J. A. H. Hirst, Retford
Rev. Canon Hulbert, M.A., Almondbury
Halifax Lit. & Phil. Soc. (S. T. Rigge)
W. Horsfall, Heckmondwike
Isaac Heywood, Mansfield
D. F. Howorth, F.S.A.S., Ashton-under-Lyne, (2)
T. Hirst, Huddersfield
C. Harvey, Barnsley
I. Hordern, Oxly-Woodhouse, Huddersfield

Ealing
J. Richardson, Headingley
F. Ramsden, Sowerby Bridge
F. Ross, F.R.H.S., Stamford Hill, London
Rev. W. S. Simpson, D.D., F.S.A., Kennington Pk. Rd., S.E.
G. Scarborough, Halifax
Joseph Sagar, Causeway, Halifax
W. Scruton, West Bowling, Bdfd.
J. Wales Smith, Leeds
Bobert Sutcliffe, J.P., Idel
Rev. T. Sutcliffe, J.P., Heptonstall
C. W. Sutton, Free Library, Manchester (2)
J. J. Stead, Heckmondwike
Evelyn P. Shirley, F.S.A., Stratford-on-Avon
F. W. Slingsbv, Piccadilly, Bdfd.
W. Smiles, M.D., H.M. Prison, Cold Bath Fields, London
Mrs. Stapylton, Myton Hall
Michael Sheard, Batley
A. B. Sewell, Bradford
T. Stratten, Hull
Rev. J. H. Stanning, M.A., Leigh Vic., Lancashire
C. Sykes, M.P., Brantingham, Brough
R. Sims, British Museum
T. Stephenson, Ilkley
John Sykes, M.D., F.S.A., Doncaster
E. Solly, F.R.S., F.S.A., Sutton, Surrey
H. P. Swaine, Brabœuf Manor, Guildford
R. Sugden, Brighouse
E. Swaine, York
S. Shaw, J.P., Stainland
T. Shaw, J.P., Allangate, Halifax
Mrs. Leopold Scarlett, Parkhurst, Dorking
Arthur Schomberg, Secud Lodge, Melksham
J. Shaw, Barnsley
H. Ecroyd Smith, Saffron Walden
J. W. Spofforth, Knottingley
W. Smith, F.S.A.S., Morley
G. E. Swithenbank, LL.D., F.S.A., Anerley Park, Surrey
Wilson Sutcliffe, J.P., Bowling
D. Sykes, Huddersfield
J. W. Sykes, Huddersfield
C. Stead, Saltaire
Jonathan Smith, Halifax

W. Rawson Shaw, Halifax
Sir C. Trevelyan, Bt., Wallington
Disney L. Thorp, M.D., Cheltenham
Rev. W. Tarbolton, Ilkley
Mrs. G. B. Thompson, Allerton, Liverpool
Thomas Turner, Old Market, Hfx.
J. Teal, Halifax (7)
J. Tattersfield, Heckmondwike (2)
W. Murray Tuke, Saffron Walden
Rev. S. Blois Turner, F.S.A., Halesworth
G. W. Tomlinson, F.S.A., Huddersfield
Stephen Tucker, *Somerset Herald*, Herald's College, London
Rev. R. V. Taylor, B.A., Richmond
T. W. Tew, J.P., Carleton Grange, Pontefract
B. Ll. Vawdrey, Tushingham Hall, Salop
W. J. Vint, Idel
Sir Albert Woods, Garter, College of Arms, E.C.
Rev. W. H. Wawn, M.A., Coley
Captain E. A. White, F.S.A., Old Elvet, Durham
J. W. Willans, F.S.S., Headingley
J. Whitley, West House, Halifax
E. Wilson, F.S.A., Beech Grove, Leeds
T. Waldron, B.A., Grammar School, Thornton, Bradford
W. J. Walker, 126, Lister Lane, Halifax
C. Wooler, Hopton
F. Sydney Waddington, Lower Clapton
J. H. Wurtzburg, Albion Works, Leeds
C. White, Chapel Lane, Bradford
H. Wagner, F.S.A., Piccadilly, W.
J. Wilkinson, Town Clerk, York
C. H. L. Woodd, J.P., Roslyn, Hampstead
J. K. Welch, J.P., 18, Billiter Street, E.C.
E. Westerton, Stationer, Knightsbridge, London
J. Webster, Gildersome
Mrs. Whitworth, Halifax
J. W. Walker, Halifax
J. Walker, Hopton
J. Watkinson, Fairfield, Huddersfield
Zech. Yewdall, Calverley
J. Yates, Masbro', Rotherham

REV.ᴰ OLIVER HEYWOOD.

A Register for Coley Chappell,

164 [4].

CHRISTENINGS.

Nouember

3 day   Nathanyell the sonn of Anthony Watterhouse
    Isacke the sonn of Tho Soothill
    Sara the daughter of Jo Lister

17 day   Judith the daughter John Saltonstall
    Ann the daughter Jere Webster

24 d   Timoth. sonn of Abra Scott 3Gy of age
    Mary daugh Michaell Hale

Decemb

1 d   Josua sonn of Tho Pannell
    Martha daugh of Petter Aumbler
    Susan daug Jeremy Smith
    Susan dau Rich. Appleyeard
    Edith dau Michael Smith
    Margaret dau Will Buttler
    Mary dau Tho. Slater

January

5 day   Jo sonn of Rich Wray
    James sonn of Robert Birkhead

19 day   Jeremy son of ffrauncis Crooke
    Sarah daugh of John Jagger

26 d   Edith daugh Abra Tempest

ffeb

day   Thomas sonn Tho Dawson
day   Isacke son Isacke Maude
day   John son Jo Hopkinson

CHRISTENINGS.

Phebe daugh Math Clay
Thomas son Jonas Roades

March
day   John son Jo Hargreues

Aprill
day   John son of Will Booth
      Susan daugh of Martin Jager
      Edward son Mich. Broadley
day   John sonn of Abra Hardisty

May
day   Mary daugh Abra Holt
day   Nathan sonn of John Mellin
day   Danyell son Danyell Niccoll
      Ann daugh of Tho Kendall

June
day   Sara daugh Andrew Pollard
day   Grace daugh Jere Holdsworth

July
day   Elizabeth daugh Jo. Gleadill
day   Martha dau Michall Emsall

August
day   John son Jo Benn
      Elizabeth dau Mart. Bachlour
24 d Mary dau Robt Parke
      John son Jo. Jewet
31 d Mary daugh Tho Haryson
      Thomas son Rich. Shoosmith

Septembr.
7 day Susan daugh Jo. Robtshaw
       Martha daugh Math Lum
28 d   Jonathan son Jonath. Crowther

CHRISTENINGS.

Octobr.

5 day Susana daugh Danyell Hemingway
26 day Martha daug Will Midgeley

Nouembr.

9 day John sonn Tho. Scott
16 d Joseph son Will. Holmes
Mary dau Jo Burneley
Phebe dau Jo Medley
Ann daugh Jo. Shepheard

Decembr

7 day Mary daugh James Scolcfield
14 day Mary dau Will Appleyeard
Tho son Mich. Driuer
21 day Danyell son Will Northend

[The names of som that were christened in the yeare 1645, which were not found till the ensueinge Register of that yeare was written ouer, and could not be put in other ways then heare, 1645.

Decem 28 day

John son James Willson
Susan dau Jo. Niccolls
John son Jo. Wadington
Willyam son Will Whittaker
Josua son Sam Whiteley
Josua son Henry Brooke
Danyell son Henry Priestley, who was Babtized on ye last Wednesday of Decembr beinge the Publicke fast.

January 4 day

Sarah dau. Jo. Eastwood of Hallifax
Jo. son Edw. Sharpe

CHRISTENINGS.

Susana dau Michaell Mitchell
feb
Mich. son Jo. Pearson
—— son Jo. Willson
[Ma] rtin son Edw. Longbottom
——son Rich. Law of Elland]

1646 May
Samuell son Mich. Smith
day Dauid son Rich ffearneside
1 day Jeremy son Mich. Willson

June
7 day Mary daugh Edw. Jackson
14 day Mary daugh Isack Jagger

July
5 day Stephen son Antho Kitchen

August
d Mercy dau Edw. Hudson

Septem.
d John son Sam. Gill

October.
day Tho son Edmund Brooke
  Mary dau Math Lum
  Lewis son Josua Brooksbanke
  Jeremy son Abrah. Smith
  Ruth dau Petter Aumbler
18 d Susan daug Will Boyes
  Jermy son Sam Bridge

Decem
6 day Mary dau Jo. Mellin
  John sonn James Priestley
day Mary dau Abra Willson
day Jeremy son Jer. Brooksbanke

CHRISTENINGS.

January
3 d   Mary dau James Ffielden

feb.
7 d   Grace dau Mich Bolton
        Anna dau Jo. Bland
        John son Will Addy
        Rich son Will Priestley
14 d   Jeremy son Jer Wells
        Ellenor dau Isack Longbothem
        Elizabeth dau Jo Holdsworth
        Mary dau James Breareley
21 d   Henry son Dauid Northend
        Susan dau Jo Smith

1647 March
28 d   Sara dau Robt Birkehead

Aprill
4 d   Danyell son Dan. Hemingway
        Jonas son Jer Holdsworth
10 day Sam son Henry Smith
        John son Rich. Smith
        Susan dau Isacke Maude
        Susan dau Jonas Roades

May
2 d   Susan dau Rich Northend
8 d   Nathan son Jere Smith
        Grace dau Jo. Wadinton
        John son Robt Smith
        Susan dau Will Buttler

June
6 d   Sam son Rich Brooksbanke
        Sara dau James Willson
27   Mary daughter of John Lister of Brier

CHRISTENINGS.

July
25   Samuel son of Daniel Nichols
        Jeremiah son of Abraha. Scott

August
1   Grandaughter of John ffurth
29   Abraham son of Mathew Lum
        Martha dau. of Thomas Harrison

September
11   Jonas son of John Priestley

October
10   John son of James Michell
17   Michael son of Michael Broadley
31   Samuel son of Henrie Spenser
        Susan dau. of Thomas Slater

November
5   Caleb son of Edward Slater
        Joshua son of John Ambler
        Samuel son of Samuel Yates
19   Mary dau. of Samuel Yeates
        these vnpayed October 1651
        James Willson
        Mathew Lum
        John longbothom
        ffrances Crooke
        John firth
        Abraham Hardysti
        Michaell Willson
        Thomas Harrison
        John Hanson
        John Ben
        abraham Tempes
27   Sarah Rushworth dau of J. Rush. of Hipholme

CHRISTENINGS.

1652 August 15

Martha daughter of Richard Apleyeard babtized

1652 August 22

Mary the dau. of Edmond Brooke

ffebey the daughter of John Wood the same day (?) [bap.] 1526

Jermeiah sonne of Daniell thorpe, baptized in the month of decem 1

Jerdmiah the sonne of ffrances Crock Baptized the 2 of janewarey 1652

Grace the dau of William Butler baptized the 9 day of Janewary

Grace the daughter of Bengemen Houmes bapt. 15 of janewary

Anteney sonne of Anteney Wattrous in, janewary bapt.

Mary the daughter of John Milner bapt. 20 d of Jenewary

february

27 Daye   Micael the son of Micael Broadley

March

6   Samuel the son of Samuel Gill

January 1655

Michael son of Richard Best

James son of james Oates of Marsh

Thomas son of Thome Whittley of Sinderhills

Anno 1655

December

2 daye   Ester dau. of John Sutliffe

28   Grace dau of Will Appleyard

· ·   John son of John Greenhill

80   Sarah dau. of Jeremiah Ramsden

January.

27   Samuel son of Abraham Hardisty

CHRISTENINGS.

february

3　　Mercy dau of Jonas Northend
John son of Robert Smith
Isaac son of Joseph Woodhead
24　　Isaac son of Isaac Smith of Hungerhill

9　　　　　　　March
Sarah dau of William Butler
Mary dau of James Mitchell

30　　　　　　March 1656
Elizabeth dau. of Edmund Brooke
Sarah dau of Matthew Clay
Levi son of Levi Crosley

6　　　　　　　April
James son of T. Oldfield
Annie dau. of J Pickering
27　　John son of Oliver Heywood
Timothy son of Andrew Watson
June　1 John son of John Whiteley
　　　2 Joseph son of John Hartley
July　13 Henry son of Nathan Sharpe
　　　20 Susana dau. of Samuel Smith
　　　27 John son of John Learoyd
Oct.　5 Thomas son of Thomas Rushworth of Barnshill
　　　John son of James Oates of Hipperholme
　　30 James son of James Bolland, Wyke
Dec.　27 Susan dau of Jonas Jagger
　　　John son of John Jagger
feb.　8 Damarth dau. of Matthew Boocock
March 22 Joshua son of John Wood of Hipperum
1657 April 21 Eliezer the son of Oliver Heywood minister of Coley
　May 17 James son of John Kershaw, Landimer
　　　Abraham son of Abraham Duckworth
　　24 Grace dau of Abraham Whitwham

CHRISTENINGS.

31 John son of John Smith of B——
      Grace dau of Samuel Brigge
June 7 Timothy son of Micael Bolton
    23 James son of John Bland
    27 Phœbe dau of Mr. Oates
July 12 Mary dau of John Sowden
Novemb.29 Mary dau of Mathew jaggar
Decemb. 6 Elizabeth d. of Joshua Barraclough
    13 Thomas s. of Abel greame
    20 Judith d. Alex. Kershaw
    Mercie the doutr of John Smith was bapt. the first day
    of May 1653

1653 Aprell 1 Joshua sonne of Isaac Smith of Northorom bap.
1655 Aprell 28 Mary the doutr of Isaac Smith of Northourom bap.
1656 feb   23 Martha doutr of Isaack Smith of Northourom bap.
1658 Jan.   8 Joseph the son of John Kershaw of Nor-woodgreen
  feb   7 John s. James Jaggar de Mathews
      14 Abraham s. Joseph Woodhead
        d Abraham Woodhead
  March 7 John s. John Hal of Thornton
      14 Susanna d John Walker
      21 James [dau] Robert Smith of Priestley green
      24 Mary d. Nathaniel Jaggar
        Jonn s. Micael Wilson
  June 20 Martha d. John Mellen, Northour.
        Joshua s Joseph Wright
  July 26 Mary d Richard Best, landimar
  Aug. 1 Mercy d. Peter Aumbler, Shelfe
        Jonathan s. John Brooke
1658 Nov. 21 Samuel s. Robert Crowther of Landshead
        Phœbe d. Henry Dugdell
  Decemb. 26 Jeremiah s. John Wood, Hipperholme
        Abraham s. Abraham Whitwham, Shelfe
1658-9 Jan. 2 Daniel s. Samuel Rushworth, Northour.

CHRISTENINGS.

	6	Ester d. John Hudson, Shelfe
feb.	6	Joshua s. Samuel Wadington of Norwood green
March	6	Patience d Isaac foster, Shelfe
May	15	Isaac s. John Kershaw, Norwood green
	17	Josiah s. John Nickol, Northourum
June	19	Judith d. William Butler
		Joshua s. John Holmes
July	17	Job s. John Woodhead
August	7	Jonas s. John Rushworth
	12	Nathaniel s. Oliver Heywood
1659 Sept.	25	Mary d. Jeremiah field
Oct.	9	Jeremiah s. John Northend, of Northourum town
Decem	11	Martha d. Nathaniel Jaggar, Shelfe
	18	Jonathan s. Joseph Wright, Hipperholme
1659-60 Jan	15	Jonathan s. Jonathan Priestley, of Priestlcy green
		Susanua d. Thomas Rushworth, of Barmeshill
febr.	12	Sarah d. Roger Stocks, Northowram
March	4	Ester d. John Brooke
	14	Martha d. Joseph field, Wyke
	19	Dinah d. Isaac Smith
1660 May	6	Susanna d. Joseph Woodhead
	13	Jonathan s. Abraham Duckworth
	20	Isaac s Isaac ffoster
July	1	Thomas s. Jeremiah Roper of Atherisgate
Aug.	19	Mercy d. Micael Bolton
		Abraham s. Abraham Woodhead
	26	Timothy s. James Mitchell
Septem.	9	Susanna d. John Kershaw, Landimar
	16	Sarah d. Robert Wilson, Hipperholme
Novem.	18	Mary d. Robert Smith, Priestley green
Decem.	11	Samuel s. Abraham Smith, Northourum
	15	William s. Thomas Hill, Shelfe
	18	Jonathan s. John Wood, Hippeiholme
1660-1 Jan.	6	Dinah d. Mathew Jaggar, jun.

CHRISTENINGS.

Decem. 30 George s. John Whiteley
1661 March 27 Martha d. John Drake
     31 Susanna d. William Hurd, Shelfe
  April   21 Lidia d. jonathan Priestley, of Priestley green
  May   26 William s. John Kershaw, Norwood green
  June   9 Joshua s. Joshua Soynier, Northourum
     23 Jeremiah s. Abraham Holt, Shelfe
     30 Ester d. Joshua Baraclough, Norwood green
      Susanna d. John Rushworth
  July   28 Mary d. Micael Woodhead, Shelfe
  Sept.   6 Elizabeth d. Jeremiah Baxter
      John s. and Grace d. John Brook
     22 Mercy d. Samell Holdsworth, Blackmires
  Decem. 1 William s. James Smith, Norwood green
      Phœbe d. Simeon Robinson
1661-2 Jan. 18 Hanna d. Joseph Wright Hipperholme
     26 Sarah d. John Holmes, Shelfe
  febru.   2 Martin s. Joseph Woodhead, Shelfe
1662 May   4 Caleb s. Jeremiah Wood, Boy-towne

This long interval of almost
ten yeares I was parted from
the excercise of my ministerial
function by the Act of Uniformity
in August 24 1662
Restored again to my work by
the Kings declaration March
1672 to ministerial imployment
in mine own house by license.

CHRISTENINGS.

1672 May 16 Hanna d. John Stephenson of Northourum
          26 John s. William Dickson of Healy, near Batley
     June   5 Elizabeth d. Jonathan Priestley of Wintreidge
             in Hipperholme
          11 David s. of Joshua Knight, Shelf
     Sep.   8 Susanna d. John Bentley of Warley
          15 Samuel s. Will. Hurd, Shelfe
          16 Mary d. John Mellen of Hipperholme
     Oct   21 Mary d. Matthew Holdsworth, Shelfe
     Novem. 1 John s. John Holmes of Shelfe
                     february 1672-3
           4 John s. William Preston, of Sutcliff wood
     ·   13 Zechariah s. John Taylour of Horton
 1673 April 1 John s. Jeremiah Watson of Northourum
     May   16 Eliezer s. Mr Joseph Dawson, of Damhead, in
             Northourum
167¾ March 8 Lidia d. Abraham Bairstow of Buttershaw
     April 29 John s. Peter Naylor Clark, living at Alvrethorp
             near Wakefield
     May   13 William s. William Clark of Morley
     June   d. of John Sutliffe
     July   3 John s John Taylour of Little Horton
           8 Abigail d Jonathan Priestley of Winteriag in
             Hipperholme
     Aug. 30 Susanna d. Willm Hurd, Shelfe
    ʹSept. 19 Hanna d. John Popwel of Heckinwyke in Burstal
             parish
     Oct   2 John s. Isaac Baulme of Boulin in Bradford parish
     Novem 23 Richard s. John Stevenson of Northourum
1675 Janu. 31 Phœbe d. Jeremiah Watson of Only house in
             Northourum
     March 1 Thomas s. Timothy Mellin of Quarry house
     April 8 Ebenezer s. John Holmes Barneshill
          13 Thomas s. William Kellet Northourum

CHRISTENINGS.

May 16 Mary d. Thomas Gill, We~tercroft, Northour.
Aug. 25 Thomas s. Thomas Wakefield of Marsh in
Southourum
1675 Novemb. 19 Samuel s. Mr. Joseph Dawson of Damheadborn
Nov. 14. bap.
18 Abraham s. John Butterworth
28 John s. John Benne, Shelf
Decem. 1 Susanna d. Hen. Burkhead of Heckinwyke
1676 April 80 John s. John Gill of Southourum
June 22 Joshua s. Joshua Cordingley of Heaton
1676 Sep. 5 Josiah s. Alvery Newzam of Heckenwyke
baptized
10 John s. William Raundsley of Tuttill bap. in my
house
18 Eliezer s. James Tetley, Priestley green bap iu
his house
Oct. 1 Martha d. Abraham Bairstow of High Bentley
bapt in my house
5 Mary d Thomas Bentley of Harewoodwell in
Warley bap. in his house
14 Abigail d. James Cordingley of Hightown bap. in
his house
1676-7 Jan 15 Hanna d William Butler, of Shaw lane near
Illingworth bap. in my house
March 11 Grace d. Thomas Gill of Westercroft bap.
1677 Aprel 9 Mary d. John Sutliffe of Norcliff bap.
17 Sarah d. John Butterworth, Warley
June 4 Joshua s. David Pye of Boulin bap. at my house
5 Joshua s. William Maude of Halifax bap. iu
Warley
July 8 Joshua s. John Kershaw, junr, of Wyke bap. at
my house.
10 Jonathan s. Richard Tenant at Bramhup
22 Joseph s. William Kellet of Northourum

CHRISTENINGS.

23 Hanna d Timothy Mellen

Sep   12 Eli s. Mr. Joseph Dawson of Damhead in Northourum

Oct.   15 Sarah d. John Popplewell of Heckinwyke

1677Novem 12 Elizabeth d. Mr Thomas Wakefield of Marsh bap.

Dec   6 Abraham s. Abraham Whitaker of Tingley bap. at Morley

24 John s. John Heywood of Little Leaver, near Bolton, Lancashire

167⅞ Jan   2 Martha d Mr. Thomas Sharp of little Horton near Bradford, bap.

feb.   24 Lidia d. John Gill

March   4 Thomas s. Thomas Walker, Westercroft Martha his daughter being twins, bap.

9 Joseph s. John Drake, of Shelf.

11 John s. John Burkhead of Heckonwyke

13 Sarah d. Mathew Holdworth, Shelf.

1678 March 18 Lidia d. of Joseph Oates of little Horton

26 Ezekiel s. Jonas Hainworth of Thornton

1678 May   24 Nathaniel Holden bap. at Halifax, aged 22 marryed to Hannah Worrel

July   1 John s. Paul Baraclough

30 David s. Thomas Leech of Riddlesden hall

Aug.   8 Jonathan s. James Hadock of Warley

9 Rebecca d. Isaac Balm of Boulin

25 Sarah d. John Whiteley of Hud-hill

Sep.   5 Mary d John Bancroft, of Warley

Oct.   4 Mary d. George Wilkinson of Swinden

1678October30 Tobias s. Timothy Mellen of Place bap.

Nov.   17 Susanna d. Thomas Gill of Westercroft and Martha her sister being twins.

Sarah d. John Sutliff of Northourum

26 David s. John Hey of Gisburn parish

Eliezer s. Rich. Mitchel of Marton parish in Craven

CHRISTENINGS.

Dec. 3 Joshua s. Alvery Neuzam of Heckenwike
4 Joshua s. John Bend of Northourum
29 Mary d. Edward Preston of Shelf
Jan. 1678-9 1 Mary d. John Butterworth, Warley
12 Rachel d. Abrahan Bairstow of High Bentley, bap.
1679 March 3 Ebenezer s. Richard Oldroyd, Deusbury
20 Martha d. James Holsted, Warley
1679 May 13 Anne d. Joseph Bryges of Warly
20 John s. Robert Smith of Southourum
June 2 Mary d. John Stevenson of Northourum
July 9 Hanna d. Richard Tenant, bramhup
22 Elizabeth d. Mr. Sam Crabtree of Tong
Sep. 29 Ester d. Timothy Kershaw, Wyke
1679 Oct. 19 John s. John Rushworth of Shelf bap.
21 Mary d. John ffoster of Thornton
Nov. 10 John s. John Popplewel of Heckonwyke
28 Martha d. Benjamin Butterworth of Warley
1680 Jan. 5 Mary d. William Clark of Morley
feb 4 Samuel s Mr. Thos. Wakefield of Marsh in Southourum
March 22 Sarah d. David Pye of Boulin
23 Jonah s. Jonas Hainworth of Thornton
May 3 Joseph s. Joseph Oates, Wibsey
12 Joshua s. Thomas Walker, Westercroft
1680 May 20 Joshua s. Abraham Ashworth, Warley, bap.
28 Hanna d. Joshua Rhodes of Horton
30 Elizabeth d. John Gill, Southourum
June 15 Martha d. William Hodgson, Bowling
July 1 John s. John Sutcliffe, Northourum
22 Phœbe d. Mr Joseph Dawson bap. She was born Lords Day morning July 18.
29 Nathaniel s. William Naylor of Quarry house
August 1 Joseph s. John Benne of Shelf
16 Nathaniel s. Anthony Lea of high bentley

CHRISTENINGS.

Oct.	3	Lidia d. Samuel Whitley of Shelf
1680 Oct.		Ruth d. Richa'd Oldroyd, Deusbury
Nov.	24	John s. John Butterworth bap.
	28	Elihu s. Robert Smith of Southourum
Dec.	7	James s. James Holsted, Warly. bap. at his house
	30	Jonadab s. James Haddock, Warley
		Benjamin s. Nathaniel Tetley, Warley
March	14	Mary d. John Kershaw, junr, Wyke
1681 April	5	John s. John Bancroft, Warly
	6	Mary d. John Burkhead of Heckmondwyke
	6	Mary d. Alvery Newzam
	8	Daniel s. Thomas Gill, Southourum
1681 May	10	Elkanah s. John Bury, Allerton, bap.
	31	Timothy s. John Ramsden, Northourum
June	6	Abraham s. Abraham Bairstow of High bentley
Sep	1	Sarah d. Timothy Bancroft, Warly
Dec.	24	John s. James Greave Northourum
168¼ Jan	19	Enoch s. James Halsted, Warley
	22	Adam s. John Sutcliff, Northourum
	30	Josiah s. John Stevenson
1682 Mch	28	Jeremiah s. Samuel Tetlaw
		Mary d. Thomas Walker, Ouru
1682 June	12	Hannah d. William Hodgson of Boulin
		Jere s. Joshua Rhodes, little Horton
		John s. Barnabas Ward, little Horton
		Tho. s. Joseph Oates of Horton
Sep.	11	John s. James Cordingley, High Town
	14	Hannah d. Abraham Ashworth, Warley
Oct	18	Isaac s. Isaac Balm junr of Boulin
Nov.	7	Mary d. John Hirth of wheatley
		Hannah d. John Bury, Allerton
	12	John s. John Naylor, little Horton
	13	Sarah d. Mr. Thomas Wakefield, Southourum

COLEY OLD CHURCH.

CHRISTENINGS.

	18	Hannah d. Tim. Paulard, North-ourum
168¼ ffebr	16	Joshua s. John Hanson, Mixenden
Mar.	20	Hopewell d. John Butterworth, Warley
168¾ Mar.	20	Sarah d. Benjamin Butterworth, Warley
		Susanna d Henry Howarth, Warley
1683 Mar.	29	Deborah d John Marsden, Sowerby
April	12	James s. Tho Gill of Southourum
		Martha d. Joseph Briars, Warley
		Joseph s. Robt. Scholfield, Warley
May	7	Martha d. John Kirshaw junr., Wyke
	21	Hannah d John Gill, Halifax
June	18	Hannah d. James Halsted
		Rebecca d. Timo Bancroft, Warley
Sep.	18	Hannah d. James Oates of Wyke
Oct	19	Hannah d. Jere. Layroid of Ovenden
	23	John s. Abrahan Bairstow, High Bentley
1684 ffeb.	21	Benjamin s. T. Reiner of Hickmondwike, a year old
		Hannah d. [Alv.] Neuzam of Hickmondwike
ffebr.	26	Judith d. Stephen Hall, Warley
Mar.	2	Abraham s. John Naylor, Wibsey
	11	Grace d. Abraham Milner, Westercroft
Apr.	1	Joseph s. Simeon Ashworth, Sowerby Dean
May	22	John s. John Bury, Shipden Head
	27	John s. Edward Hanson, Wyke
	28	Sarah d. Anthony Lea, High Bentley
June	9	John s. James Halsted
	4	Mary d. Richard Tenant, Bramhup
Sep.	22	Mary d Nathl Longbothom
Oct	31	Samuel s. Barnabas Ward
Jan.	5	Ruth d. Mr Tho. Wakefield, Marsh

𝕷𝖔𝖓𝖌 𝕴𝖓𝖙𝖊𝖗𝖒𝖎𝖘𝖘𝖎𝖔𝖓.

[*Time of Persecution.*]

1686 Mar.	8	Dinah d. Nathl Tetley, Warley
1687 May	16	James s. Tho. Sale of ffairweathergreen

CHRISTENINGS.

	19	James s. Edward Ashworth, Warley
May	24	John s. Joseph Brears, Warley
	26	James s. James Greaves, Bank top
	29	Joshua s. John Dickson, Heatonroyds near Shepley
June	9	Robt s. John Wright, Bingley
July	8	Mary d. Joseph Priestley, Westercroft
	22	Mary and Hannah d. Samuel Tetley of Horton
Aug.	16	John s James Turner, Sowerby bridge
ffeb.	8	John s. Richd. Garnet, Leeds
Mar.	10	Jeremiah s. Joseph Wood
July	26	Hannah d. James Halsted
Aug.	22	Martha d. John Hanson, Rhodes hall
Sep.	6	Caleb s. Abraham Ashworth
	26	Abigail d. John ffirth, Wheatley
	28	Elkanah s. Jere Baxter
Oct.	5	Rachel d. Isaac Balm, Boulin
	17	John s Tho. Gill of Southourum
Nov.	7	Hannah d. John Marsden, Sowerby
	13	John s. Benj. Butterworth
Dec.	16	Abra s. Abra ffirth of Little Horton
Jan.	10	Anne d. John Kirshaw, Wyke
	23	John s Matthew Holdsworth, Shelf
	26	Joshua s Jonathan Rigg, Sowerby
	26	John s. Joseph Haliday, Northour.
Mar.	9	Mary d. Rich. Hall, of Chappel le brears
	22	John s. John Armitage, junr., Kirkburton
1688 Mar.	29	Hannah d. Joseph Simpson, Bramhup
May	12	Joseph s. John Milne
Aug.	19	Lydia d. Jere Layroid, the first in the meeting place
Apr.	12	Susanna d. Stephen Hall, Warley
	12	Tho s. John ffarrer, Warley
	30	Joseph s. Joshua Wright
May	1	Grace d. James Oates
	17	John s. Simeon Ashworth, Soyland
June	26	Martha d. Robt Scholfield, Warley
Aug.	26	John s. Isaac Smith of Collier Syke
Sep.	11	Anne d. ffrancis Brook of Shutt
	11	James s. John Butterworth, Warley
	27	Esther d. John Sutcliff

CHRISTENINGS.

Oct	26	Tho s. George Bottomley, Shipden
Nov.	19	Wm s. Mr. Tho Wakefield
	28	Timothy s. James Greaves
Jan.	2	Hannah d. Tho. Hodgson of little Horton
ffeb	10	Susanna d. John Rushworth
Mar.	24	Daniel s. Nathanl. Longbothom
1689 Apr.	17	Mary d. Tho. Thornton
May	15	Mary d. Wm. Stead of Idle
Nov.	6	Judith d. Timothy Bottomley, Dighton
88 Jan.	7	Mary d Joseph Priestley, Westercroft
88 Jan	28	John s Tho Sale of fairweathergreen
1689 Mar.	29	John s. Jonathan Wood
May	19	Joseph s. James ffletcher
June	27	Sarah d Abram Brigg
July	22	Richard s. Josiah Harger
	26	Mary d. John Hanson
	31	Rebecca d. George Stocks, Hipperholm
Aug	12	Susanna d Jere Baxter
	28	Tho. s. Joseph Wooller
	28	Willm s. Saml Tetley
Sep.	10	Sarah d Robt Walker, Bingley
Oct	10	Sarah d. Jonathan Rigg
Nov.	8	Joshua s Abra Ashworth
	15	Mary d. John ffarrer, Warley
ffebr	2	Mary d. Joseph Wood
	9	Obadiah s. James Scholefield
	11	Mary d. Robt Scholfield, Warly
	19	Mary d John Oldfield, Damhead
Mar.	13	John s. Laurence Slater, Idle
	14	Mary d Thos Hodgson of Little Horton
	14	Ezra s. Isaac Taylor
Apr.	7	Mary d. John Milne, Northourum
	23	Joshua s. James Hainworth, Thornton
1689 Jan	7	Margaret d. John Dickson
Mar.	17	Eliz d. Joseph Haliday
1690 May	20	Eliz d. Mr. Nathl Priestley
May	23	Saml s. John Garnet, of Idle
June	1	Saml s Josiah Bolton
	5	Matthew s. George Moorhouse
	13	Mary d. Isaac Smith

CHRISTENINGS.

	24	Sarah d James Tiron
July	26	Edwd. s. Edwd. Hanson, Wyke
Aug.	4	Saml s. Willm. Lupton, Wakefield
Sep.	11	John s. John Hanson, Rhodes Hall
Oct	16	Rebecca d. Benj. Butterworth
	21	Mary d. Joshua Wright
	26	Abel s. Cornelius Clark
Nov.	20	Joseph s. James Oates
Dec.	4	Benj. s. Mr Josiah Oates, Chickinley
	9	Jere s. Abra. Brigg
	21	Eliz. d. John Scot of Alverthorpe
	22	Willm s Wm Lilly
	30	Joseph s. John Kirshaw, Wyke
Jan.	25	John s Jere Layroid
	28	Saml s. Stephen Hall
ffeb.	6	John s. Wm. Naylor
	18	Tho s. Tho. Brown, of Wakefield
Mar	16	Lydia d. Tho. Hodgson
	16	Isaac s. Abra. ffirth
	16	Susanna d. —— Baraclough
1691 Mar.	27	John s. Timo. Dighton
Mar.	5	Tim. s. James Greaves
Apr.	13	Tho s. Tho. Naylor, Wakefield
	26	Joseph s. Joshua Stocks
	26	Jere. s. Jere. Baxter
May	25	Ednah d. James Halsted
	26	Sarah d. Tho. Gill
June	14	Mary d Saml Denton
		Abra s. John Butterworth
July	30	Jonathan s Jon. Rigg
Aug.	7	Jane d Mr. Tho. Wakefield
Aug.	19	Han. dr —— Brigg of Holbeck
Nov.	6	Jonathan s. John Oldfield
Jan.	11	Joseph s. John Milne
	17	Eliz. d. Stephen Loxly
	17	Martha d John Scot
	22	Mary d Isaac Armiston
	25	Jabez s. Tim Bancroft
ffeb.	26	Lydia d Wm Roundsley
Mar	16	Saml s Joseph Hollings

CHRISTENINGS.

	16	John s John Wilmot
1692 Apr	3	Judith d Wm. ffoster
	15	Martha d. Isaac Smith
	13	Joseph s Jonathan Wood
May	4	Dorothy d Mr Nathl Priestley
	10	Sarah d. Abra. Ashworth
	11	Phœbe d. J. Stocks
Jan.	3	Martha d. Saml Tetley
	8	Sarah d Nathan fernside of Horton
	21	Esther d Michael Woorsnam of Darcy Lever
July	21	Jonas s John Naylor, Haworth
Aug.	13	Judith d. Mr John Brooksbank, Ealand
Sep.	9	Josiah s Joshua Stansfield, Horton
	18	Martha d. Abra Brigg
Oct.	17	Joshua s. Tho ffarrand, Bradford
	17	Wm. s. James Walks, Bradford
Nov.	2	John s Anthony Naylor
	2	Jacob s. Edwd Ashworth
Jan	9	Lydia d. Tim Hargrar, Wyke
Mar.	13	Mary d. Richd Kirshaw, Wyke
1693 Apr.	14	Eliz. d. John Learoyd
	27	Matthew s Joseph Oates
May	24	Mary d Saml Hamar, of Rochdale
	28	Jere s Joshua Stocks
	9	Rachel d Tho Hodgson, Horton
	9	Wm s. Tim Ward and Anne d. John Dickson in Horton
	29	Judith d John Hanson
June	15	Hannah d. John ffarrar
	30	Jere s. Jere Learoyd
July	17	Mary d. John Scott, at Allerthorp
	24	Tabitha d. Henry Lancaster
	24	Mary d. John Sonyer
Aug.	9	Eliz d. Jere Baxter
	9	Grace d. John Sharp
	31	John s Mr John Hough
Sep.	18	Jonas s. Tim Dighton
Nov.	22	Hannah d Joshua Wright
Dec.	18	Isaac Wilson, a married man, son to a Quaker, and his son Benjamin

CHRISTENINGS.

Jan.	28	Benj. s. Benj. Butterworth
	28	Jonathan s. Joshua Sonyer
	31	Jonathan s. Paul Greenwood
Mar.	5	Joseph s. Joseph Wood
	5	Sarah d Joseph Wood
	2	Stephen s. Stephen Hall
	2	Benj. s. John Butterworth
	23	Eliz. d. John Craven
1694 Apr.	2	Mary d. Wm Garth at Idle
	2	John s. Rich. Cowley
	8	Han. d. Robt Walker, of Bingley
	23	Abra. s. John Coulin of Wibsey
June	9	Wm. s. Mr Tho. Whitaker of Leeds
		James s. Anthony Naylor
July	4	Abra. s. Abra. Ashworth
July	23	Lydia d James Oates, Wyke
Aug.	10	Laurence Lord
	24	Benj. s. Jonathan Wood
	27	Isaac s. Isaac Smith, of place
Oct	7	George s. Robt Hatfield, of Tinsel
Dec	1	Joseph s Joseph Wilkinson
	28	Grace d. John Learoyd
1695 Apr.	8	James s. Nathan Halsted bap., Warley
1695 Apr.	12	Thomas s Thomas foster in Denham
	15	Judith d. Robert Scolfield of Warley
	26	Obadiah s. Joseph Hollins, Allerton
May	29	John s. John farrar, Warley
June	4	James s. Mr. James Haigh, Halifax
	16	John s. Jeremiah Baxter, Northourum
July	16	Jonas s. Jonas foster, Denham
	26	Phœbe d. John Priestley, Westercroft
Sep.	9	John and William sons of Mr John gaunt, twins, a Scotchman in Halifax
	11	Lydia d. William Pierson, Holdsworth

Mary d. Stephen Hall of Warley bap Dec. 4, 1695
Phœbe d. John Craven of Westercroft bap. Dec. 18, 1695
Martha d. Richard Kershaw, Wyke, bap. Jan. 7. 1695-6
Jonathan s. Nathaniel Booth, Northourum bap. Jan. 13. 96
Mary d. Antony Naylor Jan. 21
Martha d. John Squire feb 25

CHRISTENINGS.

Edward s. John Hanson of Rhodes Hall feb 28. 1695-6
Samuel s. Wm. Naylor Mch. 16
1696 Martha d. Jonathan Rig in Warley, ap 29
John s. John Oldfield, Northourum May 1
Grace d. Henry Mitchel, Sourby May 5
Abraham s. Thomas foster, Denham May 7, 1696
Mary d. Mr. Antony Buntyne of Ratchdall June 11. 1696
John s. Edward Ash——, Warly June 24   :
Judith d. John Priestley bap. July 31. 1696
Mary d. Michael Woodhead Aug. 17. 96
Joseph s. Paul Greenwood Aug. 17. 96
Daniel s John Sharp Sep 6. 1696
Joshua s. Joshua Wright. Oct 15. 1696
Elkanah s. James Greaves bap Jan 8. 1696-7
Hanna d. Robt. Scolfield bapt. feb 16. 1697
Jonathan s. Jonathan Wood bap Apr. 18. 1697
Mary d. Nathaniel Booth bap. June 14, 1697
Elizabeth d. John farrar bap. May 7. 1697
Mary d. Joseph Wilkinson, Shelf bap. May 16. 1697
Isaac s. Anthony Naylor baptized Tuesday Aug. 17 1697
Mary d. Michael Ingham baptized Oct. 1697
Hanna d. Thomas Ibison, bap in Bradshaw Nov. 1. 1697
Thomas s. John Bury, Northourum Nov 1. 1697
Judith d. John foster, Rebecca d Jonas foster of Denham
     both bap. Nov. 15. 97
Mary d John Bently of Wadhouse bap. Nov. 31. 1697
Joseph s. Joseph Wilkinson, Rivy.   Joshua s.   Richard
     Kershaw, Wyke both bap. in my chapel Jan. 16th, 169⅞
Mary d. Nathan Halsted, Warley bap. Jan. 19 169⅞
Susanna d. John Hurd bap. in my chappel feb. 6. 1697-8
Sarah d. Mr. Nath. Priestley, Ovenden feb 11. 169⅞
James s. James Kershaw of Holdworth bap feb. 27. 1697-8
Abigail d. John Craven bap. Mch. 13. 1697-8
Hannah d. John Priestly bap. June 14. 1698
Joseph s. Jeremiah Baxter bap. July 6. 1698
Sarah d. John Learoyd bap July 11. 1698
Sarah d. John Bentley of only-house bap. Aug. 15 98
Daniel s. David Mitchel bap. Aug. 21. 1698
Lydia d. Joseph Hollins Sep. 6 1698
Abraham s. Thomas Whitaker of Norwood green bap Nov.
     21. 1698

CHRISTENINGS.

Hanna d. John Milnes bap. Dec. 16. 1698
Susanna d. James Wallis bap. feb. 14. 1698-9
Martha d. Samuel Shepheard bap. feb. 17. 98-9
John s. John Sharp bap. Mch. 6. 1698-9
Isaac s. Joseph Wilkinson bap. Mch. 12. 1699
Isaac son of Mr. Mathew Smith, bap. Apr. 21. 1699
Mr Michael Donwel bap. May 5 1699
[Jeremiah] s. Samuel Paulard bap. May 7. 1699
Elizabeth d. Thomas Wilkinson of Clayton bap. July 23.
 1699
John s. John Smith bap. July 23. 99
Jonathan s. Jonathan Scot bap. Aug. 13. 1699
James s. Edward Hanson of Wyke bap. Sep. 13. 1699
Abigail d. George Longbothom bap. Sep. 20. 1699
Martha d. Joshua Wright, bap. Oct. 4 '99
Sarah d John farrar, Warly, bap. Oct 26. 99
Lidia d. Nathaniel Booth bap Nov. 5, 1699
Hannah d. John Bently.   Anna d. John Hanson bap.
 Nov. 13. 1699
Nathaniel s. of John Priestley bap. Dec. 20. 1699
Sarah d. of Joseph Wilkinson bap. feb. 2. 1699-700
Jonathan s. Jeremiah Learoyd bap. Apr. 10. 1700
Mary d. Ezekiel Hainworth bap. Apr. 14 700
Stephen s. John Ambler bap. May 16 1700
John s. John foster, Denham bap. May 19. 1700
John s. John Bently onlyhouse bap. June 5. 1700
John s. John Craven June 16. 1700
John s. Michael Ingham June 17. 1700
Alice d. John Stansfield, Sourby bap. Aug. 8. 1700
Nathan son of Jeremiah Baxter baptized Nov. 3. 1700
William s. John Hurd bap feb 23. 1700-1 in my chappel
Thomas s. Mr. Nathaniel Priestley bap. Mch. 27. 1701
Hanna Crowther a young woman at Joshua Stocks bap. in
 my house Apr. 22. 1701
Martha d. Jonathan Brian of Sinderhills bap. Apr. 28. 1701
Hanna d. William Wilkinson bap. May 1. 1701
William s. Samuel Shepheard bap. May 1 1701
James s. James Wallis bap. June 10. 1701 at his house
Tamar d. John Wilkinson of Horton bap. June 16. 1701
Mary d. John Priestly bap. July 24, 1701

CHRISTENINGS.

David s. Jeremiah Learoyd bap. in my chappel July 27. 1701
Martha d. Antony Whitely bap. Aug. 31. 1701
Joseph s. Mr. Jonathan Wright bap Nov. 18. 1701 by Mr
   Peters
Edward s. John Bently, Wadhouse bap Nov. 18. 1701
Jonathan s. Abraham Ekroyd bap. Jan. 16. 170½
John s. Nathanael Booth bap. Jan. 18. 170½
Thomas s. Jeremiah Baxter bap. feb. 11. 170½
Mary d John Bently of only house bap feb 11. 170½

𝔐𝔞𝔯𝔮𝔦𝔞𝔤𝔢𝔰.

1646 March 23. Henr. Best and Grace his wife
1647 May 31 James Hopkinson and Marie Hird
1647 June 2 John Bothomley and Judith his wife
1647 [June] 12 Edward Nicholls & Phebe his wife
[1655]   John Squire Mary Hoard Matthew Jaggar wh.
          Mary his wife
1655 febr. 19 James Jaggar Mary Whitteley
1656 July 14 Micael Wilson Sarah Hosfield
[1657]   Jeremiah fletcher
1658 Nov. 2 Jeremiah ffield Judith Walker maryed at Coley
1660 oct 31 James Kitson Sarah Denton maryed at Coley
1662 feb., 4 Peter Ambler Mary Wood maryed

[Interval, see Baptisms.]

1672 June 19 John s. John Burkhead of Gummersall in Burstall
          parish and Anne d. John Nelson of Medley
          married
1672 Aug. 1 John s. Joseph Priestley of York and Sarah
          Lister of the over briar married
Abraham Whittaker of Tingley, Woodkirk parish and Elizabeth
   Walker of Burstall parish, publisht, marryed May 1. 1674
James Tetley of Norwoodgreen and Martha Bairstow were marryed
   May 11. 1674
John, eldest son of John Kershaw of Norwoodgreen marryed
   Martha d. Joshua Walker of Rushworth Hall at Bradford Sep
   27. 1676
Jonathan Priestley of Winteredge marryed Mrs Mary Nelson
   at Coley Chappell May 29. 1677
Thomas Dodghon and Hanna Nalour marryed June 20, 1677
William Clay and Mary Wilson married at Coley Chappel by Mr.

MARRIAGES.

Hovy feb. 5. 167⅞

James Halsted of Warley & Anne Bolton married ffeb. 6. 167⅞

Mr John Mitchel of Halifax and Mary Wilson of Slede Sike in Lightcliffe married Mar. 28. 1678 she being but 15 years of age

Mr. Hawksworth of Hawksworth married Mrs ——, March 1678 having but 24 hours acquaintance one with another

Nathl Holden, apprentice with Th. Dunne, loose Apr. 20, married Hannah Worrel Apr. 23, 1678

John Ellis of Morley and Elizabeth Pierson of Tingley marryed May 17. 1678, published at Woodkirk

Tho. Holdsworth of Moorfield & Mary Bentley of Booth town married May 7. 1678

Ralph Higson & Judith Swift June 10

Mr John Milner of Pudsey & Mr Halls dr. of Swillington married July 4. 78

old Michael Booth of Comon House & Wid. Brook of Brighouse married July 31

Robert Smith of Priestley green married Joshua Hopkins daughter of Northourn. Aug. 6

John Hartley & Grace Brook married Aug. 20

Joshua Owen & Sarah Mitchel married Aug 21

Col. Duckinfield of Duckinfield and Judith Nathl Bottomleys daughtr near Peniston married Aug 20 (78) Sir Robt Dukinfelds Lady dying of childbed the same week

John Brown and a dr. of Mr Swifts of Peniston married Aug 6. (78)

Mr. Kirk of Cookridg & a dr. of Mr. Lockwoods wifes married July 16 (78) shee 17 years of age

Mr. Abra Langley & Grace Whitley married Sep. 25 (78)

Mr. Shuttleworth of Clethero married Mrs Sunderland of fairweather green Oct 8 (78) her husband left her £5000 in money 80£ panu. in Land, he a wanting man 24 years old has little

Jere Newby of Lightcliffe married John Philips widow near Booth Town Oct. (78)

John Hanson of Lightcliffe and Grace Holdsworth married Oct 30. (78)

Mr. John Priestley of York & Mr. Middlebrooks Daughter married Nov. 26. (78)

Saml Hopkinson of Sowerby & Martha Midgeley married Nov. 30 (78)

MARRIAGES.

Jo son of John Newby & Grace Cordingley Dec 11

Lord Edlington (Scot) & Sr Tho Wentworths Lady married ffeb 4 (78)

Mr Richard Briars & Sarah Marshall ffeb 11

Mr Hough & Mrs Bentley married ffeb. 25 (78)

John Armitage of Lidiat at Kirkburton parish & Mary Moorehouse married July 21. 1679

Tim Rushworth of Coley & Mary   married March 3. (78)

William Robuck Morley & Rachel fosse (!) of Top liff married Nov 3. 79

Mr Holt of Castleton married Lady Granthams Daughter p. Mr. Wood at ffixby Rastrick ffeb 24. 78

Mr Joshua Horton of Sowerby married Mrs Grey's Daughter of Chester ffeb 27. 78

James ffletcher of N.ourum & Martha Woodhead May 8. 1679

John Scot of Leebridge aged 78 married Hannah Yates his servant abt 20 years old

Adam fferniside of little Leaver married Mr Tho Cromptons sisters daughter of Asley he 76 she a young woman Apr. 79

Mr. Bramley of Sowerby married widow Beverley an Alewife there May 15

Michael Best & Mrs Laurence Apr. 19. 1679

Wm Naylor &   Denton married May 15. 1679

Danl Walker of Lightcliffe married one from Leeds formerly his servt. May 13 (79)

Saml Haliday & Lydia Hoyl married May 17

Mr. Wilkinson, minr at Illingworth & John Illingworths Daughter married June 5

Wm ffenton & Sarah Chipping June 10

Saml Nicol & Judith Hanson June 26

Mr. Edm. Ogden of Rochdale & Martha dr. of Mr. Tilsley married July (79)

John Brooksbank & Tim Wadsworths daughter Aug 2

—— Clarkson & James Philips daughter of Hipperholme July

Wm Hodgson of Boulin married a dr. of Rich. Ash of Rodley Sep. 3

Anthony Lea & Mary Northend married Sep. 3. 1679

Timo. Crowther & Mary Crosley married June 1679

Tim. Paulard & Grace Whitaker Sept

Mr Edwd Langley & Mary dr. Mr. Stephen Ellis married Nov. 26

MARRIAGES.

Tho. Reiner & Phoebe Hoyl married Nov. 27

James Oates & Hannah Smith ffeb. 17

Mr. Gilbert Brooksbank & Sarah Bretcliffe Mar. 6

Mr. ffrancis Maud of Alverthorpe & Mary Walker of Walterclof married Apr. 6. 1680

John Ramsden & Grace Smith Ap. 26

Joseph Hainworth & Eliz. Smith Apr. 27

Joseph Woller & Hannah Aked of Bradford Apr. 28

Saml Holdsworth to Alice Mellen Jan 14 1679-80 abt 34 years of age

Mr James Oates & Mrs Susanna Murgatroyd married Jan 21. 1679

Tim Bolton & Ellen Dewhirst at Wakefield Oct. 14, 1680, after he married R. Shuttleworth's daughter (86)

Tim Bancroft & Susan   Oct 25 1680

Joseph Conder, Leeds & Eliz Wadsworth Nov 29

Esther Heywood & James Lomax of Brekmitt Jan 21

James Greaves & Susan Townsend ffeb. 3

—— s. Edmd Brook & dr. John Stocks ffebr. 9

Jonathan Crowther & Bridget Mellen Apr. 4, 1681

Mr. Bairstow of Chester married Dorothy dr. Mr. Waterhouse of Bradford, Apr. 22

Nathl. Longbothom & James Greenwood's daughter May 18

John Dun & Martha ffurness married June 14. 1681

John Rhodes & d. of —— Rhodes June 9

Robt Ledgard, Leeds & Eliz. d. Mark ffreeman, May 31

Edwd Paulard & Martha Garnet July 25

Mr. Sotwel & widw Greaves July

Mr. Townley & Mrs Elenor Brook of Newhouse, Aug 4

Alvery Gibson and Mary at John Stephensons Aug 28

John Oates & wid Duckworth, Sept

Joseph Priestley & Mary Best Oct 3

Mr. Wright & Mrs. Elenor Cotton at Peniston, Oct. 26

Mr. Gleadston Lecturer at Bradford married old Mr. Tenants d. of Burnsay in Craven Dec. 7. 1681

John Gumersal & Dorothy Northend Jan 30. 1681

Tho Naylor & Adding Holdsworth Jan 25

Mr Rich Thorp & Mrs Coulston Mar 8

Rich Cook & Izabel Hodgson Apr 18. 1682

Mr. Josiah Oates & Hannah Fenton Mar. 29

MARRIAGES.

Nathl Booth to John Kitsons daughter May 3
Mr Meek of Slaughwait & —— of Huthersfield, May 10
Wm Ellis & Lydia Worrel May 25
—— Middleton & Mrs Mitchel d. of Tho. Hind, Halifax May 22,
    parted Sep. 1683, her mother buried May 18. 1682
Wm. Kirk & Sarah Northend May 20, 1682
Mr Giles Dolliffe & Dau. of George Tillotson, Aug. 1682
Mr John Billingsley of Mansfield & Mrs Dorcas Jordan of Mans-
    field, Aug 22
Mr. Starky stole away Mr Hilton of Park Dau (was to marry Mr
    ffarrington that week) married about 12 a clock in the night at
    Dr. Lows in Bolton, Sept
Mr Saml ffurnesse & Jane Breatcliffe Sep 26 (unknown to Rela-
    tions tho' for main consenting)
Jonathan Kighley & Wid. Wilson Sept. 27
Jonathan ffirth & Eliz. Riddlesden Oct 24
Mr Saml Eaton of Manchester & Mr Marlers dau. Sep 22
Mr John Lister & Mrs Bathshua Pickering Nov. 15
Jere Learoyd & Mary Park Nov. 30
John Wadsworth & Mrs Cambdena Kirby
John Reyner & Mrs Twin Kirby Dec. 26
Mr Wm Cotton & Mrs Westby, Ranfield married Mar. 27. 1683
Mr Jere Bentley of Ealand & Judith Walker of Walterclough
    Apr 14. She bore a son Sept 22
Mr Christopher Richardson & Mrs Ruth ffarrand May 17
Stephen Hall & Danl Bates dr. May 3
Jere Brooksbank & wid. Holroyds dr May 23
Geo Bottomley & J. Nelsons dr. June 12
Mr Robt Gledhill & Mrs Marsden June 29
Andrew Watson & wid. Paulard Sep 23
Saml Bradley & Deborah Hodgson Oct 4
Mr Smith & Mr Harrisons dr. Oct. 16
John Bentley of Bradford & Han. Wright Oct 25
Mr John Brooksbank & Mrs Bathshua Marshall Nov 21. 1683
Benj. Nicolson & Esther Crowther ffebr 11. 1683
John Mitchel stole away Abra. Walkers Datr. married her ffebr
    16. she 15 year old
Mr Tim Smith of Leeds & Mrs Knightly Hickson Jan. 1
Mr John Rooks of Rhodes Hall & Mrs Hopkinson of Loftas, his
    own cousin, May 27

MARRIAGES.

John Hanson & Mary Walker May 29
John Bland & Mary Tetlaw Oct
Abra Ashworth & Mary Batley Nov. 25
ffrancis Brook & Sarah Rushworth
Rich Scarborough & Henry Graim Datr Dec. 30. 1684
Joshua Wright & Han. Walker married May 14. 1686
John Milne & Margaret Day Nov. 22
Saml Wade of High Bentley & Wood ffeb 13
Mr Hanson Lecturer at Halifax & Mr Anth. ffoxcrofts dr. of
  Woodhouse Mar 29. 87
Joseph Haliday & Eliz. Baxter Apr. 6
John Hodgson & Widow Blacket Apr. 9
Danl Tempest & Ruth Ambler Apr 22
Henry Naylor & Martha Greenwood Apr 26
Jonathan Priestley & Mary Chadwick June 15
Thos Hodgson & Grace July 18
Mr. Rooks of Rhodes Hall & Mr Cooks dr. (who had bin Vicar
  of Leeds) married Dec 8 His former wife was buried April 26
James Okey of Bolton & John Grundy of Rakes Datr married
  May 1688 died in Sept, 1688
Mr Charles Herle of London & Mrs. Partington of Manchester
  June 14
John Crowther of Stowps in Shipden married —— of Leeds
  Dec. 20
Mr John Ray of Gumersall & Susanna dr. of Mr. Dickson clark
  of Whitchurch ffebr
John Oldfield & Patience Longbothom Apr. 30. 1689
John Craven & Mary Drake, June 24
Mr Nathl Priestley & Mrs Jane ffournesse July 11
Saml Appleyard & Martha Hollings July 21
Joseph Brooksbank & Sarah Naylor Sept 8. 1689, both dead
  Mar. 31. 1690
Joshua Sonier & Grace Hodgson Jan 14. 1689-90
James Harrison & Mr Naylor of Alverthorps datr Mary Jan 6
Mr —— Corlesse minister of long Marston near York & Dorothy
  datr of Mr Bryan Dickson married ffebr 6
Mr John Hatfield & Mrs Mary Hallowes Apr 3. 1690
Mr John Lister of Maningham & Sam Lister of Overbriars datr
  Apr 13
—— Thornton & Susan Rushworth Apr. 28

MARRIAGES.

Joshua Stocks & Mercy Tetlaw Apr 29
Mr Joseph Wadsworth & Mrs Crook May 10
Mr. Nic. Kirshaw & Anne Wilkinson in Craven May 20. 1690
Mr Jere Bentley & Eliz. Graim Aug 7 1690
Tho ffarrand & Judith Scarborough of Bradford married at the
    meeting place in N.ourum Aug 25
Mr. John Crompton of Breadmit & Mrs Eliz. Coulborn Sep 1
Jonathan Rigg & Han Tetlaw Sep 23
John Learoyd & Sarah Parkinson Sep 25
Joseph Thorp & Grace Hulms Sep 30
Charles Best (at 16 years) and Jane Oxley servt to Wid. Brooks-
    bank Nov 4
Japhet Hield & Martha Ledgard Dec 1
John Stansfield and Mrs Han. Bath Dec. 25
David Dean and Wid Butterworth ffeb. 2
James Brooksbank and Eliz Gleadal ffeb 4 1690-1
Mr Joseph Holroyd called Esq. and Widow Kighley Jun 19. 1691
John Walker and Judith ffoster June 28
Mr John Kirk of Alverthorpe and Mrs Rachel Burdet Silkston
    July 30
Anthony Naylor and Jane Baumford of Rochdale married at
    N.ouru. Chappel Dec. 16
Nathan Heywood and Anne Kay Dec 29
Dr. Colton and Mrs Mary Ward (Mr. Ralph Wards only child),
    Dec. 30
Mr. Michl. Gargrave and Mrs. Middlebrook ffebr
John Sonier and Mary Broadley May 10. 1692
Mr Sager of Alverthorp and Captain Pools Datr May 18 1692
Tim. Booth and —— Hemingway Sept 1
John Kellet and —— Sep. 5
Joshua Taylor and Judith Bolton Sep. 8 (92) she died Sept 24
    (92)
Widow Turner married her man at Coley Ch. Nov. 14 calld
    Lancashire a poor lad and a bad one, not 20 and she above 60
Abra. Illingworth and Anne Blackbrough married by Mr. Smith
    Dec. 8
—— Wright and a maid of Mr Rooks Dec 16
Mr. Heald and Mrs Eliz. Hough married Apr.
—— Dewhirst of Lightcliffe and Martha Stocks married May 2.
    1693

MARRIAGES.

Rich Scarborough and Mrs Mitchel (Abra Walkers datr) June 11
Mr Joseph Wood of ffold and John Ramsdens Datr May 29
Mr Ingram of Leeds and Mrs Lydia Kirk of Roiston June 27
Mr John Longbothom of London and Mr. Abr Halls Datr of
   Booth Town Aug 8
Joseph Wilkinson of Shelf and Susanna Ambler, Sept 5
John   of Burstall and Bathshua Holdsworth of Hickmond-
   wyke Sep 21
Abra. Holt of Booth Town and Esther Moor Nov 4
Mr Matthew Smith of Mixenden and Susanna Datr of Lieutenant
   Sharp of Horton Nov 14
John Bentley of Sowerby and Mary Slater of Shelf Apr 10 (94)
Mr ffuthergal Sheriffe of York and Mrs Martha Kirk May 1.
   1694
Joseph Northen and John Holdsworths Datr Apr. 24. 1694
Nathl Booth and Sarah Day June 26. 1694
John Priestley and Mary Swift Sep. 16
Tho Hodgson and Abigail Priestley Sept 27
Tho Priestley and Elizabeth Kitchingman Oct 28
Mr John Heywood and Mrs Eliz. Stacy Oct 2
Abra Scot and Widow Rhodes Oct 8
Mr Saml Brook Preacher at Whitby married —— of London,
   Sep.
Tim Vicars and Nathl Croslands daughter Oct 31
James Tetlaw and Widow Hurd Jan 1
Mr Nathl Robinson and Mr Brooksbanks dr of Ealand Mary,
   ffeb. 14
Dr Prescot and Mrs Mitchell of Scout, May 7 (95)
Mr Whately of Skipton, Apothecary, and Mrs Smith whose hus-
   band died in Y. Castle, May 7
Mr Saml Lister of Shipden Hall and Dorothy Priestley, May 16,
   1695
Mr Anthony Buxton of Rochdale and Mr ffirths datr of Height,
   May 29, 1695

---

*look into my little Book of velum bound having one clasp there
you'l find 210 marriages of several persons*

Mr John Hough and Lydia datr. of Mr Richd Sykes of Leeds,
   July 25

MARRIAGES.

Mr John Hough of Halifax and Mrs Debora Syke of Leeds married at Rodwell on July 25. 1695

Ebenezer Nalor and Zipporah Boocock marryed at Halifax Nov 26. 1695

Isaac Sonier and Elizabeth Milner married at Bradford May 7. 1696

John Bently of Northourum and Susanna Mitchel married at Halifax May 7. 1696

John Hurd of Shelf and Sarah Buckly of William Clays in Northourum married at Halifax May 12, 1696

Mr George town and Mrs Clare married thursday June 11. 1696

Mr John Holdsworth of Spen married Mary Banke at Burstall June 11, 1696

—— and Martha Lister married June 9. 1696 at Bradford

John s. Isaac Balm married Anne Stead of Bradford there June 15. 1696

Jonas Dean Mixenden and Martha Scolfield marryed at Halifax Aug 18. 1696. He dyed that day month

Mr James farrar of Thewood marryed daughter of Widow Briarly of Ratchdal Aug. 1696

Dec 9. 1696, Isaac farrar and Phœbe Clay married at Halifax Church without the knowledg or consent of parents on either side he had stollen her affections being but 17 years of age a sad grief to her tender-hearted father

John Nolson of Shipden marryed Widow Wade of High-bently at Coley chappell feb. 1. 1696-7 Mr Parret joyned them

John Smith my clark and Rebecca Viccars marryed at Halifax feb. 11. 1696-7 daughter of John Viccars of Thorp near Idle

Mr Abraham Hall of Booths Town and Jane d. of Mr Beamont of Darton, mar. there feb 25. 96-7

Alderman Stanhup of Leeds son and Hanna Reiner of Milnes Brige married Apr. 1697

John Sonier mar. Ellen Ingham of Warly, William Ingham dr. apr. 29. 97

Abraham Scot stole his wife brought her to Haslihurst May 12. 97

Ambrose Ingham marryed Aug 10. 1697

Mr Samuel Wadsworth of Horbury Mrs Welcom Kerby mar. tuesday, May 25, 1697

Richard Kighley of Sowerby and Widow Blakebrough mar. at Sowrby June 1. 97

MARRIAGES.

Mr Abraham Langley of Priestley and Ms Roseendale marryed July 1697

Mr. John Smith of Wakefield and Mtris Mitchel marryed Aug 2. 1697.

Mr Thomas Hall & Mtris Joanna Cotton marryed July 15 1697

Henry Naylor & Mtris Susanna Hallowel mar. at Rachdal Sept 20. 1697

John Wadsworth of Holdsworth mar. dr of James Chadwick of Warly Oct. 1697

Robert Brierley & — Bairstow marryed at Ealand Nov 17, 97 his old wife was drowned Oct 8, 97

Mr John Allison, Ovenden & Anne d. of Mr. Edward Langly, Hipperholm marryed Dec 30. 1697

Mr Nathan Sharp schoolmaster of Hipperholm mar. Anne Priestley

Mr John Walker mar. feb 169⅞ he married — dr to Wm. Rawson feb. 19. 98

William Lister of Bingly mar. — Dobson of Cottingly feb 18 1698 both of these young men stole their wives

Mr Brian Dickson of Hunslet Lane marryed feb 22. 169⅞

The son of Mr. Hatfield of Laughtor marryed the dr. of Mr. Rich ·of Bulhouse Mch. 1698

Abraham Ashworth & Phœbe Craven marryed Apr. 8. 1698

Mr Townly a Lanc. gentleman marryed dr. of Robt Mason of Booths Town, Apr. 25. 98.

Samuel Holdworth mar. dr. of James Gregson both of Northourum Apr. 25, 98

Charles Higson of Halifax mar.   of Brighouse at Halifax April 25, 98 and many more marriages in Halifax. 8 couples married

James Brooksbank mar. Mary Bently of Sowrby Wednesday April 27. 1698 at Illingworth Chappel.

James Wallis & Elizabeth d. Tho. Bently mar at Halifax May 2. 98

Enoch s. John firth mar. Martha d. Timothy Stansfield at Halifax June 3, 1698

James Kighly mar. Anne d. James Hall his own cozen June 18. 98

Mr Jonas Blamires mar. Lydia Nickol June 23. 1698 at Burstall, went to Durham that day

MARRIAGES.

Mr Whity s. of Jo. Whity Esq of Carburton in Nottinghamshire and Mrs Bridget Taylor Esq Taylors dr. Wallinwells July 28. 98

William Cryer of Heton & Sarah Learoyd marryed at Carverly Aug 22 1698

Thomas Gill of Southowram & Sarah Ekroyd mar. at Halifax Nov 23. 1698.

Tho. Got of Bingly and Elizabeth Parkinson sister to Sarah Learoyd mar. at Bradford Dec. 22, 1698

Timothy Bancroft & Elizabeth —— mar. at Halifax Apr. 10. 1699

James Barrow & Martha fletcher marryed on tuesday Apr 25. 1699

Timothy Stocks marryed Apr. 1699

Mr. Nathanael Heywood my nephew married, a third time, to dr. Mr. Truman of Learoyd May 25. 1699

Mr James Lister, Apothecary in Halifax & d. Willm Issot of Horbury June 1699

Sir John Middleton and Mrs Lambert mar. June 22, 99

Mr —— a souldier and Ms Mary frankland marryed that week

Joseph Croft & Mary Oldfield mar. at Halifax Sep 26. 1699

Mr Wm. Benson, minister at Knaresbro mar. d. of Mr Ralph Ward of York Sep. 27. 99

Mr. Green of Robert-town in Burstall psh. and Achsah d. Daniel Walker mar. Oct. 23 1699 at Burstall

Timothy Oldfield & d. of Ralph Dickson mar. at Leeds Nov. 20. 1699

Isaac Holroyd of Hipperholm and John Hills widow of Stump Crosse mar. Dec. 4. 1699

My son Eliezer and Hellen d. of Mr. John Rothera of Dranfield, mar. at Hansworth Jan 18 1699-700

Dr. Richardson & Mr. Crosseleys daughter marryed feb. 9. 700 at Luddenden

William Wilkinson of Wyke & Elizabeth Smith, widow, marryed May 1700 at Halifax

Mr Joseph Heywood and Mtris Martha Leaver marryed at Bolton May 14 1700 tuesday morning

John Kellet and Hannah Ward marryed at Bradford friday May 3, 1700

Joseph Jackson of Leeds & Dorothy Brooksbank of Ealand

MARRIAGES.

marryed Aug. 22, 1700

Timothy Crowther & Isabel Bolton mar. at Halifax Sep. 9 both of Warley

Richard Kershaw of Wyke & Hannah marryed at Halifax Oct. 1700

Jonathan Holdworth & Elizabeth Gregson marryed at Halifax Nov. 3. 1700

Mr Jonathan Wright & Mtris Corlesse, widow (Mr Bryan Dicksons daughter) marryed at Leeds Nov. 20. 1700

John Rudman marryed Mary Appleyard at Halifax Dec 5. 1700 : an old man to an old woman

Mr William Horton of Barsland and Sir Richard Musgraves daughter married at Ripponden Dec. 12. 1700

John Terry of High Bently marryed Mary Lister of Wibsey Mr. John Listers daughter Jan. 1700-1

Mr. Ward preacher at Thornton chappel and Martha Bently marryed at Huthersfield feb 25. 1700-1

John Terry & Mary Oates marryed at Halifax Apr. 21. 1701

William Northend & Martha Sunderland marryed at Halifax June 14. 1701

Mr Samuel Smith of York & Mtris Margaret franckland of Rawthmel marryed June 1701

Michael Rushworth & Rebecca fox marryed at Halifax thursday Oct. 2. 1701

James Paulard & Mary Coulin quakers marryed at their meeting-place at Halifax Oct 15. 1701

Nathan Tilson & Mary Hughs marryed at Halifax Dec 30. 1701

Mr. William Perkins of Richmond preacher marryed Alice d. Martha Mitchel of Halifax Apr. 9. 1702 at Halifax Church

John Holdworth of Northourum & Judith Butler marryed at Illingworth Chappel by Mr. Wilkinson Apr. 20. 1702

Burials.

the wife of Samuel Ramsden

Mary Whitteley November 28. 1655

too children of John Rushworth buryed at Coley March 5. 1657

a child of Micael Smith buried March 7. 1657

BURIALS.

Susanna d. John Rushworth buryed at Coley Novem. 20. 1660
Henry Ekroyd of Deanhouse died suddenly Nov. 6. 1675 aged 63
Tho. Nicolson of Sowerby aged 80
John Hopkinson of Sowerby aged 86 both buried Oct. 24, 1676
Widow Best of Holdsworth buried ffeb. 13, aged 92
Mr. Sam. Sunderland of Bingley Parish ffeb 4, aged 74, a very
    rich man
Dr. Hitch, Dean of York Parson at Guisely ffeb. 16. aged 82, a
    very rich man
Josiah Collier in Guisely Parish died the same day, aged 82
James Oldfield of Warley buried June 1. 1677 aged 73. rich
Matthew Clay of N.ouru June 18, aged 72, poor
Mr. Hawksworth of Hawksworth in Otley Parish buried at
    Guiseley Dec. 11. abt 60. Justice, very rich
James Scarborough of Halifax ffeb 4. aged 70. rich
Sr John Savil June 12 aged   A Papist
Sr George Dolton of Heath Hall by Wakefield June
Sir John Brights Lady of Bradsworth June 26, aged 50
Mr John Angier of Denton died Sep. 1. aged 72
Joseph Kitchin of ffarsley Sep. 6. aged 74
Mr Josiah Holdsworth, minr. died in Wakefield Oct 18. aged 75
Mr. Rich. Blacket of Shaw near Halifax died Nov. 6 aged 73
Mr Peter Sunderland of fairweather green, Dec. rich
Phœbe wife of Jonathan Priestley of Winteriag dyed March 2
    was buryed Mch 5 1674-5 at Halifax
Phœbe d. of Abra. Holt of Cockil in Shelf dyed Mch 21, buryed
    at Halifax Mch 24 1674-5
Henry Ekroyd of Deanhouse dyed suddenly Nov 6. was buryed
    at Coley Nov 8. 1675
old Robert Wood was buryed Wednesday Nov. 24. 1675 at
    Halifax aged 88.
Simeon Robisons wife buryed at Coley March 21.ͺ1675-6
John Learoyd bur. Mch. 28
Hannah Hardgr buryed at Halifax, Sat April 30. 1676
Anne White buryed at Coley, May 27. 1676
Susanna wife of John Brooksbank, Shelf, bur. at Halifax June 5.
    1676
Mary wife of Thomas Priestley buried at Halifax June 19. 1676
Abraham Duckworth bur. at Halifax Sat. june 17. 1676
Robert Bruer, Shelf bur at Halifax June 22. 76

Richard Appleyard aged 80 bur. at Halifax July 12. 1676

Will Walker aged 80 bur. at Halifax July 5. 1676

John Burnley of Shelf bur. at Coley July 23 1676 lay 11 weekes
in great misery almost eaten away with vermin, head in sores

Richard Boococks wife bur. at Halifax Aug 6. 1676

Richard Boocock her husband bur. Aug 14. 1676 aged 93 they
had lived together 55 yeares in Shelf

Micael Broadly of the Hoyle in Hipperholme bur. Aug. 21. 1676

Lidia d. Mr Joseph Dawson bur. at Halifax Sep 19. 1676, 5
years

Elizabeth wife Nathan Crowther, aged 70, died Sep 20, bur. at
Halifax Sep 25. 1676 munday

James Mitchel of Norwoodgreen dyed Dec. 31, bur. at Halifax
Jan. 3. 76-7

The d. of Abraham Bairstow, High Bentley bur. at Halifax Jan
15 1676-7   another dr. of his bur. about 6 weeks agoe.

Nicolas servant to Josh Whitley bur. ffeb. 12 1676-7

Will. Walker of Folds bur. ffeb. 18

Samuel Spencer's wife, dyed of child bearing, bur. at Halifax
June 10 1677

Hanna wife of Jeremiah Watson bur. at Halifax June 12. 1677

Mathew Clay of Northourum bur. at Halifax June 18. 1677 being
aged 72

James s. John Bland of Norwoodgreen, aged 20, bur. at Halifax
June 30. 1677

John Bests wife of Landimer went to pontefract on tuesday with
her son Charles, had fainting fits yet was hearty on friday following; dyed there on Sat. July 21, 1677, bur. 23

Mary Nickoll d. of John Kershaw of Norwoodgreen dyed of a
consumption July 31, buryed at Halifax, Aug 3. 1677

Sarah Hardgre dyed at James Tetlaws, bur. at Halifax Aug 20.
1677

Mercy dr. James Brooksbank of Lower Oxeheys, bur. at Halifax
Sep. 15. dyed of a violent bleeding in her mouth Sep 10 at 8
o'clock evening

Nathaniel Lea (Widow Lea son of High bentley,) being consumptive, became fevered, dyed Sep 28, bur. at Halifax Oct 1.
Young men carried him 1677

Jane Milner of Leeds bur. Jan 7. 1677, aged 70

Mr. Lister, Vicar of Wakefield Jan 17. aged 80.   vicar 50 years

BURIALS.

Mr Tho. Lister of Shipden Hall Jan 30. aged 80. blind 12
Rich Brigg of Healy died at Michaelmas 1677 aged 70
Ralph Low, of Denton Jan.   aged 74
Sibilla Watson of Halifax died in 1677 aged 63
John Greenwoods wife of Sowerby Nov. aged 64
Mrs Dearden of Sowerby June   aged 60
Sir Godfrey Copley, High Sheriff Yorkshire died [ffeb 17. 1678
aged 53
John ffirth, Ripponden Jan 24 aged 60
John Platts of Sowerby. ffeb aged abt 60
Sr Rich. Houghton of Houghton Tower ffeb. aged 60
Michael Briggs of Batley ffeb. 28. aged 66
Rich Scolcroft Tenant to Mr. Ol. Heywood. Oct. aged 82. 1677
Sr Tho Wentworth of Brittain Hall buried Dec 8. 1675. aged 64
Sr Matthew Wentworth of Br. H. his Bro coming to the Estate
died March 1677, aged 60
Mrs Labern of Leeds died Mar. 10. 1678, aged 80 ; a rich widow
Mr. Holt of Castleton bur. Dec. 16. 1675, aged 80, very rich
Tho. Pickles of Colne brigg died Sept. aged 80. rich
Alderman Briary of York Sept. aged 64
Mr Lionel Copley of Rotheram died at London bur. in Yorkshire
Dec. 4. 1677. aged 60. rich
Col. John Dukinfield (Sir Robts uncle) died in Essex, bur. at
Denton Chapel ffeb. 15. 1677
Susanna Midgley of Sowerby died Mar. 20. 1678, aged 86
Grace Gawkroger of Sowerby, bur. Apr. 2. aged 99
Ester Wilson born in Knaresborough forest, late servant at John
Kershaws dyed at Will Clays Nov 1. bur. at Halifax Nov 3.
1677, sick of a fever 21 d
Mary wife of Joshua Soyner of Wall close hauing lyen on her
bed two yeares in great pain and sores, dep. Jan. 8. bur. at
Halifax Jan 10. 167$\frac{7}{8}$
Mary wife Richard Robinson of Norwoodgreen was delivered of
a child and died about 3 weeks after ; bur at Halifax Jan
16. 167$\frac{7}{8}$
Mr Wm Drake, Justice of Peace in Craven buried at Thornton
Mar 13. 1678, aged 53
Tho. Evans of Manchester March, aged 60, a good man
Mr John Wilton a minr in Wiltshire March aged 79 very rich
Mr John Denhams mothers Brother

BURIALS.

Mr Taylor, Alderman of Leverpool was upon the Exchange walking at 10, dead at 12 a clock, buried Apr 12 aged 60

An Aldermans wife bur. Apr 15

Another Alderman the week before, all old

Henry Burkhead of Lightcliffe bur Ap 17 aged 70

Mary wife of John Wood of Skircote bur. Apr 14 aged 64. never spoke after she was struck

Rose Watson of Norwoodgreen died Apr. 12. 1678, aged 67, a choice good woman but poor, lay weak many years

Mr Henry Wadsworth near Luddingden was well and dead in an hours time, buried in his garden Apr 10. aged 66. a great Quaker, very rich

Abigail d. John Nickol in the Hough dyed of a dropsy June 21, buryed at Halifax June 22

Grace d. George Boyl of high-bentley buryed at Halifax July 24. 1678. Of a consumption.

Isaac s. John Nickol dyed July 31. 1678. Mary (his mother) d. of John Kershaw dyed that day twelve month, vid supra

John s. John Wells of Northouram Green bur. at Halifax Aug 7

Eliz. Robinson of Pendle buried Apr. 12 aged 90. grandmother to Tho Leech wife, 40 year old

Emmat a poor woman in Bingley Parish buried Apr 2, aged 100. Some say 102, had cost the parish above £40 in poor leys

Mr. Glendal a minr. in Chester died abt a year ago, aged 80

Grace Philip (mother to Mr John. Denham died Apr 19 near Wibsey, aged 89

John Bottomley of Deaf Mill died May 2. aged 63

John Best of Landimer dyed there Nov. 23. was buryed at Halifax Nov 26. 1678 aged 27

Mary ffletcher buried at Halifax May 16 aged 60 (or 68)

Sr Philip Musgrave in Cumberland a great Persecutor died 1678 aged 80

James and Edward Turner of Manchester, Brothers, Sick'ned both on a day, 4 days sick buried May 11, aged abt. 60

Mrs Hall of Newton Heath buried at Manchester May 30, aged 94

Alice Shuttleworth of Wakefield buried July 28 1677, aged 80

Edward Hudson of Northourum buried at Halifax Jan 14. 1678-9 aged 72

Edith Brooksbank buryed at Halifax Feb. 4. 1678-9 aged about 63

Martha d. Richard Hoyl of Godley bur. at Halifax feb 5. 1678-9 aged 17 years

Phœbe wife of Thomas Paulard of Blakehil bur. at Halifax feb 15 1678-9 aged 58

Phœbe wife of John Stancliff of Hagstocks dyed March 6. 1678-9 was buryed at Halifax Mch. 10. of a fortnight sicknes, aged 49

Jeremiah Watson of Northourum dyed of a consumption Mch 23, buried at Halifax Mch 25, 1679 aged 27

Abraham Holt of Cockhil bur. at Halifax Aug. 25 1679 aged 70

Alex Kershaw, Inkeeper, in Littleborough died Dec. 1677, aged 74

Mr. Little, parson of Kildwick many years died June 1678 aged 80 had been in dotage vncapable of preaching many years. Mr. Paulard was his Curate.

Mr Wm Barton of Martins in Leicester died in May aged 80. Preached Sabbath before. Composer of Hymns

Danl Mitchel of Horley green near Halifax died July 17. 1678 was drunk there Saturday before aged 71, a sad man

Wm Sanderson of Silkston Parish went a Juryman to York Thursday, died Monday, buried July 18, aged 60

Thomas Hill of Shelf died poor at J. Sunderland was buried at Halifax, thursday Nov 29. 1679

Jonathan Crowthers wife of Northourum buried at Halifax Dec. 2. 1679 dyed suddenly

Anne Nunwick of Shelf buried at Halifax Dec 16. 1679 dyed suddenly

John Jagger widow of Shelf buried at Halifax Dec 16. 1679

Mathew Boocock buried on tuesday Dec. 3 1679, aged 58

Mathew Jagger buried at Halifax March 28. 1680, aged 58

Ester Duckworth of Barnes hill buryed at Halifax March 30. 1680

Rachel Boocock (daughter to Mathew Boocock) buried at Halifax May 6, 1680

Anne wife of Tho. Beck of Headingly in Leeds Parish a zealous Christian died Apr 4 1678, aged 62

Mr. Thos. Brooks, Minr in London died Aug. 1678 aged 72, had married a young wife a little before

Col. Birch of Birch Hall died Aug. 5 abt 70

Robt. Robinson died Aug 21, aged 76 (Mr Angiers hearer)

William Kellets wife of Northfield yate in Northourum buried at Halifax June 27 1680 marryed again to —— at Halifax Oct

BURIALS.

11. 1680

James Smith of Northourum very well on Lords Day Aug 25,
   died 27 buried 30 his sister buried day before ancient 1678
Mr Tho. Brown Inkceper in Kighley buried Oct 3. aged 64 had
   married a young woman left her all his Estate
Eliz Pierson of Woodside Oct 13 aged 66
Ellis Bury buried at Swillington Oct 13, aged 60. was of great
   use at Bramley
Rich Rawlinson of Wibsey Slack buried Oct 24 aged 76
Mary Burkhead buried at Burstall Nov 4 aged 50. left 6 children,
   a good woman
John Burroughs near Bramhup buried at Addle Nov 5. aged 60.
   a good man usefull, much lamented
Mr Ward of Pontefract died Nov 3. 1678 abt 70 a great ffriend
   and favourer of meetings. very rich
Mr. Pailer near York that married Lady Cary, a good man, died
   Oct. aged 63
Joseph Wormwell an old man near Steneland died of an Impost
   Nov of abt. a quarter of an hours warning
Christopher Ramsden of Shaw lane near Holdsworth died Dec. 13,
   aged 70.   They immediately went to Halifax to a Phisician
   for his son George who died also before they got to town, both
   of 2 or 3 days sickness both buried on a day
Mr. Bazaleel Angier, (Bro to Mr Angier of Denton) of Dedham
   died Oct 30. aged 66.
John Reddihough of Illingworth died suddenly Nov. abt 70.
   Professor. friend to Mr. Nath. Heyd.
Thomas Slater's wife buried at Halifax May 1681
Sibell Medley in N.ourum died suddenly buried Dec 27 1678,
   aged 90
Edwd Hudson of N.ourum died Jan 11. aged 72
Anne Hepworth of Norwood-green died Jan 13 aged 81. poor
Mary Denton by Halifax free school buried Jan 16 aged 72, a
   good woman
Mr. Yates of Warrington a N. C. Minr struck with a Palsie, lost
   his Intellectualls, lay long, died Nov. his wife died ffeb. after
Luke ffirth of Barsland came constantly to N.ourn on Lords days
   many years, heard Mr. Heywood at Stubbings Dec. 26, his
   wife died that day, he sickned that night, died Jan 4. aged 61
Michael Maud lived most of his time in Halifax, removed last

BURIALS.

May to Luddenden, died, would need be buried at Halifax. Mr ffarrer sent his Hors-litter, carried him thither Jan 23, aged 62 1678

Sarah wife of Joseph furnasse buryed at Halifax March 28. 1682.

Mrs Sharp (Mr Tho. Sharps mother) of little Horton was at Mrs Waterhouse funeral Jan 21, died Jan 31, 1678 aged 63

Edith Brooksbank of Norwood-green, died ffeb 1. aged 68, long bed rid

Mr. George a parliamt man 97 years old, had bin Parliamt man in K James time, died Jan 25 having sitten 17 years. Sevll of the Parl. died at that time

Edw. Briggs an old Kendal carrier, a good man, great ffriend to minrs, (bro't up a son a scholar, Preacher, not confirming went beyond sea, died) this good old man died Dec. 4, aged 64

Phebe wife of Tho. Paulard of B(l)akehill died ffeb. 14. aged 59

John West of Sowerby died Jan 23 aged 65

Martha Holdsworth died at Oxheys ffebr. 20. aged 68.

Mr Durant Pastor of a Church at Sheffield died ffebr 11 1678, aged 66

Mr Noble, a learned man, formerly minr at Smeton died ffebr. 12 aged 74

Mr Whitehead a N. C. Minr. in Lanc. died ffeb. aged 70

James ffrisco's wife of Ratcliffe died of a dropsie Mar 10. aged 70

Saml Threaplands wife (mother to the Schoolmr. of Hipperholm bur. at Bradford Mar 31. 1679, aged 70

Mrs. Hough, Parson of Thornton's wife, died ffeb 21. 1678

Mr. Edge a N. C. Mr. at Gosworth in Cheshire died ffebr. 21. 1678 suddenly of an Impost

Mary wife of John Nicols died July 31, 1677 her only son Isaac Nicols died July 31 1678

Mr Hardcastle died suddenly Oct. 1

Major Taylor of Wallen Walls died Mar. 29. 1679 aged 55 had 5000 li a year

Mr Joshua Earnshaw, near Hulmfirth died Mar 5, aged 67

Mr Joshua Horton of Sowerby died of stone Apr. 7, 1679, aged 60. Justice of Peace, had 1000 li a year, a pious man

Mr Daniel Greenwood of Halifax struck with a Palsy, lay 5 years under it, buried Apr 28. aged 57

Mr James Saile, minr, formerly of New Church in Leeds, struck with a Palsey lay several years, died Apr. 17, buried at

Calverly Apr. 21. 1679, aged 60.

Mr Tho Calvert of York formerly Preacher at Minster buried at York Apr. aged 75

Mrs Spawford, wife to Mr Sp. a N. C. Minr at Silkston formerly, died Apr. aged 94

Edith Holden mother to Sam Bentleys wife of Halifax buried June 3 aged 97

Brian Bentley Poet at Halifax June 9 aged 64, well descended

James Milne near Rochdale died July 1, aged 67, good

Bernard Dawson Bro to Abra. D. Mr J. D. ffather died at his Bros beyond York, June, aged 74

John Moorhouse in Burton Parish near Lydiatt died June, aged 76

Abra. Holt of Cockhil died Aug. 21, aged 70

Mrs Crook of Riddlesden Hall, Tho Leechs Aunt, died Aug 22 1679, aged 66

Robt Turner of Motram Parish died Aug 26 aged 76 : a Hearer at Denton

Robt Collier died Aug. 26, aged 86, both Elders at Denton

John Burkhead of Hickinwyke died Sep. 18. aged 67. a good man

John Normanden of Sowerby buried Sept 8, aged 79

John Waters of Malton banks in Bingley Parish buried Sept. aged 61

Capt Pockley near Selby died in York Sept, aged 60

Mrs Cudworth (widow to a minr) died at Wakefield, Sept 17 aged 63

John Issot of Horbury, well Monday, died next day Sep 23, aged 73. Mr Marshall Elder

Ashton Jones, Inkeeper in Halifax died Sept 21 (77) aged 61

Jonas Rodes of Wibsey fell in the ffield on Monday, died Monday after Sep. 28, aged 80

Daniel Rich of Peniston Parish uncle to Sylv. Rich of Bullouse died Oct 1. 1679, aged 76

Lady Watson of York buried Oct 6, abt 70 Mr Williams and Mr Ward preacht weekly at her house

Coll. Bethel or Sr. Hugh died Oct 1. aged 64 chosen Parliamt. man for Headon

Dr Robt Wilde of Oundley died of 2 or hours sickness abt Aug 1. aged 69,

BURIALS.

Mrs Dawson of Leeds buried Nov. 4, aged 78, had N. C. Minrs
to preach in her house

Mary Dickinson wife to Jcre. D. buried at Halifax Nov. 13
aged 54

John Harpur of Ainsworth died Oct, aged 81

Lady Wilbraham of Woodhey in Cheshire, died Nov. aged 81 Mr
John Heywood had bin Chaplain wth her

Mr Sam Mauds wife buried at Halifax Nov 24. aged 81

Mr Gurnal of Suffolk died Oct, at his Intermt clark names the
Psalm, none sung, but all fell aweeping for their great lose so
the minr.........aged 7...

Tho Moorhouse of Kirkburton Parish buried Nov. 29. 1679
aged 70

Anne Nunwick died at Saml Wilsons Shelf buried Dec. 17 aged
62, unmarried

Mr Trimlet an anabaptist a man of note in London lost his Estate
by his turn, kept gratis by Mr Ralph Spencer near Lceds till
they grew weary of him, died Dec, aged 82

Alice   sister to Ruth Holdwat died at Norwood green
buried Dec. 9, aged ——

Nathan Sharp of Wyke buried Nov. aged 82

Peter Omroyds wife buried at Heptonstal Jan 1 the day of her
birth aged 85

Grace Turner died at Sam. Hopkinson in Sowerby Dec. 18.
aged 73

Mr. Heber died at Staunton in Craven, Dec 24, aged 73 was
considerable in the wars

Mr John Andrews of little Leaver died Dec. aged 64, had been
Capt in Parliaments Army

Michl Watson of Norwood Green bur. Nov. 1

Mr James Emmaut a Lanc. man of a considerable family buried
at Kildwick in Craven Jan. 8. 1679, aged 81

Robt Bairstow of Blakehill died Jan 10. aged 73.

Mr Lever of Chamber near Bolton buried Dec. (same day Mr
Andr was) aged 82

Robt fferniside of N.ourum buried Jan 2, aged 81

John Saltonstall, Wyke, buried Jan 2-, aged 74

Mrs Mary Drake, Pontefract, buried ffebr. 4. aged 58

Rebccca Hamond of Scholmore near Horton buried ffeb 11. aged
88

Ester Hoyl (Lukes widw. buried ffeb 16. aged 80
Robt Cloudsly of Leeds died Nov. aged 84
Richard Lawson, one of Mr Jollys Society, died ffeb. aged 83
Sr Ralph Assheton of Whaley (a member of the long Parliamt. &
  of this) died at London ffeb burd at Downham Mar 3. 1679
  aged 75
Jere. Gleadhill of Thornton buried Mar. 8. aged 64, rich, had bin
  at Halifax Sat. before
Mr. Tho. Idle of Holbeck buried at Leeds Mar 12, left 2
  Daughters to Mr Dixons guardianship 100 li a year a piece,
  1000 li a piece in money, aged 60, of good repute
Sarah Baraclough near Wibsey buried Mar. 13, aged 59
Mrs. ffarrand of Bingley, (2d wife to Mr Robt, Benj ffather) died
  Mar, 24. aged abt 80, rich widow. Mr O. Heywood. ffriend
  and hearer
Widow Rhodes buried at Rochdale Mar 25, 1680 aged 72
John Ratcliffes wife of Sowerby buried Apr 27 abt 80, had bin
  married 52 years
Mr. ffarrand Schoolmaster at Almandbury near 4— years bur
  Ap. 29, about 80.
Dr Tho. Godwin died in London March, near 80. 1680
Mrs Hough of Thornton died ffebr 21, 1678
Mr Edge a N. C. Minr. at Gosworth in Cheshire died June 21.
  1678, its thought of an Impost [See *ante*. J. H. T.]
Mr Hardcastle died suddenly Oct 1 (78)
Isaac Sergeants daughter near Woodkirk died of childbearing
  buried in the new burying place Sept 15 (78) endured much,
  the story dreadfull, Dr Johnson of Pontefract acted the midwife
Mrs Cook Mr Sales datr. of Pudsey died in child-bearing Oct 11
A woman in Calvery parish was delivered of a child, it died, she
  recovered, was Churcht, that time 5 weeks deliver'd of another
  living child, Sept 1678
Mrs Cotton of Denbigh died in childbed Oct 9. 78
Mrs. Judith ffinch (Mr Hortons datr of Barsld. liv'd in Kent, her
  husband died, she travelled, bore a child, died, both buried
  together at London, carried 60 miles, left 6 little children,
  Oct 12. (78)
Richard Scarbroughs wife died of a child bed, ffever Nov. 15 (78)
A woman died suddenly who liv'd at Wm Walkers near Walterclough Dec 21

Nathl Webster that married Mary Mr Waterhouse dr. got the foul disease they say at London in Oct, died Dec. 28, buried at Bradford

Mrs. Waterhouse of Bradford died suddenly Jan. 18

Jonathan Bentley wife of Halifax bank top buried Jan. 22

Mr Etherington, minr at Sowerby (I think) died suddenly Jan 4 on Saturday. Preacht Sabbath before

Jonas Rushworths wife of Denham gate was at Halifax on Saturday Jan 25 (78) came home, went to bed, found herself cold, askt her Husband to come to bed, put herself into his bosom, instantly breathed her last

Jeremiah Kirshaw's wife of Wyke died in childbed ffebr. 10

Mr Nettleton's wife of Heaton died in childbed buried Mar. 17

Mrs Rooks of Roids Hall Mr Croslands datr, deliverd of a datr Mar 23   [Crossed off.]

Susan Brigg, with child by Tim Stocks, he ran away refusing to marry her, was deliver'd and died, Aug 18. 1679. Roger Stocks took care of it

Mrs Oates of Chickenly died of the 5th child Aug 27. 1679

Tho. Paulard of Norwood Green died suddenly July 19. 1692

John Stancliffs maid died of an Impost at cloths Hedge, Oct. 12. 1692

A man of Okenshaw fell down dead as he was getting on horse back at Dr Richardsons Oct. 31

John Dickson of Halifax shopkeeper died suddenly Dec 31

John Baraclough of Okenshaw died eating a piece of Pye crust to his dinner Jan 17, aged 91

Joseph Galkroger of Sowerby going from Halifax died at Josiah Stanfields Jan 21

Mrs Esther Lister of Shipden Hall died in bed by her husband Jan 26, aged 60

George Boyl of Shelf was laughing, fell down in a palsey fitt in the ffold May 8, at Jos Listers near Wibsey Slack 1693, aged 75. He was of the same family near High Town that the Earl of Burlington came from

Mr Michael Gargreave wife (Mr Middlebroughs widow) near Bramley died suddenly buried May 29, 1693

Mrs Hatfield of Hatfield died Suddenly Sept. 2

Mr. Robt. Chadwick of Manchester died suddenly Sept 9

James Kighly of Thornton fell down dead (digging for Potatos)

BURIALS.

Oct 16, aged about 56

Ralph Idle an oyledrawer in Leeds was at Church Lords day twice, found dead in his bed Monday morning Nov. 13. A rich Batchelor

James Kighley of Morton bank found dead in his bed Apr 21. 1694

Mr Thornton preacher at Horsford, usher at Bingley, went out well, found dead on Rundles more Apr 21

Peter Heywood of little Lever fell down, died going to Bury fair Apr 21. Mr O. Heywd preacht his funeral at Bolton, May 23 on Job 9. 23. Aged 54

John Kitson of Syke in Burstall Parish eat his dinner well died next day June 6 1694, aged 60

Jere Marsden wife of Walmsley in Lanc. making hey with her husband fell a coughing, he took her in his Arms gave 2 sighs, breathed her last July 9

Nathl Charlesworth of Sowerby bridge found dead in bed Oct 13

Martha Vicars of Greece in Halifax found dead in bed Apr 10 1695, aged 60

John Clark of Morley died Apr. 25 a lusty young man workt day before

Mr Nathl Heywoods wife of Ormskirk deliver'd of a son, baptizd that day fortnight, he greatly rejoyced in having a living wife and son Nathl. Lords day after left her well, preacht, in afternoon sent for out of Chapel after he had been half an hour, ran fast found her dead. Apr. 1695

Richard ffarrars wife of Pudsey went to a ffeast near Otley, pretty well in the Journey with her husband, could not eat there, died after dinner July 27

Old Widw Banks of Hansworth in Burstall Parish (mother to Mr Wm Banks Watchmaker, died suddenly Sept. 4

Mrs. Langley of Barnesley (Mrs Deykins mother) buried Oct 10, not well 2 or 3 days

John Bairstows wife of Illingworth died Oct 18

Robt Leach poor and wicked, had been drinking on Lords Day, came home, fell into raging fitts, died in 2 or 3 days Nov. 1695

Robt Bell on of the Waits in Halifax went to bed well, fell ill, died, buried May 16. 1696

Two women in Bradford, one found dead in bed, the other died

BURIALS.

Dr Illingworth a schoolmaster died Aug. 20 well night before

Mr Wainwright Postmaster at ffcrybridge eat dinner well, died before 8 a clock, Dec 1

Andrew Hartleys wife of Comon Wood span 3 trippets Mar. 22. died next morning

Joseph Walker of Bingley at meeting Lords day twice died tuesday morning Apr. 13 1697, Palsie, aged 71

Mr Saml Ibison of Leeds died in the way at Hunslet Sept 3

Wid Ambler in Northowram well and dead in an hour or two buried Oct

Judith Drake found dead in bed Dec 7 1697

Mr Wm Green of Hightown well and dead in abt a hours time, 4—li a year, much money ffebr 5, aged 40, a great Drinker

Esther Scolcroft near Bolton found dead in bed ffebr

Robt Ramsden of Stony Royd died suddenly Septr 23 1699 aged 70

Mr Sandiford near Oldham in Lanc. died in the road from Manchester Dec 1699 Mr Sam Thorp married his daughter soon after

The Clark of Rippenden led the PS. before it was sung, fell down dead Jan 28

Mr Sam Crowther minr at Wibsey died June 4 1680 aged abt 40

John Heywood (Mr. O. H. fathers only Bro. buried at Bolton July 31. aged 77

Mr Henry Ashurst of Hackney died Nov. aged 66

Mr Moses Jenkins of Hackney died Dec 7, aged 82, had bin usefull

Tim Bentley Bro to Mr Eli Bentley died Jan 9, abt 54

Dan Drake of Northouram died Jan 18. Ant. Waterhouse of Blake hill buried same day Jan 20. aged 80

Mrs Farrar, Justice ffarrars wife of Ewood died at York Jan. aged 55

Jere ffarrar of Robertstown buried ffebr 7. aged 60. preachers ffather

Mr Abr. Dyson of Eland buried ffebr 15 aged 80, rich

Mr James Dyson of Westwood buried his wife at Slaugwait ffebr 18, aged 42 years, a sad loss to 7 little children

Mrs Savil of Greetland died suddenly, buried Mar. 2. aged 63

Mr Isaac Sharp of little Horton buried his wife Mar 8, aged 56.

E

lay long in a consumption

Mr Milner a N.C. Minr buried Mar 9. aged 52, preacht at Lady Rhodes usually, very usefull

Martha Hanson of Royds Hall bur. March 10 aged 52 a gangrene in her back

Mr Gleave of Rochdale died Mar 20. aged 73

Mr Valentine near Eccles, Lanc. buried Mar. 14, his son the Monday after, had 7 children, the old man near 80

Mr Bovil vicar at Rotheram buried Apr. 12. 1681. ag 56

Lady Rhodes of Houghton buried Apr 22 at 12 in night aged 72

Mr Godfrey Rhodes, her son, bur Apr, 27. aged 50

Tho. Slaters wife of Northourum buried May 5, aged 60

Nathan Crowther uncle to Joseph buried June 18, ag. 82, rich

Edwd Northend (ffather to Jonas) buried June 23 aged 82

John Wells of Northourum Green buried July 12, aged 98

Mr Gill reader at Halifax buried Dec 22, about 84

James Smith of Norwood Green died Mar 12, ag. 80

Mrs Bagnall, mother in law to Mr Tho. Sharp of Horton died Mar 12. aged 58.

Mr. Saml Newton a N.C. Minr buried at Rivington Lanc. Mar 11. 168½ aged 48. a worthy man

Mrs Angier of Dedham (Mr Beza. wife) died ffebr. 21 aged 63

Mary Ashton (Mr Angier of Dentons old maid) died suddenly at J. Johnsons Mar. 10, abt 70

Mrs Whitworth of Droilsden buried at Manchester Mar. 25, 1682, aged 76

Mr Simons Parson of Middleton buried Mar 28 aged 88

Mrs Smith buried out of Salford ffebr. 23. 1681 aged 63

Mrs Howarth (Dr H. widow) Mr. H. Ashursts sister buried at Manchester Apr 6. aged 63. good

Mary Dickenson (Mrs ffourness mother) buried Apr 8. aged 83

James Dickenson her husband fell ill in the street at Halifax May 6 dyed by that time they got him into a house, aged 80

Mrs Ramsden (wife to Mr Hen. R. Vicar of Halifax) died at Eland May 11, aged 72, a good woman

Mary Boy widw in Northourum buried June 8, aged 72

Mr John Archer near Kendal died May 20, aged 71, had bin Justice of Peace

Mrs Risley buried at Sowerby June 12 aged 40 parted 10 years from her husband

BURIALS.

Mr. Tho. Case of London (one of the last of the Assembly of Divines at Westmr. 1642 buried June 3. aged 86

Isaac Smith of Northourum buried June 14, aged 76

Mr Webster a Dr of Physic & preacher died at Clithero. June aged 74

Joseph Bleymires of Revy, an old professor, died June 17, aged 75

John Walkers widow at Hoyl bur. July 30, aged 70

Duke of Lauthersdale a Scotman a great Politician, an intimate ffriend of the Kings, but no friend to his native country died Aug. aged 70

Mr Wm Holland of Heaton, Lanc third Bro. of that House that enjoyed the Estate 600 li p. annum : before the Estate came to him he was parson of Malpas in Cheshire, died July aged 76

Mary Crowther of Lands Head in Northourum buried Sept 30. aged 53

Isaac Smith's widw of Collier Syke in Northourum buried Nov. 2. aged 70.

Eliz. Northen of Northfieldyate in Northourum died at North brig Nov 11. aged 76. 1682

Sr Wm Ingolsby of Ripley was at Church on Lords Day, died morning after Nov 6, aged 63, an honest Justice, left a very vast estate

Lady Barnick buried at Newton by Tadcaster Oct. Mr Corlase preacht, comended her for piety humility, charity, above 80

John Brearcliffe, Apothecary in Halifax died of a ffever Dec 4. aged 63

Tim Starkey of Shelf drunk 4 Jacks of Brandy with D.M.O. it dried up his body, was in horrible pain, died in 8 days buried Dec 4. aged 60

James Brigg of the Mountain in Shelf was seized Dec 8, died 12 aged 82

Grace Butler (mother to Ja & Jer. Brooksbank) died Dec 16, aged 82

Mr Hutchinson, Alderman of Leeds, died Dec 1 aged 60

Prince Rupert (Prince of the Palatinate in Germany, K. James Daughters son, buried Nov. 8. aged 63

Robt Tillotson, ffather to Dr. Tillotson buried at Sowerby ffebr. 22, aged 91

BURIALS.

Mr Sam Clark (that writ Martyrologys &c, buried at Hammer-smith near Lond. Dec 29. aged 84

Mr Wentworth of Wooley Justice of Peace (ffather to Sr Michl) buried ffebr 26 aged 60

Martha Brigg of Northourum buried Mar 23. aged 72

Grace Wood of Edg-end by Illingworth buried Mar 28. 1683 She left 900 li in Bonds Bills &c to Tho & Fra Priestley, except Legacys. aged 74

Phebe wife of Andrew Watson of Northourum buried May 8. one of ours

Mary Greenwood Danl G. widow buried May 9 aged 50 Her heart broken by a bad son in Prison at London

Susanna Clay Matthew Clays wife of Northourum buried May 22, aged 78

Old Saml Holdsworths wife of Barnshill in Northourum buried June 1, aged 80

Mr Billingsley of Mansfield formerly Minr at Chesterfield buried May 29. 1683, aged 56 a very worthy minr

Mr Wright a minr in Darbyshire died abt the same time

Dr Rich. Stern A.Bp of York died June 17 buried in State, 34 Coaches—June 22, abt 80

Mr —— Preacher at Hardger Church Chaplain to Sir Tho. Armitage died June 17

Mr Kay Preacher at New Church at Leeds died June 19, aged 55 a moderate man

Mrs Ellis (wife to Mr Steven Ellis) died in Halifax buried there July 9

—— Lister near Bradford burd July 23, aged 80. Mr Jo. Listers grandffather

Mr. Rich. Langley of Priestley green buried Aug 29. aged 64, rich

Mrs Brook of Newhouse in Huthersfield Parish buried Sep 3, aged 66

Jere Holdsworth call'd Beard, of the Height buried at Thornton Sept 6. aged 80

Wm Rhodes of the Mountain died suddenly Sept 9, aged 73

Mr John Dearden of Sowerby buried Sept 13, aged 66 rich

Jere Rossendale of Skircote buried Oct 15, aged 80, very rich

Michael Best of Landimer in Shelf buried Oct 18

Edward Hanson of Royds Hall buried Nov. 14. aged 76

BURIALS.

James Scalberts wife of Elland Ha. buried Nov 19, aged 60

John Batleys wife of Halifax buried Nov 21, abt 70

Dinah Tetlaw of Norwoodgreen, died Nov 21. aged 74, a choice Christian

Mr Armitage of little Town buried Nov 27, aged 53 had bin a great Traveller

John Hargreaves wife in Halifax died of a few days sickness Dec. 24. an active woman, he was Coroner

Justice Heber of Marton died of Small Pox Oct 1. aged 36, a moderate man

His wife died of the same disease Oct 18, left 2 children

Mich. Wilsons wife of Eland buried Jan 7 abt 40 a pious woman

Mr Sylvanus Rich of Bulhouse buried Dec 26. aged 60

John Woodheads wife of Shelf buried Jan 14. aged 50

Charles Hill liv'd with his son at Stump Cross buried Jan 17 aged 93

John Illingworths wife (Mr Wilkinsons mother in law) buried ffebr 1

James Briggs wife of Mountain buried ffebr. 6. aged 70

Lady ffairfax, Lord Henry ff. wife daughter to Lady Darnick buried at Otley ffeb. 16. aged 41

Th Wilkinson ffather to Mr. Wilk. of Illingworth died ffeb 15. aged 70

Sam Denton of Holdsworth died ffebr 24, aged 70

John Rhodes, clark of Illingworth died ffebr 24, aged 80

Jonathan Vicars of Greece in Halifax buried ffeb. 28. ag. 60

Martha Bland John Blands wife of Norwoodgreen buried Mar. 22. aged 62

Mr. Hanson Capt Hansons son of Woodhouse buried Mar 23 aged 50, fallen in great decay

Mr. Wm. Rookes of Royds Hall buried at Wibsey Mar 18 abt 48

Hen. Spencer of Westercroft buried Apr 1. 1684, aged 63

Michl Bests wife Apr 8.

Sr Roger Bradshaw of Hay near Wigan, Lanc. Justice & Deputy Lieutenant buried Apr. 4

Mr Robt Hyde of Denton Hall buried Apr 1. aged 82. A good ffriend to Mr. Angier

Mrs. Hiet of Kilshaw wife to Mr. Hiet of Cros-stone died Apr. aged 80

Capt. Tho. Taylor of Brighouse died Apr 27. A rich Quaker,

aged 63

Mr. Cotes of Rawden an eminent N. C. Minr. late of
Nottinghamshire went to his sons in Darbyshire fell into a
Palsie Lords Day May 11. died —— aged 67

Widow Nettleton buried at Dewsbury May 14, aged 77

Mr Joshua Kirshaw Parson of Ripley, died May —— aged 55,
his wife sick

Mr Barker born in York a C. Minr. in the North died May,
aged 50, a good sholar, sober man, a great estate

Mr. Saml Sykes Alderman of Leeds buried May 30, a merchant
& moderate man, aged 56

Wm. Hield of Priestley an Apothecary buried June 8

Mr Moor Minr of Howarth buried July 15, aged 63

Dr Jonathan Maud of Halifax buried July 31, aged 71, of
pregnant parts, much learning

Esther Learoyd buried at Halifax Aug 12, aged 58

Ellen Sharp died Sep 5, aged 75

Lord Delamere buried at Bowden in Cheshire, Sept 9, aged 63

Mr Wm. Farrar of Thewood Justice of Peace 30 years. Struck
wth a Palsie at his son in laws

Mr Greenwoods at Stapleton Oct 8. burd Oct 11 aged 66

Dr. Cart of Manchester died of a ffever Sept. a notable
Physitian, a minrs. son, aged 40

Mich. Wainhouse died of a surfeit got by Intemperance Oct 18,
at Cross in Halifax married James Mitchels widow aged 48

Capt Taylors wife of Brighouse died Oct 28 buried in their
Garden with head upwards standing upright by her Husband,
Daughter, &c. Quakers, aged 60

Robt Coulins wife of Northourum a Quaker buried at Sowerby-
bridge Nov. 17. aged 60

Tho. Soytels wife of Northourum, Jere Swifts mother, buried
Dec. 9, aged 74

Jennet Shosmith a notable midwife abt Coley died at Horton
May 26, aged 85

Mr Hulmes a Limner born in London, married Anne Northen
Daughter Esther, shorten'd his days by Intemperance died at
Ant. Northens in N. buried Dec. 19. at Mr ffourness charg
aged 50

Mr John Tilsley of Manchester formerly minr N.C. at Dean
Church buried there Dec 9. an Admirable man. aged 70

Martha Bairstow Robt B. wid. of Blakehill died Dec 26

Mr. Bat of Okewell a young man slain by Mr. Gream at Barne (t) near London buried at Burstall Dec. 30

Mr. O. H. in York Castle

Eliz Baxter (Jere B. wife) died Jan 13. aged 56, languisht 10 years

John Kirshaw of Norwoodgreen died July 9. aged 72, 1686

Mrs. Whitehurst of Lidget near Bradford buried in her Husbands meeting place July 20. He married again Oct 20, 1686

Mrs Root of Wakefield died of a ffever, buried there July 26 Her eldest son John abt a fortnight before. 1686

Mr Jonathan Maud of Halifax buried Aug. 4. confest he had killed himself with drinking

Mr Wm Field of Bradford buried Aug 24, left 300 li p. an. great Legacies, no child 30 year old

Wm Butler of Northourum died Sept 3. aged 77, a pious man

Mary wife of Jonathan Priestley died Nov 15, aged 51, a cancer in her breast 2 years

John Nicols of Northourum died Nov 18 languisht long, aged 73

Robt Naylor father to Hen & Ant. died Nov 18, aged 72, rich

Godsgift Kirby only son to Mr K. died Nov 22. aged 28 a young preacher—hopefull

Widw Brooksbank of Eland died Nov 30. aged 73, her husband John Br — not a year before

Mich. Gibson old clark at Coley Ch. buried Dec. 10. aged 84

Mr. Crook a N.C. minr. formerly at Denby, liv'd long in Wakefield, died of the Gout in his throat Jan. 9, aged 53

—— Wells wife of Northourum-green, aged 86

Mr Ralph Ardernes daughter came to visit James Stansfields wife her cousin at Bowood near Sowerby fell sick of small pox buried at Sowerby Jan 20, aged 18. Some sad circumstances

Grace Eckroyd of Shelf buried at Coley ffebr 17 taken up by knaves in the night, buried at Halifax ffebr. 20. aged 80

John Booth near Coley buried Mar 23. aged 75. An old professor

Mr. ffairbank Vicar of Bingley died Apr 2, languisht long, aged 80. 1687

John Mitchel of Crow Nest in Lightcliffe (that married Abr. Walkers daughter ffeb. 16. 1683,) buried Apr 8, not 21, surfeit fever.

Mrs Rooks of Royds Hall buried at Wibsey Apr 26

BURIALS.

Mrs Hutton of Popleton near York sister to Tho. Lord ffairfax
buried June 10. aged 68, a gracious woman

Richard Harisons wife of Wakefield buried June 2, aged 66, a
diligent hearer at Alverthorpe

John Illingworth of Illingworth buried at Halifax June 22, ag. 62

James Dickson of Wakefield buried July 11. in a palsy 17 years,
aged 61

Col. Venables of Chester buried July 26 famous in his day, abt 70

Mr Robt Pickering buried at Beeston Sep 2. aged 70

Dr. Hook buried a son Aug 13. 1687 a scholar, came from Cambridge, and Aug 31 buried his only Daughter

Mr Drake of Manchester buried at Thornton, Oct 14

Mr Robt Chadderton a choice minr in Lanc. buried at Prestwick
Oct 15

Sarah Bentley of Sowerby (mother to Mr. Bentley) buried Oct 31,
ag. 85

Phebe Dawson bur. same day, ag. 7—

George Duke of Buckingham died suddenly behind York July

Alderman Dawson of York died Oct, aged 75, an ancient Professor

Isaac Hollins of Clayton Junr, buried Dec 1. surfeit, young man

John Hollins wife of Allerton bur. Dec. 2. aged 66

Dorothy Brearcliffe of Halifax burd Dec. 4 aged 65

Mr. Core formerly Preacher at Tong, a N.C. preacht in a Barn
there, died Dec 14, aged near 80

Widw Hilton of Droilsden Lanc, James Hiltons mother, buried
May 3, aged 91

Justice Henry Marsden of Gisburn died Jan. 4, aged 62.
1200li. p. an.

Mr John Issot minr at John Heys in Craven died Jan 12 at
R. Mitchels

Mr John Levers wife of Bolton in Lanc. buried Jan. 12

Sarah Okey married a little while to John Fletcher of Bolton bur.
Jan. 12

Mr Saml ffourness of Ovenden burd ffebr 23 A young man
dispatcht with Intemperance

Sr Wm Lowther near Kippax buried ffebr. 24 had bin merchant,
Justice

John Wainhouse of Pyenests wife died ffebr 27

Tho. Soytel of N.ourum buried Mar, 28, aged 80, 1688

Lord Henry ffairfax of Denton buried at Denton Chap. Ap 15.

BURIALS.

ag. 60

Countess Dowager of Strafford buried at Hutton Roberts Apr 18

Abigail Hoyl Rich Hoyls daughter & Tho Priestley wife of Halifax, both young, buried May 14

Ellenor Russel of Salford (Aunt to Mr. O. H.) died Mar 1. abt 80

Anne Walker (Mr Langleys Dau) Abra Walkers wife of Water-clough buried June 18

Mrs Shaw (mother to Mr Antrobus of Halifax buried in her wedding shift July 27, had 14 children, aged 85

Wid. Rossendale near Halifax buried Sep. 4. abt 70

Mr Jonathan Hall of Booth Town buried Oct 18. aged 60. rich

Sr John Bright of Badsworth bur. Oct 21 A mighty man of wealth had bin Colonel was in torturing pain 2 years, aged 66

Mrs Cook mother to Mr Rooks of Royds ha. her husband Vicar of Leeds buried at Wibsey Oct 19

Mr Doughty Schoolmaster at Halifax ffree School buried Oct 13 aged 76

Mr. Hunter minr at Leverpool

Mrs Maud, Dr M. widow) buried Oct 28. ag. 67

Dr Bury of ffell church bur. Nov. 14

Mr Wilkinson (Attorney near Huthersfield bur. Dec 1. abt 60 left his eldest son £600 p. an

Mr Rycroft a minr born near Illingworth buried Oct.

Major Sedascur a Lords son in Germany fled into England 1640, an officer in Parl. Army, died at Heath Hall, buried at Norman-ton Dec 4. aged 76

Mr. ffarran Vicar of Otley buried Dec 21, a fat man, aged 52

Dr Stanhup buried at Guisely Dec 24

Mr John Gunter a N.C. minr. Lord Whartons Steward at Healy died Oct. aged 65

Mr James Hulm a N.C. minr at Kendal died Nov, aged 58, born in Rochdale Parish

Dr Rich. Hook Vicar of Halifax from 1662 languisht under grievous pain of a ffistula died Jan 1. aged 67

John Coates of Hipperholm buried ffebr. 7. Mr Ellison preacht, aged 63, rich

Nathl Spencer buried at Selby Jan. Laurence's son, Sarah's Bro.

—— Ramsden of Park Nook buried ffeb. 12, ag. 56

Mrs Mary Dinely buried at Bramhup ffeb 20. aged 82, married 59 years

BURIALS.

Mrs Blithman of Newcastle (her sister) a fortnight before, Sr John Stanhups Datrs.

Mrs Jollie died at her son Mr. Tho. Jollies buried ffebr. 22, aged 92, a gracious woman

Mr Rose of Norton in Darbyshire, a N.C. minr (married Mr Primes dr.) buried ffebr 27

Mrs Mary Kirby (Mr Josh. K.ye minrs. widw. buried in her Garden by her Husband who was buried 12 years before, Mar 11, aged 68

Mr Hulme Schoolmaster at Newton Heath died suddenly Sept 4. 1679, aged 70

Robt only son to Robt Ramsden of Stony-royd near Halifax fell down in their ffield, died Oct 9, 1679

Mrs ffourness (Mr. Tobiemmff. minister at Bury widw died suddenly in Manchester ffebr. 1680, aged 77

Justice Hartley of Strangways by Manchr. rode abt in the ffields, Lords day night, died next morning, June 18, 1681

Mr John Jollie a N.C. minr at Gorton died suddenly June 17, 1682

Sr John Brights Lady died suddenly in Journey from London Nov 1682, married last summer

Mr. Gartside of Rochdale, Steward of Lord Byrons court there, went to York to be married and that very morning the marriage should have bin, died, Jan. 1683

Mr Oliver a N.C. minr Lady Norcliffes chaplain died suddenly, not 2 days sick July 10. 1686

Isaac Waterhouse of Washerlane found dead in bed Aug 12, 1687

Mrs Clay of Clayhouse died suddenly Apr. 16. 1687

Mr George Thornhil of ffixby Justice of Peace died suddenly Aug. burd. at Elland Aug 19, 1687, left 9 children his wife big of the 10th

Mr James Lever of Bolton fell down dead as he was reaching for a book, ffebr. 1687

Two Daughters of John Holdsworths of Whinniroyd died of less than 2 days sickness Mar 23 & 24

Mr Turner near Doncaster a great Drinker, very fat, £700 p. an. had bin hunting, came home, died suddenly, buried Oct 21. 1688

Mr Hammond Rhodes a C. Minr. walkt to Esq. Woombles of Woomble died suddenly, Aug.

BURIALS.

Mr Robt Lever of Darcy Lever died suddenly Oct 3, aged 80

Mr Boardman born in Bolton minr. in Cheshire, buried Oct. 5

Robt Hanson of Hove Edge died suddenly Oct.

Wm Bins of Landimer Sykes in Northourum going to bed fainted away Nov. 16, aged 82

Mr. Sandal Vicar of Calverley died of a palsey suddenly burd Nov 12. aged 68

Mr Henry Swift Vicar of Peniston died suddenly Oct 31, 1689, aged 68

Anne Bairstow of Northourum (sister to Martha Mr Heywoods old maid) lived with her Bro Jere. B. found dead in her bed Mar. 28. 1690. Her sister Oswald Tenants wife died suddenly, buried Apr. 3. aged 57

Mr Wright Steward to Sr Michl Wentworth of Wooley died suddenly in his bed of a hours warning Apr 13. 1690

Sam. Wardman of Landimer died suddenly Nov 30. aged 67

Mr. John Flavel minr at Dartmouth died suddenly July 1691

Mrs Whitaker having bin married 3 years at last bore a child Aug 20. recover'd well, that day fortnight Sept 3 was chearfull & well, laying her child in the cradle dropt down & died

Mr. May of York well & dead in 24 hours. Aug

John Learoyds son of High Bentley at Leeds on Tuesday, dead before morning Dec. 2

Robt Ramsden of Siddal Hall buried Apr. 10, aged 62, rich. 1689

Rich. Jepson Bayliffe of Halifax that took Mr, O. H. buried Apr. 11

Mr. Steven Ellis that occasion'd the plundering of Mr. O. H. for preaching buried Apr. 19, aged 75

Mr Armitage a N.C. minr. at Holbeck buried Apr 20. aged 77

Mr. Waddington of Otterburn died Mar. last aged 73, had 1000li. p. an.

Timothy Sutcliffe of Northourum buried Apr. 22, aged 75

John Holdsworth of Alverthorpe buried Apr 27, aged 73, a good man

Sarah Walker of Walterclough buried May 3. aged 50

Mary Baxter of Walterclough buried June 5

Mr Edward Sill a N.C. minr liv'd in Salford buried June 10 had preacht at Eccles—great Lamentation, Mr. O. H. helpt to lay him in his grave, abt 50

Mrs Mallison, widw to a N.C. Minr. buried at Manchester June

BURIALS.

12, aged 74

Ottawell Whitworth buried at Rochdale June 15, aged 57, a honest Professor

Mr. Tim. Root died at Hawden of a Dropsie June 24, aged 54. Conform'd but languisht long not able to preach

Mr Ramsden of Crostone in Steneland a young man 1000£ p. an. married Mr Calverleys Daughter lately, very fat, died at Esheld, buried at Guisely July 25, aged 22

Mr Wentworth of Empsal a young Heir of £3000 p. an. came to Thornton with his half Bro. Lister died of Small Pox, Aug 8, aged 18

Mr John Lager of Allerton, Steward at Bradford Court, buried Aug, 31, aged 60

Mrs. Sarah Brear of New Hall buried at Ealand Sept. 7. aged 33. She was Mr. Marshalls dr.

Old Colonel Dukinfield (Sir Robt ffather died Sep. aged 74, a usefull man

Danl Walker of Lightcliffe buried his wife Oct. 22

Danl Walker himself buried Oct 26 left a daughter Achsah abt 6 years of age, themselves abt 40

Robt Dinely of Bramhup Hall in Otley Parish buried Nov. 14. ag. 83. kept up meetings in his Hall

Mr Pemberton Vicar of Bradford buried his wife Nov. 20, aged 40

Mr. Galkrogers ffather (of Haworth) buried Nov 21, ag. 80

Ruth Tetlaw of Norwoodgreen buried Nov 22, aged 75

Widow Nicolson sister to J. Priestley bur. at Luddenden Nov 23. aged 60

Mr Thorp of Cinderhills bur. his wife Nov. 24

Mr Wm Williamson of Newton Heath buried at Manchester Nov 9. aged 66. a great Tradesman, got £300 p. an. Distracted many years

Nathl Longbothom of Northourum buried Dec. 4. aged 41

Lady Katharine Hewet, of York, buried Nov. aged 62

Joseph Priestley of Good greaves above Sowerby bur. Dec. 26, aged 72

Mr. Brook of Smithouse in Lightcliffe buried at Burstall Jan 23, a great Drinker, Jacobite, Scoffer at Presb.

Capt Lister of Maningham bur. ffebr 9. aged 60. a great man in his time

Mr Gilbert Brooksbank of Eland bur. ffebr 16, aged 40, languisht

BURIALS.

long

Mrs. Horton of Barslaud (Justice H. wife) buried ffebr. 17, aged 83

Mr Mark ffreeman of Leeds buried ffebr. 25, aged 68

Gregory ffreeman his Bro. bur. abt a fortnight before (a Prodigall cost his Bro. Mark much trouble

Tho. Oates of Wyke buried Mar 19. aged 73. Mr O.H.-landlord at Norwoodgreen had near 60 li p. an. by his ffather in law death, but now poor

Henry Priestley of Baitings died at Belfast in Ireland where he went to sell goods, buried there Mar 1, aged 22, a pious man

John Kirk of Alverthorp buried at Woodkirk Mar 24, aged 56 very rich

John Stansfield's wife buried at Sowerby Mar 25. 1690, aged 40 long under weakness

Sarah wife of Joseph Brookbank buried at Wakefield Mar 25

Joseph s. James Brooksbank died Mar. 30

Mr Tho. Lister son of Mr Saml L. of Shipden Hall buried Apr. 5. aged 34

Tho. Dawson of Morley (Mr D. Bro.) buried Apr 25, aged 50

Mr Robinson Preacher at Crostone died Apr 28, had bin at Alehouse that day—a wife, 2 child. aged 56

Jennet Snell died at Wm Clays May 1. Wm Clay & she had liv'd 49 years, together, aged 80. a good woman

Esther Marshall a Professor at Norwoodgreen bur Apr 23, aged 81

Mr Heathcot of Chesterfield in Darbyshire bur. Apr 28. aged 73

Jane Hey (John Heys mother in Craven) bur Mar. aged 74

Mr Henry Coulburn of Radcliffe bridge in Lanc. bur. Mar. aged 49

Mr. Peter Naylor minr. at Alverthorp buried June 2, ag. 54. 2 coaches, 12 minrs. Mr Whitaker preacht Zech 1. 5. His distemper began in his foot

Mr Wadsworth of Swath Hall died June 2, had 4 wives left but one daughter, aged 64

John Wordsworth of Horbury that married Cambdena Kirby died May 18, ag. 35, left 3 child. much debt, honest but shiftless

Mr Wood of Norton in Darbyshire a N.C. minr. died April 1. aged 65

Sr John Ramsden died June 7

Tho. Woodhouse of Hipperholm died June 20, aged 86, poor

Mr. Turner of Wakefield, Clerk of Peace, Steward to Marquess

BURIALS.

Halifax died June young, ingenious, lovely

Mr. Jackson Vicar of Doncaster buried July 17 aged 82

Martha, Joseph Croft wife of Coley Hall buried July 23

Mr Nicolas Brooksbank of Eland a Preacher buried July 28

Mr Wm Ingrams wife of Leeds Aug 6. pined herself to death, fretting at her husband for taking 700 li. wch she had reserved for her ffriends

Mr Saml Angiers wife of Dukinfield died of a Tympany buried at Manchester July 26. Mr ffr. Mosley her uncle preacht ffuneral

Mr Moorhouse Vicar of Rotheram died Aug 5. an old man, had bin a N.C. 8 years, succeeded Mr Bovil

Saml Threapland (Dr Thr. ffather) bur. Aug. 11. aged 74

Mr Nathan Whitleys wife of Rooks burd. Sep 15, aged 82

Joseph Hollings of Liversidge Hall buried a son Sept. 15. another Sept 30 both of small pox

Susanna wife of Arthur Hey of N.ourumgreen bur. Oct 18. aged 80

Joshua Stansfields wife of Little Horton buried Oct 26

Tho Ledgard of Idle buried Nov. 1

Tho Priestley's wife of Holdsworth (Mary) buried Nov 11. aged 69

Jonas Greenwood (called Prophet Jonas) buried Nov 27, aged 62

Mr Robt Sevile of Greetland died Dec 12. aged 85, 500 li. p. an, exceedingly debaucht

Dorothy Bolton aged 75 buried at Wakefield Dec 17 died with her daught M Kirk (Mr O.H. old neighbour

Rich Mitchel of Marton Scar in Craven died Dec. 25. aged 52

John Dickenson heard Mr Smith on thursday Dec 25 bur. Jan 1. small pox, purples, hopefull

Mrs Witter (Mr W. wife) of Sowerby buried Jan 12, a consumption

Mr Ramsbothom Preacher at Henley bur Jan 17

Abra Sunderland buried at Heptonstall Jan. 16, had 19 child. aged 101

Edmund Brooks wife of Shelf Jan 24, aged 72, married 50 years

Mr Hugh Currer buried at Kildwick ffebr 2. aged 81, had fallen out with his son & children, left Pro. 30.17·to be preacht at his ffuneral, but his son a Justice of Peace would not permit it

Mr Guy minr at Littlebro' born in Bolton buried Jan 26

Mr Tho Crompton a N.C. Minr of Asley Chap. Lanc. buried Jan

BURIALS.

16. aged 82
Esther Lum, John L. daughter. Mar 4
Mr Edmund Hough Vicar of Halifax, Apr 3 Mr Corlase preacht
Lady Delamere died abt Apr 16—
Sr Ralph Knight ffather to Mrs Taylor of Wallinwells died
    Apr. 20. aged 73
Mrs Copley Mr Houghs mother in law died at Vicaridge Apr 17.
    aged 83
Mr James Longbothom of London died Apr 9. aged 64, a good
    ffriend to Mr H.
Dr Lamplaugh ABp. of York formerly Bp of Exeter died May
James Hardmans mother near Heywood died Apr. aged 86
Mr Hague minr. at Ranfield died May 9. aged 46
Mr John Heywood of Taunton near Ashton under Lyne buried
    Jan. 3, aged 60
Mr Cowper minr at Ardsley, Ap. ag. 53
Mary Dawson sister to Joseph Lister Jan 23, aged 75
Matthew Clay's wife of N. July 1.
Marg. John Rushworths wife at Coley July 22, aged 73. a good
    woman
Mrs Ramsden, Esq R. widow, of Langley Hall July 27. aged 71
Mrs Townley (Justice mother) of Newhouse Aug 10. a Lanc.
    woman
Mr John Lister (Mr Sam. L. son of Shipden Hall, a sad young
    man bur. Aug. 9
Mr Kent minr at Denby Aug 31
Mr Shaw N.C. minr near Barnsley. Sep 3
Mary wife of James Wilson in Prestwich Parish Sept 23
Mr John Denham of London Sept 19
Mr Wm Hulm of Kersley Oct 29, aged 60
Mr John Lever Vicar of Bolton Oct 31, ag. 65, 4 child.
Justice Calverley Nov 10. ag. 55
Robt Allison junr of Ovenden Nov 25 by Booth Town cast of his
    Hors. in drink
Jos. Priestley of White Windows mother Jan 15
Mr Ja Creswick a N.C. minr. Jan 20. ag. 73
Tim Crowther of North. Jan 25
Robt Boyl Esq & Mr Baxter Dec
Mr Robt Moore, —— Hall, Lanc.
Esq Beaumont of Whitley H. Mar. 7 abt 40

BURIALS.

Mr Tho Priestley Apoth. M. 8. ag. 36
Mr Ralph Ward, N.C. Min. in York, Mar. 13. ag. 62
Isabel Josh Whitleys wife Ap 15. ag. 61
James Smethurst of Manchester Ap. 21 1692
Lord Willoughby near Rivington, March, aged 91
John Rushworth of Coley Ch. July 2, aged 78
Sr. Wm. Wentworth June, should have been heir to E. Strafford

------

*In my little book with one clasp you'l find 144 sudden deaths,
their names, time of their death*

Mr John Lever, N.C. Minr at Bolton July 4, ag. 58
Mr Benson N.C. at Kellet, aged 76
Mr Zach. Taylor N.C. ag. 74 [1692]
Phoebe d. Joshua Soynier of Northourum bur. at Halifax June
18. 1683
Silence d. John Learoyd of Northourum buryed friday June 22.
1683

------

*Look into that little book before-mentioned and you'l find from
A.D. 1678, to A.D. 1695 the names of 1075 dead of ordinary
diseases most of them ancient or persons of quality that I have
taken notice of within my cognisance.   O.H.*

1679. Mr James Oates of Hollins (son to Mr James Oates of
    Marsh, bap. Jan 1655) dyed July 17th at 6 a clock in the
    morning buried at Halifax July 22, 1695
1680. Samuel Midgly that was prisoner in York Castle 1685,
    waited on us, hath been prisoner 3 times in Halifax jail for
    debt dyed there, bur. July 18. '95, aged 66
1681 Mr Gregson the Attorney of Bradford that had ruined
    many to inrich himself dyed on Lords Day morning July 21
    '95. buryed at Bradford July 24.   Mr Pemberton preacht
1682. Sir Edward Mosely of Hulm Hall was buryed at Manchester
    July 31 1695, aged 74
1683 Mtris. Brereton of Sowerby buryed there Aug 12. 1695
1683 William Midgly father to Dr. and Attourney Midgly was
    buryed at Luddenden Aug 21 '95, aged 81, Mr Sunderland
    preacht ·

BURIALS.

1684 Thomas Priestley of Holdworth 7th son of Thomas Priestley (only John left) dyed at one a clock Sept 17 bur. at Halifax Sept. 19. 1695 an hopefull young man of 30 y. of age left a young wife with child

1685 Mr Martin Hotham grocer in York was struck with a palsey continued some yeares, dyed was buryed Sept 1695, aged 58

1686 Mr Henry Newcom an eminent N.C. Minister in Manchester languisht under frequent faintings, dyed was buried Sept 20, 1695, 68 years of ag.

1687 My dear and only sister Esther Whitehead dyed tuesday night Oct 22. was buryed at Bolton Oct 25, 1695 a gracious woman

1688 Mtris Hobson of York a Nonconformist ministers widow was buryed Oct. 24. 1695

Dr Conant of or near Northampton died Mar. 12 1693 in the 86th year of his age

1689 Thomas Oldfield of Warly mother buryed at Halifax dyed suddenly aged 91, Nov, 3. '95

1690 Sybil Woodhead of Shelf buryed at Halifax Nov 4, '95 aged 75

1691 Abraham Harrison of Halifax buryed there Nov 4. '95

1692 Mrs Martha Woodhead (ordinarily called old queen of Cockil was buryed at Coley chappel. I preacht a funeral sermon the same day at my chappel Nov 13, 1695 aged 68

1693 William Hurd of Shelf dyed that day buryed at Halifax Nov 15, 1695, aged 70

1694 Mr Abraham Walker of Walterclough buried at Halifax Nov 20, 1695 aged 66

1695 John Oldfield of Shipden mill buried at Halifax Nov 26, 1695, aged 72

1696 Martha wife of Henry Naylor of Lightbezzles dyed of child bearing Nov 26, buryed at Ripponden Nov 29. 1695

1697 Richard Naylor of Wakefield buried there Nov. 23, 95 after a very long tedious sicknes a good man, aged 60

1698 Timothy Rudiord of Warley bur. at Halifax Dec. 5. 95, aged about 58

1699 John Hey of Pudsey came to John Rhodes to be cured of dropsy by Dr. Threapland dyed there Dec, 6, buryed at Bradford Dec. 9. 95, aged 65

1700 Jeremiah Jagger had his leg broke at Halifax, dyed at

BURIALS.

John Akroyds in Shelf, jury went on him, bur. Halifax Dec 18
1701 Mtris Rooks of Rhodes Hall dyed of child bearing Dec 17,
95, buryed at Wibsey chappel Dec. 20
1702 Obadiah Dawson dyed at York was buryed there Dec 21. 95
1703 Lord (Pre)ston [Juram] dyed Dec. 24, 1699
1703 Thomas Townend buryed at Halifax Dec. 22, 95 aged 70
1704 Thomas Hanson of Brighouse dyed Jan 2. buryed at
Eland Jan 6. 1695-6, aged 64
1705 Jeremiah Baxter of Northourum my good neighbour dyed
Jan 3, buryed at Halifax Jan. '96 aged 68
1706 Mr John Blakebrough of Warly the usefull man in
administring physick, my phisitian, fell sick of a violent feaver
dyed a fortnight after Jan 7. was buryed at Halifax Jan 10.
1695-6, aged 44
1707 Abigail Jackson of Hipperholme buryed at Coley chappel
Jan 13, 95-6, aged 80 had bin blind 16 years, necessity.
1708 Thomas Carver wife buried on tuesday Jan. 14. 1695, at
Halifax aged 54
1709 William Scot of Halifax buryed there Jan 17. 96 aged 60
1710 Alexander Holbrooks wife was buryed at Halifax Dec 1695
1711 Mr Alexander Nowel of Read near Padium died Dec. 1695,
aged 66, a little after his father, a vicious man, had been
prisoner for debt, a violent persecutor.
1712 Nathan Tilsons wife of Sourby bridg bur. at Halifax Jan 22.
96. ag. 66
1713 Ralph Higson of Halifax dyed Jan, 21. funeral solemnly
observed Jan 23
1714 Edmund Walker, Huthersfield bur. there Jan. 22. 1695-6.
a rich man
1715 David Brig of Carhous, Shelf, bur. at Halifax Jan 31.
1695-6, aged 66
1716 Mtrs Sharp of Bradford (mother to the present Archbp.
of York buryed at Bradford feb 7. 1695-6 aged 76
1717 Lady Armitage (this Sir John of Kirkleys mother buryed
from Hardger hall at Hardger church feb 10 1695-6. aged 70
1718 John Blakebrough the father of Dr. Bl. buryed feb 12.
95-6. aged 66
1719 The right Honourable my good Lord Wharton dyed at
Hamstead feb 5. 1695-6 buryed at Wooburn aged 82
1720 Mr John Lister of Horton buryed at Bradford feb 17. 95

BURIALS.

1721 Abigail Oldfield, Shibden, bur. at Halifax feb. 1695-6 aged 60

1722 Mary wife Jonathan Lacock a quaker buryed at Harwood well feb 25, 1695-6 aged 60, my old house-fellow at Landimer

1723 Mary wife John Sonier of bank top buryed at Halifax feb 26, 95-6, dyed of child bearing. I hope a gracious woman

1724 Mary Ryley of Sowerby never married, aged 86 buryed at Sowerby Chappel feb 26, 1695-6

1725 Michael Barret of Sowrby with whom Mr. Wiltar boarded dyed feb 27, at 2 a clock in the morning buryed there March 1, 1695-6, aged 81

1726 Robert Sutlives wife buryed at Sowerby feb. 6 1695-6 had been 20 years servant to Mr Horton of Sowrby, aged, 60, my old hearer

1727 William Got of Bradshaw bur. at Halifax Mch 2, aged 75

1728 Susanna Oldfield dyed at Godly where she was born buryed at Halifax March 3, 95-6 communicant with us, aged 77

1729 Samuel Hemingway of Shipden buryed at Halifax March 9. 1695-6. aged 65

1730 Joshua Hodgson of Hagstocks a quaker was buried at Harwood well, March 13. 1696

1731 Thomas Reiners 2d. wife buryed at Burstall March 16, 96

1732 Mr Mathew Widdups wife buryed at Halifax March 18. 1695-6. aged 59

1733 Mr Joshua Dearden (chief constable) of Sowrby dyed March 26, 1696, buryed at Halifax March 30 1696, aged 36, prejudiced himself by brandy

1734 Mr Robert Seddon a N.C. Minister preacht at the Meeting place in Bolton was seized with a palsy dyed Mch, 21. buryed at Ringly Chapel Mch 24. 1695-6, aged 68

1735 Robert Wright of Wyke elder brother to Joseph Wright, dyed on Thursday morning, Apr 16, 1696. buryed at Lightcliff aged 84

1736 Mtris Empsall of Wyke senior, buryed at Hardger church Apr 15. 1696, aged 63

1737 Thomas Pitts of Wakefield buried there Apr. 16, 1696, aged 52

1738 Richard Ramsden of Halifax dyed of a fever Ap. 18, 96 aged 36

1738 Mtris Yates of Manchester (mother to Justice Yates) buryed

BURIALS.

there Apr. 1696, aged 70

1739 Mr Ashly minister at a meeting place in Hull buryed March, 1696, aged 56

1740 Martin Dawson of Idle buryed at Carverly April 15. 1696 aged 88

1741 John Broadly of Halifax dyed Apr 29. buryed at Halifax May 1. 1696, aged 68

1742 Joseph Wood of Bramley died May 4. buryed May 6. 1696. aged 64

1743 Richard Colbecks wife of Halifax buryed there May 6. aged 6—

1744 Mr John Mitchel of Scout bur. Halifax May 9. 1696, aged 37, shortened his time

1745 Edward Nettleton of Cockil buryed at Coley May 11, 1696, aged 77

1746 John Lea of Sowrby bur. there May 11. 1696, as Ant. Lea told me

1747 Sarah Illingworth of Holdworth buryed at Halifax May 16, 1696, aged 67

Mr Rossendale buryed at Halifax May 27. 1696

1748 Mtris Hanna Levit (Mrs Diner Robinsons dr) bur. at Halifax May 16, 1696. aged 64

1749 Mr Jeremiah Roscendale went with his wife to London on Lords Day 3, 96, the news came he was dead there May 19. shortened his days by intemperance. ag. 27

1750 Mr Abraham Lockwood, my good friend, was buryed at Kirkburton May 20, 1696, aged 71

1751 Mathew Sunderland buryed at Halifax May 21. 96, aged 76. an old souldier called Sarjent

1752 Joseph Wood (my clark) a very gracious man, bur. at Halifax May 25, 1696, aged 38, lay long of a leg

1753 Martha Green of Northourum bur. at Halifax May 30. 1696, aged 69 .

1754 William Naylors wife bur. at Halifax May 30. 96, aged 42

1755 Luke Crossley, Halifax, buryed there May 31, 96, aged 40

1756 Jonathan Lacock a quaker, buryed at Harwood well June 2. 96, aged 71

1757 John Jackson a quaker of Halifax bur. June 4. 96. ag 54

1758 John Nelsons wife, Shipden, bur. at Halifax June 9. 96 dyed of a fever aged 42

BURIALS.

1759 Richard Walker of Ratcliff bridg a strong Quaker, buryed at Knot mills, June 8, 96, aged 80

1760 Jeremiah Woods wife of Stopes bur. at Halifax June 9. 1696, aged 64

1761 William Naylor my child in Christ, a zealous Christian, bur. at Halifax June 16, 1696, aged 41

1762 Abraham Hodgsons wife a quaker buryed at Hare woodwell June 21, 1696, aged 74

1763 Mtris Hopkins, mother to John Nelsons wife bur. at Halifax June 19. 1696, aged 74

1764 Mr. Willm Penne the great Quaker at London dyed May 1696 aged 63

1765 James Bates, Warly, bur. at Halifax, June 21. 1696, aged 82

1766 Mtris Sarah Langly of Priestley buryed with great solemnity at Halifax June 25. 1696, aged 74

1767 Benjamin Bates of Halifax dyed of a feaver June 29. 69

1768 Martha his wife buryed the same day, aged 70

1769 Judith Dean of Northouram bur. at Halifax July 3, 96 aged 60

1770 Mr Robert Ramsden of Quarl house, fever, buryed July 4, 96

1771 Mrs Phoebe Bently of Halifax buryed there July 7, 1696, aged 62, Mr Dan. Bently widow

1772 Robert Smiths wife buried at Coley Chappel, July 6, 1696, aged 73

1773 Nathaniel Crowther of Halifax died suddenly buryed July 7. 97 [sic] aged 81

1774 Mr Cornelius Todd a N.C. minr, dyed, buryed July 1696. aged 63

1775 Mr Aspinwall, N.C. ministr at Warrington dyed June, 1696, aged 60

1776 Mathew Cagil of Lightcliff buryed there July 14. 96 of feaver.

1777 Joseph Listers wife of Thornhill bridg buryed July 20 1696 aged 70.

1778 Widow Brighous and her man buryed at Ealand July 21, 96, she 64 old both dyed of feaver

1779 Jonathan Crowther buryed at Halifax July 22 96, of a feaver, 55 old

BURIALS.

1780 Thomas Trueman dyed July 22 under Dr Threaplands hands, buryed at Halifax July 27, 96, aged 74

1781 Mr Samuel Dawson dyed July 24, bur at Morley July 27. 96.

1782 Rachel wife of Daniel Gill dyèd July 23 buryed at Halifax july 26, 96, aged 55, had born 13 children

1783 Mrs Bradshaw sister Mrs Peel of Grindlestone bank buryed July 29. 1696, aged 72

1784 Katharin Ledgard of Idle (the upholdler of the meeting there) dyed Aug 1. buryed at Calverly Aug 3, ag. 55

1785 Bernard Hartly of Halifax buryed there Aug 4. 96. ag. 62

1786 Mr Andrew Taylor of York buryed Aug. 3. 1696, ag 75

1787 Robt Hardcastle bur. at Bingly Aug 13. 1696, age 72

1788 Thomas Reiner of Millbrig bur. at Burstall Aug 12. 96

1789 John Ramsdens wife of Stubbinge buryed at Halifax Aug 20, 1696, aged 56

1790 Roger Thornelly of Bolton buryed Aug. 18. 1696, ag. 80

1791 William Ellis wife of Halifax bur. there Aug 23. 96

1792 Judith Platts of Sowerby buryed there Aug 25. 96 aged 78

1193 Judith wife of Jeremiah field buryed at Bradford Aug 31, 96. aged 60

1194 Richard Morley buryed at Halifax Aug 6. 1696 aged 81

1195 Abraham Brown of Northourum bur. at Halifax Aug 30. 1696 aged 93

1196 Mr John Kershaw of Hoyl House, buryed at Tong Sept 3, 1696. a rich but — aged 50

1197 Mr John Park Usher at Hipperholm school buryed at Coley Sept 8. 96

1198 Jonas Dean of Mixenden, aged, of a feaver Sept 18. 1696, buryed at Halifax Sept 21

1199 Samuel Woodhead of Northourum buryed at Halifax Sept 21. 96

1200 Sir Michael Wentworth Bart buryed at Woolley Sept 1696

1201 Mr George Richardson of Woodall dyed on thursday night Oct 1. 1696, buryed at Caverly Oct 5. 96

1202 Abraham Sunderland of Shelf buryed of a fever at Halifax Oct 13. 96

1203 Jeremiah Ryly bur. at Ealaud Oct 4, 1696, aged 65

1204 John Whitaker of Halifax a Quaker dyed Oct. 27 buryed 29

1205 Robert Duckworth of Halifax a Quaker bur. at Harwood

BURIALS.

well Oct 30. 1696, a speaker, dyed of feaver

1206 Michael Boys wife of only house bur. at Halifax Nov 7. 96

1207 Grace wife of Thomas Gill dyed of a feaver buryed at Halifax Nov 10. 1696 aged 50

1208 Samuel Brig of Shelf hall buryed at Halifax Nov 13. '96 aged 81

1209 Richard Gray, gravemaker at Halifax buryed Nov 28. 96 aged 60

1210 John Sharp of Norwood green buryed at Bradford Dec. 2. 96

1211 Lidia wife Samuel Haliday bur. at Halifax Nov 30, 96

1212 Abraham Woodhead wife of gyles hill bur. at Halifax Dec. 96

1213 Michael Best of Holdworth bur. at Halifax Dec 12. 96, aged 50

1214 John Stancliff of Bayly Hall bur at Halifax Dec. 14. 96 aged 67

1215 Mercy Drake John Cravens mother in law buryed at Halifax Dec. 23. 96, aged 70

1216 Joseph Watkinson of Illingworth bur. at Halifax Dec 23. 1696 aged 66

1217 Robert Smith of Shelf buryed at Coley chappel Dec. 24. 96. aged 86

1218 Mary Ingham an Inkeeper in Halifax buryed there Dec 25, 96, aged 81.

1219 Mary Taylor of Northfield bur. at Halifax Dec 26. 96. aged 80

1220 William Cordingly of Heaton bur. at Burstal Jan 7. 1696-7 aged 56

1221 Sarah Bates of Warly bur. at Halifax Dec 23. 96, aged 57. Religious

1222 Mr Joshua Drake of York my good friend dyed Jan 10. 1696-7 buryed Jan 13. aged 44

1223 John Holdworth of Boulshey in Northourum, buryed at Halifax Jan 21. 1696.7, aged 83

1224 Ellenor Brooksbank of Oxheys buryed at Halifax Jan 22. 96-7 aged 85

1225 Widow —— of Halifax bur. same day aged 80

1226 John Simpson of Staneland bur. at Ealand Jan 25, 1696-7 aged 61

BURIALS.

1227 Joseph Watkinson wife was bur. at Halifax Jan 26. 97, aged 63

1228 Nathan Sharp wife bur. at Burstal feb. 1. 95, aged 94

1229 Mr Ralph Wood mynister at Ripponden bur. there feb 16. 1696.7 aged 72

1230 Mtris Atkinson bur. at Burstall feb 17 96-7 aged 73. I . was told by Tim Reiner feb 19. that 14 heads of family were buryed out of Heckmondwyke within this twelve months some of feaver, many of a diabetus of late

1231 Widow Sharp Willm Sharp mother of Godley bur. at Halifax of a Canker in her mouth feb 27. 1696-7 aged 68

1232 Esther Hurd of Shelf Willm Hurds widow buryed at Halifax feb 27. 96-7 aged 64

1233 Williams Inghams wife of Warly bur. at Luddenden feb 24, 1696-7 aged 70

1234 Mr Richard Dickinson dyed of a consumption buryed at Cockey chappel March 17. 1696-7 ag 40.

1235 John Eccles of Woodhous a quaker was buryed by Hardgr moor. March 22, 1696.7

1236 Ambrose Inghams wife was buryed at Halifax March 23, 1696.7 aged 70

1237 Timothy Normantons wife bur at Sowerby March 31, 1697 aged 70

1238 Michael Smith of Hove Edge buryed at Lightcliffe Ap. 1. 97, aged 81

1239 James Bolton of Warly buryed at Halifax Apr. 2, 97 aged 62

1240 Widow Crossely buryed at Rippenden Apr. 7. 1697, aged

1241 Stephen Milner of Skircot bur. at Halifax Ap. 9. 97 ag. 72

1242 Benjamin Boy, of whom I bought this house, buryed at Halifax Apr 11. 97 aged 60.

1243 Widow Holroyd mother to Jer Brooksbanks wife bur. at Ealand Apr. 12. 1697, aged 70

1244 Joshua Walker of Bingley bur. there Apr. 15, 1697, aged 70

1245 Joseph Wrights wife bur at Halifax Ap. 16. 97 aged 84

1246 Joseph Listers wife Sarah bur. at Bingley Ap. 19. 1697, ag. 65

1247 Richard Reiners wife of Milns brig bur. at Burstall Apr. 19. 97. aged 70

BURIALS.

1248 Mtris Gilham of Manchester buryed there Apr 20. 97, aged 76

1249 Abraham Broadly bur. at Halifax, Ap. 24. 97 aged 72

1250 Nathan Tilson of Sowrby Bridg long in a palsey, married 4th wife Apr 15. dyed Apr. 22, bur. at Halifax Ap 25. 1697 aged 80

1251 Margaret Midgley of Halifax bur. there Apr 27. 97 aged 70

1252 Ellen fielding an old woman that ' lived at High bently buryed Apr. 24. 97 aged 70

1253 Judith Hoyl of Northourum bur. at Halifax Apr 29 1697 aged 65

1254 Esther Kay formerly of Halifax dyed at Sowrby bridg May 1. buryed May 4. 97. aged 63

1255 Widow Ask of Rodley buryed at Calverly Apr 97 aged 70

1256 Mr John Priestley of York bur. tuesday May 11. 97 aged 43

1257 James Brooksbanks wife bur. at Halifax May 18. '97 aged 65

1258 Mr Whittel of Ealand bur there May 25, 97 aged 59

1259 Mr Richardson of Newel buryed his wife at Bradford May 26, 97, aged 58

1260 Edward Hodgson of Holdworth bur. his wife at Illingworth June 2. 97. aged 76

1261 Edward Gills wife bur. at Halifax June 5. 97. aged 66

1262 Abraham Walworth of Ringly an old puritan buryed May 23, 97 100 y. old

1263 Dr Wickam Dean of York bur Apr. 1697 aged 78

1264 Widow fenton of Holbeck bur. there June 10. 1697 aged 90

1265 Mr Ellistons of Bersland bur June 16, 1697, very rich, at Ealand

1266 William Rushworth bur. at Bingley, june 19. 96 aged 74

1267 Mr William Colburn parson of Motram buryed there June 9. 97, aged 66

1268 Thomas Kays wife bur. at Halifax June 24, 1697 aged 64

1269 Mr Chetham of Turton tower in Lanc. justice of Peace buryed at Manchester June 1697, aged 55

1270 Grace wife of Jonathan Tattersall bur. at Halifax June 24, 1697, aged 66

1271 Jonathan Tattersall her husband bur. July 2. 97, ag 70

1272 Mr Thomas fell buryed at Bingly July 3, 1697. ag 68

1273 Mr John Wadsworths wife of Holdworth bur. at Halifax July 5, 97

1274 Mr Nathaniel Vincent, minister in Southwark dyed June 1697

1275 Thomas Butterfield of Halifax chandler buryed there July 16, 97 aged 62

1276 Mary Leaver of Little Leaver my tenant, buryed at Bolton June 25, 97, aged 69

1277 John Crook bur. at Halifax July 20, 1697 of a pleursy ag 44

1278 My Lady Mozely of Hulm by Manchester dyed July 8. 97, aged 63

1278 Martha wife of William Cordingly of Burstall parish bur. there July 1697, her husband lately

1279 Abraham Sharp of Boulin bur. at Bradford, a rich man, Aug 2. 97, aged 50

1280 Sir John Hewley of Bell Hall bur. at Saviours Church in York Aug 24. 1697 aged 79

1281 Jacob farrar of Warly bur. at Luddenden Sep. 1. 1697, aged 71

1282 Mr Danl Sykes of Knottingly bur. Sep. 3. 1697, aged 60

1283 John Grays wife bur. at Halifax Sep. 12. 1697, aged 68

1284 Widow Stead of Ovenden bur. at Halifax Sep 13. 97 aged 70

1285 Joseph Haliday, our neighbour, bur at Halifax Sept 13. 97, aged 32

1286 Mr Richard Whitehurst dyed preacher at Burlinton Sept 5 1697 aged 60. Mrs Whitehurst his wife dyed Aug. 31. both of a feaver

1288 Mr Matthew Baxter of Attercliff a N.C. Minr. dyed Sept. 12 '97, aged 60

1289 John Thorntons wife of Horton bur at Bradford Sep 27. 97 aged 56

1290 James Threapland of Wibsey bur Sep 26. 97

1291 John Thomas wife bur. at Halifax Oct 2. 1697

1292 Mr Gilbt Rigby (Justice of Peace in Halifax dyed at 5 aclock afternoon on Wednesday Oct 20, 1697, aged 34 the funeral solemnity was at Halifax on Monday Oct 25 he was carryed in a coach into Lanc. on tuesday Oct 26 to be buryed at Preston in the evening of Oct 27

1293 Laurence Lomax my old friend in Ainsworth removed with his wife to   brought to Middleton to be buryed Sept

BURIALS.

1697 aged 81

1294 Mr Throp of Bolton only son (called Squire Throp) was buryed there Oct 28, 97 aged 50

1295 Mr Waterhouse of Ponfrit bur there Oct 1697 aged 80

1296 John Bury of Ecclesall buryed at Bradford Nov 9. 97 aged 83

1297 Timothy Netherwood wife bur. at Halifax Nov 17. 97 of a consumption

1298 Tho. Hodgson of Boulin bur. at Bradford Nov 20. 97 of feaver

1299 Mathew Holdworths wife bur. at Halifax Nov 23. 97 aged 60. palsy

1300 Simeon Lord in Shipden bur at Halifax Nov 28. 1697

1301 William Ramsden milner at Coley mill buryed at Coley Chappel Dec 1. 97 aged 59

1302 Mr Oddy schoolmaster in   lane Leeds buryed there Dec 3. 97 aged 58

1303 Captain Peter Seddon bur. at Ringly chappel Dec 4, 1697 aged 82

1304 Margaret Heywood my mother in law buryed at Bolton Dec 11. 97 aged 77 of long languishing

1305 Mr John Witter minister at Sowerby buryed there Dec 27. 1697 aged 66. Mr Wilkinson preacht. funeral on Heb. 9. 27

1306 Susanna Cousin sister to Abr. Holt buryed at Halifax from Shipden hall Dec 28. 1797, aged 7—

1307 James Halsted of Warly and Hanna his wife

1308 were buryed in one grave at Halifax Jan 1. 1697-8. aged 50

1309 Susanna Robinson dyed at Th. Rhodes in Horton bur. at Bradford Dec 31. 1697 aged 70. a professor

1310 Joshua Cordingly of Heaton bur. at Burstall Jan 1697-8 aged 52, one of Mr Dawsons hearers

1311 John Medley of Northourum bur. at Halifax Jan 14 1697-8. of a feaver having had 14 children. 10 living, poor man, aged 56

1312 Abraham Hardistys wife of Northourum green bur. at Halifax Jan 29. 1697-8 aged 78

1313 Mr Ramsden of Crowston that lived an exceeding dissolute life, shortened his days by intemperance, dyed young Jan 30. 1697-8 aged 27 bur. at Ealand feb 4. 97-8.

1314 George Ramsden R.R. son buryed at Halifax feb 3, 1697-8 a young man killed himself by intemperance

BURIALS.

1315 Mr Hopkin of Clayhouse dyed after the like manner bur, Mch 22. 1698

1316 Mr Wm Green of Hightown dyed feb 5. 1698 a sad drinker aged 40

1317 Timothy Normanton of Sowrby buryed there feb 9, 1697-8, aged 74

1318 Joshua Cordingly bur. at Burstall feb 7. 98

1319 Earl of Burlington died at London brought to York to be buryed feb 8. 98. aged 86

1320 Mr Paulard vicar of Kildwick in Craven buryed there feb 14, 1697-8, aged 50

1321 Martha Smith wife Isaac Bently of Northourum bur. at Halifax, feb 22. 1697-8. aged 66

1322 Thomas Sailes of fairweathergreen bur. at Bradford feb 21. 9⅞ aged 56

1323 William Bunys wife of Northourum bur. feb, 23. 97-8 aged 60

1324 Mr. Sagar of Blackburn a N.C. Minister, dyed feb 13. 97-8 seized with a palsey, aged 56

1325 Mr. finch a N.C. minister of Norwich dyed feb 1697-8 aged 63

1326 Mr Richardson of Bradford bur. there feb 26, 1697-8 aged 46

1327 Joseph fournesse bur: at Halifax Mch 5. 98 aged 73

1328 Isaac Sonier bur. at Halifax Mch 8. 98

1329 Mr Samuel Angier my nephew, a N.C. Minr at Leverpool bur. Wednesday feb 23, 1698, aged 40

1330 William Blamires an old man bur at Halifax Mch 13. 1698

1331 Sarah wife of John Fenton of Halifax bur. there Mch 11. 98 aged 55

1332 Mr Reynolds of Nottingham an eminent N.C. Minr. dyed Mch. 1698

1333 Thomas Dounes wife bur at Halifax Apr 3. 1698. ag 56

1334 Abraham foster of Denham buryed at Howarth April 2. 98, aged 74

1335 Paul Kay a fidler bur. at Halifax Apr 5. 98 Mr Bairstow preacht funeral

1336 John Hill of Stump Crosse bur. at Halifax Apr 22, 98, aged 55

1337 Thomas Bins of Northourum bur. at Coley Chappel Apr. 27. 98, aged 61

1338 Jeremiah Empsall of Norwoodgreen bur. at Halifax May 6, 1698, aged 69

BURIALS.

1339 John Knowles of Shipden bur. Halifax May 6. 98 aged 53

1340 Hugh Ramsden of Golker by Slaighwait where we were wont to preach bur. at Huthersfield May 10. 98. aged 54

1341 Miles Partinton my old tenant in little Leaver bur. Apr. 1 1698 in Bolton aged 67

1342 Mary furnesse of Shipden bur at Halifax May. 98, ag 66.

1343 John Richardsons wife of Halifax bur. there May 27, 1698 aged 71

1344 Nathaniel Hogg of Leeds bur, there May 22, 1698 aged 54

1345 John Stot of Littleborough bur. at Ratchdall May 26 1698 aged 67

1346 John Viccars of Idle bur at Carverly June 2. 1698 aged 52

1347 Mr John Kirk of flanshaw hall bur. at Wakefield June 10. 1698, aged 30

1348 Timothy Tatersall of Warly bur. at Halifax June 14. 98. aged 74

1349 John Ekroyd bur. at Thornton Chappel June 15 98 aged 47, was marryed to Sarah Maud 20 weeks

1350 Mtris Oates of Hollins bur. at Halifax June 23. 1698 age 34

1351 Henry Bently bur. at Sowrby June 25. 98

1352 Mr Roger Kenion Clark of peace in Lancashire dyed June 12. 1698 aged 63

1353 James Barrows wife of Shipden bur at Halifax July 5, 1698, aged 64

1354 Abraham Swallow buryed at Ambry July 7. 1698, aged 78

1355 Henry Spencers wife of Shelf-hall buryed at Halifax July 10. 1698 aged 80

1356 Mr Richard Taylor of Milns Brig buryed at Huthersfield May 3, 98. aged 84

1357 William Ingham of Warly bur. at Luddinden Aug. 29. 98, dyed suddenly, aged 86

1358 Mtrs Martha Sharp d. to Ms. faith Sharp of little Horton buryed at Bradford Aug. 29. 98, aged 20

1359 William Robinson of Deanhead bur. at Halifax Sept. 7. 1698, aged 42.

1360 James Robinson his brother bur there in one grave the same day Sept 7. 98, aged 40

1361 Judith widow of George Ramsden bur at Halifax Sept 17.

BURIALS.

98 aged 40

1362 Sarah wife of Timothy Bancroft bur. at Halifax Sept 23, 98. aged 50

1363 Jonas Tillotsons wife bur. at Howarth Sept, 23, 98 aged 63

1364 Mr Richard frankland of Rauthmel in Craven dyed Oct 1. buried at Giggleswick Oct 5, 1698, aged 68

1365 William Gill of Northourum bur. at Halifax Oct 24. 98. aged 78

1366 Joseph Butterworth bur. at Halifax Oct 25. 98. aged 76

1367 James Murgatroyds wife of Warly bur. at Halifax. Oct 30. 98

1368 Mr Peter Ashton preacher at Ealand bur. there Nov. 3. 98, aged 45

1369 Mercy Stocks of Northourum bur. at Halifax Nov. 4. 1698 aged 41

1370 John Hilton of little Leaver bur. at Bolton Nov. 5. 1698. aged 74

1371 Rebecca Crompton bur. at Bolton Nov. 7. 98. ag. 76

1372 John Scots wife (sister to John Northen) buryed at Halifax Nov. 29. 98

1373 Jeremiah Jaggers wife bur. at Halifax. Dec 16. 1698. aged 60

1374 Martha Gill bur. at Halifax Dec 17. 98., aged 58

1375 Jacob farrars wife bur. at Luddenden Dec 17, 1698, aged 70

1376 Ephraim Moor Clark at Coley Chappel dyed on friday was buryed at Coley Dec 26. 98, aged 50

1377 Mtris —— sister to Lieutenant Sharp of Horton dyed at Rauthmel June 1698, 100 years of age

1378 Mr Roger Throp of Bolton bur. there Nov. 98. ag. 74

1379 Mr Thomas Horton of Barsland Justice of peace dyed Jan 2. was buryed at Ealand Jan 7. 1698-9 aged 48

1380 Mtris Mary Hatten Vicar of Deans wife my wives neece dyed Dec. 1698 aged 53

1381 Mr Langdal Sunderland formerly of Coley-hall dyed at Ackton near Ponfret Dec. 1698 aged 81

1382 Phoebe King dyed at Barwick Oct. 1698, aged 85

1383 Mr Hanson parson of Thornton in Craven buryed there Jan 26. 98-9 was grown exceeding fat, aged 40

BURIALS.

1384 Mr Christopher Richardson ðf Leverpool dyed Dec. 1698-9. aged 81

1385 Isaac Bently living in the clarks house at Coley chappel dyed Lords Day morning feb 5 99. aged 71

1386 Abraham Healys wife of Bradshaw bur at Halifax feb 11 98-9. aged 60

1387 Mr Tho. Westbys wife of Raufield dyed feb 11. 1698-9 of a feaver upon child bearing

1388 Jane wife of Anthony Naylor of Warly dyed feb. 15. 1698-9 bur. at Luddenden 17

1389 Phoebe Stocks of Oxheys bur. at Coley-Chappel feb. 26, 1699 aged 61

1390 Sarah Dickson Daniel Dicksons wife at James Brooksbanks bur at Halifax Mch 24. 1698-9 aged 40

1391 Dr Edward Stillingfleet Bishop of Worcester dyed March 1699. aged 66

1392 Mtris Mabil Wood (alias Rylands) dyed in London Apr 1699, aged 81

1393 Mr Donwell of Leeds bur his wife April 14. 1699. a merchant Londoner

1394 Mr John Pickering of Tingly bur. in his burying place Apr 22, 1699 aged 74

1395 Richard Taylor Esq of Wallinwells in Nottinghamshire dyed Apr 20 at 4 o'clock afternoon bur at Carleton privately Ap, 22, aged 50

1396 Sarah wife of Samuel Wadington dyed Apr. buryed at Lightcliff Apr 28. aged 75.

1397 Mr Jeremiah Bowr of Bradford postmaster bur there Apr. 28. 99. aged 88

1398 Ant. Petty went to his work being a mason on Apr. 24. well, dyed Apr 25, aged 64

1399 Anthony Croyze's wife of Ovenden buryed at Halifax Apr 30. 1699 an old woman above 80

1400 Mr Ralph Spencers daughter marryed to Mr Hatfield dyed of her 2d child at London Apr. 1699 aged about 34

1401 James Halsted a louely gracious young man a fine scholar bur. at Halifax May 10. 1699

1402 Mr John Smith preacher at Deanhead bur. there May 19. 1699 aged 82

1403 Mrs Rusby dyed at Rooks, N. Whitley sister ; two women

BURIALS.

in Ealand the youngest of these 4 was above 80 y. of age all
buryed in that one week as J.P. informs me.
1404 Peter Bradbury a taylor in Wakefield (a good man and my
kind friend bur there May 19. 99. ag. 59
1405 Mr Henry Murgatroyd's wife bur at Luddenden May 20.
1699 above 80 years of age
1406 Mtris Angier, my sister in law, dyed Apr. 99. ag. 68.
James Oates told me June 2. 99 that 8 aged people are dead
at Norwoodgreen within last twelve months
1407 Henry flather of Brighouse bur. at Ealand June 13. 99
aged 50
1408 Robert Masons wife of Booths town bur. at Halifax June 16
1699
1409 Mr Richard Richardson of Newel bur. at Bradford June 21.
1699 had lyen a half year of a hurt, aged 50
1410 Robert Gleadhill butcher in Halifax bur there June 21.
1699, a bad man, clipper as tis sd. left 2000 li, aged 61
1411 Thomas Mason of Over-brear in our neighbourhood dyed at
10 a clock Lords Day July 9. 1699 bur. at Halifax July 12.
long consumptive
1412 John Appleyard, Shelf, bur at Halifax on Saturday July 15
1699, aged 72
1413 Grace wife Timothy Paulard of Rans bur. at Halifax July
21. 1699, consumption, ag. 41
1414 Dr Bates of London dyed July 14. 1699 being 74 years
of age
1415 Joseph Wright of Lightcliff bur. at Halifax July 28, 99
aged 84
1416 Lewes Brooksbank bur. Halifax July 28, 99 ag 54
1417 Mtris Sagar mother to Mr Sagar dyed, bur. at Wakefield
July 1699
1418 Sarah d. Mr. Abraham Hall of Booths town bur at Halifax
July 31. 99
1419 Isabel Oddy of Wibsey bur. at Bradford Aug 10. 1699
aged 3
1420 John Marsden of Marsden bur there Aug 9 1699, aged 92,
a pious man
1421 Mr Timothy Manlove minister dyed of a feaver at Newcastle
Aug 4, bur Aug 5. 99 newly gone from Leeds
1422 Grace wife of Joseph Croft bur at Halifax Aug 15. 99

BURIALS.

aged 56
1423 Mr francis Moseley one of the fellows in Manchester buryed
Aug 17. 1699, aged 74
1424 Mtris Reasby of Thornton bur. at Bradford Aug. 19. 1699,
aged 72
1425 Mr firth minister at Mansfield many years of feaver disabled
long dyed 99 aged 82
1426 Mr Thomas Ledgard of Bradford bur. there Aug. 18. 99
aged 78-80
1427 Mr William Hawden minister dyed at Wakefield, bur. at
Morley Aug 28. 99 aged 84
1428 Mr Thomas Crompton of Toxteth Park having been in
Darbishire returning dyed at Apothecary Holbrooks in Manchester was carried thence to be buried at —— Sept 2. 99 aged
64
1429 Sir Rowland Bellows of Smithels dyed near Maxfield in
Cheshire brought to Bolton bur. there Sept 7, 1699, a papist,
aged 60
1430 Mr John Ray of Gummersall dyed of a feaver Sept 17,
buryed at Burstall Sept 20 99, aged 40. preacher at Pudsey
and Closes
1431 Mr. Robt Ramsden of Stonyroid was found dead in his bed
Sat. morning, Sep 23, '99 bur. at Halifax Sep. 26. aged 70
1432 Adam fernisides wife in Darcy leaver bur. at Bolton Sep 29,
1699 aged 63
1433 Matthew Boococks widow bur Oct 11. 99 at Coley, aged
68
1434 Anne Northen of this town bur at Halifax Oct 19. 1699
aged 78
1435 Jonas Woodhead killed in a colepit bur. at Halifax Oct 23.
99 aged 60
1436 Mr. Mathew Mede of London an eminent minister bur Oct.
99 aged 77
1437 Mris Sarah Hodgson of York bur. Sept. 1699 aged 80
our old intimate
1428 Mr Prigham Vicar of Silkston bur. there Oct 1699 aged 72
1429 Richard H pworths wife bur at Halifax Oct 25 1699
aged 60
1430 Gabriel Bently bur. at Ealand Oct. 23, 1699 aged 71,
long lame

G

BURIALS.

1431 Timothy Crowthers wife of Warly bur. at Luddenden Nov 8. 1699 aged 54

1431 James ferniside of little Leaver bur. at Bolton Nov 3. 99. aged 68.

1432 Mtris Alice Ward sister to Mary Brooksbank bur. at Ribchester Nov 3. 99, aged 73

1433 John Win of Bradford, Quaker Speaker, bur there Nov 20. 1699 aged 61

1434 John Butterworth dyed at Edenborough Oct. 99. ag 56

1435 Mr Benjamin farrands wife was bur at Bingly [Nov 24. 1699 aged 74, her son David came out of the? south, fell sick, buried with her

1436 Mr Robert Ledgard of Chappeltown buryed at Leeds Nov. 25. 1699, a pious man my good friend, aged 50

1437 Joanna wife of Robt Baggil of Halifax bur. there Dec. 1. 99, aged 56

1438 Sir Thomas Rookby judg dyed at London Nov. 26, 99 aged 60. brought to be buried in Yorkshire

1439 Mr David Parkinson of Bradford wife buryed there Dec 8. 99, aged 50

1440 Thomas Jackson of Leeds bur. Dec. 12, 1699, aged 59

1441 Mtris Cotton brought dead out of Cheshire to Peniston to be buryed by her husband there Nov. 30. 99. ag. 76

1442 Paul Greenwood bur. at Halifax Dec. 16. 99 aged 49

1443 Alderman Massy of Leeds bur Nov. 99. ag 63

1444 Richard Wilkinson bur. at Bingly Dec. 99. aged 68

1445 Simeon Robinson bur at Coley Chappel Jan 5 1700. aged 71

1446 Mtris Richardson of high fernly bur. at Tong, Jan 8. 1699 -700

1447 Mary Hall bur. from John Learoyds at Halifax Jan 11. 1699 aged 76

1448 Mr. Birch Vicar of Preston an honest conformist dyed Jan 12. 700, aged 50

1449 Richard Kighlys wife of Sowrby bur. there Jan. 17. 700 aged 60

1450 William Ilbeck that kept [over-George tavern in Halifax bur. there Jan 21, 1699-700. aged 64

1451 Samuel Nickol bur. at Halifax Jan. 29 700, aged 46

BURIALS.

1452 Thomas Nobles wife of Halifax bur. there Jan 30. 99. aged 50

1458 John Hemingway of Bank top bur. at Halifax feb. 1. 1699-700 aged 46

1459 Jonathan Haliday of Halifax bur. there feb 7. 700 aged 82

1460 William Thorp of Shelf bur. at Halifax feb 9. 700 aged 87

1461 Sarah wife of Joshua Owen of Halifax bur. feb 10. 700. aged 60

1462 Mr William Bagshaw of Darbishire a choyce minister bur Jan 1699. aged 72.

[1462 Crossed off.]

1463 Joshua Whitley of Soudhouse in Hipperholm bur at Halifax feb 14. 1699-700, aged 79

1464 Mr Benjamin farrand of Bingley bur there feb 13 '700 aged 74

1465 Mr Robt Constantine formerly parson of Oldham lived and dyed in Manchester bur. at Oldham Dec 16. 99 aged 80

1466 Mr Lun preacher at Wibsey buryed there feb 17. 1699-700 aged 46

1467 Elizabeth Parker bur. at Halifax feb 20. 1699. aged 63. died at Warly under a cloud of debt

1468 Dr Gilpin of Newcastle bur feb 21.'700 aged 76

1469 Mtris Lake Bishop Lakes wife of Chichester dyed at Mr Edward Langleys buryed at Halifax feb 22 99-700 aged 71

1470 Robt Bagaly of Halifax bur feb 27, 99-700 ag. 67

1471 Samuel Wadington of Norwood Green bur. at Lightcliff of a days sickness feb 28. aged 77

1472 Dr Caleb Drake of Pikely bur at Pontefract feb 20, 1700. aged 50

1473 John Duckworth dyed prisoner at Halifax bur. there feb 26. aged 50

1474 Joseph Holroyd bur. at Ealand feb 28, 99 aged 50

1475 Anne Unsworth bur. at Manchester feb 13. 1700 distributed 300 books, aged 64

1476 Michael Godlys wife of Warly bur at Halifax March 7. 700 aged 80

1477 Mtris Rylands sister Hiltons mother bur at Manchester Jan 1699 aged 70

1478 Jonathan Scot of Blakehill bur at Halifax Mch 21, 1699

BURIALS.

aged 44

1479 Joseph Holroyds wife bur at Ealand Mch 10 99 11 days
after her husband, in debt, left 10 children

1480 Robert Spencer of Warly bur. at Luddenden Mch 20. 700,
aged 62—57

1481 Henry Grimes old wife dyed March 24 bur. at Halifax Mch
28 1700 aged 70

1482 John Hargreaves junr. bur at Halifax Mch 29. 700 aged
41 very fat

1483 Edward Hansons wife of Northowrum bur at Halifax April
1. 700 aged 67

1484 Mr Richard Green of Roberttown buryed at Burstall Mch
31, 700, aged 50

1485 Timothy Reiner bur at Batly Apr 4. 1700 a religious man,
aged 57

1486 Mr Ellison parson of Ashton under Line bur. Jan 16 99-
700 aged 57

1487 Edmund Brook of Shelf bur. at Halifax April 10, 1700
aged 92 died suddenly

1488 Sarah wife of Jonathan Scot bur Apr. 14, 1700 at Halifax
aged 40

1489 Mr John Clough of Halifax had been rich come down,
kept oth town, deputy constable bur there April 14, 1700,
aged 63

1490 his wife dyed the day after he was buryed had 10 sh a
month

1491 John Ellis of Bradshaw in Illingworth Ch ppelry dyed Apr.
19. bur. at Halifax [Dec] 22, 1700, aged 71

1492 Mr John Smiths wife of Wakefield (Mtris Mitchel, daughter
to Willm Wilton) dyed of small pox Lords Day Night Apr. 21.
700 bur. Apr 24. aged 40

1493 Sarah Hodgson widow of James H. butcher in Halifax
dyed April 22 bur Apr. 25 aged 58

1494 John Armitage of Lidyat my aged friend͜dyed Apr 22, bur.
26 aged 68

1495 Thomas Kitson wife of Hipperholm bur. Apr. 6. aged 40
at Halifax

1496 John Cook of London (Jo. Cook of Halifax father) dyed
Apr 26. aged 60

1497 Jeremiah Brooksbank bur. at Halifax May 10. 1700 aged

55
1498 Mr Pour of Newhall bur. at Ealand May 10. 1700, aged 40

1499 Mtris Crompton (cozen James wife) bur. at Bolton Apr 29. aged 4—

1500 James Nettleton of Cockill in Shelf bur. at Coley June 8, 1700, aged 80

1501 George Whitely bur at Lightcliff June 9, 1700 of a feaver aged 40

1502 Mary Brig bur. at Halifax dyed of a feaver, aged 40

1503 Susanna Empson bur. at Lightcliff June 5. 1700, of a sore brest, aged 50

1504 Captain Hellowel of Pikelow by Littlebrough dyed June 15, 700 aged 88, bur. at Ratchdall June 17

1505 —— Littleton in Rushworth dyed June 1700 an 100 years old

    Nathan Wood, not dead, 103 years of age

1506 William Garth of Idles bur. at Calverly June 26, 1700 of a fever, aged 86

1507 Mr John Listers wife of Ovenden (widow) buryed at Bradford June 20, 1700 aged 70, Mr Ellison preacht

1508 Mary wife of George farrar of Commonhouse in Halifax bur. July 2, 1700, aged 42, a good woman

1509 J. Manks wife a Quaker in Halifax bur. at Harwoodwell thursday July 4, 1700 aged 50

1510 Samuel Crabtree an Atheist bur. at Halifax July 7. aged 63

1511 Abraham Bairstows wife of high bently bur. July 10. aged 50

1512 James Smiths wife of Great Horton bur at Bradford July 21. 1700 aged 74

1513 John Wainhouse wife bur at Halifax July 29 aged 58

1514 Samuel Bradly of Batley bur. there Aug 2. aged 47

1515 Mr Robert Dinely of Leeds my old friend dyed June 1700

1516 Charles Best of Landiner killd himself with intemperance dyed in the 22 year of his age bur. at Halifax August 7. 1700

1517 Joshua Souier of Banktop bur. at Halifax Aug 13 1700, a good man, aged 70

1518 Thomas Gill of Southourum bur. at Halifax Aug 13. 1700 aged 50

1519 Isabel Gleadhill (sister to Mr Robt Gleadhill) Godly buryed at Bradford Aug 13. 80 years

1520 Dr Henry Sampson dyed about London, my worthy friend bur. Aug. aged 74

1521 Dr. Nicholson of York my good friend eat his dinner well Aug 10. 1700 dyed that night, a religious man of Dr. Coultous society aged 61

1522 Thomas Drake shopkeeper in Halifax inclining to Quakers dyed suddenly Aug 17. 1700, aged 50

1523 Mtris Bates (Mr Holdworth of Asty's mother, bur. at Halifax on Aug 22, 1700, aged 80

1524 Mr Ellison of Coley told me this day that a woman dyed at Bickerstaff in Lanc. of 105 years old, this is Aug. 27, 1700

1525 Mr. John Holdroyd (commonly called Esq.) was buryed at Ealand Ang 30. 1700. aged 66

1526 Mr John Mauds wife Mr Oats of Hollins daughter dyed Aug 29. buryed at Halifax Sep. 3. 1700, aged 28

1527 Samuel Hardger grown very poor, dyed Aug 30. bur. at Coley Aug 31, 1700, aged 64

1528 John firth ancient servant to Mris Lister by Wibsey Slack dyed Aug 31, 1700 aged 80

1529 Widow Holroyd (Squire Holroyds first wives mother) bur. at Ealand Sept. 7. 1700 aged 91

1530 Thomas Hodgsons wife Abigail d. of Jonathan Priestly bur. at Bradford Sept 10. 1700 aged 30

1531 Timothy Smith of Shelf bur. of a feaver at Halifax Sept 19, 1700, aged 47

    Sept. 15 1700 being Lords Day I heard of the death of these 5 just then dead

1532 Duke of Bedford a godly man worth 30000 li a year died Sep. aged 84

1533 Mr Allen of Ecclesall that marryed Justice Stanhups daughter dyed Sept. aged 58

1534 John farrars wife of Ovenden dyed of child birth Sep. 14, aged 46

1535 William Rhodes of Ovenden lyes dead to be buryed Sep 16. aged 50

1536 John Terrys wife of High bently lies dead in her house, aged 70

1537 Mr Obadiah Lee, Vicar of Wakefield bur. there Sep 17.

BURIALS.

aged 74

1538 Daniel Jackson that hath a great house on Bank top died poor Sept 20 1700 aged 60

1539 Lord Savil Marquese of Halifax dyed at Rufford in Nottinghamshire Sep 1700 aged 40

1540 Judith Wovert bur. at Halifax Oct 8. 1700 aged 82 drop down dyed suddenly

1541 John Crowther of Stopes in Shipden bur. at Halifax Oct 9. 1700 aged 52

1542 John Cordingly dyed suddenly Nov 3 bur at Burstall Nov 6. aged 60

1543 Justice Nettleton of Heaton bur. at Dewsbury Nov 6. 1700. aged 57

1544 Michael Gargreave of Horton bur. at Bradford Nov. 11. 1700 a pious man, aged 75

1545 Pope Innocent 12 dyed in Sept. 1700 aged 85

1546 Charloz, King of Spain dyed in Oct 1700 aged 40, Great Revolution expected there

1547 Judg Nevil dyed Nov. aged 60

this year 1700 dyed 7 noblemen in England
1 Duke of Gloucester heir to—
2 Visoount Lansdal
3 Viscount Hereford
4 Lord Castlehaven
5 The Earl of Exeter
6 the Duke of Bedford
7 the Marqvesse of Halifax

1548 Mr James Denham bur. at Bradford Nov 27, 1700 aged 70

1549 John Blackburn own cozen to Willm Clay bur. at Ambry Dec 2. 1700, aged 66

1550 Sarah Northen bur. at Halifax Dec. 3. 1700 aged 66, of our Society

1551 Mr Rawson bur. at Bradford Nov 29. 1700, aged 60 ; bad

1552 Mathew Jagger dyed at Godley bur at Halifax Dec. 27. 1700 aged 34

1553 Sir Edward Harley a pious man dyed Dec 1700, aged 80

1554 Mtris Emmat of Bradford buryed there Jan 1. 1700, aged 63

1555 Mtris Sail of Pudsey bur. at Cawverly Jan 6. 1700 aged 80

BURIALS.

1556 Richard Pickles of Southouram bur. at Halifax Jan 7. aged 81

1557 Mr Joseph Lister of Horton bur. at Bradford Jan 8. 701 age l 50

1558 Mr John Brook of Burstall bur. there Jan 20, 1700-1 aged 74, dyed of a sore swelling in privit.s

1559 John Wilson of ———— bur. at Halifax Jan 24. 1700-1 aged 82

1560 John Hellewel bur at Luddenden Jan 27, 1701 aged 85

1561 Martha Brig of Shipden bur. at Halifax Jan 28 aged 80

1562 Abraham Mitchel of Halifax bur. there Jan 31. 1700-1 aged 40

1563 Lord faulkenbridge brought down from London to York on Wednesday Jan 29, 1700-1 to be carryed unto the north to be interr'd, aged 60

1564 Abraham Hanworth of Clayton bur. at Thornton Jan. 29 1700-1. aged 88

1565 Thomas Carvel of Halifax bur. there feb. 3. 1700-1 aged 84

1566 John Kitsons wife of Syke bur at Burstall feb 3. 1700-1. aged 76

1567 Mr Richard Hardwick servant bur. at Batly feb 8. 1700-1 aged 70

1568 Alderman Ibison bur. at Leeds feb. 13. aged 70

1569 John Hargreaves bur. at Halifax feb 19. aged 72

1570 Esther Bridg of Savil green bur. at Halifax feb 20 1700-1 aged 77

1571 Phoebe wife of Jonathan Threapland bur. at Halifax feb. 27. 1700-1 aged 74

1572 Joshua Sugden of Savil green bur at Halifax March 4. 1700-1. aged 63

1573 Phoebe Melley bur at Halifax March 23 1700-1, an old woman, 88 years of age

1574 John Reiner of Batly bur there Mch 23, 1700-1 a good man aged 60.

1575 Mr John Carington preacher at Lancaster N.C. dyed Mch. 1700-1. aged 4—

1576 Nathan Garnet of Barneshill bur. at Halifax Apr 3. 1701. aged 72 had a cancer in his mouth 3 years

1577 Abraham Greenwoods wife bur. at Luddenden Apr. 2,

BURIALS.

1701. aged 72

1578 William Preston bur. at Halifax Apr 6. 1701, aged 61.
marryed A. Holt daur

1579 Mtris Crow her (wife to a preacher at Wibsey) bur. there
Apr 11, 1701, aged 63

1580 John foster of Denham bur. at Thornton Chappel Apr 9.
1701, a good man aged 84, drove beasts on friday dyed Lords
Day morning

1581 John foster (another of that name) of Denham bur at
Thornton Apr 9. 1701, aged 63

1582 Robert Priestleys wife of Warly bur. at Halifax Apr. 14.
1701 aged 63

1583 Susanna Butler of Northowrum bur. at Halifax April 18.
1701. aged 87 almost

1584 Widow Longbothom of Booths town bur. at Halifax May 1.
1701. aged 62

1585 Abraham Greenwood wife of Warly bur. at Luddenden
April 1701. aged 75

1586 John Walker of Bingly bur there Apr. 30. 1701 aged 66

1587 John Smith my Clark dyed of Smallpox bur at Halifax
May 7. 1701

1588 John Dickson a gracious christian. bur. at Ringly in Lanc.
May 8 1701. aged 82

1589 Samuel Barker of Shipden bur. at Halifax May 14. 1701,
aged 82

1590 Mr. J. Midgly Attourny in Halifax buryed there May
20. aged 50

1591 R. Naylors wife, widow, buryed at Luddenden May 1701,
aged 88

1592 John Amblers wife bur. at Halifax May 24. 1701 of
Northourum aged 66

1593 Mr. John Drake of York dyed May 19, 1701 aged 51

1594 Mr Christopher Jackson of York dyed May 22 1701. aged
60. Minister at Crux Church

1595 Mtris Hague of Cockill in Shelf bur. at Coley June 10.
1701 grown poor, aged 64, called Queen of Cockill

1596 Thomas Pierson of Warly bur at Halifax June 11. 1701 a
godly man, aged 34

1597 Mr Hepworth Vicar of Burstall buryed there July 14, 1701,
a very bad man, aged 50

BURIALS.

1598 Mr. Berons son preacher at Sowrbybridg bur. at Bradford July 18

1599 Mtris Longbothom came sick to Booths-town July 7, was buryed at Halifax July 22 1701 aged 30

1600 Jeremiah Wood buryed at Halifax July 24, 1701 aged 77

1601 Mr Thornhill of Fixby brought from London, bur at Ealand July 16, 1701 aged 22

1602 Samuel Smallpage a pious poor man buryed at Halifax July 1701, aged 77

1603 John Wainhouse of Broad yates in Warly bur. at Halifax Aug 7. 1701, aged 78

1604 Mary Bins of Westercroft bur. at Coley Aug 17. 1701 aged 70

1605 John Hanson of Shelf buryed at Halifax Aug 21. 1701 aged 79

1686 Jonathan Holdworths wife bur. at Halifax Aug 30. 1701 aged 80

1687 Mr Robt Eaton a N.C. Minister bur. at Manchester Aug 25. 1701 aged 70

1688 Mr Joseph Holroyds wife bur. at Halifax, of child. Sept. 2. 1701

1689 Thomas Snawden, mason, bur. at Halifax Sep. 4. 1701 aged 40

1690 Gervas Brown of Tong bur. there on Saturday, Sept 7. 1701, aged 80

1691 James 2d late King of England dyed in france Aug 1701, aged 68

1692 James Halls wife of Horton buryed at Bradford Oct 15, 1701 aged 63

1693 Thomas Milner of Skircot buryed at Halifax Oct 16. 1701, aged 80

1694 Mr Empson of Wyke bur. at Hardger Oct 17. 1701, aged 80 years, father to Attourney

1695 Thomas Robinson of Leeds buryed there Oct 18 1701, aged 63

1696 Mr Dison, schoolmaster of Drighlinton 24 yeares dyed of Apoplexy bur. at Burstall Nov 2 1701

1697 John Scot of Hall-houses bur. at Halifax Nov 9. 1701, aged 52

1698 Mr Lister of Thornton in Craven Esq dyed in the South

BURIALS.

unmarried left Sir John Kays youngest son 1500 **a year**, brought to be buryed at Almondbury Nov

1699 John Wilson formerly clark at Halifax dyed Sat Nov, 14, buryed there Nov 17. 1701, aged 63

1700 Samuel Clark of Morley bur. there Nov 19. 1701 married Judith Swift, aged 30

1701 M [ichael] Maud of Bingly Parish, in Cottingly bur. there Oct. 1701 aged 62

1702 Mtris Donwell of Leeds bur. Dec 6. 1701 aged 73 **a pious woman**

1703 Alderman Skelton of Leeds dyed Nov. 1701, 84 years

1704 Mtris Milner a pious woman bur. at Leeds Dec 12. 1701. aged 74

1705 Edmund Marsden a rich covetous old man buryed at Halifax Dec 27 1701 aged 70

1706 Mr Thomas Leach of Riddlesden hall my good friend bur. his wife at Bingly Jan 7. 170½ aged 50

1707 John Benton of Halifax glazier bur there Dec 30. 1701 aged 58

1708 Ann Booth widow of North field yate in Northourum bur. at Halifax Jan 10. 1701-2, aged 60

1709 Mary Drake of Northourum maid buryed at Halifax Jan. 13, 170½, aged 65

1710 Thomas Coates dyed in Halifax prison, jury empaneld for him Jan 9. 1702, aged 64

1711 William Garth of Idle bur. at Calverly friday Jan 23. 170½, aged 56

1712 Mr John Sagar of Allerton buryed at Bradford Jan. 26, 1702 aged 40.

1713 Daniel Bates of Warly bur. at Halifax feb 5. 170½, aged 76

1714 Isabel Timothy Crowthers wife bur. at Halifax feb 5. 170½ aged 41

1715 Mr Modesly in Cheshire bur. Dec 5. 1700

1716 John Hartly of Northourum bur at Halifax feb 26. 170½ aged 84

1717 Mr Henry Murgatroyd of Luddenden bur. there March 1702, very aged but bad man, aged 94 or 95.

1718 Mr. Galkroger preacher at Howarth baptised a child at Kirk on feb, 4, dyed March 1. buryed March 5. 1702, aged 63, a very rich man

BURIALS.

1719 Dr. Breary parson of Guisely worth 400 li a year, bur. there March 1702 aged 60, a fat man, he marryed Dr Hitchs daughter.

1720 King William 3d our good king dyed Lords day morning March 8 170¼, 52 yeares of age, much lamented.

1721 Stephen Hurds wife of Hipperholm buryed at Coley March 17. 1702, aged 74

1722 John Lambert of Caulton Esq, buryed at Malme in Craven, March 18, 170¼, aged 63

1723 John Brigs wife of Shipden bur. at Halifax Mch. 18, 170¼ aged 66

1724 William Ray joyner, of Halifax, buryed there March 25, 1702, aged 72

1725 Mtris Westby of Hague bur. at Ravenfield March 25, 1702, aged 72

1726 Mathew foster, of Cottingly had not been well but breathed his soul exp—ly by his wife Apr. 11. 1702, aged 74.

1727 Mr William Bagshaw of Glossup in Darbishire a worthy N. C. minister dyed Apr 8 1702 aged 74, my dear brother

1728 Richard Walker of Bingly, long melancholy, now better, was found dead in his bed, buryed April 17, 1702, aged 64

1729 Dr. Gale Dean of York bur. in state April 15. 1702, aged 60

1730 Henry Murgatroyd liuing at John Sugden buryed Apr. 21, 1705, aged 40.

———◆———

The following five baptisms should have been inserted on page 32. They are misplaced in Mr. Heywood's Register.

———◆———

1682 April 23 Henry s. John Pickles bap.

,, May 30 Mary d. Anthony Lea of High Bentley

,, Sep. 18 John s. Wm. Clay of N.ourum

,, Nov. 17 Lydia d. Joseph Priestley of Westercroft

1683 April 16 John s. John Ramsden of Shipden Head

On pages 48 and 80 will be found references to 'a little velum book with one clasp.' These notices occur on page 56 of Mr. Heywood's MS. along with the following memoranda :—*The children that I have baptized at home and abroad from A.D. 1682 till A.D. 1695 you may find in a little book with one clasp bound in velume the names and number whereof is 213 till Dec. 28. 1694, there you may find them. Turn back 13 leaves and you'l find them taken out of that Book.*

DECLARATION OF INDULGENCES.

It should be stated that Mr. Heywood's Register is arranged for three columns to a page, for baptisms, marriages, and burials or "ffunerals," as he sometimes heads it ; but he seems to have utilized vacant columns and spac s in the Register by transcribing from 'the little velum book with one clasp' the entries he refers to. This accounts for many of the columns being written in a slightly more modern hand. The whole of the entries to within a few days of his death are, however, in his own handwriting. It is worthy of remark that two pages are left blank before Mr. Dickenson, his successor, resumes the entries, and not one word as to Mr. Heywood's death and burial occurs. He, who had been so particular in noting the deaths of his friends, and who was succeeded by a minister as particular as himself, has no line in his own book in which his death is recorded. Yet those two blank pages speak volumes. Even the Revs. Dr. Fawcett, Richard Slate, and Joseph Hunter, have not exhausted the lessons to be derived from the life and writings of good Oliver Heywood.

Before proceeding to copy from Mr. Dickenson's portion of the Register, we will digress by supplying a large quantity of unpublished notes bearing on the ecclesiastical history of the West Riding of Yorkshire from 1672 to 1700. In 1672 Charles the Second issued his DECLARATION OF INDULGENCES. From the thousands of applications for licenses to preach, or for preachi g places, (now preserved at the Public Record Office, Lon lon,) the following list for Yorkshire has been compiled by Mr. Marsh. The *Indulgence* lasted only till 1673, but the number of applicants shows that the severe laws from 1662 had not been effectual in securing conformity.

Preacher.   Meeting House.   Place.   Denomination.

The abbreviations used are as follows:—O.H., Own House;
P., Presbyterian; C., Congregational; B., Baptist; A., Anabaptist; I., Independent.

—   ...John Armitage.........Kirkburton...........P
Armitage Robert ...Lillbury House ......Holbeck ....P
Robert Armitage was ejected from a living at Holbeck, and
died in 1689; aged 78.
Astley Richard......John Robinson ......Kingston-on-Hull ...I.
Bagshaw William...William Garlicke......Denting ....P.
—   ...John Balme...........Bradford.............C.
Bentley Eli .........O.H. ....Halifax ....P.
—   ...Timothy Bentley......Halifax ....P.
Bayley Sam .........O.H. ....Morley ....C.
Benton William ...O.H. ....Thornsco ....·...P.
William Benton was ejected from the curacy of Thornsco, and
afterwards became a maltster. He died in 1688.
Birbweek Thomas...O.H. ....Sheffield.............P.
Bloome Matthew ...Arthur Powell.........Attercliffe ....P.
Matthew Bloome was ejected from a living at Sheffield, and
afterwards turned maltster, but continued preaching as well.
He was once imprisoned in York Castle, and died in 1686.
—   ...Mathew Bloome ......Arcliffe ....P.
—   ...Nat. Bothamley ......Cowthorne ....P.
—   ...The Brick House......Briggate, Leeds......P.
Browning
Theophilus ......William Wombwell ...York ....B.
Burdsall Thomas ...   —   ...York ....P.
Thos. Burdsall was ejected from the curacy of Selby, and
afterwards became chaplain to Mrs. Hutton, of Popleton,
sister of Lord T. Fairfax. He died in 1686.
Calvert James ......O.H. ....York ....P.
James Calvert was ejected from a living at Topcliff. In 1675
he became chaplain to Sir W. Strickland, and afterwards
filled the same office in the house of Sir W. Middleton. He
died in 1698.
Clayton Luke ......   —   ...Rotherham...........P.
Luke Clayton was ejected from the vicarage of Rotherham. He
was the first minister after the Bartholomew Act to be imprisoned in York Castle. He died in 1674; aged 50.
Clayton Samuel ...O.H. ....Rotherham...........P.

| Preacher. | Meeting House. | Place. | Denomination. |

Coates Samuel ......O.H. ....Wath ....P.
Collier Josiah ......Sarah Grimshaw ......Guiseley ....I.
Cooke Robert ......Elizabeth Wentworth.Browdsworth ....P.
Coope Richard ......O.H. ....Tonge ....An.
Richard Coope, D.D., was ejected from Tong Chapel, and afterwards practised physic. He died in 1688.
Darnton John ......O.H. ....West Tanfould ......P.
Dawson Joseph......O.H. ....Birsteld ....P.
Joseph Dawson was ejected from Thornton Chapel, and he died in 1709 ; aged 73. Four of his sons entered the ministry, and the youngest had seven sons, all of whom became Dissenting ministers, but left the profession, and four became ministers of the Church of England.
— ...Joseph Dawson ......Birstol ....P.
Dawson Joseph......O.H. ....Halifax ....P.
— ...Sibbe Dawson ....Leeds..................C.
Denton John.........John Steen ....Osgoodby Grange,
                                             N. Riding.........P.
Denton Nathan.. ...Silvanus Rich ....nr. Peniston ....C.
Nathan Denton was ejected from a living at Bolton-upon-Dearn. He was living in 1713. A son entered the ministry.
— ...James Dixon............Wakefield,
                                             Northgate ......P.
Donkinson John ... — ...York ....P.
Dickinson Robt. ...O.H. ....Fishlake..............C.
— ...Hiram Duffield ......Sherborne ....C.
Duncanson James...O.H. ....Selby ....P.
James Duncanson was ejected from the curacy of Sand-Hutton.
Durant Robert......Fisher ....Sheffield..............C.
— ...Samuel Ellison..... ...Leeds..................P.
Forbes Henry ......James Brook............Ellingthorpe ....P.
Ford Cornelius...... — ...Healy Manor ....P.
Frankland Richard. — ...Rusholme ....P.
Gargrave Michael...O.H. ....Bradford..............P.
— ...William Garlick ......Dunting ....P.
Grant Jonathan ...O.H. ....Hurnescoe Grange...P.
Gunter John.........O.H. ....Helaugh..............C.
John Gunter was ejected from the rectory of Bedal. For a time he was chaplain to the merchant adventurers at Hamburg ; then he returned and was appointed chaplain to

| Preacher. | Meeting House. | Place. | Denomination. |

Oliver Cromwell. Lord Wharton was a very good friend to Gunter. He died in 1688, aged 63.

— ...Thomas Haigh ......Haslehea l ....P.

— ...John Hall ....Bradford..............P.

Hancocke Rowland..O.H. ....Shercliffe ....P.

— ...O.H. ....Shercliffe ....A.

Rowland Hancock was ejected from the curacy of Bradfield, and was once imprisoned in York Castle. He died 1685.

Handow William ...O.H. ....Sherborne ....P.

— ...John Hardaker ......Guiseley ....I.

Hartley James ...... — ...Guiseley ....I.

— ...O.H. ....Kildwich Craven C. & I,

Hawdon William ...White House ....Sherborne ....P.

— ...John Herd ....Eckelsell, Bradford...C.

Heywood Oliver ...O.H. ....Halifax ....P.

— ...John Butterworth......Halifax ....P.

Oliver Heywood was ejected from the curacy of Coley. He suffered very much from persecution in the Ecclesiastical Courts, and was imprisoned in York Castle. Yet he never ceased his ministerial labours when out of custody. Two of his sons entered the ministry.

— ...Thomas High ... ...Halsthead House, Penistone ....C.

Hobson John ......Kirksandal Hall, Yorkshire ....:......C.

Hobson Richard ...James Brooke ....Ellenthorpe ....P.

Holdsworth Josiah..O.H. ....Wakefield ....P.

Josiah Holdsworth was ejected from Popleton, near York, and he died in 1677, aged 75.

— ...William Hookby......Shell re ....P.

Joshua Horton ......Meeting house.........Quarrel-hill, Sowerby, P.

Houldsworth Josiah.Eliz. Reyner ....Sutton ....C.

Josiah Houldsworth was ejected from the curacy of Sutton, and afterwards became chaplain to Sir Rl. Houghton, of Houghton Tower, Lancashire. He died in 1685, aged 50.

Hull John............O.H. ....Thornton, Bradford..C.

— ...John Hull ....nr. Northallerton ...P.

— ...Hutton's house.........Popleton ....P.

— ...Joseph Jackson ..,....Leeds ....C.

Jaile James ....James Moxon ....Leeds ....P.

Preacher.	Meeting House.	Place.	Denomination.

essot [Issot] John, jun. ...O.H. ....Harberry ....C.

Johnson Thomas ....Sandall Magna ......P.

Thomas Johnson was ejected from the vicarage of Sherburn.

Kirby, M.A., Josiah.O.H. ....Wakefield ....P.

Josiah Kirby, M.A., was ejected from a living at Wakefield. He was several times imprisoned at Lambeth and York Castle. In 1676 he died at Wakefield, aged 59, and, being excommunicated, was buried in his own garden. (Nonconformists' Memorial.)

   —   ...The Kiln House ......Flanshaw Lane,

                       Wakefield ....C.

Lamb Nathaniel ...O.H. ....York ....P.

   —   ...Mrs. Lassell ....Mountgrat's ....P.

   —   ...Thomas Ledgard......Calverley ....P.

Long John ....Wakefield ....P.

Luck William ....Bridlington ...,......P.

William Luck was ejected from the curacy of Bridlington.

Tucker William ....Bridlington ....P.

   —   ...William Luke ....Bridlington ....P.

Marshall Christr. ...O.H. ....Topcliffe Hall,

                       Yorkshire ....C.

   —   ...Christopher Marshall..West Ardsley ......C.

Maulton Richard ....Beverley ....P.

   —   ...A new meeting house..Blackfriar's-gate,

                       Kingston-on-Hull.P.

   —   ...Meeting house.........Idle ....C.

Milner Jeremiah ...Lady Rhodes ....Haughton ....C.

Jeremiah Milner was ejected from Rothwell, near Leeds, and afterwards preached in a chapel belonging to Lady Rhodes. He died in 1681, aged 41.

   —   ...Robert Morley.........Tadcaster ....C.

   —   ...Robert Morewood ...Selby ....P.

Nailor Peter.........Boniface Cooper ......Pomfret ....P.

Nesse Christopher.....................Leeds ....C.

Christopher Nesse, M.A., was ejected from a living at Leeds. He was excommunicated, and then retired in London. In 1705 he died, aged 84, and was buried at Bunhill-fields.

Newton Edward ...William Harrison ...Parish of All Saints,

                       Leeds ....P.

Noble John ....Leonard Ward.........West Riding ....P.

H

Preacher.	Meeting House.	Place.	Denomination.

John Noble, M.A., was ejected from a living at Smeeton, and died in 1679, aged 68.

Oliver Thomas ......John Mares...... .....Newland ....I.
Packland John ......John Newton ....Anterly, near Hull ...I.
—   ...James Peckring...... Parish of St. Michael's. Leeds...............P.
Pluxton John   ......George Taylor.........   —   P.
—   ...John Prior ....Shipley ....P.
Proctor, M.A.,
Anthony ....   —   Kirkby Massard ......P.
Prime Edward ......O.H.....................Sheffield...............P.
—   ...Robert   Britsworth's malthouse ....Sheffield ....P.
—   ...Sir Henry Quentine...Beverley ....P.
—   ...Christopher Richard-son ....Shiplangton............P.
Richardson Chris-topher ....William Cotton ......Denby............ ...P.
Christopher Richardson was ejected from the Rectory of Kirkheaton. He died 1698, aged 80.
Rogers John.........O.H. ....Lartington ....P.
Rookes John.........O.H. ....Westhall, Hatfield...C.
Root Thomas.........Samuel Goodall......Lee ....P.
Sale Jas. ............O.H. ....Leeds ....P.
James Sale was ejected from a living at Leeds, and he died in 1679.
Sharpe, M.A., Thos.O.H. ....Leeds ....P.
Thos. Sharpe, M.A., was ejected from the curacy of Addle. He died in Leeds, 1693, aged 59.
Sharpnell Henry ...   —   Bradford ....B.
Shaw Joseph   ...William Rookby ......Arkworth...............P.
Snowden John ......O.H. ....Sherbourne............P.
—   ...Ralph Spencer.........Hurlstey...............P.
—   ...Samuel Stables.........Calverley ....P.
Stretton Richard ...James Richardson ...Cawood ....P.
—-   ...Andrew Taylor.........Michaelgate, York ...I.
Taylor Richard......Mr. Fisher ....Sheffield...............C.
Richard Taylor was ejected from Long Haughton, and died in 1681, aged 40.
Taylor Richard......John Wadsworth......Swath ....C.

Preacher.	Meeting House.	Place.	Denomination.
Thelwell John	......O.H.	....................Whiston	................I·
Thorp Richard	......O.H.	..................Hopton	................P·
—	...John Tod	...............Tadcaster	............P·
Treggatt Mark	......Kirksandall Hall	......Yorkshire	............C.
—	...Room or rooms in Trinity House	......Greasebrooke	.........P.
—	...Josiah Walker	........Bingley	................P.
Walker Thos.	......O.H.	..................Horton, Bradford	...A.
Ward, George	......O.H.	..................Bradford	................P.
Ward Noah	.........O.H.	..................Little Askham	......P.

Noah Ward was a student at the time of the ejectment of the
Nonconformists. He became chaplain to Sir John Went-
worth, and afterwards was an itinerant preacher all his life.
He died in 1699, aged 59.

Ward Ralph	.........Brian Dawson	.........Ousegate	................I.
Warham Richard	...— Milcock	...........Badsworth	............P.
—	...The Lady Watson	...Saviour Gate, York	...I.
—	...Alice Wentworth	......Broadsworth	.........P.
Whitechurch Rich..	— Westhall	...........Hatfield	..............C.

Richard Whitechurch was ejected from Leighton-in-the-Mooning,
and he died in 1697.

Williams Peter	............O.H.	....................York	..............P.

Peter Williams was ejected from a living at York, and afterwards lectured in the house of Lady Watson. He died
1680, aged 55

Wilson Joseph ....Newland, near King-
ston-on-Hull ......P.

Joseph Wilson was ejected from a living at Beverley, and died
in 1678.

Wilson Joseph	......Richard Barnes	......Kingston-on-Hull	...P.
Woolhouse Robert..	O.H.	..................Chapwell	..............C.
—	...Orsula Wrightson	......Aulne	..................P.

APPLICATION NOT APPROVED.

Trinity House, in Greasebrook, Rotherham, York, belonging to
the Earl of Strafford, for a Presbyterian congregation.

The following notes I gathered some years ago from the West
Riding Sessions Rolls. They are so voluminous that I shall

content myself by little more than a bare recital.

Thomas Bentley, constable of Southowram, procured an indictment against Thomas Wakefield and others, for not attending the Parish Church at Halifax, and not receiving the Sacrament, 1675. Also against the said Thomas for calling the constable a fforsworne rogue, and saying the King's precept was a ffratching paper. Thomas Wakefield's name will be found frequently in the preceding pages from Heywood's Register.

Sarah Hurd, on Sunday, March 7th (old style), 1674, in a very disorderly and seditious manner, com'd into the Church of Bradford in time of divine service, and did then and there by some indecent and clamorous speeches disturb the minister in his prayer and the whole congregation in their devotion.

Nicholas Shippen, and Elizabeth his wife, of Barnbow, summoned for not attending church : Pontefract Sessions, 1675.

William Taylor and Elinor his wife, of Scoles, for the same, 1675.

At Doncaster Sessions, 1677, six indictments were preferred against David Noble, of Heckmondwike, and his hearers for holding a Conventicle at Batley.

Joshua Smith, of Halifax, was committed, 1679, for refusing the oath of Allegiance tendered to him. Ordered to be brought to Doncaster Sessions. He was a noted Quaker.

Robert Harrison and twenty-two others, of Garforth, Aberford, &c., bound to answer for Recusancies : Wetherby Sessions, January, 1678.

Henry Barrows, Constable, of Skipton, under a warrant for apprehending Popishe Recusants, took John Cotton, of Skipton, a papist, who called the constable " a pittifull rogue and rascall."

Peticon of John Ffox Bayliffe of the Maner of Wakefield haueing a prisnor one Robt Seele a papist, one Thomas Kirshawe of ye same religion came riding to my dore asking if the prisor. was gone. John ffox replyed and tould ye said Kirshawe yt ye said Seele was sett att liberty and yt Mr Thome Watterton came and lent him money to release ye sd Seele alsoe ffoxe tould Kirshawe if there was an honest man in Yorkeshire of a papist he thought yt Mr Watterton was one with that Kirshawe replyed againe yt a papist was as good a man as he and as good a religion, ffox tould him noe, ffor he tooke ye oath of Suprmise and ye oath of allegiance.

POPISH RECUSANTS.

---◆---

Skipton, ffeb. 1678.

Broughton.—Stephen Tempest gent. Ann wife of Tho Tempest, Esq. Robert Tempest Gent. Mary Brogden. James Wooffenden.

Hebden.—Francis Ward.

Mitton.—John Singleton, Jane his wife. Eliz. wife of Thomas Shawe. Anne wife of Willm Hindle. Ellen wife of John Usherwood.

Wigglesworth.—Mary Livesey, Eliabeth Harrison, ffrances Harrison.

Ingleton.—Thomas Baynes, Isabell his wife. Widow Calvert. Jeffrey Leak, Cicilly his wife. Anth. Leake, Agnes his wife. Thomas Leak, and Eliz his wife. Richard Beesley, Agnes his wife. John Taylor, Isabell his wife, Richard his son, Agnes his daughter.

Rathmell.—Willm Husband, Ann his wife, John and Sarah his children.

fforest of Bolland.—Roger Parker, Gent. James Driver, Robt Rawman, Edward Hesleth, Anne Swinglehurst, Eliz. Turner, Tho. Driver, Mary Swinglehurst, Eliz Swinglehurst.

Skipton.—John Cotham, Eliz Butler.

SKIPTON ORDER BOOK, Oct. 1678.

Whereas the lawes and Statutes against Popish Recusants, &c· These are therefore in his Mats. Name and in pursuance of the said pclaymasion to require and command yoᵘ that yoᵘ omitt not for any Libtye, calling to yoʳ assistance the sevrall petty constables within yᵉ Libtye and others, but forthewith apprehend the bodyes of all such popish Recusants and make search in their sevrall houses for them as are mencioned in the schedule hereunto annexed, or any that are so reputed and them convey before a J.P., to find sureties for good behaviour. Anthony Bland Constable of Burnsall to have 15s allowed him for conveying George Long, a Popish recusant, to Wetherby Sess.

Claroe Recusants : Recognizances, 1679.

Knaresbbrough.—Mat Harrison Jnd. Wm Casse Ind. Ann Parker Ind. Isabell Simpson Ind. Willm Cowton Ind. Ann Young. Edw Bickerdyke. ffrancis Bridge. Rich. Casse.

Ind   George Casse.   Bridgett ux Rich Casse Ind.   John
Tucker.   Willm Ffawcett Ind.   Eliz ux George Smith Ind.
Tho Jefferson Ind.   Barbery ux Peter Simpson.   John ffawcett
Ind. [icted.]

Stainley.—Hen. Swayle Bart.   George Penington.   Leo. Cowper.
John ffish.

Weatherby.—Chris. Hardcastle Ind.   Tho Immerson.

Ripley.—Thomas Pallerser Ind.   Willm Rayner Ind.   Law.
Hodgson Ind.   Martin Hodgson.

Linton.—Symon Swayle.   Isabell ux ejus.   Ann Robinson.
Isabell Wilford.

Burrow Brigges.—Rich Waddington Ind.

Minskipp.—Mich. Wright Ind.   Rich Earle Ind.   Peter Earle
Ind.   Chris. Smith Ind.   Ann Gray Ind.   Isabell ffearsey.

Clint.—John Mawtus.   Chris. Mawtus Senior Ind.   Chris.
Mawtus Ind.   Tho Kenerdayle.   Tho Hardcastley Ind.   Rob
Joy Ind.   John Tompson.   Edw Wells Ind.   Peter Shawe.
John Milner.   James Shawe.

Copgrave.—Ninney Morras.

ffainscliffe.—Kat. Smith.   Tho Milner.

Awdfeild.—Phillip Mawtus Ind.

Rocliffe.—Janet Trees.   Edward Channeler.   Willm Trees Ind.
Ann Young.

Plumpton.—John Parker Ind.

Spofforth.—Rob. Sumpter.

Stainebeckdowne.—Tho. Browne Ind.   ffran. Toppan.   Tho
ffryeare Ind.   Rob. Graine.

Winsley.—James Whelehouse Ind.   James Mawde.

Harthwith.—Mat. Burnett Ind.

Harrogate.—Tho Squire Ind.

Panell.—Edw Tompson Ind.   Ralph Raynere Ind.

fferansbye.—Anthony Beckwith.

Nesfeild.—Tho Moore & Vx.   Andrew Hard-wick.

Barrobye.—Willm Shillitoe.

Mickley.—Chris. Coates.

POPISH RECUSANTS, 1679.

WESTRIDD } Ad genal session pac dm Regis tent apd Pontefract
Com Ebor } in le Westridd Com. prd. vicessimo nono die Aprilis

Anno Regni Caro Scdi dei gra &c vicesimo primo
coram Johe Kay Barto Willmo Ingleby Barto Thome
Yarburgh mil Johe Boynton mil Waltro Calverley
Willmo Lowther Willmo Hamond Thome Yarburgh
Jaspo Blythman Welbur Norton Willmo Ellis,
Bradwardne Tindall, Henrico Edmunds Thome
ffairefax Johe Beilby Thome ffawx & Willmo Farrer
Aris Justic. Die Dom. Regis ad pacem ibm.

WHEREAS...................all of.................in this
Rideing stand presented by the Grand Enquests for the Breache
of Seval Acts of Parliamt. made agt. Popish Recusants in the
Reignes of or. late Soveraigne Lady Queene Eliz : & or. late
Soveraigne Lord King James both of blessed memory these are
therefore in his matyes name strictly to charge & comand you &
every of you that imediately upon receipt hereof you omitt not for
any Libtye but enter the same and attach the bodyes of the
said.................................and them forthwith
convey before some of his matyes Justice of peace for the said
Rideing pvided sufficient suertyes as well for their psonall
appeance at the next Gnall Quarter Sessions of the Peace to be
holden at Rotheram for the said Rideing as allsoe that in the
meanetime they keepe the peace & be of the Good Behavior
ffaile not herein as you will answer the contrary at yor pills [peril]
dated at the said Sessions the day & yeare above said.

To all Balliffs Constables   P me
within the said Rideing but   Johes Peables Cl. pax
espially to the Constable of———   ibm

Wintersett ....Crosse gen & Thomas Scarrer.
Clayton in ffrickley..Michael Anne Esq Lawrence Chamney
    Katherine his wife Katherine Champney
    his daughter ffrances wife of Edw Tyas
    John Whittikers Margt. his wife
Handsworth.........Eliz. Berry Eliz : Barker & Sarah Hutching
Whittgift ....Mary Clerke and Mary Clerke
Cridling Stubbs ...Mary Briggs George Briggs Eliz Briggs
    ffrances Briggs
Sheifeild ....Thomas Aire Widdow Abdye Widd Champer-
    know, Bridget ux Edw : Murphey Edward
    Murphey yongr, Murphey sonne of Edmund
    Garrett Murphey and his wife ffrancis Radcliffe
    and Anne his wife

Purston Jag : ......Anne hamerton Anne Hodgson Mary Darley
          & Judith Adiman
Skelbrough ....Thomas Hornecastle and Alice his wife
          [Non invent sunt.]
fferrifryston ....Anne wife of Wm : Bedford James Calvert
          Richard Iles & his wife Eliz : Cowpland
          Hellen Jackson Mary Iles, Jos : Haire Margrt.
          Norton Elizabeth Shillitoe Mary wife of Rob.
          Speight Tho Stocks Gabriel Toothill Alice
          his wife Dorothy Wright
          [no invent.]
Hallam ....John Barker & his wife
ffullwood ....George ffox
Burrwallis...........Michael Anne Esq Mary Copley Thomas
          Hornecastle ffrancis Kendall Anne Mudde
          Grace Smith Josias Smith Kath. Walton
          Grace Woodhead Sarah ffossard
Ecclesfeild ....George Aire Mary Hall George Hall Eliz :
          Hall Eliz : Mathewman & Gregory Revill
Reedneste...........Willm Smith
Drax.................John Collen & Sarah his wife Willm Russam
          Anne Russam widdow
Smeaton ....Phillip Heppinstall George Holgate Eliz :
          wife of Phillip Heppinstall Peter Hepinstall
          his sonne
Hampall ....Stephen Ayre Jane Ayre Stephen Horne
          Thomas Lawrance & wife
Goole ....Anthony Empson & Dorothy his wife
Woodsetts...........George Eyre gen
Swinfleete...........Eliz. Ray & Mary Spinke
Stubbs Walden......John and Scicilly Pearsey Rich Wassney
Snaith ....Michal Gawbutt
Hooke ....Isabell wife of Tho. Empson Tho. Empson &
          Mary his wife
Bradfeild ....John Brittlebank Michal Browne & Scicilly
          his wife Rose ffenton Geo Hilton Anne Revill
          John Wildsmith & his wife Hanna Revill &
          Gartritt Revill
      Appended is—
          Bradfield the 20th 1679. These are to certifie this
          Honble Court that Michael Brown & Cicilly his

wife are ffrequent comers to Church
Wittnesse our hands

Thomas Ibittson   John Hoole Mins.
Joseph Watearhouse   Edward Taylear churchwarden
George Thomson

The following are notes from the respective Constables:—

South Emsall ......July the 22th (1679)

> There is noe Popish Recusants in or
> Constablerie save one Ellen Marris whoe is
> Escapte and not to bee founde. By the
> Constable William Haber
>   mke

Clayton in ffrickley..July yᵉ 22th 1679

> These are to certifie the Right Worshipfull his
> Maties Justices of yₑ Peace that accordinge to
> a warrt. sent from the Clerke of the Peace
> concerninge Popish recusants, I have to the
> vtmost of my power endeavoured to have
> taken the body of the said Recusants, wᵗʰ the
> Churchwardens Assistance, & other, but they
> have either hid themselves, or fled away.
>   Christopher Hurst, Constable

Hauercroft ....July ye 22th 1679 These may certifie his
> Maties Justices of peace that Laurence
> Clarkeson hath not any Settlement in this
> towneshipp of Hauercroft : And that ffrances
> Clarkeson Widdow is very old and Infirme
> and not able to come or Ride vnto this place.
>   John Clarkson, Constable

ffetherston Bill ......July ye 22nd 1679

> As for Mr Thomas Hippon & Mrs Alis Hippon
> they became bound before Mr Whyte to
> apeare at this Sessions.
> As for Mr John Hippon Margarett Thimbleby
> and Alice the wife of John Spinke they are
> non est Inuentus.
> As for John Spinke & Mrs Brigitt Scholey I
> have given them notice to be heare accordinge
> to Order
>   marke
>   William Malinson
>   Constable

Burghwallis ....July the 22th 1679
These are to certifye that I Robert Sykes
Constable have in obedience of a warrt.
touching certaine recusants in our pish have
made due search att sundry times since I
received the said warrt For all the psons
therein nominated, but can find none of them
to carry to the Justices of Peace according
to the direcons of the said warrant
Nevertheles I doe certify that Mr Ann &
Thomas Horncastle have taken the oath of
Allegiance & given such bond as of them hath
been required
And Mary Copley & Sarah ffoster have also
taken the same oath and have sundry times
since the last sessions repaired to our Church
and have received the Sacrament there and
soe hath ffrances Kendall done but for any of
the rest they have reformed nothing.

Hutton Pannell ...Margret Purdye wife of William Purdye
These are to certifie that her husband is a
very poore aged and infirme man and shee the
said Margret a very poore weake and almost
blind and deafe woman and about 85 yeares
old and vnable to travell
this 8th of July 1679 Thos Stanhope, Robt
Turner, &c.
Certificate from John Marshe, Min. to same
effect.

Airmin in Snaith
  Parish ....July 21th 1679
Elizabeth wife of Wm Jackson who was lately
a Roman Catholick hath now revoked the
same and is become Conformable to ye Church
of England
        Ri : Petty Cu : ibid
               mke
        Robt   Hesletyne Churchwarden

Wakefield ....Mem. That Mr Germane Poole of Wakefield
a Recusant at Leeds Sessions took both oathes
and at this Sessions brought a certificate of

his conformity, according to the Statute and
was discharged. Leeds, July 1679
Memorandum of this date.
Recusants who took onely the oath of
allegiance, & had the oath of Supremacy
tendred but refused
ffrances Shippen wife of Peter of Scholes
Robert Bartlett of Weatherby
Isabell Stokes of K. Fenton
Agatha Hardwick of Grimsdike
Eliz. wife of John Stokes of Scholes
Mary Sh—— of Barmbow, vid
Anne ———— of Scholes
W ———— of Carleton
———— of Barwick
Elizth. Shippen of Barnbow
Eliz. Butcher of same

IN SKIPTON BUNDLE, JULY 1679 :

Hebden...............ffrancis Warde
Linton ....John Swale, & Isabel his wife & Eliz : Well-
foote.
ffountaines Earth...Elizth Burrell Katherine wife of John
Craven, Elizabeth Hardcastle widdow Dorothy
Pasley widd Elizabeth Swaileson Maudlin
wife of Richard Thomson
Stainebeckdowne ...ffrancis wife of William Baynes Thomas ffrear
Mary wife of William Geldart Mary Gill Anne
Grange Robert Grange Richard Gill Anne
Lowpe Jane wife of Peter Grange Jennet wife
of John Harrison Anne Gill Mary wife of
Robert Leathley Jona Rayner George Smith
ffrancis Shaw & his wife Anne Suttle Ralph
Suttle & Jane Suttle Thomas Thopham &
ffrances his sister Mary wife of Matthew Ray
Anne Thackery
Stainebeckup ......John Tully Eliz : his wife Anne Shaw wife of
ffra : Margrt Bayne
Buckden ....Widow Sadler
Midleton ....Andrew Hardwike Wm Gill Ellen his wife
Anne wife of Jo: Walton Isabell Bickerdike

Tho Harrison Eliz : wife of Math. Hawks-
worth John Harrison Ellen wife of Chr.
Hodgeson John Gill Phillip Loftehouse &
Anne his wife Margt. wife of Tho Hodgson

Nesfeild   ....Abraham Atkinson & Anne his wife Thomas
Moore ffrances his wife Mrs Ellen ffarrand
Willm Moore

Audfeild in Studley.Phillip Mautus Richard Mautus Sarah Mautus
Barbary Mautus Prusella Mautus

Boulton   ....Thomas Fletcher Issabell Willden

Plumpton ....William Atkinson ffrances his wife ffrances
Bickerdike widd. ffrancis Briggs Elizabeth his
wife Edward Bickerdike & Issabell his wife
Ellen Briggs Thomasin the wife of John Coats
ffaith ffeming [sic] widd. Mary the wife of
Samll. Lathom Bryan Marser and Mary his
wife Hellen Plumpton John Swaile Elizabeth
his wife Robert Swaile Mary wife of John
Parker Anne Swaile widd John Trongleton
Margt Ramsden Margt Norton widd Jane
Norton of Plumpton & Anne wife of Robert
Sumptor of Spofforth

Burnsall   ....George Longe

Farnham   ....Kath. Atkinson Barbara Bickerdike Willm
Plumpton Ellen his wife Anne Lashells
" We have no such woman as Kath Atkinson
Barbara Bickerdike is very sick " Constable's
Mem.

Roecliffe   ....Edward Challensor, Dorothy Foster Dorothy
Holden William Treese & his wife & John his
sonne John Treese Isabell Warde Anne Yonge
Mary Yonge John Yonge Jane his wife Anne
Yonge his daughter
Mem : from Constable states " Anne Younge
widdow and Mary her Daughter are gone out
our Constablerye. John Yeounge is a servant
at Sr Willm Tanckred's without our Con-
stablrye but his poore Children are within us.
Dorethy Houlden and Dorethy ffoster goe both
to Church and had a certificate from our
Minister. Issabell Warde wee cannot find.

The rest carryed before Sr Wm Ingleby and he lett them goe."

Stainley cum Cayton Dorothy Robinson & Katherine Ripley
Constable writes " Kath. Ripley is above four score yeares of age and is maintained by our parish and is not able to goe before any of his maties Justiseas."

Arkendale............Anthony Beckwith Christian his wife & Anne Scarrow

Minskipp ....Ellen Earle Mary Earle Anne Gray Isabell Harrison Jane Norman Mical Wright Chr. Smith

Skipton...............John Catton

ffolifoote ....Anne wife of William Chapman ffrances wife of William Chadwick Grace wife of William Lund
Certif. from Timothy Platts Curate & others states that all three attend Church and receive Sacrament

Horton ....Alice wife of Willm Parkinson

Ingleton ....Thomas Baines & Issabell his wife Widdow Calvert Jeffery Leake & Cicilly his wife Anthony Leake Agnes his wife Eliz : wife of Thomas Leake John Taylor and Issabell his wife Richard & Agnes their children
Certi : John Lodge Curate & others that John Taylor is sick and likely to die and his wife is near her delivery and not able to travell

Grindleton ....Elizth Turner Margt Tayler widd. Jane wife of Thomas Wright

Knaresbrough ......William Cowton William Casse Emmanuel his sonne William Casse yongr Elizabeth ffawcett Anne the wife of Tho Jefferson Ellen his daughter Anne wife of Thomas Parker Katherine Wheelehouse Anne ffletcher George Casse
Note. " Could not take them. Constable discharged "

Greene Hamerton...Anne ux Willm Marmaduke

Wiglesworth.........Mary Livesey
Rathmell ....Anne wife of Willm Husband & John his
                     sonne.
                     Certificates as follow
Brearton ....Anne wife of John Siser. She is of good
                     behaviour and delicate health
                          given by John Levet, Vic. & others
Ripley ....Dorothy Atkinson   non est invent
                     Catherin Challenner   ,,   ,,   ,,
                     Jane Haldesworth   ,,   ,,   ,,
                     Jennet her sister   ,,   ,,   ,,
                     Jennet wife of George Mitton   ,,
                     Willm Hakin   ,,   ,,   ,,
                     Anne Hodgson dangerous sicke
                     Grace ux ffrancis Gale extreame sicke
                     Mary Thomson non est inventa
                     Ellen Nursay   ,,   ,,   ,,
                                    Robert Nursey, Constable
Killinghall...........July the 16. 1679
                     "William Wardman and Alice Wardman is
                     not to be found in Kilinghal and I have made
                     dilligent search
                                    Thomas Bradfielde Constable
Bilton cum Harrogate.Thomas Grimstone and Mary Squire not to
                     be found

SUSPECTED POPISH RECUSANTS, JANUARY, 1680.

Hooke.—Thomas Empson & Isabell his wife, Mary his daughter,
   Anthony his son
Goule.—Anthony   Empson & ux eius.   Willm Empson.
   Catherine Empson spinster
Swinnfleet.—John Pennithorne, Mary Spinke, Jone Spinke,
   Elizabeth Raper
Snaith.—Michaell Talbott and Katherine his wife
Whitgift.—Mary wife of Wm Clarke Junior
Little Smeaton.—Phillip Heppenstall and Issabell his wife (aged
   about 40) Their son Peter (about 15)

Bramwith.—Mr. Nathan Cooke

ffeatherstone.—Mr Thos. Ippon, Mr John Ippon, Mr Aleis Ippon [sic] Mr Margret Thimellbee [sic] John Spink and Alies his wife

Langsett.—Margery Hage, Margaret Blackburne Anne Hage spinster John Brownell their servant

Havercroft.—ffrances Clarkson Widdow Laronnce Clarkson the son of ffrancis Clarkson

ffery fryston.—James Calvert and Martha his wife Edwd Howcroft Richard Tempistt Edward Marchill.—*Servants of Mr Canelvaert* Mary Illes Richard Illes and Mary his wife Thomas Stocks Dorty Bramllay.—Sauerveants of Richard Illes Mr Elling Jackson and Jane her Dowther Anne Bedford Eller Eller Elizabeth Shilato and Ellizibeth her douwther Marye Hight, Wlte. Tutill Margret Norton Joseph Haier and frances his wife

Stappleton.—Mr John Gatenby and Lucy his wife

Cridlin.—George Briggs, Eliza his wife, Mary his Mother frances his sister

Campsall.—Ann Baytes Widdow.

Tanshell.—Samuel Jackson and Ann Jackson his wife

Knottingley.—Isabell wife of Mychell Gage

Norton.—Ann dr of Thomas Goodridge (15 yrs old)

Purston Jackling.—Phillip Hamerton Senior Phillip Hammerton and his wife, William Hutchison. Margrett Constable, Elizabeth Robbinson John Hamerton Ann Hodgson, John Darley and Mary his wife Michael Darley, Betteris Darley Mary Darley and Thomas Champney.

Stubbs Walten.—Cicylie Perry (40 or 50 years of age) Mr Thos. Pearie, Mrs Mary. Anthony.

Rotherham.—Jane wife of John Chadwicke, Robt Hall of Bentley

Barnebrough.—Basvile Moore Esq., and his wife Mary, ffrances, Bridgitt his children, Mrs Julian his servant Mrs Alice Luland

Tickhill.—Ralph Hansby Esq. and his wife, his son 20 years of age Ralph, ffrances above 16 years, Walter about 9 years

Burghwallis.—Mr Michaell Anne Joseph Smith Grace Smith Anne Mudd, Grace Woodward

Kirkeby.—Mary wife of Mr ffrancis Armitage

Hooton Roberts.—Elizth wife of Edward Pierson, Senr

Handsworth.—Thos Hutchinson and Sarah his wife, and four young children. Joney the wife of George Greaves. Thos

.

Parker & Elizth his wife

Hallom.—George ffox gent, and Mary his wife, *servants*—John ffox Gervase Sales, Elizabeth Wolstenholme, Katherine Constable Ersula Ottawell. Children—Willm & George

Houghton.—Thos Prince and Anne his wife, Margt. Bilcliffe. Mary Bilcliffe ye Elder, Mathew Bilcliffe, Anne Bilcliffe Thomas ffleminge

Clayton.—Lawrence Champney and Catherine his wife, John Whitekers and Margarett his wife, Alse the wife of Edward Tyas, ffrances the wife of Richard Gascoyne, Michael Anne Esq and his wife

Bradfeild.—Eliz. Revill Widd., Eliz. Wildsmith Widd., Geartrick Revill, Ann Revill, Mary Smalfeild, John Wildsmith and his wife, George Hillton and his wife, Roseman Fenton, John Brittilbanck, Will. fenton, Jane Dungworth, Rowland Revill, Ursely Revill

Ecclesfield.—George Eyre aged 20, ffrancis Wild pentioner aged 75.

Hampsall, Stubbs.—Thomas Laurence & Anne his wife, Issabell Gelstropp

Skelbrooke.—Alice wife of Thomas Horncastle

Sheffeild Towne.—ffrancis Rattcliffe and Anne his wife Mary aged 18, Henry 16, Thomas 12, *servants* to ffrancis Rattcliffe— Willm Savage, John Rose, Thomas Hodgkinson, Katherine Stevenson and Millison Torre. Edmund Murphey and Bridgett his wife, Anne his daughter, 22 years, Mary 20, Mary Rose his servant. Elizabeth Champernoone, Mary Abdye, Jane Oldom, Elizabeth Ellis.

Roundhay.—Richard Aspinwall and Mary his wife, Anne Leigh, poore, 60 yrs old.

Shadwell.—Mrs ffrances Thompson Mrs Cupgrace Thompson Mary Sheppon

Scarcroft.—John. Ryther, Gent, and Mary his wife

Kippax.—Richard Grococke and Eliz. uxor ej. Thos, Luke, John, filii. Eliz. Grococke filia

Snydall.—Robert Hyemsworth, Gennit Hyemsworth Widdow Mary Wright, Mrs Elizabeth Nettelton, Widdow Theasby, Grace Theasby, Barbara Theasby, Jane Pease Widdow, Ann Dougless

Walton.—Thos Waterton, Esq., and Catran his wife. Thos Kirshey and Winwefred his wife

Catteran wife of George buxtan Mrs Brigit Constable Mrs Elizth Benson

Crofton.—Joseph Ward and Margritt his wife, Robart Seele and ffranceas his wife

Ilkley.—Ellinge wife of John Barnes and Margrett Gibbons the said John Barnes his servant

Abberford.—Peter Slater & Mary his wife, Margrett and Cathren his daughters, Wm. Tindsdall & Ursale his Wife, Wm Slater, John Milner — Patsinton, Anthone ffulshurst and Ann his wife, Robert Harison, John Heptenstall and Elizabett his wife, George his sonne, Elinge Peper, John Peper hir sonne, Mare Addaman wife of John Ademan, Ellisabeth Sarvant, Mare hir dowghter Petronell Cousett, Marey hir doughter Mary Heptonstall Philep Ealond and Marey his wife and Ellisabeth his daughter, Ellisabeth Hey

Garforth.—Thomas Hunt, Bennett Johnson, Dorothy wife of Willm Samson, Mary wife of Thomas Barugh, Ane Marshall, widdow, Mary Varley, widdow, ffrancis Varley, Thomas Cantalett

Barwick in Elmett.—Francis Johnson and Elisabeth his wife, Marke Brunton and Alice his wife, Marke Brunton his son, Edmonod Hunt and Mary his wife, William Shelletoe and Mary his wife, Elinor Belhouse, Nicholas Shippen and Elisabeth his wife, Elisabeth Butcher, John her son, Alice Shoore, Katherine Sheppen, John Sheppen and Elinor his wife, Wm Smith and Anne his wife, Wm Taylor, Elisabeth Stowker, Andrew Slayter and Elisabeth his wife, Elisabeth Slaytor his daughter, ffrances Shippen widow, John her son, Katherine her daughter, John Holdcroft, William Hardwicke and Agatha his wife, Eliner Plumpton

Nether Shitlinton.—None

Whitwood.—None

Thornhill   „

Cheret.— Noe papishes

fflocton   „

Whitley   „

Staineland   „

Kirkburton   „   ·

Morton   „

Aldmanbury   „

Bingley   „

Bolling. None
Rawden. None
Stanley ,,
Yeadon ,,
Hothersfield ,,
Bramhope. ,, Secondly we have noe other Absenters from the Church as Qvaker nor any others that refvse to come to devine service or sermon. Thirdly All Hves & Cryes and other warrants have bene dvly excevted & our Stocks are in good repaire

Carleton.—No papists &c.
Wakefeild.—No papists
Horsforth— ,,
Saxton.—John Cresey and Mary his wife, Isabell the wife of Marmeduke Robeson, Margritt wife of Will. Shirdey, Ann bywater, widdow, Richard Gibsonn, Thomas Core
Burton fullings.—Jane Lund, very ould woman
Braton com Thorpe Willaby.— —ran Penington widow and hir doughter Ann aged about 9, her son John, 16
Sheerburne.—Elizabeth Barker
Lumby in Huddleston.—No popish recusant. John Simpson a servant, absent from church a month
Gateforth.—Henry Smith & his wife, Henry and Cathran their children, Elizebeth Richardson
Camelsforth.—Michael Hessay and Anne his wife, Peter his son about 11 yeares old, Hugh Brumley and Mary his wife, Nicholas Awdas an old man, Robert Riccald a single man, Issabell the wife of John Cliffe, Mary the wife of Gabriel Palmer, Jony the wife of Willm Hogley
Selby.—Thomas Wright and Ann his wife, Ellin Darton their servant, John Stroyham gent.

Carleton.—Margret Goforth and Elizabeth ffuler servants to Sr Miles Stapilton, Mrs Mary Chamnay, widow, John Newal, John Tomson and Jane Harrison her servants, Barbara Chamnay singlewoman, Thomas Kendall and Barbara Tomson servants to Mary Kendall, John Etherington and Anne his wife, Mary their daughter 11 years old, Mary Wentforth, singlewoman, Willm Awdas, Catherine Stephenson, widow, Margrett Kirkley widow, Catherine Ingram widow, Anne the wife of James Peares, Alice the wife of Robte Walker, Mary the wife of George Jubb, John Sothaby and Annie his wife.

South Milforth.—Mary Prince, a poore woman near foure score yeares of age wife of Thomas Prince a poore man

Barkston.—Willm Nicholson, Mary and Ann Nicolson, Villian wife of Anthony Saxton

Kirke ffenton.—Mrs Barbaray Simson Widd, Isabell wife of William Stoker

Dra.r.—Sarah Collins, Anne Rushem

Clifforth.—Henrie Puleine gent, Elizabett Gelstrupp

Bramham.—John Hurray and Mary his wife, Mathew Chalener and Isabell his wife, and Thomas Darley and Elling his wife belonging to Peter Liberty in York

Aberforth & Leutherton.—Ann Houlcroft, Margarit Houlcroft, Anthony bell

---

CONVENTICLE ACT.

Forasmuch as Joseph Hubert an old Irishman was brought to the Sesss. being suspected to be a Popish Priest and to have had a head in the popish plott who being required to fynd suretyes for his good behavyor hath refused to doe the same, committed to York Castle.—Wakefield, Jan., 1680.

A Conventicle, held at Heckmondwike, March 12th, 1681, was reported, when Josias Holdsworth was preaching at the house of Isabell Rayner, and persons were there from Gomersall, Batley, Mirfield, Heckmondwike and other places. It 1682 it is recorded in the Leeds Session Call Book that for six or seven years great numbers of people have gone to Topliffe Hall to an Independent Conventicle, and that Josias Holdsworth, of Heckmondwike, preached there in May last, when sixty persons were present.

At Rotherham Sessions, August, 1681, we meet with the traverse of Margaret Blackburn, of Langsett, a Recusant.

Doncaster, Jan., 1682.—Wm Bridges Rector of *Castleford* certifies that Thomas Fleming of Houghton for several years a popish Recusant did 3 or 4 months agone declare his sorrow for persisting so long in that his recusancy whereupon he procured his absolution from the Ecclesiastical Court and since that time hath duly resorted to his parish church of Castleford as a member of the Church of England.—Dated 15 Jan. 1682.

Similar certificate by Sam. Hundle curate of KIRK BRANWITH and others, that Jane wife of Francis Kertshaw of Braithwait hath for some Lords days last paist com'd to the church to divine service and behaved herself orderly and decently, and is resolved

to continew a dutiful and observant churchwoman for the future."
Dated 15 Jan. 1682.

Doncaster, Jan. 1682, certificate—that Thomas Bishop of our
toune of Hatfield hath bene of late several lords dayes at our
parish church durcing the time of divine service & doth promise
to be a common frequenter of the same.   Dated Jan. 15, 1682.
Signed by Simon Simpson the minister and others.

Mr Yarbrough's record of a Conventicle "Speaking or praying,"
in 1682.

Certificate dated 17 April, 1683,—John Collins hath & doth
in all things behave himself as a true conformeable son of the
Church of England as now established.—Signed Jo Brewer,
curate of Drax.

West Ridd) Decimo die Julii Anno R. Regs, Carol Sedi nunc
Com Ebor   ) Angliæ &c. xxvto Annoque Dom. 1683.

Memorial of the account of ye moneyes menconed in ye Record
Certifyed at ye last Qr. Sessions of ye peace houlden at Weatherby
for ye sd Rydd. by Tho: Parker & Chr Wilkinson Esqres two of
his Matys Justices of peace for ye same (forfeited as in ye sd
Record is menconed in an unlawful assembly Conventickle or
meeting held in the dwellinghouse of Wm. Holgate in Sawley
upon Sunday ye 10th day of December last undr Colour of
Exercise of Religion in other manner than according to ye Liturgy
and practice of ye Church of England

A pticular of such moneyes & forfeitures as have beene pd into
ye hands of the sd Justices since the sd Qr Sessions held at
Weatherby amounting in all to the sume of ten pounds his Matys
third pte of ye same being three pound six shillings and eightpence
tendred into ye Cort of ye genrale Qr. Sessions of ye peace held
at Skipton ye 10th day of July 1683 And by the Apointmt of
ye same by the sd Justices paid to Mr.   deputy
sheriffe for ye County afforesd to his Matys use.

	£	s.	d.
Thos. Driver of Gisburne	00	05	00
John Aspenale of Standen in ye County of Lancre	00	05	00
John Aspenall in respect of ye poverty of the abovenamed Wm Holgate	09	10	00
Suma	10	00	00

His Matys third pte of ye } 03 06 08
sd sume of £10 is ... }

Wetherby Sessions, Jan. 1682, According to the Record in
which John Lawson of Sawley husbandman and Richard Hayte
of the same husbandman are the informants whose information is
dated 29th December 1682 & is made at Gisburne before Thos.
Heber, Thos. Parker Henry Marsden and Chr. Wilkinson, the
conventicle was on the 10th December, at Holgates house in
Sawley and there were found present Will. Holgate and Tho.
Driver of Gisburne, John Scott of Sawley, Elizabeth Scott of the
same, spinster, Ric. Cowburne of Clytherow in Lancashire, yeom.,
and John Aspenagh of Standen in same County yeoman. Holgate
was fined £20 & the others 5 shillings each.

The return of ye Constable of Askwith, Wetherby, Jan. 1682.
These persons hereafter named absent themselves from ye church
—Robert Smith & Jane his wife & John Brown his Servant,
Isabell Thackeray, Dorathy Shutt, Elizabeth Shutt, Ffrancis
Kendall, Christopher Greenwood, Edmund Greenwood, Margrett
Smith, Henry Thomson, Elizabeth his wife, Edward Thomson,
Jane Gill, Thomas Crooke, John Brown of ye fold, George
Darraine & Eliz. his wife, Will. Blakey, Thomas Pauson, &
Eliz. his wife, All these be called Quakers. December 28th,
Wee found these persons assembled in an house belonging to
Henry Thomson, Senior. Henry Thomson Senr. de Askith,
John Overend of Guisley, Will: Bradley of Swinesty, Jane Smith,
Peter Hardcastle, John Barber of Leathley with several others yt
refused to declare their names. December 31th we came to the
same place and entring the house found the parlour door made
fast soe yt we could not enter but suppose some persons were
there and then assembled but we know not who they were.

<table>
<tr><td>his
Antony T ffell Constable
mark</td><td>his
Lawrence L K Kendall Overseer.
mke</td></tr>
</table>

Joseph Hargreaves Churchwarden

1682, Dec. 31, Sabbath day. Meeting at house of Benjn.
Parker of Thornton, Butcher, where, besides the family, were
Thomas Higson of Kelbrooke Hatter, Joseph Higson of Easeby
Linnen Webster, John Parker of Acronley in Lancashire, Rich
Boothman, of Salterforth, husbandman, Willm Ellis of Broughton

husbandman, all of them reputed Quakers, silently sitting in ye house, not a speaker amongst them.

Joseph Higson confessed before Justice Assheton that he was present, but would not tell who else was there neither would he subscribe to his confession.

Benjn. Parker confessed there was a meeting at his house but who were there or what it was about would not confess, and would not sign the confession respecting himself.

1683 Jeremiah Grimsaw of Rawden and many others indicted for being at a Conventicle there.

July ye 7th (82

Recud. then of Christopher Tauckred, Esqr, the sume of six pound thirteen shillings & four pence, (to be distributed among the poor of the town & parish of Little Ousburn, as the statute in that case directs) being the third pt. of the sume of Twenty pounds which was levied by distress on the goods of Richard Blythman; for suffering a conventicle to be holden at his house, Wee say recud by us

> John Abbay
> William leak
> Overseers for ye poor.
> Barnsley, Oct. 1682, Rolls.

Thomas Cowper of Knottingley a Quaker indicted for being at an vnlawfull conventickle, contemptuously refused to plead to the indictment, fyned tenn pound, which he refused to pay; to be conveyed to be imprisoned.   Barnsley, Oct. 1682.

Joseph Bailey of Denby, Edward Dickinson of the same, Robt Ellis of Penniston and Thos Cowper of Knottingley, Quakers, for absence from church three Sondayes, refused to find sureties: committed to gaol.

Joshua [Green] of Denby, Matthew Burdett of Nether Denby, Thomas Spavald of Bawtry, William Hill of Thorne, indicted and convicted upon a Premunire refused to take the oath of allegiance. Committed to gaol.   Barnsley, Oct, 1682.

John Turner of Cawthorne, Quaker, being absent from church for three Sundays, required to find sureties but refused; committed to York Castle.

Robert Clarkson of Pontefract, a Quaker, contemptuously refused to take the oath of allegiance; committed to gaoler of York.

Thomas Cooper of Knottingley (who was speaking or praying), Sarah his wife, Thomas Scafe of Pontefract, Samuell Wiedye of Pontefract, Richard Crabtree of Owston, Abraham Brigg of Kildwicke Parish, Peter Barrett of Carleton, on Dec. 24 last, held a conventicle at the house of Elizth. Stones.

Barnsley, Oct. 1682.

Tho. Midlebrook of Thorne, Robt Hallyfax, Henry Rustell, Thos. Brewley & Ro. Smith of Thorne, Joseph Clark of Rawmarsh, Hen Huntington of fferybridge, ffra. Boothes of Smawfitt, Quakers, committed. Barnsley Oct. 1682.

Mark Trickett (ejected minister) both preached and prayed at Tanshelf: committed. 1682.

POPISH RECUSANTS AND DESENTERS.

Wakefield, July, 1683.

Lotherton cum Aberforth.—Anthony Bell, Robert Sawer, Ann Holcroft, Ann Barker.

Carleton cum Camblesforth.—Sir Miles Stapilton Bart, John Tayler, John Collin, Elizth Chapman, John Sothebie, gent, and Ann his wife, John Titherington and Ann his wife, William Awdas & Cath. his wife, John Britton, Michaell Hessley, Isabel Cliffe, Mary Palmer, Johne wife of Willm Hoyley Quakers 1683. James Marshall of Idle towpp. ffynd £20
Ephraim Sandall of Idle   ,,   £20
John Adcock of Idle   ,,   iijs.

Dec. 6. 1683. On Sunday last 11 a.m, the Ch.wardens of Weston being informed of a conventicle in a house belonging to Henry Thompson of Askwith; they found Henry Thompson Senior, Shoemaker, Christopher Greenwood of Askwith, Laborer, Edwd Greenwood Junr of same, laborer, Edward Thompson of ye same, cordwainer, John Browne of ye same, Laborer, Elizth ye wife of George Darwen of the same, laborer, Jane the wife of Robt Smith of the same mason, Dorathye wife of William Shutt of ye same labr., ffrancis Kendall of ye same laborer, Elizabeth Shutt of same spinster, Henry Thompson of Weston cordwainer, John Pawson of ye same, Catherine Ackman of ye same spinster, Mary Smith of ye same spinster, Robert Barber of Leathley cordwainer, John Myers of Otley linen webster, Mary the wife of John Blakey of Denton, laborer, Alice the wife of John Bainbridge of Lyndley, laborer, William Bradley of Swinstye, Walter ffawcett of Haverey Parke, labourer.

29 Novr. Thursday, 1683 in a house at Askwith, they found
Joshua Dawson of Addingham, yoom. George Myers of same
husbandman, John Myers of Otley Linnen webster, Samuell
Thornton of Beckwith Shaw, Labr., John Bainbridge of Lyndley,
Labr, John Ouerend, clothier, Robt Smith of Askwith mason,
Wm Bradley of Swinstee cordwainer, ffrancis Kendall, Walter
ffawcett, &c.

John Elum, John Whittiker Thomas Holmes & William
Midgley of Halifax and Joshua Smith, Thomas Barber and John
ffirth of Sowerby, and Robert Cowlinge of Northowrame, brought
before Justices Farrer & Horton by order of Ambrose Pudsay.
Esquire, High Sherriffe : They refused to give bond : Committed
to York Castle. Leeds, July 1683.

Joshua Smith a quaker fined £60, same date.

John Wordsworth of Horbury indicted for being psent at a
conventicle, refuses to enter into recognizance Committed to
York Castle. Leeds, July 1683.

John Wright of Grindleton in Waddington is a true soune to
our comon mother the church of England.

Certified, (Leeds Sess: July 1683,) Willm Calverley pastor ibid.
Jo : Assheton
Tho. Parker
Henri Marsden
Chr. Heber
Chr. Wilkinson.
[These 5 were J.Ps.]

CONVENTICLE AT SKIPTON, NOV. 26. 1682.

	lb	s	d
Abbigaill Stott Wid. for suffering the sd conventicle wittingly to be held in her house £20, but adjudged not able warrant sent out to levye vpon her goods and chattells only £10 pt. thereof	10	00	00
Abbigall Stott her daughter for being psent and a hearer	00	05	00
Braidley. Edward Wadkinson and Jane his wife hearers	00	10	00
Jtm. a ffine of 10lb pt of Abbigall Stott fine of £20	10	00	00
Skipton. John Hall, Taylor, Speaker for Teacheing there fined 20lb but he adjudged not able	09	00	00

Jtm. Elizabeth his wife a bearer	00	05	00
Empsay. Richard Thompson Labr. & Anne his wife hearers	00	10	00
Jtm. fine £5 upon Richard, pt. of John Hall fine	05	00	00
Carleton pish. Peter Barrett labr. bearer ...	00	05	00
fined, part of John Hall fine	02	10	00
John Smith and his wife hearers ...	00	10	00
fined part of John Hall fine	02	10	00
Skipton. John Cowper Labr. and Alice his wife, hearers	00	10	00
Jtm. fined pt. of John Hall fine... ..	01	00	00
Thomas Smith & Anne his wife labor, hearers	00	10	00
ffrancis Dune laborer hearer	00	05	00
Jane Bowcocke wid. hearer	00	05	00
Joshua Bowcocke labr. hearer	00	05	00

Sum of 44lb. 00s. 00d.

27° die 9 bris 34° Car 2ᵈⁱ.
        Hen Fairfax
        Tho. Fairfax

Conventicle att ye house of Willm Sidgswick of fflasby when Willm Morehouse of Craco in Burnsall yeoman, preached ; Christr Morehouse of Hetton, Tho. Morehouse of Hetton, Rich. Ibatson of Rilston yeomen, & others present.

Knaresbro' Oct. 1683.

CONVENTICLE 19 DEC. 1683, AT DENT.

Fines. Richard Harrison	14	14	00
Jon Mason	00	05	00
Mary Mason, Gilbert Lund, Rebecca Lund, Jon Hugonson, Mar. Hugonson, James Capestick, Antho Mason, Eliz. Greenwood, Eliz. Lund, George Capestick Senr, Geo Capestick Junr., Chr. Capestick, Emma Capestick, Jon Dent, each 00 05 00	03	10	00

Total £18 09 00

The Kings third pte of the same is £06 03s. 00d.

UNLAWFUL ASSEMBLY (CONVENTICLE) AT HOUSE OF
HENRY THOMPSON OF ASKWITH, 29 NOV. 1683:

Committed to gaol for being present—

Samuel Thornton of Beckwithshaw, labor.	
Stephen Marshall of Yeadon	,,
Abm Marshall of Burley	,,
Robt Smyth of Askwith	mason
ffrancis Kendall ,,	laborer
Joshua Dawson Adingham	yeoman
George Myers ,,	,,

All discharged.

Thurgoland, Oct. 1683.—Absenters from Church—Ann Morton,
widd., Josias Coldwell & Mary his wife.

Munk Breton.— Jonathan Broadhead & Jane his wife, Will
Broadhead & Hannah his wife, Will Selvister & Elizabeth his
wife, Henry Ellis, Alice Hill Widd., Joseph Sawnderson, all
quakers

Clayton.—Laurence Champney & Katherine his wife, Thomas
Champney, John Whitcker & Margt. his wife, Alice ye wife of
Edward Tyas, Frances ye wife of Richard Gaskin, Michael
Anne Esq., & ffrances his wife

DISSENTERS FROM CHURCH, OCTOBER 4TH, 1683.

Wakefield Sessions, 1683.

Walton cum Breton.—Mr. Thomas Watterton and his wife
Catherine, Thomas Kirshaw and his wife Winnifred

Lowton.— Gervis Hamand Esq, & Katren his wife, Thomas
Challander and Mary his wife, Thomas Marshall and Anne his
wife, all supoased papest

Braton.— John Walker, Joseph Arnell, Rich. ffoster, Thos
Collin, Cathcren Peninton

Ossett.—Thos Pasley, Tho Schorey, popish Recusants. Tho
Naylor, John Atacke, John Rider, James Rider Jun, John
Claughton, Will. Claughton, Ann Claughton, John Bradford,
Martha Pickard, Quakers

Cleckheaton.—James Graue, William Pearson, Quakers

Saxton cu Scarthingwell.—Joan wife of Willm Hamand, Esq.,
Widow Bywater and John her son, Willm Wright and Ellin
his wife, Widdow Bellerby, Richard Gilliam and Mary his wife,
Steven and Mary Gilliam theire children, ffrancis the wife of

Willm Allison, Isabell wife of Marmaduke Robinson, Christopher
Barker, Margaret his wife. Noe Conventiclers
Ryther cum Osendyke.—Cattran Wright, John Wright, Elezebeth
Wright, Mary Leafe, Edward Sedall, Susanna Sedall, Tho.
Sedall, Cattran Sedall
Wareley.—Abraham Wadsworth and Bridgett his wife and Benj.
his son, Richard Lawson and his wife, and Wm Coppley
Shelley.—John Robuck & Sarah his wife, John Kay and
Elizth. his wife, Willm Kay, Daniell Broadhead, Joshua
Sanderson
Midgley.— Quackers. Jos. Wadsworth, John Turner, Sam
Turner, Mary Wiggen, Henry Bettes & and his wife, Abraham
Hellewell & his wife
Gateforth.—Henry Smith & his wife, & Elizabeth Richardson
Chrigleston.—John Reyner
Crofton.—Robert Seele and ffrances his wife, Joseph Ward and
Margrett his wife—popish recusants. Caterine ffirth stands
excomunicate. Jennit Jefferson & Thomas Jefferson her son
in law that lives in incest
Aberforth.—Peter Slater and Mary his wife, William Tinsdaile
and Vrsulay his wife, William Slater and Matthew Tinsdaile,
John Milner
Rothwell.—ffrancis Raner, chrisfor Roods, Will moor, Joseph
Lupton, Abraham Buterfield Susan his wife, Edmond Walker,
Elizabeth Moor, Gilbert Crauen
Barkston.—William Nicholson, Mary his mother, Ann his sister,
Julian wife of Anthony Saxton, Mary Cowthet, papists. Mar-
garet wife of William Nicholson a dissenter
Kirk Ffenton.—Charles Barker & Elizabeth his wife, Christopher
Batley and Anne his wife.
Ledsham.—Richard Gent. (? Sykes) Mrs Sykes and ye daughter
of Mr Sikes
hodersfilld.—Edmond Horsfall & Sara his wife, Edmond Kaye
and Sara his wife, and Mary Kaye, ffilleph Horsfall, Anna
Marsden, John Brooke, Richard Brooke, Quakers
Parlinton.—*Papists*, Robert Harison, Thomas hepenstell, George
Hepenstell, Elizabeth Hepenstell, John Peper, Ellin Peper,
Dorothy Samson, Mary Hepenstell, Mary Sarvan. *Quakers*
John Harrison & Mary his wife
Monk ffriston.—a poore widow, quaker
Maningham.—John Jowett of Breck Lane

Selby.—There is none that absents from the church but Quakers That are already psented and are prisoners at York And are vnder Bayle when they come to Selby. Mrs Wright now married to Mr Potman a ptestant

Qrarmby.—John Marslland & Doraty his wife qvakers

Battley.—Samuell Hurd, James Janson, John Bradley, Nicholas Talbut

—————◆—————

Leeds.—Lawrence Benson Lect. of Leeds tests. that Richard Atkinson attends church, and promises to take ye Sacrament next Lords Day

John Ryder of Ossett ffyne 100li. Robert Lumbe of West Ardsley ffyne 100li. Committed to York Castle till they pay it : ffyned for refuseing the oath of allegeance. Quakers

Grace nx. Ja. Pearson for being at a conventicle sub. fyne 40s. 1683

Jacob Earnshaw, Dewsbury, for conventicle £10, Rotherham Sess., July 1683. He sent an apology to the magistrates and promised to go to church.

Wm Taylor, Scholes, popish recusant, refused to take the oath of allegiance

Ger. Canby, Selby, Quaker for conventicle ... 40s. fyne
Rob. Scott. Stainr., Quaker ,, ... 10s. ,,
Jo Leake Selby ,, ,, ... 40s. ,,
Anthony Collyer, Selby ,, ,, ... £3 ,,

Quakers.—Jo : Walker, of Brayton, for conventicle £3 fyne Roth. 1683. Hen. Jackson, of Holmfirth, refused to take the oath of allegiance, quaker, £10, 1683.

John Earnshaw, Dewsbury for a conventicle, £10, petition to have it forgiven and he would become a good Churchman. 1683

Joshua Rande, 6 Oct. 1682, I doe pmise to come noe more to any vulawfull conventicles, Roth. July 1683

John Burgess and Henry Dickinson of Hooton Pannell, Quakers, committed to Castle at York. Roth. July 1683

Skipton Sessions, 1683, report of a conventicle at the house of Samuel Watson, gent., Stainforth in Gigleswick

Preston Jaclin, Oct. 1683.—Absent from church three weeks : Philip Hamerton & his wife, Henry Addison & his wife, John Darley & his wife, John Spink & his wife, Sall. Shillitoe Quaker, ffrancis Shillitoe Quaker

Langsett.—Dissenters : Hen. Dickinson & ux, Mary ux Dan Marsden, John Coldwell & ux, Geo Trout & ux, Jn Greene & ux, Margaret Haigh vid. Ann Haigh, Margt Blackbourne, Jn Brownell, Jane Brownell, Jn Wordsworth

Remington Constable reports—July 29, 1684, Wm Oddy & his wife, Tho Dryver & his wife, Jo Baldwin & his wife, Ja. Hoult now prisoner at York Castle, & Johnas Chapman all reputed Quakers, absent from church

Conventicle at Wm Masons Stonehouse in Dent, recorded at Knaresbro, Oct. 1684

Tempest Illingworth, of Tong, Labr., indicted for speaking severall maliciouse and oprobrious words in contempt and derogation of the booke of Comon Prayer, Leeds, July 1687

The foregoing notes corroborate the statements made in some histories that the time of greatest persecution under the Stuarts was in 1683-4. Other particulars respecting the persecution of the Quakers will be found in *Besse's Sufferings*, and of other Nonconformists in *Calamy's Lives of the Ejected*, but I am not aware that anyone has gathered full materials for a history of the Yorkshire Sufferers.

We have now reached the period of the " Glorious Revolution," and I am delighted to be able to place in a permanent form a list of the Founders of Nonconformist Congregations in the West Riding ; a list, probably complete, which I gathered from the numerous bundles of Sessions Rolls preserved at Wakefield. My extracts extend from 1689 to 1700. They are entered under the so-called TOLERATION ACT.

---- ◆ ————

TOLERATION ACT.

Leeds, the 19th July, 1689,—These are to Certify their maiestys Justices of ye peace att ye Quarter Sessions Held att Leeds the day Above that there is a Congregation of Protestant dissenters doe Assemble to worship God publickly att ye house of Tho Ledgard in the Town of Idle and pish of Calverley.

Tho Ledgard
John Stead.

[Same wording] —House of Isaac Balm in Boulcing in ye pish of Bradford. Isaac Balm, John Garnett.

We have made choice of John Brooksbankes house in Ealand in the vicaridge of Hallifax for the public ser-

vice of God according to a late Act of Parliament made
in the first year of the reigne of King Will and Queen
Mary entitled an Act for exempting their Majesty's protestant
Subjects from certain penal Lawes.

Jno Brooksbanke   John Lister.

House of Wm Kighley of Kighley—   Leeds, July 1689
,,   Thomas Leach of West Riddlesden in Morton   ,,
,,   Joshua Walker of Bingley   ,,

A Congregation or Assembly of Protestant Subjects Dissenting
from the Church of England doe hold their meeting for religious
worship on the Lords Dayes in Toplife Hall, Woodkirk, and they
hold other occasional meetings at Jo. Pickerings house at Tingley;
signed by

Jo. Pickering   Tho Atkinson

These are to Certify &c. . . . . that there is a Congregation of
Protestant Dissenters doe Assemble to worship God Publicly att
a Publick place built by ye Inhabitants of Idle for yt purpose in
Idle Town.

Jonathan Wright.   Leeds, July 1689.

To certify yt Joseph Dawson of Morley Clerk doth make
choice of his owne dwellinghouse in Morley to assemble in for ye
service of God according as is allowed by a late Act of Parliament
made &c.

Joseph Dawson
John Coppendale.

July 1689—House of Oliver Heywood, Clerk, Northouram.

July 1689—Nathanaell Preistley of Ovenden, Clerk, doth make
choice of ye house of John Butterworth in Wareley to assemble
in for ye service of God

An Assembly of dissenting protestants in and about Bradford
& Bradfordale do make choice of the House of Rich. Whitehurst
Clerk, Lidgate near Clayton.

House of John Aske of Lancffeild in heptonstall
,,   Thomas Johnson of Painthorpe in Sandall Magna

[Same wording as Idel Chapel, above.]—At a publick place
built by the inhabitants for that purpose at the Towne of Morley
In the parish of Batley

John Coppendale,   John Lister.

July 31, 1689, We desire that the barn in Newgate ad Tanshelf

belonging to John Watson may be allowed as a place for religious worship as by Act of Parlt allowed
> Timothy Lyle, John Mell, John Pickeringe.

July 31, 1689, Ditto for house late Mrs Abigail Mandevile of Rotherham,
> Wm Langley, John Broughton.

July 31, 1689, Ditto, house of Mrs Elizabeth Nodder of Woodhouse in Hansworth,
> Wm Ellis.

——————Ditto, house of John Armitage of Waldale Leedyate in Kirkburton Parish
> John Armitage.

July 31, 1689, Ditto, Barn late Richard Spoons of Stannington in Bradfield
> Richard Greaves, Nicholas Stead.

July 31, 1689, Ditto, House of Margt. Moake of Sheffield.
> George Shore, John Clayton.

July 31, 1689, Ditto, New-hall in Sheffield
> John Sanderson, Francis Girdler.

July 31, 1689, Ditto, building or barn of Margt. Stainforth of Attercliffe
> Joseph Nicholson, Wm. Wadsworth.

July 31, 1689, Ditto, house of James Wright in Attercliffe
> James Wright.

July 31, 1689, Ditto, house of Edw Penne (?) in Sheffield
> Edw Peinne (?).

July 31, 1689, Ditto, house of Mr Elkanah Rich called Benthom (? Bulhouse) in Pennistone
> Francis Haigh, Isaack Wordsworth.

July 31, 1689, Ditto, Thorney Grass House in Fishlake in possession of Thomas ffairburn.
> Thomas Perkins, Thomas ffairborne.

July 1689, House and Chappell of Wm R—————— Esq, Great Houghton.

July 1689, House of John Wordsworth, Smith Hall, in Worsburgh.

——————— House of Mr—— Kirkby, Wakefield.

——————— Idle Chappell to be restored to Church of England.

——————— House of Mr. Wm. Howden, Wakefield, for dissenters.

The dwellinghouse of John Moore of Rawden is intended for a
publick meeting place for Protestant dissenters the adherers
having no other design but to glorify God and edify one another,
desiring ye health, peace, prosperity and safety of their
Majesties King William & Queen Mary, & the good of the
Kingdome,   Therefore we whose names are here subscribed
desire this worthy Bench to grant us a Licence,   God save the
King and Queen.

> John Moore, Josias Marshall, Jeremiah Marshall,
> John Marshall, Ezekiel Butler, John Hardacer, Abrm
> Hollings, 1689.

Oct. 1689, House of Joseph Hall, Thorne, near Wakefield
> Joseph Hall.

Oct. 8, 1689, Barn, Widdow Hill at Windall in Calverley
> Richard Simson, Willim Garth, Joshuah Sandall, Tim
> Collier, John Hardacer, John Moore.

Oct. 8, 1689, House of Richard Wheatley, called Northrop in
Murfield,
> Richard Wheatley.

Oct. 8, 1689, House of George Heie of Linley in Quarmbie
> George Heie.

Oct. 8, 1689, House of Michael Norton, Quarmby
> Michael Norton.

The people called Quakers [Brighouse Monthly Meeting] have
the following places for worship and give notice to the Justices :—
One at Stansfeld at house of James Stansfeild.
>   ,,   ,,   James Bancroft.
>   ,,   ,,   John ffeelding.

Four in Langfield at houses of Thomas Sutcliffe, Anthony
Crossley, John Greenwood, Joshua ffcelding.

One each at houses of Abraham Shakelton, of Wareley, Henry
Broadbelt of Midgley, Joshua Smith of Sowerby, Abraham
Hodgson of Scircoate, Jonathan Laycocke of Scircoate.

One at Robert Cowlings of Northowram, Daniel Sutcliffes of
Stansfeld, John Eccles of Nether Woodhouse, Jonas Prestons
of Rastrick, Richard Hansons of Brighouse, Thomas Greens in
Longliversedge, William Pearsons at Okenshaye, Edmond
Horsfalls of Greenhouse, John Marshlands of Quarmbye,
Timothy Hoyles of Broadcarr, Robert Walkers of Staincliffe,
Martha Phillips house of Bowlinge, William Cookes of the
same, John Winns of Bradford, Jonas Bonds house of Bolton,

Thomas Bonds house Ecclesall, John Kays house of Birkhouse in Shelley.

One meeting place in the hamlet of Wooldale,

One at the houses of Henry Jackson of Tottyes, John Bradford of Ossett, John Attack of the same,

One at Joseph Naylors of Ardsley, Richard Lawtons of Midgley, John Whaleys of Langfeld.

We desire that these meeting places may be registered : James Bancroft, John Eckles, Henry Jackson, Thomas Roberts, John Bradford, Joseph Naylor.

Oct. 10, 1689, House of James Smith, Haworth
   James Smith.

Oct. 10, 1689, House of Henry Nayler, Lighthazles in Sourbey
   Henry Nayler.

Oct. 8, 1689, Chappell of Tosside for dissenters
   Henry Robinson.

To be referred to the Archbishop and if not granted case to be brought to Wetherby Sessions.

Oct. 8, 1689, Houses of John Bullock & Henry Robinson of Sawley and Tosside
   Henry Robinson.

Oct. 8, 1689, Houses of Mr Richard Ffrankland of Rathmell, John Wilkinson of Halton West, George Wilkinson of Lower Scale, James Brogden of Slickhouse
   John Hey.

Oct. 8, 1689, QUAKERS' PLACES—

One at ffarrfeild in Addingham at George Myers house
 ,, Gatecroft in ,, at Joshua Dawsons house by course
 ,, Silsden in Kildwick at Thomas Bleakeys house ,,
One at Bradeley in ,, at Mathew Luptons house
One, by course, at houses of John Hall in Skipton, Abigail Stott in Skipton, Peter Hardcastle in Hartwith, Kirkby Malzeard parish, Miles Oddy in Netherdale, Rippon, Peter Moor, Bewerley in Netherdale, William Reedshaw at Beckwithshaw in Panhall
One meeting house in ffarrfeilds in Addingham built for yt purpose,
One meeting house at Arkendale at the house of Jane Clarkson, one meeting house at Knaresborough at Mary Middleton house,
One meeting house at Henry Thompson, Senr, house in Askwith, Weston parish by course, One at the houses of Robert Smith in Askwith, Edmund Greenwood in Askwith, John Myers of Thackeray in ffewston, John Overend in Guiseley,

James Marshall of Idle Thorpe, Margret Walker of Yeadon, Sarah Grimeshaw of Rawdon, Henry Thompson of Weston, ffrancis Emmott of Westsikegreen in Hampsthwaite

> We desire these meeting places may be registered—George Myers, Peter Hardcastle, Willm Readshaw, Miles Oddy Senr, Henry Thompson Junr, John Barber, John Overend, Chris. Greenwood

Oct 8, 1689, *Quakers*—

One at Setle built on Purpose

One meeting house at Bentham built for yt purpose

One at ye houses of Samuel Watson of Stainforth in Giggles Wicke, George Atkinson at Roamhouses in Giggleswicke, John Moore in Clapham Parish, Henry Bayley of the Hill in Mitton parish, John Walbanke, Mary Peel, William Birkett, Nicholas ffrankeland, Thomas Turner all of Slaiteburne parish

One at Benjamin Parkers in Thorneton, James Dawtery in Carolton parish

One each at ye houses of Richard Boothman of Salterforth, Thomas Wood of Marton parish, Margaret King of Marton, William King of Stainton, William Ellis of Broughton parish, James Walton of Earby in Thorneton

One at fflasby in Gargreave built for yt purpose

One at houses of John Tomlinson in Gargreave, Phinehas Parkinson at Belbuske, William Anderson in Malham, Richard Wilkinson of Knowbanke, William Moorehouse in Cracoe, James Conyers in Rilsden, Christopher Moorehouse in Hetton, Willm Ellis in Aerton, James Tennant at Scarrhouse in Arncliph, James Scott in Hawkeswicke, Richard Harrison in Dent, Edmund Winne in Grisedale, Richard Wilson in Garsdale, Matthew Hogg at Harrogate, William Dickinson of Bilton cum Harragate

One at Brigg flatts in Sedbergh

> We desire that these places may be recorded—Geo Myers, Peter Hardcastle, James Tennant, Miles Oddy Senr, John Overend, Willm Readshaw, John Barber, Henry Thomson Jr., Chris Greenwood

To this is added :—

One each at houses of Ingram Holmes of Dearstones, in Skipton, John Moore at Brownhill in Skipton, Henry Whittaker of Rawdon

DISSENTING MEETING HOUSES,
Barnsley Sessions, 15 Oct., 1689.

These are defaced and decayed by damp.

(1) My dwelling house, Bolton sup Dearne,
Nathan Denton.

(2) Mansion House, Beale als. Beage Hall, residence of Jas. Creswick,
James Creswick

(8) *Quakers*—
One at High flatts at Edward Dickenson ——
1 at Wm Marsdens ——
1 at Abraham Roberts ——
1 at Caleb Broadhead ——
1 at Wm Keys ——
1 at Richard Brook ——
1 at Wm Keys of ——
1 at Hen Dison of Lower ——
1 at Thos Barkers ——
1 at Jo : Firth ——
1 at Tho Mittons of Barkishland
1 at Hen Dickensons at Shephouse
1 at Jo ——— in Lang ——
1 at Ralph Sanderson
1 at Jo. Charlesworth ——
1 at Jonathan Woodhouse ——
1 at ——
1 at Wm Shawes at Hill
1 at Geo Shawes at Brookeside
1 at Richard Websters in Sheffield
1 at Hen Robucks in Casbrook
1 at Godfrey Newbolds
1 at Robert Haslams in Hansworth
1 at Godfrey Watkinsons
1 at Jo : Beales in Rotherham
1 at ffra Ellis in Denington
1 at Hen Milners in Brampton
1 at Sarah Ffletchers in Barnsley Widd.
1 public meeting place in Thorne
4 at Pollington   [Names illegible]
5 at Rawcliffe   [Names illegible]
1 each at Richard Cookes, Elizth Womersley, — Sharpe,

1689—Meeting place for Dissenters at Darington at George Jacksons
— Whitesides, & 10 others ; one at Oakes

MEETING HOUSES REGISTERED AT WETHERBY SESSIONS JAN. 1689.

Barn belonging to Thomas Cockshott in Kildwick.
Signed—John Dickonson, Martin Dickonson, John Wright, John Dugdale, John Barrett

Meeting house for Quakers at House of Wm Holgate, Sawley Manor
Wm Holgate, Edward Mavor, Christo Knapton

Another at John Tippins, of same Manor, crossed out

Meeting house for Quakers at house of Thomas Masons in Wetherby, at Richard Stables in Bramham, Christopher Knaptons in Sherburne, Mary Tenants at Beamsley in Skipton. One at Edward Moores in Wetherby crossed out.
Signed—Wm Holgate, Edward Moore, Chris. Knapton.

Barn of Christopher Edmondson in Barnoldsweek.
John Dickonson, Martin Dickonson, John Wright, John Dugdale, John Barrett.

Houses of Jane Moreley and Christopher Willson both in Adlingefleet.
Edwd Jackson, Lane End Kildwicke.

LEEDS, 1689,

House of Samuel Hurd, Stancliffe in Batley.
John Leadbeter, Jonathan Jagger, Samuell Hird.

„ William Hepworth of Morefield in Morefield [Mirfield] parish.
Samuel Dey.

That an assembly of Discenting Protestants at Alverthorpe in the parish of Wackfeild do make Choyce of A Misedge belongin the dweling house Mr Peter Naylor Clarke to assemble in for Relidgous Worshipe Acording as is alowed by a late Acte &c.
Peter Bradbury, John Ray, Daniell Sykes.

Wee shall (God willing) Assemble & meet at Kipping house in Thornton in Bradfordale & at Jonas Deans House in Mixenden in ye parish of Hallifax.
Matthew Smith, Jno Hall, Joseph Lister, Jonas Deane, John Hanson, John Berry.

House of Joseph Walker of Burstall, called ye closes.
John Ray, Richard Atkinson, John Kitson.
House of John Leadbeater, Whitelees in Batley.
David Noble, John Holdsworth.
House of Mr William Kirby, Wakefield.
Cornelius Clarke, William Handen.
That Thomas Sharp of Little Horton nigh Bradford Clerk doth make choice of his own house to assemble in &c.
This may certify the Court that the dwelling house of Abraham Dixon of Bowling in the parrish of Bradford and County of York is intended & by the adherers thereto agreed upon for a publick meeting place for protestant dessenters having no other desire but to glorifie god & edifie one another desiring the health, peace prosperity & safty of their majesties King William and Queen Mary & the good of the Kingdome. Therefore we whose names are here subscribed do desire this honourable & worthy Bench to grant us a Licence.

Robert Burnell
Abr Dixon God save the King &
Jo. Hardakers Queen.
Pontefract, April, 1690.

We shall (God willing) assemble and meet to celebrate Gods worship at Paul Helliwell's house in Stansfield in the parish of Heptonstall, Pont. Ap. 1690.
Ditto : for John Haworth's house in Langfield in Heptonstall.
Pont. Ap. 1690.
Barn belonging to Richard Kendall of Sawley in Craven registered for protestant dissenters.

Richd Kendall, Richd Brewer, Giles Hargreaves, Wm Slater, Richard Brigg. Skipton, July, 1690.
Barn at Tong for Meetings recorded on the petition of John Goodall. Wakefield, Jan. 1690.
Barn in the occupation of Thos Beeston of Ashold in Otley Parish.

Timothy Collier, John Hardacer, Josias Marshall, Richard Simson, John Moore.
Leeds, July 1690.
John Rhodes house of Haworth registered for worship
Knaresbro, Oct. 1690.
Bradsworth Hall in the occupation of Mrs Susannah Wentworth recorded as a place for a congregation of religious worshippers

on the petition of Robt Cooke.   Donc. Jan, 1690.

Petition to have the house of Mr John Mandeville, Rotherham, recorded as Meeting House,   Wm Cooper.   Granted.
> Rotherham, July 1691.

Ditto—Benj. Westby's house, Raufeild,   ,,   ,,

Dwelling house of John Smithies of Little Horton recorded as place of religious meeting.   Wfd. Jan 1691.

> Signed—Saml Swayne, John Smythies, John Butterfield, Robt Parkinson.

Highfield House, Southowram, recorded as Meeting House,
> Wfd. Jan. 1691.

Upper Binns house [Southowram] (James Scholefield's) recorded.
> Wfd. Jan. 1691.

Henry Firth's Barn, Hunsworth, Burstall, recorded,
> Pont. Ap. 1691.

The Quakers gave notice, Wetherby, January 1691, of the following meeting places,—

Att our Publick Meeting house at Brig flatts in the parish of Sedbergh,

At the dwelling houses of John Blaykling, Richard Willan, John Holmes, ffrancis Blaykling, John Atkinson, Thomas Hawden, John Knewstob, All in the Parish of Sedbergh.

At the dwelling houses of James Greenwood, Richard Harrison, George Capstack, Samuell Winn, Anthony Mason, Myles Burton, all in Dent.

At houses of Edward Rawe, Richard Wilson, William Raw in Garsdale ; Edmond Wynn, Michaell Dawson in Grisdale.

> Signed, Edward Moore, John Burleigh.

So ordered.

John Wormall's house at Allerthorp for Quakers Meeting House,
> Signed, John Bradford, John Kidd, John Candler.
> Wfd. Oct. 1691.

We some of the Inhabitants of Bramham & Clifford have chosen a house called Petty House in Clifford for preaching place.
> Lancelott Smithies,   Leeds, July 1691.

House of Samuel Naylor of Skelmanthorpe for a place of Public Worship.
> Signed Henry Jackson, Joseph Naylor
> Leeds July 1691.

House of Michael Sheard in Hopton near Mirfield, for a place for religious worship.   Pont. Ap. 1692.

A new house at Bullhouse in Penistone recorded as place for
worship—   Pont. Ap. 1692.

House of Mrs Abigail Mandevale in Rotherham recorded as place
for religious worship.   Donc. Jan. 1692.

House of Thomas Fether of Northis in Haworth for dissenting
meeting place.

> Signed—Thos. ffether, John Holmes, Robert Heaton,
> Nicholas Dickson, Michael Pighells, Chr. Holmes,
> George ffether, John Moore, Joseph Pighells.
>   Leeds July 1693.

House of Martha Mitchell of Slenmerow in Slaidburne recorded
as Preaching Place.

> Signed—John Hey.   Skip. July 1693.

House of Henry Wood, clothier, ffarnhell in Kildwick, recorded
as Preaching place   Skip. July 1693.

Houses of John Hall and John Cooper, adjoining to the Green in
the New Markett, Skipton, fitt & convenient place for Public
Worship desired to be recorded.   Skip. July 1693.

House of Beatrix Sayll Widd, Pudsay, recorded

> Signed—Richard Hutton.   Wfd. Oct. 1694.

House of Abm Heinworth in Pudsey, and the barn, recorded for
religious worship.   Pont. Ap. 1694.

Wee the peopell of the Lord Who is called by the name of
Quakers Doe make Choise of Robert Lumm & Elizabeth Rain-
house in Wakefield & Hellin Spray of the same for Meetein
houses for to Worship God In & wee have formerly subscribed;
and James Asquith house at Heaton Common side, Dewsbury,
& our Burying place adjoyning to the highway betwene Wakefeild
and Agbrigg.

> Signed—Robert Lomm, Elizabeth lomm, Joseph Naylor,
> his   marke, James Asquith, John Bradford.
>   Wfd. Jan. 1694.

House of Wm Lupton of Olerthorpe, Wakefield, ⎫   recorded
  „   John Holdsworth of Spenn, Burstal,   ⎬   for worship.
                                            ⎭
                                            Wfd. Jan. 1694.

  „   Tho Whaley of Winterburne
  „   John Walker of Bingley
  „   Tho Leach Junr, Morton Banks
  „   Joseph Hammond, Bingley

,, Martha Marshall, Bingley
,, Joseph Hollings, Allerton in Bradfordale.
,, Joseph Wright, Hippholme.

Wak. Jan. 1694.

We (Quakers) desire to have 'the following places registered as places for Religious Worship—

House of Robt Willan, Dent,
,, Martha Eliss, Riggton,
,, Alexander Hopwood, Tadcaster.
Signed—John Burleigh, Edward Moore,
Wetherby, Jan. 1694.

House of Phillip Harrup, Greenay Hill, Rippon, recorded
Wetherby, Jan. 1694.

Houses of Tho Jefray, Church Marton.
,, John Constantine, Elslacke.
,, Samuell Taylforth, Rilston.
,, Will. Elles [Airton] Weth. Jan. 1694.

House of Joseph Webster, Whiteley, Thornhill, for meeting of Quakers,
Signed John Bradford, Wm Claughton, John Claughton,
Joseph Webster. Wakefield, Oct. 1695.

Barne late Wm Lepton's, Pudsey, for preachings
Signed, Richard Hutton, Abraham Haineworth, John
Rudde, Richard ffarrer. Wfd. Oct. 1695.

House of Robt Ramsden, Southowram.
Signed, Wm Naylor. Wfd. Oct. 1695.

House of John Wright, Kighley, for Protest, Dissenters.
Signed, John Holmes, Michaell Pighells, Robt Merall.

House at Shewbroad, Langfield, for Publique Worship,
Wfd. Jan. 1695.
Signed, Daniell Sutcliff, Thos Sutcliff, James Banscroft,
Jno Greenwood, John ffielden, Jos ffeilden.

House of Robert Duckworth in Halifax for Quaquers.
Signed—Jonathan Laycocke, Henry Dyson, Robert
Duckworth. Wakef. Jan. 1695.

House of John Jackson in Halifax, for religious Worship,
Signed, John Jackson, Geo Hargreaves, Joshua
Laycocke. Wfd. Jan. 1695.

House of Thomas fferrand of Bradford for religious worship,
Wfd. Jan. 1695.

John Moore desires a certificate as being a protestant dissenting Minister, and desires also his House in Guiseley for meeting place,   Leeds July 1695.

House of Matthew Smith of Mixindin, Ovenden, } recorded
and that of Charles Gaukroger of } Leeds, July,
Errenden } 1695.
Signed, Jonas Deane.

House of Robt Whitehead in Sadleworth for a congregation of protest : Dissenters—
Signed, John Rhodes.   Leeds, July, 1695.

House of Mr Joseph Lister in Bingley recorded   ,,   ,,
,, Hugh Ramsden in Golcar   ,,   ,,   ,,
Signed— Joseph Heeley.

House of John Heawards, Tansbelf, for religious worship.
Signed, John Huntington.   Pont. Ap. 1695.

Meeting places for people called " Quakers " recorded—for the house of John Box, husbandman, Barmbrough, and the house of John Burgesse of Morehouse in Hutton-pannell.
Pont. Ap. 1695.

James Garth's New building in Heaton recorded   ,,   ,,
House of Samuell Sykes merchant at Cawood ,,   ,,   ,,
Thomas Pollard's Barne in Bolling   ,,   ,,   ,,

            (John Tippin of Grainge in Sawley,
            | John Scott, Longam Roe, Sawley,
Houses of { Willm Oddye, Gylls, Rimington in Gisborne,
            | Willm Watson, Loyne, Middop in Gisborne,
            (Thomas Desver(?) of Gasegill, Rimington in Gisburne,
                      recorded Knaresbro' Oct. 1695.
Signed for all—Ralph Pawson.

House of Joseph Clark, Rawmarsh } for
,, Lorence Pearson, Tinsley } Quakers.
Rotherham July, 1695.

Signed—Thomas Oldham.

House of William Catforth, Rawckliffe } for
,, Robt Bowland   ,, } Quakers.
,, Wm Walker   ,, }
,, George Box of Trumflitt } for
,, John Dearman of Brafit } Quakers.   Barnsley,
,, Caleb Lee of Aston }   Oct. 1695.

House of Giles Shaw, Quick — recorded, Wfd. Oct. 1696.

  ,,   Edmund Buckley, Quick ,,   ,,   ,,

  ,,   John Wharton, Tadcaster ,,   ,,   ,,

  ,,   Nathanl Priestley, Ovenden ,,   ,,   ,,

Halifax—The bearer hereof comes upon my errand viz to procure a license for a Publick Meeting House newly erected in Halifax. If you'l please to lend him yr assistance yt he may be quickly dispatch'd 'twill extremely oblige

Sr yr aff. Kins. & Servt
Nath Priestley.

Ovenden Oct ye 8. 96.

Quakers—People of God called Quakers, certifie—

One at Wm. Shaw's the Hill in Bradfield

  ,,   Geo Shaw's Brookhouse, ,,

  ,,   ffran. West Carrbrook, Sheffield,

  ,,   Thos. Ward's liberties, Sheffield town.   Oct. 1696.

House of Samuell Haigh, Marsden recorded for place for Religious Worship.

Wfd. Jan. 1696.

House of Thomas Hodgson, Bradford, recorded.

Wfd. Jan. 1696.

House at [Pontefract] wherein I now dwell may be recorded as place for Religious Worship :—

      John Heywood.   April 1696, Pontefract Sess.

House of Jo : Cordingley, Liversedge, recorded.

Pont. Ap. 1696.

  ,,   Jeremiah Hillas, Norwood, for Quakers.

Pont. Ap. 1696.

House and Barne of Robt. Gawtherappe of Carleton recorded.

Pont. Ap. 1696.

Part of House called Lupsit House, being the part in possession of Mr Joshua Sager recorded.   July, 1696.

House of John Stansfeld of Sowerby recorded.

Leeds, July 1696.

Houses of (Quakers)

    viz—John Drake, Bradford Parish,

        Will Clayton Haworth Parish

        Jonas Smith   ,,

        Jonathn Widdop Bingley Parish

        Jeremie Heaton   ,,

        Richard Shakelton   ,,

John Hird,   Kighley Parish
Will Smith   ,,
John Smith   ,,
Thom. Briggs   ,,
Jeremie Briggs   ,,
Jonas Turner   ,,
James Ramsden   ,,
Will. Davie of Kildwicke Parish
John Wade   ,,

Leeds, July 1696.

Please send by the Bearer a Licence for a Prot. Dissent. Meeting to be holden at House of Robt Hancocke, Sheffield. The bearer will pay what law requires.

Barns. Oct. 1696.

House of John Moore, Horsforth, Dissenting meeting House recorded.   Leeds, July 1697.

Certify that ye Dissenting Protestants in & about Wakefield do set apart ye New erected Place at Westgate End for a meeting place.

Joseph Conder   July 15, 1697.

Leeds, July 1697.

We, Protestant Dissenters—appoint house of James Taylor of the Cross in Saddleworth in the West Riding for worship of God.

James Taylor, James Hayward, Isaac Wilde, John Kennerley, Caleb Broadhead, Henry Dickenson, Hen Jackson.

Roth. July 1697.

House of Joshua Brooksbank, Broomhall in Gunthwait in Penistone. " for my Friends," called Quakers

Roth. July 1697.

House of Richard Lee, Newton in Bolland, recorded :
John Hey.   Skip. 1697.

Houses of Miles Oddy & Peter Hardcastle in Dacre cu Bewerley

Pont. Ap. 1697.

Barne of Mr. Wright in Winsor Lane, Knarsbrough.

James Talor Minnister, John Wright, William Thompson, George Cass, Wm. Benson, &c.

Pont. Ap. 1697.

House & Barn of John Blackburne, Sutton recorded.

Pont. Ap. 1698.

House of Richard Ward, Hillam in Monk ffrystone and
  ,,   Edmund Hemingway ,,   ,,   ,,   recorded
for Quakers—Signed Richd Ward, George Bocook, Joseph
Dickinson, Edmund Hemingway, Robt Clarkson.

Pont. Ap. 1698.

Meeting House by & in ye Burying place of ye people called
Quakers Joyning on a Lane called Southgate in Pontefract and
set apart for ye Publique Worship of God after their maner.
Robt. Clarkson, Ferdinando Buck, Joshua Marsden.

Pont. Ap. 1698.

New Erected house in Monck Bretton called West Croft House
recorded.   Wfd. Oct. 1698.

Houses of Michll Broadley, Henry ffarrar, John Hollings, Benj.
Ferrand at Harden Grange, Richard Wilkinson & Thos.
Whaley, all in Bingley Parish be recorded.

Skip. July 1698.

House of Henry King, Langber in Marton,   ⎫ Signed—
  ,,   Wm. King's Oucliffe in Carleton, ⎬ Hen. King
  ,,   John King, West Marton,   ⎭ Sk. July 698.
  ,,   Wm. Slater, Langcroft in Kildwick.

Houses of William Windle of Barnoldsweek Coates, Richard
Stoney of Cromacke in Clapham. Mathew ffrankland of Clapdell
in Clapham, Stephen Egland, of Selside in Horton : all for
Quakers.

Henry King, Thomas Wood.   Pont. Ap. 1699.

Houses of Sarah Coates & Daniel Parker Earby, Thomas
Womersley in ffishlake, Abraham Beaumont of fenwick.

Pontefract, April, 1699.

A publick Meeting House in ye Townshipp of Rastrick in ye
parish of Yealand [Elland] : Also ye house of James Greaves
in Okenshey for Quakers.

Samuel Grimshaw.   Pont. Ap. 1699.

House of Will Rokeby. Esq, of Scella   ,,   ,,   ,,
        John Pigot
  ,,   John Chappel of Burton near Barnsley   ,,

House of Wm. Mitchell of Bolling.

Signed—Wm Mitchell, Abraham Barraclough, George
Hey, John Smethies, Samuell Swaine, Mathew
Thornton, Abraham Dixon, Saml Thornton, John
Hutchinson, Wm Thornton.   Leeds, July. 1699.

New erected Chappell, Barnsley, Wak. Jan. 1699.
Joseph Deykin.
House of Richard Reyner in Halifax.
    Signed—Sarah Jackson, Joshua Laycock, Richard
        Reyner.   Wfd. Jan. 1699.
House of Thos Marriot, gentl. of uphill. Sheffield   Oct 1699.
„   John Clarke of Ramar, for Quakers.   „
„   Mary Rastricke, Rawdon.   „
„   John Hattersley, Sheffield.   „
„   Joseph Dickenson. Woodhall, Womersley.   „

POPISH RECUSANTS.

It would be interesting to continue the search from 1700 to
1800, but it does not come within the period of this Register.
I will conclude my notes from the West Riding Sessions Rolls
with another list of Roman Catholics.

Mrs Catherine Palmes a Roman Catholick how living at the
house of Mr Thomas Waterton of Walton in ye west rideing hath
by undue means and practises got into her custody Ann
ffrances Stringer daughter of Wm. and Christabella Stringer,
Gentleman and Gentlewoman, protestants, (an infant) and detains
her from her mother, ordered that she be given up.
        Sr. John Powell, Justice of Assize.
            Wakefield October, 1690.
The Chief Constables issued orders to bring Papists to Justices
to take the oaths ; also to disarm them, and seize their horses
above the value of £5 which were to be sold.   Their arms,
(guns, &c.) to be taken for their Majesties service—Skipton,
July 1691.   This was effected upon
        Wm Husband of Bentham, Gent.,
        Thos. Grimes of Austwick,
        Arthur Ingleby, of Lawkland, Esq.,
        Richard Beesley of Twiselton, Gent.
The following Papists were reported at Leeds Session, Augt.
1691.
Spofforth—John Middleton Esq : & Jaine his wife, Squire
Plumpton, Henry Pullan, Abm Atkinson, Will. Gill, James
Hawkesworth, Gabriel Loadman, George Crooke, Catherine
Smithson, Ann Shearewood, Elizth Loftas, John Swaile, Ann
Sumpster and Ann her daughter. [See Middleton below.]
Brearton—Ralph Grimston.

Wetherby—Thomas Emm.rson.

Ripley—Wm Pallister, Lawrence Hodgson, Martin Hodgson, John Eavson, Wm. Hawkin, Dorathy Plenom, Widd., Mary Hodgson, Wid., ffrances Hakeins, singlewoman, Anne Hodgson, singlewoman, John Matson Labr., Michaell Mawd, Wm Dobson & Jane his wife, Alice ye wife of Wm Pallister.

Plumpton—Wm Atkinson & Ffrances his wife, Widow Bickerdike & John her son, Wm Mercer, John Parker & Mary his wife, Edwd Bickerdike & Isabel his wife, Mrs Hellen Plumpton, Ann Swaile, Barbary Clayton, Edwd Briggs & Eliz. his wife, John Swaile and his wife, ffrancis Briggs, Ellen Briggs widow, Thomasin Coats, Margt. ye wife of John Knowles, Stephen Shann & Eliza Pullen.

Stainbeck Downe—Geo Smith, ffrancis topham, Thos Topham, Rich Gill, Thos Fryer, Ralph Suttle, Francis Shaw, Thos. Browne.

Stainbeck Up—Thomas Jully.

Fountaine Earth—Thomas Spence.

Midleton—John Midleton Esq., & his wife, Abraham Atkinson & Wm Gill their servants, Andrew Hardwick, Thos. Hawksworth, Philip Lofthouse & Ann his wife, Ellinor the wife of Christopher Hodgson, William Gill, Wm Harrison, Thos. Harrison, Margt. wife of Thos Hodgson.

Nesfeild—Thos. Moon & ffrances his wife, Wm Moon, Abm Atkinson & Ann his wife & Thos his son.

Knarsbrough—Thos Jefferson, Geo. Cass, Emanuel Cass, Wm. Deubon, Richard Cass, Lyolett Slater, Mathew Harrison, Stephen Cass, Wm. Colbon, John Linton, Joseph Harrison, Geo. Smith.

Hartwith com Hinsley—Mathew Burnit, Jas. Whelous, Wm. Crosland, James Maudes.

Aserelay—Chas. Dufil, George Runfit, Henry Duffil, Mathew Duffil, Michell Duffil.

Audfeild—Richard Mautus.

Norton—Thos Gudridge & ffrances his wife.

fferry friston—Jas Calvert, Martha his wife, & 2 maid servants. Mrs Mary Iles, Richard Tempest, Thos. Stockes, Richard Barker, John Scott, Jude his wife, Mary Speight, Elizabeth Shillito, Ann Bedford, Joseph Harre & his wife, Margret Norden, Elizabeth Cowplon.

Wistow—Mary Brogden, Eliz Morritt.

Staineley Cu. Caton—Solomon Swale Barronett, Mr Alderage Swale, Will Kilburn & his wife, Anthony Bretherick & his wife, George Pennington & his wife, Leonard Coup & his wife, Francis Benson & his wife, John Barton & his wife, Thos Wheelehouse & his wife, John Thompson, Sarvant, John Wright, Sarvant

Roundhey—Richard Aspinwall Laborr, Stephen Lodge Laborr, Anthony Lodge Husbandman, Ann the wife of Robt Lee.

Linton—Thos. Whitham, John Whitham, Edwd Moore.

KILLINGHALL CU. HAMLETTS—

> *Killinghall*—Wm Wardman, Alice Wardman his mother.
>
> *Harrigate*—Mr. Jo. Fawcett Robt. Young and his wife, Barbary ye wife of Peeter Simson, Elizabeth Simpson his daughter, Henry Young, Thos. Squire & Mary his wife, Mrs Mary Copley.
>
> *In Pannell*—Edward Thompson, & Julian his wife, Ralph Reynard & Elizth his wife, Robt. Reynard, Wm Reynard.

Minskip—Christr. Smith, Peter Earle, Thomas Darley, Charles Lowrey, Michael Wright.

Borough Bridge—Mr Francis Calvert, Mr John Calvert, Mr Ambrose Jackson, Mr Geo. Hammerton, Robt Bartle.

Burton Leonard—Stephen Umpleby & Jane his wife, John Swale & Ellin his wife, Elizth. Baynes, widow.

Arkendall—Robert Hargreaves, Widdow Beckwith, Elizth Smith.

Tadcaster—Ann ye wife of Thomas Taylor, Gentln.

Sicklinghall—No papist nor dissenter but Thomas Brown a poor labourer.

Timble—Mr Wm Hardisty.

fetherston—Mr John Hepron, Mrs Alice Hepron.

South Kirby—Mrs Mary Armitage, John Marshall.

Castleford—Anne Norton, Sarah Atak.

Bramham—Matthew Challenger & his wife.

Purston Jackling—Mr Mathew Hammerton & his wife, Mr Edward Killingbecke, Mrs Winifrid Killingbeck, Mr Luke Brittan, Mr Attwood, Willm Darley, Jane Darley, Katheran Darley, Mary Prince, (last four servants,) Mr George Steemson & his wife, John Spinke & his wife, Joseph Stringer & his wife, John Darley & his wife, Michaell Darley, John Darley Junior, Anne Darley, ffrances Darley, Anne Darley their servant, Edward Owram & his wife.

Houghton—Matthew Billcliffe, Ann his wife, Margrett & Mary Billcliffe.

Knottingley—Katherine Geys, & Ellin Wood.

Tickhill—Henry Beslay, Ralph Hansbey, the wife of Thomas farnworth, the wife of Jonathan Adeson.

Bentham in Eucross—Cudbert Parkinson, Robert Turner, Mr Wm Husband of Lankishire.

Crofton—Joseph Ward Robert Steele.

Hallam—Wm ffox gent., Wife of John Casollton.

Kimberworth—Henry Rattliffe & his brother Robert Rattliff, Ann Rattliffe their mother.

Bawtry—Henry Scott Labourr.

Bradfeild—Rowland Revell, Edward Cheshire & his wife, George Hilton and his wife, John Wildsmith & his wife, Gregorie Revell, Gartrude Revell, Ann Revell, Mary ffox, Rosamond ffenton, John Brittlebanke.

Auston cu Membrs—Elizabeth wife of John Shuttleworth, William Everritt her sonne, John Marshall her nephew aged about 16.

Rotherham—John Chadwick, Wm Jessop, Garvis Sailes.

Clayton cu Ffrickley—Michael Anne, Esq, & Ffrances his wife, Thomas Champney & Anne his wife, Catherine Champney widd., Margt ye wife of Alexr Watkin, Barbarah Marsden, Richard Gaskin, & ffrances his wife, & Eliz the wife of Thomas Lawton.

Kettlewell—Lawrence Dent.

Sheffield—Edmund Murphey, Edward Murphey, Agneis wife of Mr Tho. ffreeman, Elizabeth wife of John Ellis, Jane Aldam widd., Mary Aldam maide, Elizabeth Champernoone widow, Mrs Abdy widow, Hellen Walker neese to George Walker.

Hansworth— Joseph Crownshaw, Thomas Parker, Thomas Huchinson.

Austwicke— Arthur Ingleby Esq., Thomas Grime, Thomas Foxcrofte.

Ingleton—Mr Richard Beeslay & Agnes his·wife, Isabell Tayllor, Isabell Redmayne, Thomas Leake & Eliz. his wife, Agnes Leake widow.

Rathmell—George Mottley, John Husband, Thomas Tindall.

Broughton—Thomas Tempest Esq., Stephen Tempest gent., Richard Tempest gent, John Tempest Labourer, Robert Tempest Labor, Thomas Yorke Labor, Edward Yorke Labor, Stephen Yorke Labor, Christopher Oxnerd Labor, Stephen

Oxnerd Labor, Mrs Elizth Yorke Widow, William Lofthouse Labor, Adam Lofthouse Labour., Bridget ye wife of xpher Oxnerd, Margery Tempest & Jane Tempest singlewomen.

Carleton—James Singleton gent., Henry Singleton (removed).

Skipton—Mr John Mitchell Attorney at Law, John Cotham.

Harcrcroft—Laorence Clarkson, ffrances Clarkson.

Langside—John Browne, Robert Blackburn.

Skelbrook—Thomas Horncastle & Alice his wife, ffrances his daughter. This Thomas Horncastle is servant to Mr Michael Anne of Burghwallis.

Burwallis—Michael Anne Esq., & Jane his wife.

Scriven & Tentergate—John Tucker, Anthony Cass, Daniel Dodshion.

Hooton Roberts—Elizabeth Pearson, Vid. about 70.

Grewelthorp—Mary Atkinson, Jane Walker.

Stotton—Sir Walter Vavasour Bartt & Jane his Lady, Richard Green, George Wilson, Mathew Tinsdall, Richard Swayle & his wife.

Stubbs Walden—Mrs Cisalle Pearcy, Mrs Dorathy Pearey, Mrs Mary Pearcy, Elizabeth Singalton.

Armin—Elizabeth Jackson.

Little Smeaton—Phillip Heptenstall & Isabell his wife, Peter Heptenstall & Ann his wife.

Larton—Elizabeth Raynard.

Whitgift—Mary Cleark.

Hurst cum Hurst—Ann Arnitt.

Kirkby Malzeard—Elizabeth Hemsworth, Mary Harieson.

Thorp Audlin—Ann ffearnley.

Otley—Jane wife of Richard Birch, Mary wife of John Ffarnell.

Brotherton—Thos Allison & Jane his wife, Anthany Jefferson, Richard Jefferson.

Gowle—Dorathy Emson & her sons William & Gregory.

Snayth—Mr Tallbot & his son Dowderst.

Barkeston—Wm Ringcrosse & Ann his wife, Julian Sapton Widdow, Margratt Nicholeson Widdow, Margratt Sisan.

Clint cu. Hambletts—John Tompson, Thomas Hardcastle, Christ. Maulthouse, John Maulthouse, Robt Shann, Thomas Kendall, Francis flish, Robt Joy, Peter Shan, ffrancis Happerton, Thos Happerton, Christopher Smith, Edward Thorpe.

Brayton—Katherine Penington, Elizabeth Richardson.

K

ffishlake cu. Sikehouse—Clara wife of Willm Dynnis, Junr. of Sikehouse

Towton—Mr Gervas Hamond & Katherine his wife, Thomas Marshall & Ann his wife.

Saxton-cum-Scarthingwell — Mrs Johane Hamond, William Allingson & ffrances his wife, Johannah ffletcher, Isabel the wife of Marmah Duke Robinson, Marmah Duke Barker Servant, Mary Mood, Henry Mood, Johanah Mood, Anne Bywater, John Bywater and Mary his wife, Thomas Bywater, Richard Gilliam Senior, Steven Gilliam his sone, Mary Gilliam his daughter, William Sauer and Mary his wife, William Wright and Ellen his wife, Richard Wright & his wife, Catheran Wright and Robert her sonne, Anne Barker Widow, John Cressey & Mary his wife, Christopher Barker & Margaret his wife, John Speech and Anne his wife, Margaret Slater Servant, Margaret Robinson Servant, Mrs Sturdy Widow.

Haddlesey West—Anne Matthewes Spinster.

Sherburne—John Simpson & Margret his wife, John Hall & Winifrid his wife, Ann Creadway widdowe.

Leod, parish of Ryder—John Wright and his wife.

Aston cum Aughton—Cladeous Penny.

Shadwell—Mrs Cuphras Thompson, Mary Shippen, Izabell Daniel, Mr Milles Lodge (sometimes resident).

Gerford—Thomas Heptonstal, William Shillito, Edward Marshall.

Hotton Panell—Thomas Shann & Jane his wife.

Huddleston cum Lumbe—Phillip Hamerton & his wife.

Thurnscho—Mr Stephen Horne.

Thornton—Joseph Busby and his wife.

Cawood—Robt Gaell & his wife, & Ann his maide, Robt Thorold, John Clacton, Peter Dotchon & his wife, Mary Gudger, Barbara Adcock.

Barwick in Elmet—Thomas Gascoigne Esq., William Taylor, Andrew Slator, John Butcher, Willm Cooke, John Sheppen Senior, Rich. Sheppen, John Sheppen jun, Cuthbert Procter, John Holcroft, Nicolas Sheppen, Mark Brunton, Samuel Robinson, Peter Sheppen.

Follifoot—Edward Bayram & Margret his wife, Roger Deighton & Barbury his wife.

Lothertan cum Abberford—Antany Bell, John Bell, Ellin Bell.

Thorner—Thomas Prince.

Kippax—John Grocoke, Elez. Grocoke, ffrancis Johnson, Ann Coplin.

Abberford—Wm Slater, Wm Tinsdale, Peeter Slater, John Milner, Wm Tarleson.

Selby—Mr William ffoxcroft & wife, Mr George Dalltry.

Carleton cum Camlesforth—Sir Miles Stapelton Bart, Nicholas Erington Esq., Mr John Sotheby, John Reynall, Thomas Shillito, Wm Audas, Phillip Ealand, Thomas Walker, John Tomson, William Bell, Anthony Emson, Robert Richard [sic] and barbara his wife, Mary Palmmer, John Talor and Usley his wife, Mary Pearson, Nicklas lessay, Mrs holgstaf, John briton, Joney hodgley, Ladye Stapleton, Maddam Erington, Jane Askue, Dorate Askew, Mary Wenforth, John Collin, Mrs Sotheby, Elizabeth Sotheby, Mrs Champney & her sister, Cattaran Awdas, Elling Awdas, Mary Walker, Margitt Rigsby, Ann Peares, Mary Empson.

Parlinton—Mr John Gascoigne, John Pepper, John Adiman, George Heppenstall, Nicholas Messenger.

Criddleing Stubbs—George Briggs & Elizabeth his wife.

Scarcroft—John Ryther Esq, & Mary his wife, Grace Daniel, vid.

Ossett—Thomas Pashley.

Austrop—Mr Remmey George.

Shiplay—Mr Richard Tempest.

Morley—Mr William Stephenson of Howley.

Snydall—Wm. Willson, Robert Hainsworth, William Pease, Robert Wager, Thomas Pease, John ffanning Esq, and his three men Timothy Bryan, Edward Darrley, and Dennis, also Francis Parkison and Joseph Wright Junr., which have not been apprehended.

Eland cum Greetland—Richard Randell Esq.

Hallifax—John Bollard, Henry Hanson, Willm Priscod.

Barmbrough—Anne Roe.

Walton cum Bretton—Thomas Watterton Esq., Thomas Kershay, Thomas Avison, Joab Cooper.

Waddington cum Bradford—Stephen Anderton, Laurence Ward.

Thus endeth our chapter of iniquities,—a chapter we, as Protestants, ought to be ashamed of, unless Roman Catholicism is something more than a religious creed, and involves the safety and property of the country.

Part ii : Dickenson's Register.

BAPTISMS.

Elizabeth daughter of John Priestley of Westercroft, Baptized
Dec. 11. 1702

· Sarah d. Jonathan Harrar of Sinderhills, bap Jan. 14. 170⅔

Susanna d. Joseph Wilkinson of the Mountain bap. Jan. 18. 1702

Lydia d. John Craven of Westercroft, Jan. 24

Mary d. John Ambler, Shipden Head, Feb. 5. 1702

Elizabeth d. William Wilkinson of Collier Syke bap. Apr. 9. 1703

James s. James Gregson of Thorntree in Northourum bap. June
6, 1703

Mary d. John Lairoyd bap. (p Mr. Ac. Lister) July 28

Edward s. Thomas Clark of Scout Hall, bap. Aug. 19. 1703

Joseph s. Nathanael Booth of Collier Syke bap. Jan. 16, 1703

Dorothy d. Mr. Jonathan Wright bap. p. Mr. Priestley Nov. 10.
1703

John s. Mr. James Gream bap. by Mr. Parrot Nov. Born Oct. 31

Joshua s. Tho. Scholefield bap. Mar. 12 in Northour.

Samuel s. Jonas Judgson, Horton, bapt Mar. 29. 1704

Nathaniel s. Mr. Nathl. Priestley Apr. 2. 1704

Thomas s. John Moorhouse, Oxheys, nr. Norwoodgreen May 7.
1704

John s. Joshua Wilkinson, Blakehill, nr. Northourum bapt.
May 10. 1704

Mary d. Saml. Holdsworth, Green Lane bapt. June 4. 1704

Mary d. Mr. Stern born Aug. 8

—— son Mr. John Allison born Aug. 1

John s. John Simpson born Aug. 19, bapt. Aug. 20 p. Mr. Sharp

Daniel Charles s. Abra. Hemingway bap. Oct. 27. 1704. p. Mr.
Sharp

Mary d. James Kirshaw near Holdsworth bap. Nov. 12. 1704

Peter s. Abra Barret of Lim'd house, Northourum bap. Dec. 10.
1704

Abraham s. John Speith, lower Briar, bapt. Dec. 25

John s. John Bamford bap. ffeb 12

BAPTISMS.

Abigail d. John Priestley, Westercroft bap. ffeb. 16
Elizabeth d. Mr. James Gream born Mar. 19
Richard s. Mr. Rich. Milne of Stockport born Mar. 23
Mary d. Mr. Jonathan Wright, of Lightcliffe bap. Mar. 26 1705
Saml s. to Mr. Tho Clark, Scout Hall bap. Apr. 1
John s. Joshua Hartley nr. High Cross bapt. Apr. 1
Esther d. Jere. Layroid, Northourum bapt. Apr. 15
Abraham s. John Ambler, Shipden Head, bapt. Apr. 25
George s. Abraham Scot, near Shipdenhead bapt May 7
Susanna d. Simeon Jackson, Northourum bap. May 27
Dinah d. John Kellet near Northourum bap. June 3
John s. Anthony Proctor born Sep. 3. bapt. by Mr. Cliffe
Sarah d. Ephraim Elsworth bap. at Horton Sep. 16. 1705
Anne d. of Mr. Stern born Sept. 21, bap. Oct. 18 p. Mr Sharp
James s. Eliezer Tetlaw born Oct. 4 bapt Oct. 15 1705
Mary d. Jeremy Baxter of Northourum born Dec. 13. Bapt.
    Dec. 16
Hannah d. Joseph Wilkinson of the Mountain in Shelf Bapt.
    Dec. 28
Joshua s. Joshua Wilkinson of Blakehill near Northourum bapt.
    Feb. 3
Sarah d. Mr. Jackson of Leeds born Feb. 2
Thomas s. John Bentley in Shelf born ffeb. 15. Bapt Mar. 13
—— d. of Saml Riddlesden of Rooks born ffeb. 18
John s. John Woodhead, Shelf, born ffebr 19. bapt Mar. 20. p.
    Mr. Sharp
Martha d. Abraham Bairstow of High Bentley bapt. Apr. 8. 1706
Jonathan s. Jonathan Duckworth near Northourum, bap. Apr. 9
William Hartley's wife by the Comon wood was deliverd of two
    living children Apr. 27
Mary d. Anthony Whiteley, Hipperholm Lane Ends bap. June 16
John s. Robert Rusby near Batley bapt. July 1
John s. Isaac Sharp, little Horton born July 7
Sarah d. Nathanl Booth, Collier Syke bap. Aug. 7
Elizabeth d. John Moorhouse near Norwood green bap. Aug. 13
My son Thomas Dickenson was born ffriday Aug. 16. a qr. past
    Ten the forenoon 1706 : bapt Aug. 22 by Mr. Sager
John s. Mr. Nathaniel Priestley born Aug 13 bapt Sep. 6. 1706
Elizabeth d. John Wood of Bramley bapt. Sep. 23

BAPTISMS.

Stephen Farrands wife at Damhead in Northourum deliver'd of two daughters abt Sept. 19

John s. Samuel Marshall of Shelf born Sep. 29

John s. Mr. Tho Wainman minr at Bingley born Sep. 30

Mary d. Joshua Hartley near the High Cross, bap. Oct 15, died a few hours after

Jonathan s. John Priestley, Westercroft bap. Oct. 25. 1706

John Listers wife at Northbrigg, nr. Halifax deliver'd of two Daughters abt Oct 26

Christopher Dades wife at Stopes, nr Northourum deliver'd of two sons Nov, 2, call'd Thomas and John

Catherine d. Anthony Proctor born Jan. 4. 1706, bap. p. Mr. Sharp

Phebe d. Joshua Threapland bapt Jan. 7. by Mr. Cliffe

Sarah d. Thomas Clark, of Scout Hall bap. Jan. 9

Mary d. John Bamford bapt Feb. 17. 1706

Emanuel s. Abraham Gregson, Northourum born Mar. 15. had two teeth (they say) when born and other two within a fortnight after

Hannah d. Tho. Scholefield born Mar. 17, in Northourum bapt. Apr. 20

Josiah s. Mr. Rich. Milne, Stockport born Mar 29. 1707

Henry s. Tho, Oates, Shelf, bap. Apr. 21

John s. Henry Medley nr. Northourum bap May 19. 1707

Mr. Hartleys wife was delivered of a daughter Dec. 5. 1707

William s. John Clay of Northourum born June 5 bapt. July 3

Mrs Firth of Kipping deliver'd of a dead Dauter. Aug 8. 1707

Abraham s. Abraham Scott of Haslehurst, Northourum born July 26. bap Aug 29

James s. Joseph Wilkinson born Aug. 5 bap. Sep 1

Mary d. John Ambler Shibden Head, born Aug 27. bap Sep 8

Mary d. Joshua Hartley bap. Sept. 8

Mary d. Eliezer Tetlaw born Sep 2. bapt Sep. 14. 1707

James s. James Wallis Northourum born Sep 22 bapt Oct 20

Jonas s. Joseph fflodder, Northourum born Oct 10

Joseph Dickenson my second son was born on Monday a qr. past ffive in the afternoon Oct 13, bap Oct 24 p. Mr. Wright. 1707

Mary d. Wm. Hardy of Shutt near Coley Hall, born Nov. 9. bapt Nov 27 p. Mr. Sharp

BAPTISMS.

Martha d. Mr. Jonathan Wright of Lightcliffe born Nov 26, bapt Dec. 3

Mary d. John Scott, near Northourum bapt Jan 13

Joseph s. John Bentley in Shelf bap Jan 21

James s. John Firth of Wheatley born Jan 7. bap. ffebr 1. p. Mr. Hartley

Jonathan s. Anthony Whitley near Hipperholm bap. Febr. 15

Hannah d. of Robert Pickerd of Osset bap Apr. 21 1708 p. Mr. Sager

Phebe d. John Kellet, Northourum bap. June 6

Susanna d. James Kirshaw of Holdsworth bapt June 20

Elizabeth d. Elkanah Wirrall of Halifax bap July 18. 1708

Susanna d. Joseph Flodder, Northourum born Aug. 27

Henry s. Mr. Pendlebury of Leeds born Aug. 29

Elizabeth d. Mr. Milnes of Stockport born Aug 31

—— s. of Saml Applyard, Shelf born Sep. 4

William s. Jonas Lacock nr. Collier Syke, Northourum bap. Sep 5. 1708

—— s. Mr. Geo. Green, Leeds, born Sept. 24

John s. Abraham Bairstow, High Bentley born Sep. 12, bap. Oct 11

Grace d. Saml. Marshall, Shelf, born Oct. 21

Dinah d. Simeon Jackson, Northourum bap Nov. 14, 1708

Abraham s. Joshua Wilkinson bap Dec, 12

James s. John Bamford bap. Dec 13

Mary d. Thomas Clark, Scout Hall, bap Jan 26. 1708

John s. Joseph Gargrave, Bradford bap. Jan 30. p. Mr Priestley

Joshua s. Joshua Robertshaw, Collier-Syke, bap Feb. 13

Saml Midgley's wife, of Coley Hall, bare 2 children Febr. 22

John Hurds wife deliver'd of a dead child Feb. 24

Mercy d. Tho. Oates bap. at Northourum Mar. 13. 1708

John s. John Speith of lower Briar bapt. Mar. 16

James Hodgsons wife of Hanging Royd deliver'd of 2 children May 7

Mary d. Robert Rusby, near Batley, bap July 18. 1709

Anne d. Tim. Oldfield of Northourum born Aug. 17

Joshua s. Joshua Bentley, Oxheys bap. Oct. 3

Anna d. Dr Nettleton born at Haigh Hall Oct 23 bap Nov. 8. p. Mr Whitaker

BAPTISMS.

Rachel d. Abraham Bairstow of High Bentley born Sep. 29 bapt Oct 31

Susanna d. John Moorhouse nr. Norwood Green bap. Nov. 10

Samuel s. Solomon Holdsworth, Northourum born Nov. 16. bap. Nov. 22

Elizabeth Dickenson my third child was born on Wednesday abt a qr. past seven in the morning Dec. 28. 1709 bap. Jan. 11. by Mr. Priestley

Susanna d. Danl. Empsall, Norwood Green, bap. Jan 1. 1709

Hannah d. James Wallis, Northourum Green bap Jan 6. born Nov. 8

Susannah d. John Bentley, Northourum bapt Mar. 13

Deborah d. Joseph Ingham Hipperholm bap Mar 7. born Feb 12

Mary d. John Clay Northourum born Mar. 10. bap Mar. 23

Eliezer s. Widw. Tetlaw of Rooks born Mar. 22. bap Mar. 29, 1710

Joanna d. Mr. Wm. Vernon in Cheshire born Apr. 2

John s. Mr John Heywood minr at Blakeley, nr. Manchester born Apr. 9. 1710

My Bro. Foster of London had a son born May 13. 1710 abt 12 a clock. and died abt a qr. of an hour after

Hannah d. Tho. Batley nr. Leeds bap May. 29

Mary d. of John Tillotson, Shelf, bapt Oct. 3, 1710

Hannah d. Tho. Ramsden born Sep. 17. bapt Oct. 9. 1710

Mrs Ryley of Leverpool bore a child Dec 7, was married Sept 10 last. She was Widw. Baker the Innkeeper of Eland

Lydia d. John Priestley of Westercroft born Dec. 19. bap. Dec. 28. 1710

Abraham s. Mr Saml Crompton of Darby born Jan. 8. 1710

Rachel d Daniel Greenwood born Feb. 13. 1708 and Joseph s. Daniel Greenwood born Oct 15. 1710 bap. both together Jan 17. 1710. below Cinderhills

Matthias s. Tho Scholefield, Northourum bap Feb. 5 1710

Hannah d. Tho. Oates bap Feb. 18 at Northourum

James s. Tho. Swaine of Shelf bap. Feb. 28

Jeremiah s. John Swift nr Begrington John s. James Kirshaw of Holdsworth Sarah d. John Bamforth all bapt. at John Bamforth's near Begrington in Northourum, Mar. 12

Isaac s. Adam Wilson, Blakehill bap. Apr. 8. 1711

James s. John Speith, lower Briar, bap. Apr. 9

Anna d. Mr Willm. Vernon, of Cheshire born June 2. 1711

BAPTISMS.

Sarah d. Robert Wilson nr Beg'rington born May 28 bap June 11 1711

Ellen d. Tho. Clark, Scout Hall bap. June 28

Ellen d. Mr. John Heywood minr at Blakely born Aug.

Samuel s. Joshua Wilkinson, near Southourum bap. Aug. 19

Hannah d. of my Bro. Foster of London born Sep. 9. between 8 & 9 a clock being Lords Day morning 1711

Elizabeth d. Dr. Nettleton of Halifax born Nov 20. 1711

Mary d. Joseph Gargrave, Bradford, born Nov. 20

Abraham s. Joshua Ambler near Shibden Head bap Dec. 17

Hannah d. Tho. Boocock, Northourum bap Jan 5. 1711-2

Elizabeth d. Mr. John Maude, nr. Wakefield born Jan. 12

Susanna d. Jere. Smith, Blakehill bap ffeb 11

Alice d. Solomon Holdsworth, Northourum bap. ffeb. 19

Nathan s. Danl. Empsall, Norwood Green, bap. Mar 30. 1712

Mary d. Robt. Low, Scout in Northourum, bap. Apr. 6

Abraham s. Abraham Bairstow, High Bentley, bap. Apr. 8

Hannah Dickensou my ffourth child was born on Monday half an hour past six in the morning May 5. bap. May 13. by Mr. Wright. 1712

John s. of my Bro. John Dickenson born at High Shuttleworth Hall May 6, abt 11 at night bap May 26

Henry s. John Moorhouse near Norwood Green bap June 5

John s. Joseph Wilkinson of Westercroft born May 12, bap. June 9

Mary d. of Mr. Clough of Eland born Aug. 11

Thomas s. Tho. Swaine of Shelf born July 18, bap. Aug. 13. 1712

John s. Joshua Knight, Cockhill, bap. Aug. 18

Joshua s. Joshua Brooksbank of Oxheys born Aug. 23

Thomas s. James Wallis bap. at Whinniroyd Sep. 29, abt 10 weeks old

John s. John Swift near Begrington bap. Oct. 7

Jonathan s. John Wood in Green lane in Northourum bap. Nov. 25. 1712

Saml s. Mr Saml Hulme minr at Kipping, bapt. Nov 26, born Nov. 2

Susanna d. Mr John Maude near Wakefield born Nov. 27

Benjamin s. Stephen Holdsworth of Wakefield bap. Dec. 24

Sarah d. John Priestley of Westercroft born Dec. 13. bap Jan. 1

John s. Joseph Moor of Northourum bap. Jan. 16

BAPTISMS.

Susanna d. John Briggs of Halifax bap. Jan. 25

Mary d. John Metcalf of Norwood Green bap. Feb. 2

George s. Daniel Tempest, of Halifax, bap. Feb. 8 by Mr. Eli Dawson

Samuel s. Mr Eli Dawson born Jan. 19 bap. Mar. 4 by Mr. Priestley

Joseph s. Samuel Futhergill of Ossett, bap. Feb. 24

Joseph s. John Askew bap Mar. 8

Archippus s. Mr. John Heywood, minr at Blakely born Feb. 7

Ruth d. John Futhergill junr, Ossett & Sarah d. Tho. Fozard of Osset, & Christopher s. Joseph Nicholson of Alverthorp bap. Apr. 8. 1713

Mary d. Tho. Ramsden & Jabez s. John Bamforth bapt. May 5

James s. Willm. Clayton near the Lee bap May 6

Anne d. Joseph Brigg: John s. Joseph Oates & Elkanah s. Thomas Oates all bap. in my house at Northourum May 18. 1713

Martha d. Titus Greenwood of Hally Green bap. Aug 5. 1713

Elizabeth d. Robt. Rusby of Stancliffe Comon bap. Aug. 19

Bathshua d. Mr. Clough of Eland born Aug. 13

John s. Mr. Tho. Holden Halifax, born Aug. 17

Stephen s. of my Bro. Foster of London born Aug 25, abt 9 a clock at night

Gregory s. Geo. Fox near Clayton Heights bap. Sep. 29

Saml s. George Pickerd of Crigglestone bap. Oct. 15

John s. Mr. John Kirkby, minr. at Heckinwyke born Oct 22

Joseph s. Mr. Saml Hulme, of Kipping, born Nov 11, bap. Dec. 15

Joshua s. John Burton, Ossett, bap. Dec 1

Robert s. Robt. Wilson, near Begg'rington bap. Dec. 9

Mary d. Saml. Askew, Northourum, bap. Dec. 14

Jeremiah Peel & Sarah his dr. bap. at my house at Northourum Jan. 1

John s. Joshua Ingham of Hipperholm born Jan 14. bap. Jan 25

Sarah d. Caleb Ashworth born Feb. 6. bap Feb. 14 in Northourum

John Dickenson my fffth child was born Feb. 11. being Thursday abt 3 qrs p. ten a clock at night bap. Mch. 1. 1713 by Mr. Pendlebury

Joanna d. Dr. Nettleton of Halifax born Feb. 23

Elizabeth & Sarah drs. Mrs Isaac Sharp of Horton born Mch 2d

Anne d. Tho. Swaine, Shelf, bap. Mar. 11

BAPTISMS.

Grace d. Joshua Knight, Shelf, bap. Mar. 24

Nathanael s. Solomon Holdsworth, Northourum bap Mar. 29. 1714

John s. Robert Burton, Ossett, bap. Apr. 1

Elizabeth d. Mr. Wilkinson of Wareley born Mar. 29. bap. Apr. 3 by Mr. Priestley

Hannah d. Joshua Ambler, near Shibden Head, bap. Apr. 21

Francis s. Mr. John Maude, nr Wakefield born Apr. 20

Elizabeth d. Robt Low of Scout in Northourum bap. May 9

John s. Joshua Robertshaw of the Lee, Northourum born July 11. 1714

Martha d. Tho. Scholefield of Northouram bap. June 6. 1714

Willm s. Mr. Wm Pendlebury minr. in Leeds born Aug. 11

Richd s. Mr. Anthony Markham of Leeds born Aug. 21

Mary d. Mr. Rodes of Haughton born Aug. 22

Anna d. of my Bro. John Dickenson, born at Heaton Yate Aug. 21, between 8 & 9 at night

David s. Robt Pickerd, Osset bap. Sep. 2

Ruth d. Willm Scott, Alverthorp & Benjn. s. Philemon Ellis bap Oct. 19

Hannah d. Daniel Empsall, Norwood Green bap. Nov. 9

Edward s. Edward Hanson born Nov. 2. bap Dec. 9

John s. John Askew, Northourum, born Nov. 5. bap. 21

Sarah d. Abraham Bairstow, Danehouse, bap. Dec. 13

Judith d. Mr. Clough, of Eland, born Jan. 16. 1714-5

John s. Caleb Scholefield bap. Feb. 9

Richard s. Joseph Oates Norwood Green bap. Feb. 14

Martha d. Samuel Askew bap. Feb. 16 at Landimer

Mary d. Joseph Drake, Northouram bap. Mar. 20. died Apr. 6

Edward s. Mr. Rooks of Royds Hall born Mar. 23. bap. Apr. 4 p. Mr. Priestley

David s. John Swift, Begrington, bap. Ap. 7

John s. Mr. Saml. Hulme minr. at Kipping born Apr 20 Bap Apr. 28. 1715

Titus s. Widw. Greenwood (John Sonyer's dr.) Bapt. May 2

John s. Mr. John Wrightson of Leeds born May 3

Timothy s. John Speith at Hipperholm lane ends Bap. May 30

Richd. s. my Bro. Foster of London born June 19. abt. 10 a Clock at night

Susanna d. Joseph Moor Bap. Aug. 7. at Northourum

Anne d. Mr John Kirkby minr. at Heckinwyke born Sep. 22

BAPTISMS.

James s. Robert Wilson Beggrington Bap. Oct. 6

Sarah d. Joshua Wilkinson Northourum Green Bap. Oct. 10

Sarah d. Dr. Firth, Kipping born Oct. 13

John s. John Smith near High Cross in Northourum bap. Nov. 14

Nathan s. Nathan Tilson near Green Syke in Northourum bap. Nov. 14

Stephen s. John Moorhouse near Norwood Green bap. Nov. 16

Joseph s. Joseph Brigg near Coley Mill bap. Nov. 23

Richard Dickenson my sixth child born on Saturday half an hour past one in the morning Nov. 26. bap. Dec. 5. 1715 by Mr. Wright

Joseph s. John Wood Green Lane in Northourum Bap. Dec. 13. 1715

Jonas s. Joshua Robertshaw bap. at Lee Dec. 27

John s. of Willm Clark bap. at Hag Stocks Dec. 27

John s. of Dr Nettleton of Halifax born Dec. 24

George s. Mr. Joseph Brooksbank of Eland born Jan.

John s. Thomas Swaine of Shelf bap. Jan. 11

Abraham s. Caleb Ashworth of Northourum bap. Jan. 15. born Jan. 7

Willm. s. John Halliwell—and John s. John Woodhead near High Cross bap Jan 16

Joshua s. Benjn. Sowood of Place near Dumb mill bap. Jan 26

John s. Thomas Ramsden Northourum bap. Jan. 30

Titus s. Jonas Laycock, Northourum bap Jan. 30

John s. Jeremiah Peel of Northourum bap. Jan. 31

Phebe d. Abraham Pool of Shelf Moor bapt. Feb. 5

John s. Willm Thorp born Feb. 27   The first child, the Parents having bin married abt. 15 years

———— Wife of a poor lame Piper at Hill Top above Landimer was deliver'd of 3 children Mar. 31. 1716

Elizabeth d. Tho. Fozard of Ossett bap. Apr. 10. 1716

Deborah d. Josh. Knight of Cockill bap. Apr. 21

Joseph s. Joshua Ambler near Shibden Head, bap. June 15

Thomas s. of my Bro. John Dickenson of Heaton Yate. born July 2

Hannah d. Mr. Anthony Markham of Leeds born Aug. 5. 1716

Joseph s. of Joseph Milnes Landimer bap. Sept. 1

John s. Edward Hanson near Wyke bap. Sep. 13

Jonathan s. Jonathan Milner near Shipden Head bap. Sept. 4

BAPTISMS.

—— dr. Mr. Isaac Sharp of Horton born Sept. 21

Mary d. John Askew of Northourum bap. Oct. 13. born Sep. 20

Richd s. Mr. Abraham Rodes nr. Bradford born Sept. 28. 1716

Mary d. John Mallison of Norcliffe bap. Nov. 13

Hannah dr. of Bro. Richd Foster born at Alverthorpe Nov. 18 halfhour after 8 a Clock in the morning. bap. Nov. 27

Sarah d. Abraham Scholefield of Norcliffe, bap. Dec. 10

Nathl. s. John Longbothom of Blakehill bap. Jan. 16. 1716-7

Mary d. Mr. Rooks of Royds Hall born Jan. 1. bapt. Jan. 15. by Mr. Eli Dawson

Mary d. Mr. Saml. Hulme, minr at Kipping born Jan. 16. bap. Feb. 4

James s. Caleb Scholefield bap. Feb. 7. of Staups

Mary d. John Holdsworth of Northourum bapt. Feb. 17

George s. Robt. Burton of Ossett bapt. Mar. 3

Lydia d. Abraham Bairstow of Danehouse bap. Mar. 11

Sarah d. Joshua Ingham of Hipperholm bapt. Mar. 20

Richd s. Mr Alexandr. Clough of Eland born Mar. 22

James s. Joseph Milner bapt. at Hud-hill Apr 6. 1717

Mary Dickenson my seventh child born on Friday, Apr. 19 halfhour past ten in the forenoon, bap. Apr. 24 1717 by Mr Pendlebury

Saml s. John Swift near Holdsworth bap. May. 5

John s. Mr Saml Rotheram of Dronfield (who mar. Mr. Joshua Wrights dr of Hipperholm) born May 3, abt 2 a Clock at noon

Phebe d. Saml Bateman of Hipperholm lane Ends. bapt. May 17

Mary d. Mr. John Lumb of Wakefield born May. 27

Mary d. Joshua Robertshaw of Lee in Northourum bap. June 13

Mary d. Mr. Pendlebury minr at Mill Hill Chappel in Leeds born June 26

Hannah d. Mr. Kirkby, minr at Heckinwyke born July 1

Elizth d. Danl Empsall of Norwood Green bapt. July 17

David s. James Mitchel of Painthorpe bap. at Ossett. July 21

John s. of my Bro. Foster of London born July 26, abt half hour past eleven in forenoon

Mary d. Thomas Swaine of Shelf, born July 8. bap Aug. 7

Eli s. Richd Constantine of Farsley bap. at Pudsey Sept. 15

John s. Timothy Ramsden of Shittleton Hill in Northourum born Sept. 5. bap. 26

Susanna d. Wm Powner of Manchester bap Oct. 4, at New Chap.

BAPTISMS.

George s. John Tinker, Manchr. bap. Oct 9. at New Chapel
Joseph s. Samuel Askew, Northourum born Sep 5. bap. Oct. 12
Thomas s. Joseph Moor. of Boulshaw in Northournm bap. in my
house Oct. 14
Mary d. Robt. Wilson Black Myers bap. Dec. 9
Ruth d. Tho. Ramsden near Collier Syke in Northourum Bap.
Dec. 18
John s. Robt Low bap. at Onely House Jan. 6. 1717
Abram s. Solomon Holdsworth, Northourum bap Jan. 8
Sarah d. Edward Hanson of Okenshaw bap. Jan. 9
Joseph s. Jeremy Peel near Northourum bap Jan. 27
James s. Mr. Js. Hawkins minr. at Wakefield born Febr. 10.
1717-18
Elizabeth d. Mr. Joseph Brooksbank of Eland born Mar. 2
John s. John Wood of Greenlane in Northourum bapt in my house
Mar. 13
David s. Caleb Ashworth of Northourum born Mar. 10. bap.
Mar. 23
John s. Daniel Sharp of Tanhouse born Mar. 10. bapt. Mar. 23
Samuel s. Benjan. Sowood at Godley bap. Mar. 24
Ruth d. Joshua Knight of Cockill bap in my house Apr. 5. 1718
Hannah d. Jonathan Milner, near Shipdenhead bap. Apr. 14 in
my house
Hannah d. Joshua Smith of Hipperholm bap. Apr. 24
Joseph s. John Woodhead, Shelf, bapt Ap. 28, born 21
Mary d. John Williamson of Mytham bap Apr. 30
Grace d. Willm Clark of Hagstocks bap May 1
Elizabeth d. James Gregson, Northourum bap. July 13
Joshua s. Wm Tomlinson of Alverthorp bapt. July 17
Hnnaah d. Mr. Saml Rotheram of Dronfield born July 18
Ma ryd. Joseph Drake of Pudsay bap. July 23
Margaret d. Mr Anthony Markham of Leeds born July 22
Frances d. Dr. Nettleton of Halifax born July 31
Elizabeth d. my Bro-in-law Mr Stephen Foster of London born
Aug. 13. 1718
Saml. s. Mr. Moult of Leeds born Sept. 1
Susanna d. Mr. John Wrightson of Leeds born Sept. 9
Willm. s. Mr Rooks of Royd Hall born Aug. 27. bap. Aug by Mr
Eli Dawson
Jane d. Mr. John Maude of Wakefield born. Oct. 21

BAPTISMS.

Samuel s. Joseph Milner at Lands Head bap. Nov. 2. at Northourum

Obadiah s. Mr. Saml. Hulme Minr. at Kipping born Nov. 20. bap. Dec. 10

Edmund s. Tho. Swaine of Shelf bap. in his House Dec. 27

Mary d. John Halliwell near Reavy Beacon bap. in my House Dec. 27

Benjamin s. John Askew Northourum bap. Jan. 3. in my House

Sarah d. Danl. Bateman of Shelf born Dec. 7. bap. Jan. 11 in my house

Anne d. Bro. Richd Foster born at Alverthorpe Jan 3. bap. 21. 1718-9

Mary d Joshua Ambler near Shibden head bap. Feb 23

Mary d. John Smith near High Cross bap. Feb. 25

Hannah d. James Mitchel of Painthorpe bap. there Mar. 23

Mary d. of my Bro. John Dickenson of Heaton Yate born Mar. 6

Benjamin Dickenson my Eight child born at Ossett Mar 18 half hour past 4, in the morning being Wednesday bap Apr. 1 by Mr Hawkins 1719

Patience d. John Fletcher of Blakehill bap. Apr. 4. there

Willm s. John Wood in Green Lane bap. Apr. 7

Elizabeth d. Timothy Ramsden of Shittleton Hill bap Apr. 7. born Mar. 27

James s. Willm Smith of Pudsay bap Apr. 10

Elizabeth d. Saml Roundsley bap at Ossett, Apr. 12. 1719

Hannah d. John Metcalf near Coley Hall at Shutt. bap. May 18

Joseph s. Joseph Futhergill of Ossett bap. May 29

Hannah d. Abraham Bairstow of High Bentley & Anne d. Martin Woodhead of Shelf, bap June 8

James s. Joshua Robertshaw of Lee in Northourum bap. there June 15.

Anne d. Mr. Pendlebury of Leeds born June 16.

Mary d John Terry of High Bentley bap. June 22

Hannah d. John Speith of Hipprholm-lane-ends bap July 13. 1719

Joshua s. Joshua Thornes of Ossett born Aug 9. bap. 10.

Anne d. Joseph Westerman of Ossett bap. Sep. 4

Sarah d. John Swift near Ovenden bap. Sep. 15

Thomas. Mr Jno. Kirkby Minr at Heckinwyke born Aug. 29

Joseph s. Mr Alexandr. Clough of Eland born Sep. 17

BAPTISMS.

Joseph s. Joseph Drake of Northourum bap. Sep. 20
Christopher s. Mr. Brooksbank of Eland born Sep. 22. 1719
John s. Robt Kitson of Upper Brear born Oct. 6
Hannah d. Jonas Laycock of Hudhill in Northowrum bap. Nov. 3
Samuel s. Benjam. Sowood of Godley & Hannah d. John Mallison
  of Norcliff. bap. at Northourum Nov. 13

John s. Mr. Hawkins Minr at Wakefield born Oct 30
Joshua s. Mr. Saml. Rotherham of Dronfield born Nov. 6
Achsah d. of Caleb Ashworth of Northourum born Nov. 20. bap.
  Nov. 26. 1719

Benjamin s. 'of Benjamin Scott of Ossett bap. Dec. 1
Sarah d. of John Holdsworth of Blakehill bap. Dec. 16
Thomas s. of Mr. Wm. Hotham of York born Dec. 12
Tho. s. of Dr. Nettleton of Halifax born
Anne d. of Moses Holdsworth bap. Jan 6. 1719-20
Sarah d. of Joseph Moor of Boulshaw in Northourum bap. Febr. 15
Jeremiah s. of Jeremiah [Pe] el near Northourum bap. Feb. 15
Joshua s. Edward Hanson of Okenshaw bap. Mar. 17
Lydia wife of Joseph Oates of Staups & Hannah their dr. bap. in
  my house Mar. 22

Rachel d. John Williamson of Mytham bap. Apr. 6. 1720
John s. Tho. Laycock of Shelf, bap. in my house Apr. 9
John s. John Lee, Pudsay bap. Apr. 7
John s. Joshua Smith of Hipperholm bap. Apr. 26, 1720
Susanna d. Tho. Swaine of Shelf bap. Apr. 26
Sarah d. Wm. Tilson of Shelf bap. May 9
Stephen s. Mr. Joseph Foster of Ossett born Apr. 15. bap. May 9.
  by Mr. Wilkinson
Martha d. Jonath. Brigg of Northourum bap. May 29
John s. Joseph Wood, of Brian Scholes in Northourum bap. July 3
Grace d. Jonath. Milner of Shittletonhill bap. July 11
Benjamin s. John Ingham of Ossett, bap. July 28
Timothy s. John Smith of Landimer & Nathan s. Danl Sharp of
  Tanhouse bap. there Aug. 14
Hannah d. Mr. Saml Hulm, Minr at Kipping born Aug. 12, bap.
  Sep. 2
Joseph s. Joseph Hanson, born at Oxheys Aug 3, bap. Sep. 21
Jane d. Mr Wm. Rooks of Rodes Hall, born Aug. 21, bap. Aug.
  — by Mr. Eli Dawson

June 12 1700

Reverend Brother
and Sister

Your letter by your maid I received yesterday, am glad to hear
from you, but sorry for your bodily infirmity, and desire to
sympathize with you, but god will gradually wean us from and weary
us out of the world that heaven may by ... endear... this ... world which
desires or that ... which draws us... makes us unfit for heaven
I am heartly sorry for that unhappy faction amongst our friends in
... condemn upon this ... of ... it ... our ... and ... every
here ... and the like in some other places, bodes ill to the nation and our ... enjoy
... sad ... strife ... god ... it by ... plaistry I should enjoy
that ... my sick, or breath, or blood would afford I plad ... not do ... I am
... they have bred and one or else to me, but ... out ... always, and ... here
... the K ... hath ... it ... a ... hurry ... walk
... soft ... of ... his ... by ... they ...

... maintenance —

Accept this little breathing as a ... from ...

BAPTISMS.

Joseph s. Joseph Drake of Northourum bap. Sep. 20
Christopher s. Mr. Brooksbank of Eland born Sep. 22. 1719
John s. Robt Kitson of Upper Brear born Oct. 6
Hannah d. Jonas Laycock of Hudhill in Northowrum bap. Nov. 3
Samuel s. Benjam. Sowood of Godley & Hannah d. John Mallison
   of Norcliff. bap. at Northourum Nov. 13
John s. Mr. Hawkins Minr at Wakefield born Oct 30
Joshua s. Mr. Saml. Rotherham of Dronfield born Nov. 6
Achsah d. of Caleb Ashworth of Northourum born Nov. 20. bap.
   Nov. 26. 1719
Benjamin s. 'of Benjamin Scott of Ossett bap. Dec. 1
Sarah d. of John Holdsworth of Blakehill bap. Dec. 16
Thomas s. of Mr. Wm. Hotham of York born Dec. 12
Tho. s. of Dr. Nettleton of Halifax born
Anne d. of Moses Holdsworth bap. Jan 6. 1719-20
Sarah d. of Joseph Moor of Boulshaw in Northourum bap. Febr. 15
Jeremiah s. of Jeremiah [Pe] el near Northourum bap. Feb. 15
Joshua s. Edward Hanson of Okenshaw bap. Mar. 17
Lydia wife of Joseph Oates of Staups & Hannah their dr. bap. in
   my house Mar. 22
Rachel d. John Williamson of Mytham bap. Apr. 6. 1720
John s. Tho. Laycock of Shelf, bap. in my house Apr. 9
John s. John Lee, Pudsay bap. Apr. 7
John s. Joshua Smith of Hipperholm bap. Apr. 26, 1720
Susanna d. Tho. Swaine of Shelf bap. Apr. 26
Sarah d. Wm. Tilson of Shelf bap. May 9
Stephen s. Mr. Joseph Foster of Ossett born Apr. 15. bap. May 9.
   by Mr. Wilkinson
Martha d. Jonath. Brigg of Northourum bap. May 29
John s. Joseph Wood, of Brian Scholes in Northourum bap. July 3
Grace d. Jonath. Milner of Shittletonhill bap. July 11
Benjamin s. John Ingham of Ossett, bap. July 28
Timothy s. John Smith of Landimer & Nathan s. Danl Sharp of
   Tanhouse bap. there Aug. 14
Hannah d. Mr. Saml Hulm, Minr at Kipping born Aug. 12, bap.
   Sep. 2
Joseph s. Joseph Hanson, born at Oxheys Aug 3, bap. Sep. 21
Jane d. Mr Wm. Rooks of Rodes Hall, born Aug. 21, bap. Aug.
   — by Mr. Eli Dawson

Your letter by your maid I received yesterday, am glad to hear from you, but sorry for your bodily infirmity, and desire to sympathise with you, god will gradually wean us from pride and mercy is out of the road that heaven may be more welcome, that soul which desires, or that love which draws us to god, makes us meet for heaven. I am heartily sorry for that unhappy faction amongst our friends at Soverm, a sad comment upon the zeal flames — I cannot but miss something that with the like in some other places, bodies ill to the passion and one ill bred and if my ink, or breath, or blood would afford a plaister, I should enjoy for they have been and are dear to me, but what can man do? It am very jealous that Mr K hath missed it a wrong ways, and he must rather seriously repent, and solemnly declare via a publick professed way or he cannot expect that either god or man will be reconciled to him. sin will bring shame and shaming our selves is the best fruit of it. I purpose, if the lord will, to rewrite home to him, to which I have some peculiar obligations. I: glad you have so be concerned yourself in this affair, and have born to thrill by him and them, and that he shews any relentings but that's not enough them that sin, rebuke, before all things so especially purchase, and I think a time of probation of the truth of repentance may be fit. I am troubled for his prejudices, and you and silence to your letter. I am far from palliating, extenuating, or accusing any ones faults, niger in locis inge sunt in clericis Blasphemie yet its frequently observed that when men bray to clear up matters they oft run too back, make worst constructions of tolerable actions, aggravate things to the height, new prejudices are raised, inveterate, god will nothing bring storys out of it that tend to perpetuate dissentions, I wish these had been met caution and moderation used, by our christian brethren, had they sorted with some of us at first before matters came to this head, and height who knows but quick scandall had been prevented and yet for all this if both sides would by aside billious, and quietly state their case, methinks something might be done, by the ministers of Christ at a distance, for I must confess I am not capable of reaching them or conversing personally with them, nor is it fit for them to come, but some proposals of general terms of accommodation subscribed by 3 or 4 of us, and presented to them might make an experiment. how far that may give before these be a totall rupture, for I should be sorry he shilling that should be a true prophet, 20 years, let thy dissenters alone and they will destroy themselves, gods way hath its authority as much as their Apocalyptical conicks, you that live nearer, may have fairer opportunity to help them, and the difference they have for your person, gift, gravity, age and graces, is as likely, to put an Eye to the matter as any I know, and I will contribute the best assistance that lyes within my power, if you or they shall signify what you reckon is wise therein, and withall there seems some necessity of their rewriting, upon several considerations. but I cannot enlarge here, yea I must make it matter of my poor prayers that the god of all grace would humble and soften their hearts, that they may walk in the fear of the lord, and comfort of the holy ghost may be relived — Dear brother we have not many steps to our fathers house, punctr, one senses shall unanimously sing the song of moses and the lamb, in the more godly joined, and brethren now — at last — wever he longer to be jealous.
Accept this little token as a viand —
                                              your endeared sincerely obliged
                                              brother   Ol Heywood

BAPTISMS.

Tho. s. George Wiggleworth near Halifax bank, bap. in my house Aug. 28

Anne d. Mr Wilkinson of Wareley born Aug. 26

Hannah d. Joseph Smith of Osset bap Oct. 5

Sarah d Tho. Ramsden near Collier Syke in Northourum bap. Oct. 5

Timothy s. John Sharp of Blakehill born Oct 6. bap. Oct. 9. 1720

Joseph s. John Askew of Northourum born Sep. 12, bap Oct 15

Martha d. David Wood of Hill top above Landimer bap. Nov. 6

Judith d. Mr Brooksbank of Eland born Oct. 26

Sarah d. Saml. Askew, of Northourum born Oct. 14 bap Nov. 20

Mary d. Tim. Ramsden born Dec. 6. bap. Jan. 3

Eli s. James Milnes, of Staups in Northourum bap. Jan. 27

Joseph s. James Ward of Ossett bap. Feb. 23

Esther d. Robt Low near high Cross bap. Feb. 26

James s. John Halliwel in Shelf bap Mar. 27. 1721

Sarah d. John Fletcher of Blakehill bap. in my house Apr 2

Isaac s. Solomon Holdsworth bap. Apr. 10, at Saltinstall

Martha d. Joseph Drake, Northourum born. Mar. 31. bapt Apr. 23

Anne Dickenson my ninth child born on Tuesday Apr 4. 1721, a qr. before one a clock afternoon bapt Apr. 16 by Mr Priestley

David s. John Coulborn of Hipperholm born Apr. 9. bap. Apr. 25

Mary. d. Bro. Richd Foster of Flanshaw born Apr. 23. bap. May 8. 1721

Susanna d. Dr. Colton of York born Aug 1

Susanna d. John Smith, Nr. High Cross bapt. Aug. 9

Anna d Mr George Heald of Macclesfield born July 18

Elizabeth d. Wm Clark, Hag Stocks bap. Aug. 28. 1721

Benjamin s. James Mitchel of Osset bap. Aug. 31.

Elizabeth d. Mr Isaac Clegg of Manchester born Aug. 22

Timothy s. Josh. Ambler near Shibden Head bap. Sep. 10

Sarah d. John Terry of High Bentley bap. Sep. 15

Elizabeth d of my Bro in Law Mr. John Jepson of Dewsbury born Aug. 25. bap. Sep 5

Nathanl s. of Benjamin Sowood of Northourum bap. Oct. 8

L

Titus s. of Mr Joshua Cordingley Minr. at East Wood born Oct. 18
John s. of Stephen Ambler of Clayton born Oct 31. bap. Nov 29
Abraham s. of John Swift near Ovenden bap. Nov. 28. about 6
weeks old
David s. of John Holdsworth & Mary d. of John Sharp of
Blakehill bap. Dec : 5: 1721:
Elizabeth d. Abraham Bairstow of High Bentley bap: Dec: 23
Joshua s. Joshua Robertshaw of Lee in Northourum bap. Dec.
26
Elizabeth d. of my Bro. Mr Joseph Foster of Ossett born Dec.
13. bap. Dec. 28
John s. Mr Rooks of Royds Hall born Jan. 26. died Feb. 7.
Phebe d. Wid. Phebe Wood of Green Lane in Northourum bap.
Feb 14. (line of shorthand).
Susanna d. John Walker & Mary d Samuel Turner bap. at
Wall Close in Northourum Mar. 9
Sarah d. Mr Joseph Brooksbank of Eland born Mar. 11
John s. John Williamson of Mytham bap. Mar. 22
John s. John Smith bap. at Landimer Mar. 25. 1712. (one line
shorthand)
Willm s. Moses Holdsworth of Greenlane in Northourum bap.
Apr. 23
Hannah d. Joseph Oates near Norwood Green Bap. Apr. 24
John s. Jonathan Briggs, of Northourum bapt May 13. 1722
Betty d. John Longbotham of Spiggs in Northourum bap. May.
17. 1722
Mary d. Jeremiah Peel near Northourum bap. May. 28.
Hannah d. Joseph Toulson of Ossett bap. June. 13.
Edward s. Joseph Hanson of Oxheys in Shelf bap. June 27
Richard s. Bro : Richd Foster of fflanshaw born Aug : 6 : ½ hour
past 10 at night bap. Aug. 29. 1722
Hannah dr. of Tho : Bates of Bradshaw in Ovenden bap. in my
house Sep. 8
Susanna d. John Sutliffe of Shelf bap. Sept. 23
Hannah d. John Askew of Northourum bap. Oct. 9
Mary d. Joseph Drake of Northourum bap. Oct. 21
Jonas s. Jonas Laycock of Shelf bap. Nov. 19
Thomas s. Tho. Laycock of Shelf bap. Nov. 19
Mary d. James Milnes bap. Dec. 4. in Saml. Appleyard's house
in Shelf

BAPTISMS.

Esther d. Joseph Brigg near Coley mill bap. Dec. 10

Richard s. my Bro.-in-Law Mr Benjamin Foster born at New York Dec. 13

Joseph s. James Mitchell of Ossett bap. Jan. 29

Nathanael Dickenson my tenth child was born on Thursday abt one a clock in the morning or soon after Jan. 17. 1722 bap. Feb. 2. by Mr Joseph Dawson Minr. at Rochdale

Richard s. Joseph Moor of Boulshaw bap. Feb. 4. & Daniel s. Daniel Sharpe of Boulshaw bap. Feb 4

Thomas s. Dr. Colton of York born Feb 10

Robert s. Timothy Ramsden of Northourum born Feb. 13. bap. 27

Nancy d. Stephen Ambler of Clayton born Mar. 4. bap. 19

Elizabeth d Abraham Hanson of Northourum bap. Mar. 30. 1723

Hannah d. John Wright of Landshead in Northourum bap. Apr. 3. in the Chapel

Grace d. Obadiah Day of Earls Heaton near Dewsbury bap. Apr. 16

Martha d. Thomas Ramsden near Collier Syke in Northourum bap. Apr. 25

John s. Samuel Askew of Northourum born Mar. 14. bap. Apr. 28

Mary d. Wm. Wood bap. May 19. in Halifax chapel

Judith d. Mr Alexander Clough of Eland born June. bap. July 4 by Mr Bairstow

Saml s. Samuel Bateman bap. July 7

John s. John Coulborn of Hipperholm born Apr. 20. bap May 6

William s. Mr Saml Hulme minr at Kipping bap. July 18, 1723

Mary d. George Wigglesworth near Halifax bank bap. in my house July 21

Abraham s. Abraham Hall of green lane in Northourum & John s. Jonathan Milner of Shittleton hill in Northourum bap. in my house Aug. 4

John s. James Kirshaw of Holdsworth bap Aug. 21

John s. Willm Sutcliffe near Eastwood born Aug. 23

Mary d. John Rodes of Horton born Aug. 23

John s. John Stephenson of Ossett bap, Aug. 29

David s. David Wood of Hill Top above Landimer in Shelf bap. Sep. 15

Mary d. Willm Tilson of Deanhouse bap. Sep. 20

Martha d. Abel Wadsworth of Godley bap. Oct 2

BAPTISMS.

Martha d. Wm. Tomlinson of Alverthorp. bap. Oct. 9

Joseph s. Thomas Swaine of Shelf born Sep. 25 bap. Oct. 25

Hannah d. John Smith near High Cross bap. Nov. 1

John s. of my Bro. Mr Richard Foster born Oct. 31. bap. Nov. 20, & also Anne d Joseph Peace of Ossett bap. Nov. 20 at Flanshaw   (One line shorthand.)

Martha d. John Mallison bap. in my house by Mr Hulme Jan. 2

Joseph s. Joseph Healey bap. in John Bentley's house in Northourum by Mr. Wright, Dec. 29

Nancy d. John Sharp of Blake hill bap. in my house Feb. 16

Samuel s. John Sutliffe of Shelf born Feb. 17, bap. Mar. 10. in my house

Richd s. of my Bro. Joseph Foster of Ossett born Mar 3, bap Mar. 18. 1723

Elizabeth d. Benjamin Scott of Ossett born Mar. 19, bap. Mar. 20

Abraham s. John Clayton near Wibsey bap. Apr. 13. 1724

Susanna d. Joseph Hanson of Oxheys bap. there Apr. 13

Grace d. Peter Ambler of Shelf bap. Apr. 20

Daniel s. John Haliwell of Green lane in Northourum bap. Apr. 20

William s. John Terry of High Bentley bap. Apr. 21, 1724

Jonathan s. Joseph Fothergill of Ossett bap. May 12

Anne d John Archer of Ossett bap. May. 13

William s. Jonathan Brigg of Northourum bap. in my house, May 24

Abraham s. John Crabtree of Northourum born Apr. 4 bap. June 1, in my house

John s. John Hollings of Bolton bap. June 14 at Bradford New Chapel

Joseph s. John Ellis of Norwoodgreen bap. June 21 in the New Chapel at Northourum, 1724

William s. John Walker of Shelf bap. July 12. in my House

Edward s. John Hanson of Wyke & Hannah d. Sarah Williamson of Mythom, Widw. bap. July 16. in Wyke

Sarah d. Edward Laycock of Cinderhills near Coley bap. in my house July 18

Grace d. Joshua Hanson bap. July 31 in his house at Bracken-foot in the Parish of Kirkby Overblow

Anne d. Mr. Rooks of Rodes Hall born Oct. 30. bap. by Mr. Eli Dawson

BAPTISMS.

Betty d. John Booth of Northourum bap. Oct. 4.

Mary d. Stephen Ambler of Clayton bap. Oct 5

Mary d. Wid. Barber of Halifax bap. Oct 25

James s. James Milnes of Blakehill end in Northourum bap. Nov. 12

Eli s. Benjamin Sowood bap. at Dovehouse Nov. 23

Willm. s. Joshua Smith & Martha d. John Smith, bap. Dec. 27. in my House

Sarah d. of my Bro. John Dickenson of Heaton Yate born Nov. 16

John s. John Fletcher of Blakehill & Elizabeth d. John Holds-worth of Blakehill bap. in my house Jan. 10. 1724

Samuel s. Richd. Gray, bap. at Joseph Wilkinsons at Wester-croft Mar. 4

Mary d. John Coulborn near Hipperholm born Feb. 28. bap. Mar. 15

Richard Dickenson my Eleventh Child born Apr. 9 abt. 4. a clock in the morning being ffriday bapt Apr. 19. 1724 by Mr. Eli Dawson

Thomas s. Timothy Bentley of Northourum bap. Ap. 25

John s. John Banes of Thornes near Wakefield born May 2. bap. May 13

David s. John Askew bap. May 17. in his house in Northourum 1725.

Anne d. Timothy Ramsden Northourum born Apr. bap. May. 18. in his new house.

Jonathan s. Abram Garras bap. June 8. at the Inghead in Northourum

Anne d. John Roundsley of Ossett bap. June the 21

Sarah d. Danl Sharp of Boulshaw bap. in my house June 27

John s. Mr. Wm Gream of Heath near Halifax born July. 1. bap. Aug. 4. in his house by Mr. Priestley

John s. Abraham Hanson born June 24 bapt. in his house at Browside in Northourum July 21

Susanna d Mr. Saml Hulme Minr. at Kipping born July 13 bap July 28 at Holm Top in Horton

Elizabeth d. James Bland of Halifax bap. in the New Chapel there Aug. 1

Elizabeth d. Saml. Askew of Northournm, bap. Aug. 8

Elizabeth d. of my Bro in Law Mr Richd Clapham born Aug. 28.

BAPTISMS.

being Saturday abt 2 a Clock in the morning bap. in his house
Sep. 8. in Halifax

Sarah d. John Crabtree near Beggrington born Aug. 30. bap in
his house Sep. 9

Grace d. Jeremiah Peel near Northourum bap. in the New Chapel
there Sept. 12

Elizabeth d. Joseph Healey bap. Oct. 7. in his house near Clack
Heaton

Martha d. Robt Low of Northourum born Sep. 24. bap. Oct. 19

Hannah d. Joseph Drake of Northourum born Sep. 29, bap. Oct. 24

Nathanael s. Mr Jonathan Priestley of Winteredge born Oct. 12.
bap. in his house by Mr Nathl. Priestley Oct. 19. 1725

Edmund s. Tho. Swaine of Shelf born Oct. 1. bap. Oct. 28

Elizabeth d. Jonath. Milner bap. Nov. 15 at Haslehirst in Northourum

Miles s. Joseph Moor of Boulshaw in Northourum bap in his
house Dec. 12. died next day

Thomas s. Richard Roust near Landshead in Northourum bap.
Jan. 9

Sarah d. John Longbothom of Northourum bap. Jan. 16. in my
house

Elizabeth d. Joseph Wilkinson bap. at Lower Brear Dec

Hannah d. Willm. Clark of Scouthall bap. Febr. 3. 1725-6

Sarah d. John Sutliffe of Shelf bap. Febr. 21

Benjamin s. John Booth of Northourum bap. Mar. 20

Mary d. Richd. Gray bap. at Joseph Wilkinson's at Westercroft
Mar. 31

James s. James Kirshaw born at Scout Hall Mar. 17. bap. in
my house Apr. 20. 1726

Nathanl. s. John Craven bap. Apr. 24. at Landimer

Hannah d. Abel Wadsworth of Godley bap in Northourum Chappel
May 22: 1726

Benjamin s. Joshua Clark of Alverthorp bap. June 2

Hannah d. Stephen Ambler of Clayton bap. Aug. 1

Nathanael s. James Milnes bap. at Blakehill End in Northourum
Aug. 21

Joseph s. John Walker of Shelf bap. Oct. 16. born Sept. 11
[1 line shorthand]

Elizabeth d. Mr Willm Gream of Heath near Halifax born Oct 6
bap. in his house by Mr. Priestley Oct 19, 1726

BAPTISMS.

Hannah d. Mr. Jonath. Priestley of Winteredge born Oct. 25. bap. in his house Oct. 29, died Nov. 24

John s. Richd Holdsworth of Landshead born Nov. 2. bap. 9

John s. John Hanson of Wyke born Oct 27 bap. Nov. 10

Hannah d. Jeremiah Parker of Shelf bap. Nov. 13 in Northourum Chapel

Susanna d. John Haliwell of Buskin in Reavy bap. in my house June 4, 1727

Betty d. John Smith near High Cross bap. June 19

Joseph s. Richd Roust bap. at Boulshaw July 14, bur. July 24

Martha d. Timothy Ramsden of Northourum born Ju— 2 bap. July 19 in his house

Hannah d. of my Brother in Law, Mr. Richd Clapham of Halifax born July 27 being Thursday near 8 a clock in the morning bap. Aug. 15

Martha d. John Askew of Northourum bap. Aug. 16

Sarah d. Joseph Brigg near Coley Mill bap. Aug. 21. 1727

John s. Isaac Ambler of Shibden Head bap. there Aug. 23

Tho. s. Willm Charnock near Shibden Hall bap. Aug. 28

Betty d. John Hargreaves of Norwood Green bap. Sep. 11

John s. Joseph Healey bap. Oct. 23. 1727 in his house near Clackheaton

Squire s. Abraham Hanson of Browside in Northourum bap. there Nov. 13

Abraham s. George Wigglesworth near Halifax bank bap. in his house Nov. 14

Elizabeth d. Mr. Rooks of Rodes Hall born Nov. 18. bap. Nov. 21, by Mr. Eli Dawson

Abraham s. Joshua Smith of Landimer Syke born Oct. 25 bap. in my house Nov. 27

John s. Joseph Hanson of Oxheys born Nov. 17. bap. there Nov. 28.

Mary d. Jonas Laycock bap. Nov. 29

Betty d. John Sharp of Blakehill born Nov. 14. bap. Dec. 15

Mary d. Abraham Garras of Inghead in Northourum born Nov. 29 bap. Dec. 26

Anne d. William Tilson of Shelf bap. in my house Jan 9. 1726-7

Timothy s. Timothy Bentley of Northourum & Anne d. Joseph Moor of Boulshaw in Northourum bap. Mar. 19

John s. Abraham Bairstow of High Bentley bap. Mar. 20

BAPTISMS.

Joshua Dickenson my Twelfth Child was born on Wednesday Mar. 29. abt a qr. or more before 10 a clock at night, bap. May. 2 by Mr. Pendlebury 1727

——— son of Mr John Simpson born Apr. 18

Robert s. Mr. Samll. Hulme Minr. at Kipping bap. Nov. 16. at Holm top in Horton

John s. John Holdsworth of Blakehill bap. in my house Nov. 19

Grace d. John Fletcher of Blake Hill bap. in my house Jan. 7. 1728

Mary d. John Booth of Lightcliffe born Jan. 10. bap. Feb. 12

Hannah d. John Booth of Northourum bap. Febr. 24

Eli s. Richard Gray of Shelf bap. Mar. 4

William s. Jeremiah Peel near Northourum bap. Mar. 6

Stephen s. Stephen Ambler near Clayton born Apr. 1. bap. Ap. 9

Martha d. Jonath. Milner born at Collier Syke. Dec. 25. bap. Apr. 9. 1728

Mary d. Mr James Ingham of Halifax born Apr. 30. bap. May 12 by Mr. Priestley

Mary d. of my Bro. in Law Mr Samll. Hanson of Dewsbury born May 6. bap. 22

John s. William Laycock of Shelf bap. May 12

Susanna d. Samll. Askew of Northourum bap. May 19

Betty d. Tho. Wilkinson, bap. May 29, at Cinderhills near Coley

Margaret d. Tho. Swaine, of Shelf bap. Aug. 28 in his House & also John s. John Sutcliffe

Nancy d. Isaac Wilkinson of Westercroft bap. Sept. 3. born Sept. 1. 1728

Francis s. Tho. Laycock of Shelf bap. in my House Sep. 21

Abraham s. Abraham Garras of Inghead in Northourum bap. Sep. 30

John s. of my Bro. in Law Mr. Joseph Foster of Ossett born Sep. 24 bap. by Mr. Hanson

Mary d. James Kirshaw of Northourum bap. in my house Oct. 27

Sarah d. of my Bro. in Law Mr. Richd Foster of Flanshaw born Oct. 22 bap. Nov. 7 by Mr. Hanson

Joseph s. James Milnes bap. at Blakehill End in Northourum Nov 24

Samuel s. Danl. Sharp of Northourum bap. in my house Dec. 8. 1728

Mary d. Tho. Thorp of Dumb Mills bap. Dec. 27

BAPTISMS.

Joseph s. Joseph Wilkinson of Landshead in Northourum bap. Jan. 26

James s. Joseph Hanson of Oxheys bap. there Feb 3, died 5th

William s John Hanson of Wyke bap there Feb. 12

Sarah d. Isaac Ambler of Shibden Head bap. Feb. 19 in my house

Sarah d. Timothy Bentley of Northourum bap Mar. 2. in his house

Samuel s. Stephen Ambler near Clayton born Mar. 26. bap Apr. 20. 1729

John s. Abel Wadsworth near Godley bap. May 4

Hannah d. Richd Gray of Shelf bap. June 8

John s. John Illingworth of Landshead in Northourum bap. June 29 in my House

Mary d. John Smith of Shelf bap. July 20 in my house

John s. Abraham Scott of Northourum bap. Aug. 16

William s. Richd. Roust of Northourum bap. Aug. 17

William s. Willm. Tilson near Reavy Hall bap. Aug. 18

William s. Joseph Booth of Bowlshaw in Northourum bap. Oct. 24

Abraham s. Joseph Moor of Boulshaw in Northourum bap. Nov. 30

Mary d. Willm. Wood near Thornhill Briggs bap. Dec. 14, 1729

—— s. Wm. Charnock near Shibden Hall bap. in Northourum Chappel Febr 1. 1729-30

Joshua s. Joseph Hanson bap. at High Fearnley Feb. 19. bur. at Coley Apr. 23

—— dr. Mr. Saml Hulme Minr. at Kipping born 29 bap. Feb. 16. at Holm top in Horton

Hannah d. Timothy Ramsden of Northourum born Feb, bap. Mar. 2. in his house

Joseph and Hannah Children of John Holdsworth of Blakhill in Northourum bap. in my house Mar. 22

Lydia d. John Booth of Northourum bap. Apr. 4

John s. John Hargreaves of Norwoodgreen bap. in my house Apr 12 1730 the Mother was bur. the day before

Richard s. of my Bro in Law Mr Richard Clapham of Halifax born Mar. 28, bap. Apr. 13. 1730

Joseph s. Joseph Stead of Northourum bap. Apr. 20. born Mar. 23

Thomas s. Richard Holdsworth of Northourum bap. June 7

BAPTISMS.

Thomas s. John Walker of Shelf bap. June 7

Joseph s. Timothy Binns of Green lane in Northourum bap. June 28

Isaac s. Isaac Wilkinson of Westercroft born July 23, bap. Aug. 13

Jonathan s. William Laycock of Shelf bap. Sep. 13

John s. James Hanson of Woodside bap. Oct. 14

Elizabeth d. Jeremiah Peel near Northourum bap. Oct. 30

Abigail d. John Askew of Northourum bap. Dec. 6

Timothy s. John Sharp of Blakehill bap. Dec. 27

Hannah d. Abraham Garras of Inghead in Northourum bap. Dec. 30

James s. John Gregson of Landshead in Northourum bap. Dec. 30

Ellen d. George Wigglesworth bap. in Northourum Chapel Feb. 7

William s. Willm. Wood near Thornhill Briggs bap. Apr. 18. 1731

Timothy s. Timo. Scott of Lower Brear bap. May 23

William s. Richard Warburton bap. at Westercroft May 23

Martha d. Jonathan Milner of Northourum bap June 21. 1731

Esther d. Abraham Scott of Northourum bap. June 22

Mary d. Joseph Healey bap. in the Hough June 24

John s. Joseph Askew of Northourum bap. in my house July 4

Mary d. Joseph Wilkinson Junr. born in Halifax June 9. 1731

Elizabeth d. Mr. Nathanael Priestley of Northourum born July 7, bap. July 25

John s. Tim Bentley of Northourum bap. July 26

James s. John Fletcher of Blakehill in Northourum bap. Aug. 8

Grace d. John Smith of Shelf bap. Aug 15

Stephen s. Stephen Ambler near Clayton bapt. Sept. 16. 1731

Elizabeth d. Tho. Bairstow, Beggrington, bap. Sep. 16

Abraham s. James Kirshaw bap. in my house Oct. 3

John s. Jonathan Standeven bap. Oct. 4 at Lim'd House

John s. David Ryley near Coley Mill bap in my house Oct. 17

Benjamin s. James Milnes of Northourum, born & bap. Oct. 23. 1731 bur Aug. 13. 1732

Sarah d. John Hanson of Wyke bap. Nov. 1

Martha d. William Hird bap. at High Bentley Dec. 21

Sarah d. John Booth of Northourum bap. in my house Dec. 26

Abel s. Abel Wadsworth of Godley bap. Jan. 4. 173$\frac{1}{4}$

Judeth d. Tho. Wilkinson near Cinder Hills bap. Feb. 2

Samuel s. Jeremy Peel near Northourum bap. Mar. 9

Rebecca d. Timothy Scholefield of Bank Top near Halifax Mar. 13

BAPTISMS.

Joshua s. Mr. Joshua Hardcastle Minr at Bradford bap. Mar. 17

Betty d. Richd. Roust of Northourum bap. Mar. 21

James s. John Towers of Halifax bap. Apr. 10. 1732

Grace d. Daniel Sharp of Northourum bap. in my house, Apr. 23

Joshua & David sons of Michael Dawson near Beggrington born May 16. bap. May 19

Isaac s. Abraham Hanson of Green Lane in Northourum born Apr. 20. bap. May 21, in my house

Susanna d. Joseph Wilkinson of Landshead in Northourum bap. June. 19

Nathanael s. Mr. Samll Hulme Minr. at Kipping born June 17, bap. July 2 at Holme Top in Horton 1732

Samuel s. Joseph Hanson bap. July 12 at High Fearneley

John s. David Mitchel, bap. in my house July 23

James s. Mr. Nathl. Priestley of Northourum born July 30, bap. his House Aug. 20

Mercy d. Jeremy Stocks of Northourum bap. Aug. 24

John s. John Brigg, bap. in my House Sept. 17   •

Anne d. Jonathan Learoyd bap. in my House, Oct. 8

Mary & Judeth drs. James Hanson of Woodside bap. Oct. 9. 1732

Sarah d. Tho Bairstow near Beggrington bap. Oct. 16

Mary d. William Charnock of Northourum bap. Oct. 29

John s. Timothy Scott of Northourum bap. Nov. 13

Hannah d. Samll. Askew of Northourum bap. Nov. 19

Hannah d. John Greenwood of Northourum, bap, in my House Dec. 17

Betty d. William Rushworth of Shelf bap. Jan. 15

John s. Joseph Moor of Northourum bap. in the Chapel Jan. 21

Benjamin s. William Wood near Thornhill Briggs bap. at Northourum Jan. 28

Mary d. James Parkins bap. in my House Feb. 23

Peter s. Peter Ambler born & bap. at Spiggs in Northourum Febr. 28. died Immediately

John s. Jeremiah Rooks of Northourum born Mar. 7. bap. Mar. 8

Martha d. Widw. Kirshaw bap. in my house Apr. 1. 1733

Mary d. Joseph Askew of Northourum bap. Apr. 29. in my house

Anne d. Stephen Ambler of Shibden Head in Northourum bap. there July 12

BAPTISMS.

Martha d. William Laycock of Shelf bap. in my House July 28

Sarah d. Abraham Scott of Northourum bap. Aug. 19

Betty d. John Askew of Northourum born Aug. 12 bap. Sep. 9 in my house 1733

Nancy d. Isaac Scholefield bap. in my house, Sep. 30

Titus s. Timothy Scholefield born Sep. bap. Oct. 8. in his house at Bank Top, near Halifax

Susanna d. Timothy Bentley of Northourum bap. in his house Oct. 14

Isaac s. George Ellis of Norwoodgreen bap. in Northourum Chapel Nov. 11

John s. John Booth of Lightcliffe born Nov. 18. bap. in his house Dec. 17

David s. David Mitchel of Hag Stocks bap. in Northourum Chapel Dec. 30

Elizabeth d. Saml. Hanson born. Febr. 8. bap. Febr. 18. in Northourum

John s. Abraham Garras & Mary d. John Booth bap. at Ing Head in Northourum Feb. 21

John s. John Wilson of Halifax bank bap. Febr. 24. in Northourum Chapel 1733

John s. John Haliwell Junr. of Clayton Heights bap. Apr. 14. 1734. in my house

Jane d. William Tilson of Northourum bap. in my house Apr. 15

Benjamin s. John Hanson of Wyke born June 8. bap. June 18

John s. Nathanl. Priestley of Northourum born June 6. bap. June. 23. 1734

Joseph s. Willm. Wood near Thornhill Briggs bap. June 30. in Northourum Chapel

Sarah d. Isaac Wilkinson bap. in his House at Westercroft June 30

Mary d. Jonas Pierson bap. July 14. in my house

John s. Joseph Wood of Hipperholm bap. there July 31

Jonathan s. Mr. Jonathan Priestley of Winteredge born July 19, bap. Aug. 15 there

James s. Mr. James Huthwaite born at Westercroft July 30, bap. there Aug. 3 by Mr. Dodge

Samuel s. Timothy Scott of Shelf bap. Sep. 11

Thomas s. John Holdsworth of Northourum bap. Sept. 15

Sarah d. Joshua Nichol of Damhead in Northourum bap. Oct. 2

William s. Joseph 'Hanson of High Fearnley born Oct. 5. bap. Oct. 11. 1734 .

BAPTISMS.

Mary d. Jeremy Stocks of Northourum bap. Oct. 13
William s. James Parkins of Northourum bap. Oct. 26
Mary d. William Parish of Norwood Green bap. Jan. 2
Martha d. John Brigg of Northourum bap. Jan. 5 ith' Chapel
Betty d. Jeremy Peel near Northourum bap. Jan. 20, 1734-5
Betty d. George Wigglesworth of Booth Town in Northourum bap
in my house Febr. 1
Mary d. John Greenwood of Northourum bap. in my house Febr. 2
Betty d. Richard Warburton of Shelf bap. Feb. 3. 1734-5
Grace d. Grotius Clifford junr of Shelf bap. in my house Feb. 6
Joseph s. John Fletcher of Blake hill in Northourum bap. in my
house Mar. 16
Mary d. Joseph Moor of Whinniroyd bap. in my House Apr 6.
1735
Jeremiah s Jonathan Learoyd bap. in my house May 7
John s. John Sharp bap. May 10 in his house by Shibden Mill:
died next morn:
William s. Daniel Sharp of Northourum bap. in my house May 11
John s. Timothy Fauthrop born & bap. at Collier Syke May 23 ˙
William s. William Roe of Bradford bap. June 29. 1735
Nancy d. Joshua Sowden of Hove-Edge near Hipperholm bap.
Sep. 5
Thomas s. of my son John Dickenson born in London Aug. 21,
Bap. by Mr. Tim. Jollie
James s. John Harrison of Northourum bap. in my house Sept 7
Moses s. Timothy Scholefield bap in his house at Bank Top. near
Halifax Sept. 22
Hannah d. George Ellis of Norwood Green bap. Sep. 18 in my
house
James s. Wm Charnock bap. Sep. 26
Anne d. Benjamin Morley of Over Scout bap. there Nov. 6
Joshua s. Joshua Dean of Hudhill in Northourum bap. in my
house Nov. 17. 1735
Joseph s. John Wilkinson of Northourum born Nov. 17. bap.
Dec. 18
Sarah d. John Wilson of Halifax bank Top. bap. in Northourum
Chapel Dec. 14
Grace d. Joseph Askew of Northourum born Dec. 18. bap.
Dec. 19, died Jan. 4
Thomas s. Stephen Ambler of Shibden Head born Nov. bap. Dec. 25

BAPTISMS.

Jonathan s. John Fauthrop bap. at Collier Syke Jan. 15
Mary d. Joshua Gray of Westercroft, & John s. Abraham Lee of
  Landshead & Martha d. Jeremy Webster of Landshead in North-
  ourum bap. in my house Feb. 1
Samll. s. Timothy Scott bap. Febr. 28 at Upper Brear
Ellen d. James Barclett of Shelf bap. Apr. 10. 1736 in my House
Benjamin s. Benjamin Souwood bap. Apr. 11.· in Northourum
  Chapel
Charles s. Joshua Crowther bap. Apr. 18. in Horton Chapel
Sarah d. David Mitchell bap. in my house Apr. 19
Mary d. John Flather of Northourum bap. Apr. 19
Timothy s. Timothy Fauthrop bap. at Collier Syke Apr. 26. 1736
John s. John Booth of Northourum bap. May 4
John s. John Sutliffe of Northourum bap. May 9.
Samuel s. Samuel Askew of Northourum bap. May 16
Hannah d. Jeremy Wood near Micklemoss bap. May 29
Sarah d. Abraham Garras of Inghead in Northourum bap. June
  14
William s. James Swaine of Norwood Green bap. in my house
  July 9
Betty d. Timothy Bentley of Northourum bap. July 25
Mary d. Jonathan Standeven of Northourum bap. Aug. 1
Samuel s. Saml. Sheppard of Northourum bap. Aug. 22
James s. Danl. Bateman bap. Aug. 28
James s. Thomas Wallis of Whiniroyd in Northourum bap. Oct. 7
Mary d. Abraham Pyerah of Bolshaw in Northourum bap. Oct. 31
Mary d. James Scholefield of Haslehirst bap. Nov. 15
John s. James Parkins of Northourum bap. Nov. 16
Lydia d. Wm. Hird near Norwood Green bapt. in Northourum
  Chapel Dec. 26
Thomas s. Jonas Pierson of Westercroft born Dec. 21. bap. Jan.
  21. in my house
Thomas s. John Drake near Nowell Hall bap. in Wibsey Jan. 23
Jonathan s. Joshua Sowood bap. at Upper-place in Southourum
  Mar. 9
Samuel s. Timothy Binns of Greenlane bap. Mar. 14. & Mercy d.
  John Greenwood of Hagstocks bap. Mar. 14
Brian s. Isaac Wilkinson of Westercroft bap. Mar. 15
John s. Grotius Clifford Junr. of Shelf bap. in my house Apr. 9
  1737

BAPTISMS.

Sarah d. John Sharp of Northourum bap. Apr. 10. in my house

Mary d. Timothy Scott of Northourum bap. Apr. 17. in my house

Richard s. Joshua Nichol near Shibden Mill bap. Apr. 23

Mary d. Wm. Laycock of Shelf bap. Apr. 28. 1737

Samuel s. Samuel Scholefield of Sutcliffe Wood bap. May. 1

Samuel s. Richard Walmsley bap. at Horton May. 22

Grace d. Timothy Scholefield bap. June. 27

George s. George Wigglesworth bap. July. 3

Mary d. John Bartlet bap. in my house Aug. 18. he lives at Dean-house in Shelf

James s. Richd. Holdsworth of Northourum born July 25 bap. Aug. 21

Nathan s. Nathan Firth of Hungerhill born Aug. 1. bap. Aug 25

Robert s. John Wilkinson of Northourum born July 31. bap Aug. 26

Hannah d. John Flather of Northourum bap. Sept. 11

Sarah d. Joseph Moor Junr. bap. in my house Oct. 9

Betty d. Wm. Parish of Norwoodgreen bap. in my house Oct. 15

Joseph s. John Brigg of Northourum bap. Oct. 23. 1737

David s. John Harison of Northourum bap. Oct. 30

Joseph s. Abraham Garras of Northourum bap. Nov 1

Anne d. Wm. Wood near Thornhill Briggs bap. in Northourum Chapel Nov. 13

John s. Joshua Sowden near Thornhill Briggs bap. Nov. 17

Jonathan s. Jonathan Learoyd of Northourum bap. Dec. 4, 1737

Hannah d. of my son John Dickenson born in London

Phebe d. Samll. Brigg of Priestley green bap. Jan. 10

Nancy d. Benjamin Souwood bap. in Northourum Chapel Jan 29

Mary d. John Sutliffe of Northourum bap. Febr. 4

Grace d. John Holdsworth of Northourum bap. Febr. 14

Abraham s. John Fauthorp of Collier Syke & Grace & Mercy Twin drs. of Abraham Lee near Tan-house in Northouram bap. Febr. 27

Martha d. Thomas Thornton of Norwood-green bap. Mar. 11

Mercy d. William Sheppard of Lands-head in Northourum bap. Mar. 12. 1737

Rachel d. John Hanson of Wyke bap Mar. 14

Mary d. Daniel Sharp bap. in his house at Barnshill Apr. 3. 1738

Joseph s. Joseph Drake and Hannah dr Titus Laycock bap. at Tanhouse in Northourum Apr. 19

BAPTISMS.

Betty d. Isaac Scholefield bap. May. 4

Hannah d. Mr. Nathl. Priestley of Northourum born Apr. 19. bap. May 7

Hannah d. Joseph Wilkinson of Westercroft bap. May 8

Joseph s. John Booth of Northourum bap. May. 21

Becca d. George Ellis of Norwoodgreen bap. June 3

John s. Willm. Tilson bap. June 4. in Northourum Chapel

Hannah d. Jeremy Webster of Lands head in Northourum bap. June 7. 1738

Joseph s. Jeremy Wood of Green lane bap. July 8

James s. Jonathan Holdsworth of Northourum bap. Aug. 26

Joseph s. David Mitchel of Northourum bap. Sep. 18

Hannah d. Thomas Wallis of Whiniroyd in Northourum bap. Oct. 9

Amos s. John Askew junr. of Northourum born Nov. 5. bap. Dec. 10

Hannah d. Joshua Scholefield of Southourum bap. Dec. 24

David s. Isaac Hill of Northourum bap. Jan. 20

Sarah d. Wm Hird near Norwood Green bap. Jan. 27

Gilbert s. Joshua Gray of Westercroft bap. Jan. 28

Betty d. Timothy Scolefield, bap. in my House Feb 12, 1738

Thomas s. John Wilkinson of Northourum born Feb. 3. bap. Febr. 14

Jonas s. Jonas Oddy of Shelf bap. Febr. 19

Rachel d. James Wallis of Whiniroyd near Northourum bap. Mar. 5

William s. William Laycock of Shelf bap. in Northourum Chapel, Mar. 18

Jonathan s. Benjamin Jagger bap. in my house Mar. 24

Hannah d. Edmund Woan bap. at Onely house in Northourum Mar. 29. 1739

Sarah d. Abraham Pyrah bap. Apr. 29. & James s. James Parkins bap. Apr. 29 in my House

Jonathan s. Timothy Fauthrop of Collier Syke bap. May 7

Joseph s Timothy Bentley of Northourum bap. June 11. 1739

Caleb s. Caleb Ashworth bap. June 24 in Northourum Chapel

William s. Samuel Sheppard bap. June 27 in Shelf

John s. John Greenwood of Hag Stocks in Northourum bap. July 8

Mary d. William Charnock bap. in Northourum Chapel Aug. 12. 1739

BAPTISMS.

James s. Abraham Garras of Inghead in Northourum bap. Aug. 15
John s. John Sheppard bap. Aug. 21, at Blakehill
Margaret d. Wm. Sheppard bap. in my house Oct. 1
Henry s. Mr. Tho. Gream of London born Sept. 23
Betty d. William Wood near Thornhill Brigg bap. Oct. 14
Anne d. Jonas Pierson bap. in his House at Westercroft Nov. 8
Samuel s. Joshua Sowden near Thornhill Briggs bap. Nov. 26
Mark s. Isaac Hill of Northourum bap. Jan. 5
Betty d. —— Scholefield bap. Jan. 9
Mary d. John Askew Junr. bap. Jan. 9
Isaac s. Joshua Nichol near Shibden Mill bap. Feb. 10
Mary d. Joshua Souwood of Upper place in Southourum & Martha
    d. John Harrison of Northourum bap. in my house Mar. 9. 1739
Jonathan s Jonathan Holdsworth of Northourum bap. in my house
    Mar. 25, 1740
Solomon s. Wm. Laycock of Shelf bap. Apr. 13
Sarah d. John Sutliffe of Northourum bap Apr. 20
Abraham s. Tho. Hanson bap. at Collier Syke Apr. 30
Joseph s. Timothy Scott bap. in my house May 7
James s. John Swaine of Shelf bap. May 20
James s. John Brigg of Northourum bap. May 21
John s. Jeremy Webster of Northourum bap. May 27
Mary d. John Woodhead & Susanna d, Joseph Moor bap. at
    Barnshill June 5
William s. Saml. Brigg of Priestley Green, bap. June 17
John s. John Fauthrop of Boulshaw, bap. June 22
Nathanl. s. John Booth of Northourum bap. July 27
Betty d. Abraham Lee of Northourum bap. Aug. 24
Sarah d. Abraham Threapland bap. Sep. 7
Betty d. Thomas Wallis bap. in my house Oct. 28
Betty d. James Swaine of Norwood-green bap. in my house Nov.
    24. 1740
Sarah d. Matthew Boocock of Shelf bap. in my house Dec. 13
Grace d Jeremy Wood of Green-lane bap. Jan. 2. in my house
Phebe d. Abraham Firth of Norwood-green bap. in my house
    Febr. 1
John s. John Fauthrop of Collier-Syke bap. Febr. 5
Ruth. d. Timothy Scholefield of Banktop. bap. Mar. 9
Benjamin s. Timothy Fauthrop of Collier Syke bap. Apr. 1
  ohn s. John Clough & Lydia d. Wm. Dewhurst bap. Apr. 26.

BAPTISMS.

at Hill Top near Wibsey 1741

Thomas s. John Flather bap. Apr. 26. in his house in Northourum

Margaret d. John Askew of Northourum bap. at Yew Trees
Apr. 28

Elizabeth d. Nathl. Souwod bap at Lower Brier Apr 30

Sarah d. Joseph Drake of Tan-house bap. in my house May. 10

Lydia d. Henry Stephenson bap. at Sim-Carr in Northourum June
22. 1741. born May 24

Joseph s. Jeremy Stocks bap. in his house in Northourum
June 27

Martha d. Dan. Sharp bap. June 28. in my house

Eunice d. James Priestley of Longshayfoot bap. in my house
July. 12

Nathanael s. John Booth of Hove-Edge in Lightcliffe bap. Aug
26. in his house

James s. John Bartlet of Dean House in Shelf bap in my House
Aug. 28. 1741

Hannah d. Nathll. Longbottom bap. Oct. 23 at Yew Trees in
Northourum

Samuel s. John Shoosmith of Lidgiat in Hipperholm bap. Nov 1

John s. Nathan Dixon of Green Lane in Northourum bap. Nov. 4

Elizabeth d. James Scholefield bap in Northourum Nov. 14

Martha d. Abraham Pyrah & Hannah d. James Parkin of Northourum bap in my House Nov. 25

Ellen d. Wm Sheppard of Northourum bap. Febr. 14

Anne d. Francis Drake of Northourum bap. before, viz Dec. 13

Robt s. John Wiversley of Northourum bap. Feb. 25

John s. Samll. Oddy of Northourum bap. Mar. 28. 1742

Joshua s. Abraham Threapland & David s. John Greenwood bap.
in my House Apr. 18

Joseph s. John Sutcliffe bap. May 23 at Tanhouse 1742

Nathan s. Wm. Laycock of Shelf bap. June 24

William s. Grotius Clifford Junr. of Shelf bap. July 1

Francis s. Samuel Sheppard bap. in my house July 27

John s. Joseph Wilkinson of Westercroft bap. Sept. 20. 1742

Betty d. Eli Simpson of Blakehill bap. Oct. 22

Anne d Mr. Evan Stock Minr. at Clack Heaton born Sept. 30.
bap. Oct. 25. at Birkinshaw 1742

Eli s. Nathl. Souwod of Brier bap. Oct. 29

BAPTISMS.

Lydia d. John Booth of Northouram bap. Nov. 10

Abraham s. Danll Sharp & Sarah d. James Wallis & Mary d. Isaac Hill bapt. at Barnshill in Northourum Dec 20

William s. Matthew Bowcock bap. in my House Jan 16. 1743

Timothy s. John Fauthrop bap. in my House Jan. 23

Joseph s. Joshua Sowden near Thornhill Briggs bapt. Febr. 23

Elizabeth d. Jeremiah Stocks of Northourum bap. Mar. 5. 174¾

Benjamin s. John Fletcher of Hall Houses bap. in my House Mar. 20

John s. Edmd. Woan of Northourum bap. Mar. 13

John s. Samuel Scholefield of Sutliffe wood & James s. Jeremy Webster bapt. Apr. 3, 1743

Abraham & Isaac Twin Sons of Abraham Lee of Whiniroyd bap. May 23

Levi s. Silas Tias of Scout bap. June 12

James s. Tho. Hanson of Halifax Bank Top bap. June 16. 1743

—— Drake of Northourum bap. June 17

George s. Timothy Fauthrop bap. June 22 at Solomon Holdsworths

Hannah d. Joseph Drake bap. in my House June 24

Elizabeth d. John Brigg of Northourum bap. in my House July 3

Joshua s. John Harison of Northourum bap. in my House July 17

Sarah d. Joshua Gray bap. at Westercroft Aug. 11

Hannah d. Joseph Smithy's of Whichfield in Shelf bap. Aug. 13 in my House

Sarah d. John Askew of Northourum bap. Sept. 12. 1743 in my house

Ann d. Benjamin Dickenson of Northouram born 4th Sep. 1746 at 10 min. past 7, Wednesday morning bap. 22 Oct.

Mary d. Jas. Harriott of London born July 16, 1748

Thos Dickenson Harriott son of James Harriott of London born July 25th 1749

Wm. Dickenson s. of Benjamin born 30th Aug. 1748 abt 2 of the Clock in the morning on a Tuesday bap. 26th Sep. by Mr. Hesketh

Thomas s. John & Sarah Bentley born Apr. 6, bap. 23rd. 1750. [Dead.]

Hannah d. Benjamin Dickenson born Wednesday 13th June, a qr. before 7 in the morning bap. July 11 p. Mr. Hesketh 1751

Thomas s. Benjamin Dickenson born Mch. 17th, 1752 bap. 25

BAPTISMS.

Inst. born Tuesday Morn 4 o'Clock
Nancy d. Josa & Haunah Dickenson born 1787 bap. July 2, 1788
at Elen Royd House by Mr. Knight

MARRIAGES.

Samuel Drake & Dinah Smith married Nov. 30. 1702
Mr John Walker of Rivington & Mrs Deborah Gaskell mar. Jan.
Mr. John Eaton, Grccer in Warrington, & Mrs. Jane Bird married abt June 20. 1703
Mr Robert Stansfield of Bradford married Mrs. Elizabeth Sharp of Little Horton, Aug. 29. 1703
Mr Matthew Blyford of Norwich married Dorothy d. Mr Kitchingman of Skircote-green at Halifax Sept. 9. 1703
John Simpson married Mary Ramsden of Quarlers, Sep. 30. 1703
Joseph Brook & Eunice Liversidge mar. Oct. 26
Mr Peter Peters & Mrs. Mary Wilson of Loeds married Oct 12. 1703
Mr Rich. Milne of Stockport & Mrs. Lydia Stansfield of the Breck were married Oct 19. 1703
Mr Joseph Sutton & Mrs Phebe Wadsworth mar. near Christmas
Mr Tho Wainman & Mrs Sarah Walker married Dec.
Mr. George Ogden ffellow of Manchester & Mrs Alice Hawarth of Salford Nov. 7
Mr Rich. Stern and Mrs Lister of Shipden Hall married at Coley Ch. Nov 16. 1703
Tho. Scholefield & Mary Bentley mar. Nov 23
Mr Matthew Greaves of Manchester & Mrs Anne Madock of Newton Heath
Mr Latham of London & Mrs Eleanor Clayton of Manchester
Mr James Clegg Minr in Darbyshire married Mrs Champion
John Bamford & Grace Philips mar. ffebr. 8
Jonathan Holdsworth and dr. John Holdsworth Febr. 26
Abraham Hemingway of Sow'd House mar. Anne Breffit (Mr. Abra. Langleys Maid at Halifax Febr. 24. 1703
John Wilkinson mar. Grace Walker, the same day
James Maude nr. Rochdale & Widow Taylor of Scowcroft nr Middleton, mar. May 9. 1704

MARRIAGES.

James Smith & Lydia Baxter mar. May 9. 1704

Mr Richd Wainhouse of the Pye-Nest & Mrs Power, mar. May 10. 1704

Mr Penteth, near Borough Briggs & Mrs Elizabeth Newhouse of Leeds, married June 6, 1704

Mr. John Taylor Minr in the Dales and Mrs Elizabeth Ellet married abt Midsumer

Eliezer Tetlaw & Elizabeth Strickland married July 5. 1704

Mr Ralph Lathropp & Mrs Margaret Angier of Dukinfield marr. July

Mr Tho. Blinston Minr at Town of Ashton & —— Rosbottom one of his Hearers' drs. Aug 10. 1704

Mr Briggs Attorney & Mrs Mary Hall of Booth Town married Aug 10.   [Crossed off.]

Mr James Taylor of Manchester & Mrs Eliz. Percivall mar. Aug 10

Mr Richard Taylor of London (his Bro) & Mrs Mary Taylor mar. Sep 6. 1704

Timothy Stansfeld & Sarah Hege, mar. later end of Aug.

John Stansfeld of little Horton & Eliz Battersby married Sep. 14 1704

Saml. Robuck and Drake mar. Sep. 14

Mr Jere Gill Minr at Hull & Mrs Spencer married abt Michaelmas

Robert Kitson of Mytham & Elizth Lister mar. Oct. 11. 1704

Mr Bentley, near Brighouse, & Mrs Wainhouse of Halifax mar. Dec. 7. 1704

Mr Smith of Maningham & Mrs —— of Silkston mar. Nov. 1704

Josias Craven & Sarah d. —— Copper of Eccleshall mar. at Bradford Dec. 5

Anthony Proctor mar. Dec 26, 1704

Mr Eli Fenton son to Wm Fenton of Pudsey & Mrs Kay, Dr Gilpins Daughter & Dr Kay's widow of Newcastle upon Tyne mar. Dec. 29. 1704

Saml Riddlesden of the Rooks & Diana d. John Forness of Batley married ffebr. 6

Mr Richard Holden (son to Mr Nathl. H. of Halifax) & Mrs Travis of Manchester mar. Mar. 8

Mr Accepted Lister, Minr at Kipping & Mary Whitehead their housekeeper married Apr. 11

MARRIAGES.

Mr Edmd Brigg, Attorney in Halifax & Mrs Mary Hall of Booth Town mar. Apr. 11

Isaac Sharp of little Horton & Eliza Wood of Bramley mar. Apr. 18

Jonathan Scot & Phebe d. Danl Scot of Athersgate married Apr 25, own cousins

Timothy Crowther & Sarah d. Danl Scot mar Apr. 30

Geo. Addison & Mary Holdsworth (John Clay's maid mar. May 3

Joseph fflodder of Northourum & Ellen ———— mar. May 2

George Whitaker who liv'd with Abr. Scot near Shipdenhead & Sarah Bland (Landlady at Comon House's sister) mar. May 17

Mr. Stanhope & Mr Byron's Daughter of Bradford mar. June

Mr James Grimshaw & Mrs Hannah Finch mar. June 30. 1705

Mr John Witter & Mrs Peacock's dr. of Hull mar. at Halifax July 7

Mr Joshua Rayner & Madam Rhodes of Long Haughton Hall married July

Mr John Cheney a mercer in Warrington & Mrs. Anne Eaton of Manchester married

Mr. Gamaliel Brear & Mrs. Town of Eland married Aug. 7

—— Ainsworth of Hipperholme married Aug 25 1705

Mr Wm Bond Minr near Preston in Lancashire & Elizabeth d. Thomas Cumin at the Ship in Leeds mar. abt Michaelmass

Jonathan Futhergill of Osset & Mary Barnett of Morley mar. Sep. 26

Samuel Holdsworth & Judith Holdsworth of Northourum married Oct. 1

Joshua Robertshaw & Mary Gregson of Northourum mar. Oct. 8

Mr Sugden, Curate at Oldham & Mr John Lightbowns dr. of Manchester married Oct. 6, or therabt.

I and my dear wife married Oct 24. 1705

Mr. Joshua Firth of Kipping & Mrs Mary Kitchingman mar. Dec. 4

Mr John Cagill & Mrs Stead of Halifax married the same day

John Ramsden of Park Nook near Southourum & Elizabeth Robinson of Osset married in Xmas

—— Ramsden of Siddal Hall & Eli Dysons dr. mar. abt New Years day

—— of Warley & John Frost's dr. of Lightcliffe married. Jan 15

Mr John Thomas Minr at Chesterfield & Mrs Ledgard of Leeds married Jan. 16

MARRIAGES.

Rowland Myers & Susan Flodder married Mar. 12

Elkanah Wirrall & Eliza Higson married at Coley ch. Apr. 4. 1706

John Clay, Northourum & Hannah d. Widow Hodgson of Bowling nr Bradford married June 4

Ebenezer Naylor & Mary d. Mr. William Lupton, nigh Wakefield mar. June 13

John Bentley, Bradford & widow Threapland Nr. Halifax mar. Aug 14

Mr Chamberlain & Widow Whitaker of Halifax married abt Sept. 17. 1706

Mr Tho. Holden of Halifax & Elizabeth dr. Mr Josiah Stansfeld of Sowerby Married Sep 24

Mr Jonathan Maude & Wid. Hargreaves Daughter of Halifax married Sep. 26

Mr James Stansfeld of Bowood in Sowerby & Mrs Elizabeth Priestley (Mr. Kitchingman Dau.) married Sept. 29

Joseph Gargrave near Bradford & Lydia Priestley of Westercroft mar. at Coley Chappel Oct. 29. 1706

Mr Hurst, student with Mr. Coningham & Mrs Deborah Hollingworth of Manchester mar. Mr George Green & Mrs Elizabeth Ambler of Leeds mar. Nov. 14

James Priestley & Wid. Surridge of Shelf married Dec. 2

Richard Empsall nr. Snathe & —— dr. of Robert Cowlin of Northourum Quakers, married abt Candlemas

William Hardy, Bradford & Margaret Brook of Coley married Feb. 24

Tho. Lacock & —— Holroyds Daughter of Shelf married Feb. 24

John Arthington & —— Elam's daughtr, Quakers married Apr 2. 1707

Abraham Rhodes of Bierley & Anne Wood of Bramley mar. Apr. 22

Mr. Biron of Holbeck & Sarah d. Mrs. Ambler of Leeds married May 14, 1707

Mr Hartley Minr at Illingworth mar. a dr. of Mr Wilkinsons who was minr there before him May 25

Mr John Greaves an apothecary in Manchester married Mrs Jane Gilliam May 31

William Garfoot & Mary Bradshaw married June 2. They had bin servants with Joseph Eccles at Coley Hall

MARRIAGES.

old Squire and Widow Waterhouse in Shelf married June 2. This the fifth wife

Mr Robert Mason of Booth Town & Elizabeth Proctor married June 25 he above three score & she 26. Scarse three days acquaintance.

Mr Matthew Greaves of Manchester & Mrs Cope of Derbyshire married July 8

Mr Tho. Butterworth of Manchester married Mrs Frances Dukinfield dr. to Sr Robert Dukinfield abt beginning of August.

John Knight of Shelf & Henry Blakebroughs Dautr. mar Aug 13

John Smith of Ovenden & Mary Moor, near Cinderhills married Sept 22

John Firth of Wheatley & Hannah Ingham of Hipperholme married Oct 14

My Brother in Law Mr Stephen Foster & Mrs Anne Gream married at London Dec. 2. 1707

James Hall near Kipping & Widw. —— of Bradford married Dec. 9

Mr. Richmond minr at the New Church at Liverpool married Mrs Sarah Langley of Hipperholm at Coley Chapel Dec. 17. 1707

Mr. Saml Lister & Mrs Midgley of Horton married Dec. 30

Mr George Empsall & Mrs Nevill of Chect Hall married privately at Coley Chapl. Jan. 19

John Medley near Hipperholm mar. ffebr 4

John Sowden & Hannah Strickland married ffebr 9.

John Farrars son & Henry Nailors dautr. of Wareley mar. ffeb. 12. 1707

Mr Tho Reyner & Mrs Sarah Green of High Town married Mar. 22. own cousins

Thomas Nettleton Dr of Physick & Mrs Elizabeth Cotton of Haigh Hall, mar. March 30. 1708

Mr Robert Hesketh Minr. at Platt Chappel near Manchester and Mrs Hannah Sykes of Leeds mar. Apr. 6

Martin Longbottom of Northourum & Mary Cotes mar. Apr. 12

Tho. Crosley who lived wth Wm. Sharp and John Holroyd's wifes dr. of Stump Cross mar. Apr. 12

Solomon Holdsworth of Northourum and Anne Skilton of or near Mixenden Mar May 26. 1708.

John Hurd in Shelf and —— of Norwoodgreen mar. May 24

Saml Futhergill of Osset and —— abt Kirkburton married June 1

MARRIAGES.

Saml Romsbothom of Birks and Sarah King of —— married June 4

Joshua Bentley of Oxheys & Mary Sutcliffe of Norland married June 10

Mr John Bretcliffe of Stony Roid, near Halifax married dr. of Mr Edward Wainhouse of Willow Hall. June 18

Mr William Vernon abt Middlewich in Cheshire mar. Mrs. Frances Cotton of Haigh Hall, June 24. 1708

—— son of Edward Haigh the Quaker near Halifax, married Henry Nailors dr, of Warley June 30

Mr Travis and Mr Peacocks daughter of Hull married at York abt beginning July

Joshua Ingham of Hipperholm and Sarah Knight of Shelf married July 22

Mr Richd Wilson (ye Lawyer) of Mill Hill in Leeds & Mrs Blackburn mar. abt. later end of August

Wm. Haffie a Scotch Man living at Fulham, near London and Abigail Wm. Fentons dr. of Pudsey mar. Sep. 14

Mr John Smith of Wakefield and Mrs Batts of Burstall married abt middle of Sept.

Saml Starky of Blakehill and Margaret Gawthrop of Bingley mar. Oct 7

Nathl Lea of High Bentley and Elizabeth Crosley of Halifax mar. at Coley Oct 21

Willm Bentley, Bookseller in Halifax mar. Widow Milner of Eland abt beginning of Nov.

John Elsworth of Rodley married Wid. Oddy of Leeds Nov 15

Robert Arthington ye Quaker married Nov. 18

James Emmott mar. Hannah Scholefield, Mr. Matth. Smith's Maid, Nov. 30

Mr Martin Hotham, Shopkeeper in York, and Sarah d. of Mr Josias Stansfeld, Sowerby, mar. Jan. 5. 1708

Mr Saml Scot and Mrs Elizabeth Dawson of Leeds married abt. middle of Jan.

Mr John Hollings of Shepley near Bradford & Mrs Mary Rossendale, near Halifax married Feb. 24

John Driver & Susanna Swift, of Northourum mar. Mar. 7

John Greenwood of Norwood Green, married ——— March 7

Mr Nathan Arderne & Mrs Dewhirst mar. Apr. 7. 1709 nr Manchester

MARRIAGES.

Mr. Allison Parson of Thornton and Mrs Mary Langley of Hipperholm married Apr. 27

Mr Tho. Danson of Winsley, nr Knaresbro' fforest & Mrs Susan Brooksbank of Birks married April 24

—— Mitchel and —— Ekroyds dr. mar. May 26. they live in Holdsworth

John Windsor and Saml Spencer's dr. of Shelf mar. June 8.

James Whaley and Mary d. of Wid. Swift, Northourum mar. June 13

Isaac Broadley an oyl Drawer in Bradford & Mrs Anne Hutton of Pudsey mar. June 22

John Glover of Alverthorpe & Sarah Bradbury of Wakefield mar. July 1

Mr John Heywood Minr at Blakely & Mrs Mary Milne of Rochdale mar July 7.

Mr Rawson ye Attorney in Bradford & Mrs Grace Rossendale near Halifax mar. Aug. 4

Mr John Truman near Halifax mar. Mr Firths dr. of ye Heights, Aug. 17. 1707

Mr Hool Curate at Burstall & ——— mar. abt end of Aug.

George Stansfeld of Bowood & —— Lord of —— married Sep. 12

Tho Scholey at Leeds Bridge End a Chandler mar. Anne Thornton of Bramley Sep. 15

Mr. Rowbothom & Mrs Mary Lever of Bolton, married abt Michaelmas

Mr John Kay Clark at Halifax Church & Mrs Carnel mar. Oct. 6

Nathl Hurd of Rawden and Eliz. Longsden of Bramley mar. abt Michaelmas

Thomas Wilkinson, near Shipden Mill and Mary d. Timothy Stansfeld Oct. 13

Mr Sugden Minr nr. Reading, son of Mr Sugden of Shelf and Mr Brooksbanks dr. of Reading, mar. abt middle of Oct. 1709

Mr Tho. Rigg and Mr Edwd Wainhouse's eldest dr. mar. Oct 7

—— Bottomley of Shipden Mill and —— of Dewsbury mar. Nov. 14

—— Dane of Halifax and Isabel Gregson, Northourum, mar. Nov. 21

Daniel Illingworth of Sowerby married Nov. 24

Tho. Ramsden near Shipden Head and Martha Elswick his Houskeeper mar. Nov. 26

MARRIAGES.

Tho. Swaine, Shelf, and Margret Lacock Nr. Lusburn Moor in Craven Mar. Dec 1

Mr Armitage of Outwood near Wakefield and Alderman Fosters dr. of York mar. abt Dec. 1. 1709

—— Healay near Halifax and George Kitchingmans dr. Rachel mar. Dec. 4

Mr Mark Whitaker, Shopkeeper in Wakefield mar. Dec. 7

Thomas s. George Bottomley of Shipden Mill and —— of Dewsbury mar. Dec.

John Hurst and Sarah Pierson of Holdsworth mar. Jan. 22

John Watkinson of Ovenden and Judith Holdsworth of Northourum mar. Jan. 26

Jonathan Ramsden and —— Thornton mar. Feb. 6

Samuel Walker of Lightcliffe and Rebecca Longbothom, Mr. Priestleys maid of Ovenden mar. Feb. 8. 1709

Elkanah Farrar and Luke Hoyl dr. of Ovenden mar. Feb. 21

Willm Pollard of Wyke and John Ferguson's dr. of Halifax mar. Mar. 23

Willm Pollard of Marsh, near Southourum and Wid Kitson's dr. of Halifax mar. Mar. 23

Mr Saml Crompton of Darby and Mrs Anne Rodes of long Haughton Hall mar. Apr. 3. 1710

Joseph Armitage nr. Leeds and Widow Hodgshons dautr of Bowling mar. Apr. 11. 1710

Mr Richard Marsden Curate at Sowerby and Elizabeth d. Mr. James Stansfield of Bowood mar. May 3. 1710

Joshua Clark of —— and Hannah Heald, near Osset mar May 8

Mr Isaac Wilkinson, Minr at Wareley and Mrs Esther Lepis of Pontefract married May 23

Timothy Rhodes and Mary Copper nr. Bradford mar. May 25

Mr Wm Read and Mrs Elizabeth Wimersley of Leeds mar. July 5. 1710

Tho. Watmough Jail Keeper at Halifax mar. —— July 10, buried his wife abt a month before

John Heald near Osset, mar. July 20.

Joshua Hopkins and Lydia Wood of Bank Top. mar. Aug. 3

Robt Wilson and Sarah Pickerd our first servt. maid married Aug. 30

Mr. Saml Wareing of Bury and Mrs Esther Crompton of old Hall near Stand of Pilkington married Aug.

Mr Richard Halsted, Curate at Horbury and Mrs Elizabeth Wadsworth of Horbury, mar. Oct. 28. 1710

Willm Bromitt of Leeds and Mercy d. John Craven, of Westercroft married Oct 29. 1710

Abraham Woodhead of Whini-hall in Shelf and ——— Blaymires of Reavy, mar. Oct. 26

Mr. Steer of Sheffield and Jane d. Mr Clough of Stockport mar. abt middle of Nov.

Jeremiah Clay of Northourum and Martha Hodgson of Bowling, mar. Nov. 16

John Nalson Junr near Shibden Hall and Tho Dun dr. of Halifax mar. Dec.

Samuel Crowther Landshead in Northourum and Sarah Walker his housekeeper mar. Dec. 27

Mr Richard Hutton of Pudsay and Mrs Mary, Mr Thorps dr. of Hopton mar. Jan

Nathan Tilson and Mary Longbothom of Northourum married Jan. 17. 1710

Mr. Caleb Wimersley and Wid. Simms of Leeds mar. abt Candlemas

Mr John Maude, Wakefield, and Mrs Elizabeth Whitaker of Leeds mar. Feb. 7. 1710

Mr John Dunnel of Leeds and Mrs Fairburn near Doncaster mar. Feb 13

Elkanah son of Jere. Baxter of Northourum mar. Hannah Drake at London, March 1

Mr Joseph Brooksbank of Eland and Elizabeth dr. Widw. Lodge, near Halifax, married at Coley Apr 3. 1711

Mr John Milnes of Wakefield mar. Mrs Elizabeth Lepis of Pontefract May 1

John Drake and Joseph Crowthers dr. near Northourum mar. May 6

Mr John Gream near Halifax and Mrs Earnshaw of Hulm Firth mar. May 17

Mr Joseph Whitworth Minr at Coley Chappel mar. ——— Aspinwal May 31

Mr Joseph Dutton Minr at Manchester and Mrs Brown of Cheshire mar. at Buxton June 2. 1711   She has its sd near 4000 li.

Mr Joseph Beevers of New Miller Dam and Mrs Milner near Barnesley mar. June

MARRIAGES.

Robt Dautrie and Rachel Baum near Bradford mar. June 19

Jeremy Batley and Wid. Hanson of Lightcliffe mar. July 5

John Dickenson my Brother and Sarah d. John Beardsell of Blakely mar. July 10. 1711

Mr Alexander Clough, Stockport mar. Mrs. Judith d. Mr John Brooksbank of Eland Aug 15. 1711

Mr Saml Wadsworth of Wakefield mar. Sept. 3. at Coley Chapel

John Taylor of Clack Heaton mar. —— Stevenson of York abt Sep. 9

Joshua Knight Junr. of Cockill and Anne Holmes near Morley mar. Oct. 15

Mr Lister Curate at Birstall mar. Widow Swallow of Heckinwyke, abt Oct. 30

Mr Simeon Crosley near Sowerby and Mrs Dyson near Huthersfield mar. Dec. 19

John Drake near Rastrick and Susan Marshall near Norwood Green married Oct 31

Elkanah Boys near Bradford and Grace d. Grace Ramsden mar. Dec. 11

Tho. Priestley of Exley and Mary d. James Naylor mar. Dec. 11

Joshua Brooksbank of Oxheys and Sarah Best of Landimer mar. Dec. 16

John Askew and Mary Milner of Northourum mar. Dec. 27

John Scott of Shelf mar. Dec. 31

Simeon Shay and —— Townend mar. Dec 27

Mr Saml Hulme Minr at Kipping and Mrs Mary King, Horton, married Jan. 9

Mr John Fergison of Halifax and Mrs Eliz Tetlaw of Rooks married Mar. 3. 1711

Mr Henry Gream and Mrs —— mar. at London

Mr Eli Dawson and Mrs Alice Taylor mar. Apr. 14

Danl Tempest of Northourum and Sarah Marsh of Halifax, Apr. 20.

Joshua Smith of Northourum, mar. May 5

John Metcalf mar. Rebecca Ellis of Norwood Green, May 1

Mr Oldfield of Leverpool s. to Mr Oldfield of Manchester and Mrs Elizth d. Mrs Langley of Hipperholm mar. May 6

William Butler and Lydia Boys of Northourum mar. May 29

Joseph Atkinson and Mary d. Mr. Daniel —— of Leeds mar. June

MARRIAGES.

Moses Holdsworth and Anne d —— Skilton mar. June 4

Joseph Oates and Lydia Lord in Northourum mar. June 7

Joseph s. John ffuthergill of Ossett, mar. Hannah Whittle June 9

Henry Spencer of Shelf and Grace Jackson of Halifax mar. July 23

Mr Willm Walker of Lightcliffe and Widw. Ramsden late of Siddall Hall mar. July 2. And Mr. Norfolk and Mrs Ward.

John Longbothom and Mary Crosley mar. July 6

Richd Lun and Dorothy Pool mar. July 9 they had liv'd servants with Mr Joshua Wright

Caleb Ashworth and Mehetabel Day our second servant maid mar. July 23

Joseph Gott, Schoolmaster at Northourum and Susan Gregson mar. Aug. 6. 1712

Mr John Whitaker, near Manchester and Mrs. Elizabeth Priestley of Ovenden mar. Aug. 27

Thomas Pool of Halifax and —— Hall married Sept 11

Mr. Anthony Markham of Leeds and Dorothy d. of Mr Henry Gream near Halifax mar. at London Sept 11

Joseph Stead and Sarah d. John Hartley in Shelf mar. Sep. 23

Willm Gibson of Stockton, Shopkeeper and Wid. Mary Bentley of Sowood House near Coley, mar. Sep. 25

Mr. Peter Peak of Manchester and Mrs Sidebothom mar. Dec. 4. 1712

Mr Nehemiah Reyner Minr at Gorton and Mrs Jane Eaton mar. Nov. 20. 1712

Mr Edwd. Kendal of Stourbridge in Worcestershire and Mrs Anna Cotton of Haigh Hall mar.

Saml Askew and Grace Swift of Northourum mar. Jan. 13

Jeremiah Smith near Coley and —— mar. Jan. 13

Mr. John Kirkby Minr at Heckinwyke and Martha Nurssey mar. Jan. 27

Mr William Rooks of Royds Hall and Mrs Mary Rodes of Great Haughton Hall mar. Jan. 27

John Bentley of Shelf and —— d. of John Nalson mar. abt ffebr 1

Mr. Joseph Condor of Leeds and Mrs Hannah Wadsworth of Morbury married : own cousins

Mr Willm. Pendlebury Minr at Mill Hill in Leeds and Mrs Anne Fenton mar. Apr. 8

MARRIAGES.

Titus Greenwood and Mary d. John Sonyer mar. Apr. 20

Mr Thompson of Stancliffe and —— near Huthersfield mar. Apr. 23

Timothy Moy and Jane Broadbelt (lately our maid) mar. Apr. 23

Jonathan Crowther and Martha Naylor of Northourum, mar. Apr. 28

John Croyser and Lydia Holdsworth married May 2. She bare a child next day

Mr John Fairbourn of Fishlake nr. Doncaster and Mrs Sarah Crompton of old Hall near Stand in Prestwich Parish mar. April

Joshua Burnet of Wakefield and Sarah Oddey of Horton mar. June 3

Mr Joshua Firth of Kipping and Abigail d. John Dixon of Bradford June 16

Mr Robt Richmond, Minr at Clack Heaton and Mrs Lister (late of Kipping mar. July 21

John Roades and Susu Sharp of Godley mar. July 23

Mr Willm Read of Leeds and Mrs —— Hardcastle mar. July 25

Charles Hughes of Northourum and Mary d. Jere Learoyd mar. July 28

Joshua Robertshaw of Lee and Hannah d. John Berry, mar. Aug. 4

Mr Willm Richardson of High Fearneley and Madm. Kirk of Wakefield, Aug 11

Capt John Fourness and Mrs Frances Oates of Halifax mar. Sep. 14

John Watkins of Northourum and Grace Pollard married Sept. 21

John Yates of Lightcliffe and Rose Coulin married abt begining of Sept. Quakers

Henry Johnson and Mercy Bromitt (John Craven's Dautr) mar. Sep. 22

Caleb Scholefield near Southourum and Mary Smith mar. Oct. 6

Abraham Ashworth of Wareley and Sarah Ashworth mar. Oct. 8, this the ffifth wife

Saml. Riddlesden of Rooks and Mary d. John Northrop of Mirfield mar. Nov. 4

John Haliday of Northourum and Elizabeth d. Tho. Clark of Scout Hall mar. Oct. 18

Mr Richd Rodes of Great Haughton, and Mrs Martha Rich of Bullouse, mar. Nov. 18. 1713

MARRIAGES.

Mr Sheffield ye Reader at Halifax Church and Mrs Holroyd mar. Nov.

Robert Fausit of Northourum and Sarah Bolland near Wibsey mar. Nov. 25

Mr John Jolly Minr at Sparth in Lancr. mar. abt Xtmas

John Fox, miller at Coley Mill and Mary Woodhead mar. Feb. 8

Mr John Ferguson of Halifax mar. Mrs Cowper of Dumfrees in Scotland, Feb.

Mr Christopher Basnet, Minr at Leverpool and Mrs Cheney of Manchester mar. Feb. 9

Tho. Thorp of Godley and John Best's dr. Mary mar. Mar. 29. 1714

John Scott of Halifax and Hannah Stead near Wisket hill married May 13

Eliz. Kirk near Hopton mar. Apr. 1

Willm Sharp and —— of Wheatley mar. Apr. 4. They live at Blakehill End in Northourum

John Wrightson of Leeds and Judith Lea mar. Apr. 8. (sisters children.)

Eli Stansfeld of Sowerby and Mary d. John Farrar of Wareley mar. May 1

Edward Hanson of Wyke and Martha Stansfeld of Horton mar. May 6

Matthew Croyser of Green Lane in Northourum mar. May

Henry Blakebrough of Shelf and —— Settle married May 17

Richd —— and Bridget —— mar. May 17

Joseph Drake and Mary Oddey mar. May 17

Mr Robt Ramsden of Siddall Hall and Mrs Bretcliffe of Stony Royd near Halifax mar. June

Mr Richard Holden of Manchester and Mrs Marsden of Bolton mar. Aug 26

Michl Bentley of Shelf and Eliza. Wm Mann's dr. mar. Aug 25 or Sep. 1

Mr Richard Stern and Esther Mr Timothy Booth's dr. mar. Sep. 9

Mr John Wainhouse of Willow Hall and Mary d. Michl. Oldfield mar. Sep. 9

Mr Timothy Jolly, Sheffield and Mr Simond's dr. married abt. middle of Oct.

William Clark of Hagstocks in Northourum and —— Mitchel near Bingley mar. Oct. 21

MARRIAGES.

Mr Willm Hotham of York and Mrs Bendicta Cotton of Haigh married Nov 30

Mr Tho. Rigg and Mrs Truman mar. abt begining Dec.

John Brogden and —— Blackburn mar. Dec.

Tho. Oldfield of Wareley and Sarah Stansfeld of Bowwood married Jan. 13

Nath n Tilson and Wid. Bairstow Jan. 13

Joseph Milnes and Eliza. Brooksbank mar. Jan. 13

Jonath. Milner and Alice Crabtree mar. Febr. 10

Joseph Moor ye Clark at Halifax Chappel and —— Addison mar. ffeb.

Mr John Wadsworth Minr at Sheffield and Rebecca, dr. of Mr. Sylvester mar. Apr. 4

Joseph Midgley and Eliz. Kay (Dr. Nettleton's maid) mar. Apr. 18

Stephen Parkinson of Leeds, and Mrs Smith of Colne mar. Apr. 19

Willm. Sunderland near Sowerby Bridge and Judith d. of Widw. Clark of Morley Married May. 8

John Holdsworth and Grace d. of John Sharpe of Blakehill married May 17

David Baxter s. of Jeremy Baxter of Northourum and —— mar. at London June

John Priestley of White Windows and Mary Israel Wilde's d. mar. Aug. 11

Mr. Sam Rotheram of Dronfield & Mrs. Hannah Wright of Hipperholm mar. at Coley Chapel Aug. 24. 1715

Mr. David Brear of Elland & Mrs. Lodge mar. at Tork Aug. 29

Mr. Willm. Cotton of Haigh Hall & Mrs. Mary Cotton Mar. Sep. 1

Mr Abraham Rodes near Bradford & Mrs. Dorothy Priestley of Ovenden Mar. Sep. 1

James Pollard of Shipden Hall & Susan Shutel mar. Sep. 22

Mr. Saml. Wadsworth of fflanshaw and Mrs. Lamb of Wakefield mar. Sep. 29

Joseph Milner lives at Hud Hill & Mary Hartley mar. Oct. 3

Mr John Lumb & Sarah d. Mr. Robt Milnes of Wakefield mar. Oct 11. 1715

Saml Hall of Warley & Mary d. Wid. Greenwood mar. Nov 29

Joshua Ashworth of Warley & Wid. Robertshaw, married

Mr John Hotham of York & Mrs. Vanderbank of London mar. Dec. 27

Mr James Gream of Shay-Hill & Mrs Wainhouse of Pye-nest (a

N

MARRIAGES.

young widw.) mar. Jan 5

Mr. Jackson a mercer in Sheffield & Mrs. Crowther (Sister to him that owes the Staups in Northourum) mar. at Coley Chappel Jan. 10

John Mallison & Hannah Whitham mar. Jan. 18

My Bro.-in-Law Mr Richd. Foster & Mrs. Mary Lumb mar. at Chappel-Town Jan. 19

Abraham Hemingway of Booth-Royd near Dewsbury & Mary Bentley near Coley mar. Jan. 28. 1715-6

Willm Jackson of Cinderhills & dr. of Widw. Heaton mar. Jan. 29

Mr. Busk (a Swede) & Mrs Rachel Wadsworth of Leeds mar. Febr. 2

Mr Tho. Fenton of Hunslet near Leeds & Madm. –—— Haughton of Haughton Tower mar. Feb. 13

Mr Matth. Denison & Mrs Miriam Rider of Leeds mar. abt ffebr. 2

Joshua Stead & Phebe Hodgshon of Bradford mar. Feb. 14 (he stole her to the great griefe of her Father)

Mr Powell & Mrs Hannah Ambler of Leeds mar. Apr 5. 1716

John Marshall & Mary –—— mar. Apr. 9

Daniel Robinson & –—— mar. May 21

John Conway of Lightcliffe & Mary Smith of Holdsworth mar June 18

Mr Rontree of or near Leeds & Mrs Anne Simpson mar. abt 12 June

Mr Saml Dawson of Leeds & Sarah dr. of Widw. Heald of Wakefield mar. July 2

John Hurd of Shelf & Phebe Wilson of Northourum mar. July 31

Mr Nathl Holden of Halifax & Mrs Mary Mitchel of Walterclough mar. Aug. 2

Tho. Ratcliffe & Mary Goodall mar. at Coley, Aug. 9

Joseph Hanson & Grace Jackson mar. Sept. 6

John Cotes & Martha Danebrough of Wyke mar. Sep. 23

Jacob Scholefield near Southourum & Elizabeth Mann mar. Sep. 20

Michl Brigg & Grace Holdsworth mar. Sep. 20

Mr William Condor (son of Mr Joseph Condor of Leeds) & Mrs –—— mar. Sep 25

Timothy Ramsden of Shittleton Hill in Northourum & Elizabeth

MARRIAGES.

Smith of Sutton in Craven mar. Oct. 15

Abraham Horton of Bradford & — Swaine mar. Nov. 6

Mr. George Cotton & Mrs Elizabeth Milnes of Wakefield mar. Oct. 22

Mr. Joseph Hardcastle & Martha d. Widw Bradbury of Wakefield mar. abt. Nov. 12

Mr Josias Oates of Wakefield & Mrs — Norton mar. Dec. 18

Mr John Godley the Usher at Halifax Free-School & Elizabeth d. Henry Tassey of Halifax mar. Dec. 26

Charles Clarkson & Elizabeth Button of Wakefield married

Mr Joseph Dukinfield Parson of Thirsk & Mrs ——— a rich Widow mar. abt. middle Feb.

John Hanson of Wyke & Sarah Hanson near Addle mar. Feb. 28

Josias Lumb & ——— Smithson married March. 4

Mr James Wood minr at Chowbent in Lancr. & ——— Judith Brooksbank of Oxheys mar. Mar. 14

Mr Charles Greenwood & Mrs Rockett of Bradford mar.

John Best of Landimer & Hannah d. Widw Pollard of Wyke mar. Mar.

John Ramsden of Quarles & Widw. Gauthrop of Clayton Heights mar. Apr. 3

Daniel Sharp of Blakehill & Rose Burkbeck mar. Apr. 21

Joshua Smith servt. with Robt Booth at Landshead in Northourum & Jane Pierson mar. Apr. 21

Robt Porter near Halifax & Widw Farmer of Beverley mar. at York Apr. 24

John Williamson of Clack Heaton & Sarah d. of Edward Hanson near Wyke mar. June 3

Willm Bentley & Grace Denham (Mrs Crowthers old maid) mar. June 17

Joshua Kitson of Ossett & Alice Jagger mar. June 18

Mr. Heald Vicar of Huthersfield & Mrs. Walker mar abt. Midsummer

Timothy Gill o'th' Haigh mar. June 25

Mr Willm Moult minr at Call Lane Chappel in Leeds & Mrs Darling d. of Mr Crompton of Doncaster mar. June

John Nettleton & ——— Wilson of Ossett mar. July

Jeremy Bargh near Booth Town & ——— Ward near Ribbenden mar. July 14

Mr. Stancliffe Jackson of Gainsbrough & Mrs Hannah Ledgard of

MARRIAGES.

Chesterfield mar. July

John Popplewell of Heckinwyke & Eliza Jepson July 15

Mr Danl Bayley & Mrs —— dr. Nathl. Gaskell late of Manchester, married

Mr Birch s. of late Mr Birch minr at Manchester & —— dr Jonathan Lees of Manchester

Mr Thomas Bradbury minr in London mar. Mrs Mary Richmond Aug. 1, 1717

Joseph Westerman & Martha Pickerd of Ossett mar. Aug. 23

Willm Tomlinson of Alverthorpe & Mary Scott mar. Aug. 25

Mr Ebenr. Spencer of Hunslet & Mrs Bathshua Brooksbank of Eland mar. Sept.

Mr Richd Wood of ffold & Deborah d. of Widw. Ramsden of Quarles mar. Sept. 24

Mr George Town near Kin-Cross & Mrs Smith mar. Oct.

Daniel Bateman & Susan d. of James Wallis mar. Sept.

Moses Holdsworth of Northourum & Sibil dr. of —— Exley mar. Nov. 13

Willm. Priestley near Birstall & Hannah dr. of Mr. John Cooke of Halifax mar. at Coley Nov. 28

Christopher Brook near Clack-Heaton & Mary dr. of Joseph Priestley of White-Windows mar. Nov. 28

Richd. Clapham of Halifax & Judith Nicols of Eland mar. Dec. 5

John Ramsden of Park-Nook & Ruth Brigg mar. Dec. 24. at Leeds

Mr Richd Huntington & Mrs Eliza Wilson of Leeds mar Feb. 16

Mr Richd Milnes of Wakefield Junr. & Mr Pembertons dr. of Liverpool mar. Feb 18

Mr Robt Wood of ffold & Mrs —— Holdsworth of Astie mar. Feb. 28

Tho. Moss & Elizabeth Wm Stevenson's dr, of Ossett mar. Apr. 15

John Watkinson of Ovenden Moor & —— dr Abra. Kirshaw of Ovenden mar June 4.

Capt —— Samples & Mrs Sarah Gaskell of Manchester mar. May

Mr Lodge near Halifax & Mrs Rigg mar May

Mr. Tho. Bretcliffe & Mrs Byrom of Manchester mar June, abt 12th

Robt Johnson of Manchr. & Elizabeth d Mr John Birch of Ardick mar. at Gorton Chapel June 26

MARRIAGES.

Jeremiah Scholefield & Martha Smith mar. July 9, had liv'd servts with Wm. Wrights of Hipperholm

Stephen Holdsworth of Alverthorp & — Smith mar. abt June 11

Mr Saml Hollings of Allerton & Mrs Mary Wright of Hipperholm mar. at Woodkirk July 21 own sisters Children

Mr. —— Hodson of London & Mrs Jane Rooks of Royds Hall mar. Aug:

Mr. George Newson an Attorney in Lightcliffe & Mrs. — Willoughby near Bolton in Lancashire mar. Aug.

Saml. Appleyard of Shelf & Ellen Baraclough mar. Aug.

Mr Willm. Cornwall of Hull & Mrs. Sarah Brooksbank of Eland mar. Oct. 2

Mr. James Mallison Minr. at Holden & Mrs. Dorcas Almond of York mar. Sept. 2

Mr. Danl. Bentley Curate at Illingworth & Mrs. Elizabeth Wadsworth of Holdsworth mar. Oct. 28

John Naylor of Wareley & Elizabeth dr. Mr. John Farrar of Wareley mar. Nov. 5

Robt Kitson of Upper Brear & Anne d. Wm. Dean of Skircote mar. Jan. 1

Charles Best of Shelf & Mary d. Isaac Farrar of Wareley mar. Jan. 13

Edward Brook & Elizabeth Heaton near Coley Chapel mar. Jan. 13

Jonathan Brigg of Northourum & Grace Walker mar. Jan. 13

John Smith of Shelf & Mary Craven mar. Jan.

Mr Tho. Holden of Halifax & Mrs Martha Nettleton mar. Feb. 5

John Illingworth of Ossett & —— of Caspar mar. Mar. 30

John Hobson & Martha Dean of Cinderhills mar. Mar. 30

John Walker & Sarah d. John Bentley of Northourum mar. Mar. 30. 1719

Stephen Parker of Ossett mar Mar. 30

Mr Joseph Lumby of Pudsay & Hannah dr. of Wid. Wood of Bramley mar. Apr. 16

My Bro in Law Mr Joseph Foster & Hannah d. Mr John Farrar of Wareley mar. in Halifax Church Ap. 28

Mr Wm Rawson of Bradford & Jane d. of Mr Stockdale mar. Apr. 30

Mr, Midgley of Horton & Mrs Bathsheba Hollings of Bradford mar. May 21

MARRIAGES.

Jeremiah Whiteley & Mary d. Abra. Whitham of Northourum mar. May 24

Mr Fearnley & Mrs Lunns dr. both of Birstall mar. June 1

William Wigglesworth of Hunslet near Leeds & Sarah d. Wid. Hodgshon of Bowlin mar. June 8

William Tilson & Mary Bartle mar. July 7

George Wigglesworth & Ellen d. Abra. Naylor of Staups in Northouru. mar. July

Joseph Hanson & Sarah d. Joseph Wilkinson of Westercroft mar. Aug. 3

Mr Timothy Alred Minr at Morley & Mrs Mary Wilson Wid. near Hulm Firth mar. Sep. 24

Mr Sandford minr at Pomfret & Mrs Beans near Tadcaster mar.

Joseph Wood of Northourum & Mary d. John Howgate mar. Sep. 9

Josia Stansfeld & —— dr Matthew Wadsworth both of Sowerby mar. Sep. 10

Joseph Hall & Widw. Whitehead of Norland mar. Sep. 21

Saml Bentley of Shelf & Widw Philips of Howkins in Northourum mar. Sep. 22

John Sharp & Sarah Pollard of Northourum mar. Sep. 24

Joseph Smith & Rebecca Stevenson of Ossett mar. Oct. 25

Mr. John Stansfeld of Hough End in Sowerby & Mrs Elizabeth Jenkinson of Lime ditch, nr. Manchester mar Nov. 4

Dr. Colton, Minr in York & Mrs Anne d. Sr. Robt Dukinfield of Dukinfield mar. Nov. 19

Saml Webster & Eliz. d Widw. Clark both of Morley mar. Nov. 23

Abraham Naylor of Limedhouse in Northourum and Widw. Ogden of Sowerby mar. Dec. 16

Samuel Crowther, Landshead, Northourum and Martha Waon mar. Jan.

Abraham Foster of Bradford and Elizabeth d. Jeremiah Baxter of Northourum mar. at Halifax Jan. 12

James Mills and Wid. Mary Scholefield of Staups in Northourum mar. Feb. 15

Jeremiah Lupton & Mary d. Wid. Heald of Wakefield mar Mar. 14

John Coulborn and Mary Craven mar. Apr. 18

David Northen of High Bentley mar. Apr. 18

James Pierson and Wid Driver both of Landshead in Northourum mar. Apr. 20

Mr. Lineham of London and Mrs Anne Rooks of Royds Hall mar.

MARRIAGES.

at Wakefield Apr. 17

Saml Swift of Northourum and Anne Sonyer mar. May 12

Abraham Kirshaw of Ovenden and Jane d. Mr John Cooke of Halifax mar. May 19

Mr Benj. Naylor and Mrs Jane Percival of Manchester mar. May 25

Mr John Ferrand of Gainsbro' and Mrs Smith of Ailsby, May 26

Richd Lodge and Mary Futhergill of Ossett mar. June 6

Joseph Naylor of Dewsbury and Abra. Hemingway's dr. married May 12

Mr George Heald of Macclesfield and Mrs Eleanor d. of Madm Cotton of Haigh mar. July 28

Willm Jackson and Widw Hughes of Northourum mar. July 27

Tho. Kitson of High Sunderland and Elizabeth dr. Mrs Kighley mar. Aug. 3

Mr John Jepson of Dewsbury and my sister in law Mrs Mary Foster of Ossett mar. Aug. 11. 1720

Mr John Dobson minr at Ross in Herefordshire and Hannah d. Timothy Wood of Little Town mar. Aug. 18 1720

Richard North and Sarah Drake mar. Aug. 22. they live at Ossett

Luke Sutcliffe of Shelf Hall and Judith Richd Kirshaw dr. mar. Oct. 17

John Fozard and Anne Craven both near Dewsbury mar. Nov. 2

Mr Isaac Clegg of Manchester and Mrs Sarah Gream of Heath near Halifax, mar. Dec. 7

Mr Joshua Cordingley minr at East Wood and Sarah d. Mr. John Farrar of Wareley mar. Dec. 27. 1720

Mr John Mottershead and Mrs Margaret Gaskel of Manchester mar. this is her 3d husband and his 2d wife

Stephen Ambler of Shibden Head and Hannah Ramsden mar. Jan. 31, 1720

Jonathan Rawson of Rands near Halifax and Wid. Kitson mar. Apr. 18. 1721. She was wife to his late wife's brother

Joshua Smith of Northourum and Wid. —— mar. Apr. 20

Thomas Swaine, Bradford, and Mrs Susanna Simpson of Leeds mar. May 1

John Benn and Deborah Denton of Northourum mar. May 13

Mr Sam Hollings of Allerton and Mrs Sarah Wood of Bramley mar. May 15

John Gill of Southourum and Mary Rodes of Eland mar. June 22

MARRIAGES.

Jeremiah Northend and Mary Hartley near the Common Wood mar. June 27

James Kitson of Halifax and Martha d. Mr. John Cooke mar. July 13

Willm Ware Apprentice with Robt Kitson of Upper Brear and Sarah d. John Edwards of Halifax, mar. July: he 14 and she 13 year old and a half.

Mr Thomas Ferrand of Bradford and Mrs Wadsworth late wife of Mr Saml. W. of Flanshaw mar. July 25. 1721

Richd Wadsworth and Anne Witton Mr Jouath. Priestleys maid mar. Aug 24

John Sutliffe of Shelf and Martha Appleyard of Warley mar. Sep. 21. 1721

Mr Jeremiah Bairstow Minr. at Eland and Widow Martha Clay of Northourum mar at Coley Nov. 15

Mr. David Leech near Bingley and Mrs. Rachel ffenton of Hunslet mar. Dec. 19

Mr Rigby of Chowbent and Mrs. Rebecca Crompton of Old Hall mar. Nov. 28

Mr Spink of Wakefield and Mrs Eliza. Ingram mar. Jan. 3. 1721-2

Mr John Brooksbank of London and Mrs —— mar. Jan 16

Mr John Parr of Manchester and Mrs Phebe Crompton of old Hall in Prestwich Parish mar. Jan. 30

James Brook and Mary d. Wid. Woodhead of Whinnihall in Shelf mar. Feb. 4

Willm Ferguson and Mary Sheppard of Halifax mar. Febr. 6

Mr Ramsden of High Fearnley and dr. Sr. Walter Hawksworth mar. Mar. 9

Mr. Benjn. Foster my Bro. and Mrs Hannah Vaningbro mar. at New York Febr. 1

Mr Myers of Farffield near Skipton and Mrs Laycock near Halifax mar. Apr. 5 rich Quakers

John —— and Widw. Tempest of Common House in Halifax mar. Apr. 5

John Beans of Thorne near Wakefield and Anne Day (lately our maid) mar. Apr. 2

Mr. Saml Totty of Leeds and Mrs —— mar. Apr. 10

Willm. Crosley of Horton and Sarah Scholefield mar. May 10. She had been brot. up wth. John Sonyer

MARRIAGES.

Ebeuezer Heald of Wakefield and Sarah dr. of Mr. Wm. Lupton
mar. May

Mr Hoyle of Ribbenden and Mrs — Allison mar. June 13

Mr. Richd. Gilpin Lawrey of Broughton Tower in Lancra and
Mrs Faith dr. of Mr. Robert Stausfield of Bradford mar. June. 5

John Laycock near Skipton in Craven and ——— near Padiham
mar. May abt. 29

Mr John Piggles of Manchester and Mrs Brown mar. June 20

Mr. Feru Minr. in Derbyshire and Mrs Richardson of Sheffield
mar. July 25

Saml. Gargrave of Horton and Sarah Lea of Leeds (late of High-
Bentley) mar. Aug. 9

Nathl. Sutliffe of Shelf and Grace ——— mar. Sept 23

Mr. — Lightbown Minr. at Lostock in Cheshire and Mrs. Hannah
Kiblain of Batsworth in Yorkshire mar : Sept.

Mr. Crosley of Kirshaw-house near Luddenden and Mrs. Rawson
near Bradford mar. Oct. 22

Richd. Brown of Leeds and Susanna dr. Timothy Netherwood
mar. Sept. 23. 1722

John Rodes of Horton and Grace dr. John Learoyd of Northourum
mar. Oct. 3

Mr. — More of Kendall and Mrs. Anne Gream of Heath near
Halifax mar. Oct. 11

Joseph Healey of Wiskett-Hill and Mehetabel dr. John Bentley
of Northourum mar. Oct. 15

David Farrar of Warley and ——— dr. George Kitchingman of
Ovenden wood mar. Oct. 19

Dr John Heslope of White-Haven and Mrs. Mary Seal of old Hall
near Stand in Prestwich Parish mar. Nov. 14

— Hammond of Wibsey and Elizabeth Smith near Coley mar.
Nov. 29

Mr. Amor Rich of Bulhouse in Peniston Parish and Mrs. Grace
Bagshaw of Attercliffe mar. Dec. 4

Willm Brook of Hunslet and Mary d. Mr John Lister near Bradford mar. Jan 31. 172¾

Thomas Sleddall of Clayton and Wid. Dixon's dr. of Rochdale
mar. Feb. 19

John Ramsden of Wellhead by Halifax and Mrs Allison late of
Priestley Green mar. Feb. 23

Willm. Sutcliffe near Eastwood and Mary d. Joseph Wilkinson of

MARRIAGES.

Northourum mar. Febr. 26

John Crabtree and Grace Brook mar. Apr. 15

John Clayton near Wibsey and Hannah Crabtree of Shelf mar. May 21

Joseph Bottomley of Damhead in Northourum mar. June 3

Tho. Mellen of Halifax and Hannah d. Abra. Kirshaw mar. June 25

Mr Alexander Walker of Bolton and Martha d Mr. Edward Dewhirst of Bolton mar. June 2

John Booth of Northourum and Anne Beaumont of Almanbury mar. May 13

Mr Willm Greame of Heath by Halifax and Mrs Frances Kirk of Wakefield mar. at Thornhill, Aug. 6. 1723

Timothy Farrar son of Mr John F. of Warley and — Areton mar. abt. July 30

Joseph Naylor and —— mar. at London Aug. 7. left London the day following and came to live at Ossett where he was born

Joshua Hanson of Woodside near High Fearneley and Grace Iles widw, near Knaresbro' mar. Aug. 13

Mr Joshua Dobson Preacher near Rodes Hall and Elizabeth d. Mr. Smith of Mixenden mar. Aug. 28

Mr Jonas White of Allerton and Sarah d. Joshua Waddington of Bierley mar. Aug

Mr Robt Stansfield of Bradford and Mrs — Busfield mar. Sept. 3. 1723

Joshua Smith of Priestley Green and Widw. Mary Milner of Landimer Syke mar. Oct. 24

Mr Jonath Priestley of Winteredge and Mrs Hannah d. Mr Robt Milnes of Wakefield mar Oct. 29

Mr Jonth. Laycock near Halifax and Mrs ——, Quakers mar. Nov. 10

— Shoosmith and Martha —— mar. Nov. 18. She had bin servt with Wm. Sharp at Godley abt. 26 years

Willm. Sharp of Godley and Wid. Sarah Crowther of Landshead mar Nov. 30

John Scott of Halifax and Barbary Garnet of Tanhouse in Northourum, widw. mar. Nov. 30

James Wood and Susan Adam Wilson's dr. of Northourum Nov. 30

Mr. Stockdale a mercer in Halifax and —— dr. Mr. John Pres-

MARRIAGES.

cot of Halifax mar. Dec. 3

John s. Robt. Northend of Northourum and —— dr. Mr. Hemingway near Bradford mar. Jan.

John Bolton of Southourum and Catherine d. George Kitchingman of Ovenden mar. at Coley Feb. 9

Mr Thomas Clows of Manchester and Mrs Eleanor Taylor d. of Mr Richd. Taylor of London and brot. up with Mr. Richd Taylor of Manchester her step-grandfather were mar. Jan. 9. at Gorton Chapel

Robert Hardacre and Hannah d. John Elsworth of Rodley mar. Feb.

Mr —— Wilde an Apothecary in Nottingham and Eliza. d. Mr Heywood of Dronfield mar. Jan.

Mr James Huthwait minr. at Wareley and Phebe dr. Widw. Priestley of Westercroft mar. at Mansfield Mar. 31

Richd Roust and Susan d. Jeremiah Baxter of Northourum mar. Apr. 6

Mr Richard Clapham of Halifax and my sister in Law Mrs Elizabeth Foster of Ossett mar. at Thornhill May 6. 1724

Timothy Bentley and Sarah Scott both of Northourum mar. May 25

Mr William Lupton of Wakefield and Mrs Farrar of Robert Town mar. June. 29

Abraham Garras and Judith Viccars of Inghead in Northourum mar. June 16

Abraham Whitwham of Northourum and Mary Greenfield of Shelf mar. Aug. 18

John Appleyard of Shelf and —— near Hawarth mar. Aug. 24

Joseph Wilkinson of Westercroft and Mary d. John Learoyd of lower Brear mar. Aug. 27

Mr —— Smith and dr of James Alderson near Halifax mar. Sep. 3. She abt. 16 year old. She bare a child 6 weeks after

Mr Abraham Walker of Walterclough and Wid. Walker of Lightcliffe mar. Oct. 31

William Ingham of Warley and Grace d. Tho. Clark of Scout Hall mar.

John Booth, of Lightcliffe and Mary d. Mr. Jonath. Wright mar. Nov. 26

[James] Bury of Lee in Northourum and Sarah —— mar. Nov. 24

MARRIAGES.

Michael Hemingway of Halifax and Martha Mitchel mar. Dec. 1

Wm. Wood near Thornill Briggs and Mary Ingham formerly our maid mar. Jan. 13

Saml Stansfield of Horton and Lydia dr. Mr Sandford minr at Pontefract mar. Jan. 13

John Longbottom and Hannah Medley mar. Feb. 8

Richard ; aylor of Norland and Mrs Bathshua Town near Eland mar. Mar. 24

— Empson of Norwood Green and Hannah d. Elias Crosley mar Mar. 28

Richd Holdsworth and Sarah d. Elias Crosley mar. Mar. 29

William Charnock and Mary Ryley mar Mar. 30

Luke Hoile of Ovenden and —— dr. Mr. Thomas Holdsworth of Astie in Southourum mar. Apr. 3

Tho. Royston of Southourum and —— Peter Ambler's dr. mar. June. 8

Caleb Pierson of Allerton and Hannah dr. John Milnes of Northourum mar. June 14

John Craven and Mercy Armitage Servts. with Mr Jonathan Priestley of Winteredge mar. June 27

— Ambler of Shelf and Susan Stocks mar. June 29

Jeremiah Crowther of Northourum and Margaret dr. John Holroide of Hipperholm mar. July 15

Abraham Ashworth of Warley and —— mar. July 1. this the 6th wife

Mr —— of Manchester and Anne d. Mr Joseph Dawson minr in Rochdale mar. July 22. 1725

Mr Slater an Apothecary in Wakefield and Mrs Feather of South Cave mar. Aug. 3

John Kightley of Heckinwyke and Sarah d Joseph Priestley of Fieldhead near Birstall mar. Oct. 6

John Mann and Susan d. John Woodhead of Shelf mar. Aug. 21

Wm Wood of ffold in Northourum and dr John Nalson mar. Aug. 24

Mr Norton of Sawley near Knaresbro' and Mrs Furness of Halifax mar. Sept. 16

Jonath. Duckworth and Phebe Knight of Northourum Oct. 7

Mr Wright of Hull and Mrs Abigail Rotheram of Dronfield mar. Sept 12

Mr Braddock minr. in Bury and Mr Barron's dr. near Bury mar.

MARRIAGES.

Oct. 11 at Heywood Chapel
John Firth of Horton and Grace d. Mrs Blaymires of Halifax
mar. Nov. 1

Timothy Scott junr of Shelf and —— mar. Nov. 9

Mr Hodgson min. in Hull and Mr Moody's dr. of Doncaster mar.
Nov. 16

Mr Broughton Grocer in Wakefield and Grace dr. Widw. Wright
of Wakefield mar. Nov. 16

John Holdsworth of Sowood House and Mary dr. John Mortimer
of Shelf mar. Nov. 25

Jonathan Vicars of Halifax and Widw. Sarah Williamson of Mytham mar. Dec. 13

Mr. Tho. Farrar of Warley and Susan dr. Joseph Wilkinson of
Northourum mar. Feb. 16

Tho. Wilkinson of Westercroft and Elizabeth Story of th' Hough
in Northourum mar. Feb. 19

William Hanson of Britton Moor and Hannah Fox, Servt wth.
Mr Foster of Ossett. mar. Febr 22

Mr — Astley of Chowbent and Mrs Jane Dewhurst of Bolton mar.
Mar. 1

Joseph Scholefield of Halifax and Martha Sonyer of Warley-
green mar. Mar. 26. 1726

Abraham Clayton of Lee-lane in Northourum and —— mar.
June 16

Timothy Booth near Lands-head in Northourum and — mar.
June 23

Mr Joshua Jones Minr. at Manchester and Mrs — Walker mar.
July. 6

John Murgatroyd of Hipperholm lane Ends and Widw. Butterfield
near Halifax mar. Aug 9

— Armitage and Mary Whitley mar. abt. Oct. 16

Sarah Milner of Ossett married Nov. 16

Saml. Drake schoolmaster at Horbury married Nov. 19

Willm. Jackson of Northourum and Elizabeth Wales married
Nov. 27

John Smith and Mary d. John Ambler, Shibden Head, mar. Apr

Mr Robt Milnes of Wakefield and Mrs Sarah Priestley of Ovenden mar. at Coley May 12

Mr Joseph Sutton and Mrs Lepton of Hunslet Lane mar. May 4

Mr Richd Cooke of Halifax and Baptista d. of Mr Robert Milnes

MARRIAGES.

of Wakefield mar. May. 18

Mr. Clough of Leverpool and Mrs Judith d. Sr. Robt Dukinfield mar. abt middle of May

Joseph Askew of Northourum and Grace Walker mar. May 23

John Dickenson of Northourum mar. June 18

Samll Wilson of Halifax and Widw Medley of Hipperholm mar. June 19

Mr Abraham Sharp of Hipperholm and Mrs Anne Walker of Walterclough mar. June 22

William Laycock of Shelf and — Laycock mar. June 27. Brother's children

Mr James Ingham of Halifax and Elizabeth d. Wid. Priestley of Northourum mar. July 5

Tho. Settle near Hipperholm and Mary Hutcheson servt. with Mr. Priestley of Winteredge mar. July 27

John Hodgson of Bradford and — d. of Mr Tho. Leach of Kighley mar. Aug. 17

Isaac Wilkinson of Westercroft and Sarah Lister of East Morton near Bingley mar. Sep. 5

Tho. Morhouse near Hulm Firth and Mrs. Earnshaw mar. at Halifax Sep. 27

Francis Stapleton and Dorothy d. Mr Isaac Sharp of Horton mar. Oct. 24

Mr Allanson near Halifax and Mr Markin's of Willow Hall mar. Dec. 28, or 26

Obadiah Hollings of Allerton and —— of Birstall mar. Jan. 10

John Walker of Bradford and Martha d. Mr. Wright of Lightcliffe mar. Jan. 12

Mr Kennet Vicar of Bradford and Mrs — Stockdale mar. abt. Feb. 1.

Mr Saml Hanson minr at Ossett and my sister in Law Mrs Mary Jepson mar. at Wakefield Feb. 1

Mr — Hoile of Lightcliffe and Mrs Deborah Wood of Field in Northourum mar. at Coley Feb. 6

John Settle of Northourum and Mary d. Timothy Booth mar. Feb. 16

— Fletcher of Horton and Martha d. John Mortimer of Shelf mar Feb. 23

Mr John Buck minr. at Idle and Mrs — Morhouse mar. Feb. 28

Andrew Hodgson of Horton and — Thornton mar. Feb. 21

MARRIAGES.

Mr John Simpson and Mrs Dorothy Sharp of Hipperholm mar. Mar. 4

Abra. Scott of Hough in Northourum and Esther Learoyd mar. Apr. 1

Abra. Lee and — Smith mar. Apr. 3

Richd Waddington and Esther Sutcliffe of Shelf mar.

Timothy Askew and Mary Ingham of Northourum mar. Jan. 22

Timothy Binns and Mary Holdsworth of Northourum mar. Mar. 4

Nathan Netherwood and Phebe Threapland near Northourum mar. Mar. 4

Dr. of James Gregson of Northourum mar. June 8

Isaac Nicolls of Eland and Hannah d. Robt. Northend of Northourum mar. July 23

Joseph Scott of Shelf mar. July 17.

Joseph Booth of Northourum and Anne Coppindale mar. July 25

Mr Joseph Rayner and Judeth Drake of Leeds mar. Aug 5.

— Robinson of Halifax and Mary d. of Abraham Kirshaw mar. Aug. 31 unknown to her parents

John Willis of Wakefield and Mary late wife of Mr. Lister minr at Kipping afterwards wife of Mr Richmond minr at Clack Heaton, mar. Sep. 18

William Ingham of Ossett and Mary d. Wid. Smithson mar. Oct. 17

William Thomas and Wid. Hill of Northourum mar Nov. 2

Mr Thomas Wolrich and Mrs Kitching of Leeds mar. Dec. 5

Mr Gamaliel Brear of Eland and Mrs Mary Lodge mar. Dec. 8

Mr Richd Scolefield Preacher at Whitworth and Elizabeth d. Mr Dawson Minr. in Rochdale mar. Jan 8. 1728

Mr Sutton of Ribchester and Sarah d. Wid. Spencer near Shipden Hall mar. Apr. 2. about 17 years of age either.

— Thorp and Mary d. Joseph Gargrave of Horton mar. Apr. 6, 1729

Jeremy Wood and — dr Willm Gray of Shelf mar. Apr. 7

Willm Rous and Ellen Cowper (servts at Rodes hall) mar. May 12

Willm Hodgson of Holdsworth and Rachel Wilkinson his Housekeeper mar. May 21.

Oliver Gray of Shelf and Mary Deykin mar. May 26. (she not 13 year old and half.)

Grotius Clifford of Shelf and Mary Wood mar. May 27

MARRIAGES.

Thomas Rotheram mar. May 27

Tho. Cagill and Elizabeth d. Jonath. Stead of Halifax mar. June 19

Mr John Wainman minr at Pudsay mar. Mrs Sarah Hollings of Bramley June 26

Paul Greenwood of Southourum and — Blackburn of Dewsbury mar. July 3.

Mr Knox Ward of Hackney and Eliza d. Doctr Nettleton of Halifax mar. July 22

Mr Richd Hampson of Rochdale and Mrs Martha Holden (Dr Nettleton's sister) mar. Aug. 21

Mr Michl Gibson of Sladehall and Widw. Dade mar. Sept. 18

Joseph —— of Thornton and Mary d. of Dr. Firth of Kipping mar. Sept 3

— Parkinson of Craven and Wid. Tenant of Halifax mar. Sep.

Joshua Williamson of Clack Heaton and Judith Viccars of Halifax mar. Sep

— Hanson of Woodside near Wyke and Anne Wood of Bramley mar. Dec. 17

Willm. Hird and Martha Bairstow of Shelf mar. Jan. 13

— Longbottom of Northourum mar. Feb. 9

Mr — Alwood of Chesterfield and Mrs Eliz. Robinson of Gainsbro' mar. Febr.

Mr. — White of —— and Mrs. Mary Waterhouse near Chappel in Firth mar. Febr.

Mr. — Thompson Minr. at Knaresbro' and — dr. Mr. Sandford Minr. in Pontefract mar.

Mr. Hananiah Elston Minr. at Malton and Mrs. Lydia Hollings of Allerton mar. Apr. 15

Mr. Jonathan Priestley. of Winteredge and Mrs. Martha Reevley of Leeds. mar. May. 7

Joseph Wilkinson and Elizabeth Binns of Northourum mar. May 18

John Sharp and Martha —— of Northourum mar May 19

Mr Nathanl Priestley of Northourum and Mrs Haunah Holden of Halifax mar. at Coley Chap. June 18

Sr John Kay of Woodsome and Mrs —— dr. of Doctor Richardson of Bierley mar. July 28

— Oldroyd of Dewsbury moor and Ruth **Fox** near **Reavy** mar. July 27

MARRIAGES.

Joseph Wilkinson and Mary Clay of Northourum married Oct. 26

Mr. John Lambert Powell and Abigail Mr. Wainman's dr. of Bingley mar. Oct. 30

Tho. Lister near Leeds and Mary Elsworth dr. of John E. late of Rodley married abt. ay 20

Mr Benjn. Cooke of Halifax and Miss — Lawton of Rochdale married June 17

Mr Richd. Taylor of Norland and Mrs Mary Tetlaw mar. July 1

John Conway and Elizabeth Bentley mar. July 5

John Towers and Martha Kirshaw of Halifax mar. July 27

Isaac Hodgson of Leeds and —— mar. Aug. 10

Jonathan Duckworth of Northourum and —— mar. Aug. 12

Peter Naylor of Wakefield and Bithia Lister Dr Nettleton's maid mar. Aug. 5

James Parkins & Hannah Bentley of Northourum mar. Aug. 15

Jeremy Stocks & Susanna Gregson of Northourum mar. Oct. 12

John Bentley of Northourum & Wid. Duckworth mar. Oct. 19, 1731

John Brigg & —— of Northourum mar. Oct. 28

Mr Edmund Brigg of Halifax and his maid servt. mar. Nov. 11.

Jonas Cotes & —— married Nov. 11

Joshua Best of Godley and Eliza. d. of Elkanah Wirral of Booth Town mar. Nov. 21

John Flather and Grace Greenwood servts. with John Clay of Northourum mar. Jan. 13

Mr Tho Rayner and —— dr of Mr. John Cagill mar. Febr. 3

Samll. Appleyard and Martha Oddy mar Feb. 25

Willm Rushorth and Susanna Moorhouse mar Feb.

Mr. Robuck near Wakefield and Elizabeth d. Mr John Maude of Wakefield mar. Febr. 26

Mr. Shelmerdine and Mrs Eliz. Upton (Mr Richard Taylor's Niece of Manchester) mar. Oct. 28

James Hemingway and —— dr. of William Hodgson of Holdsworth mar. May 7

Mr Tho. Lax minr. at Topliffe and —— mar. June 27.

Tho. Gant, apprentice with Mr George Green of Leeds and —— dr of Widw. Priestley of Leeds mar. May. 15

Mr. Stackhouse Curate at Sowerby Brigg and Widw. Butterfield of Halifax mar. June 25

Robert Nalson and Martha d. Jonath. Longbottom of Booth

o

MARRIAGES.

Town mar. at Coley June 26

James Fletcher of Halifax and Wid. Thornton mar. June 28

Mr John Brook youngest son of Sr Tho. Brook of Norton in Cheshire and Lady Egerton of Heaton near Manchester mar.

Mr Joseph Brooksbank of Eland and Mary d. of Mr Smith of Mixenden mar. at Cockey Chapel in Lancashire Aug. 10

— Hall of Southourum and Mary I'anson mar. Aug 17

Mr James Hardman of Rochdale and Mrs —— eldest dr. Mr. George Leigh of Utrington in Cheshire mar. Oct. 19

Mr Richard Totty of Leeds and Mrs Markham of Leeds mar. Mar. 21

Benjamin Wilkinson and Elizabeth Craven of Westercroft in Northourum mar. May 22. 1733

James Robinson and — Sutliffe of Shelf mar. May 24

Jonas Pierson of Landshead in Northourum and Anne Brigg near Coley married June 24

Mr. James Huthwaite Minr. at Buttershaw and Mrs. Sarah Bristow mar. at London Aug. 27. 1733

Edward Ledgard and Anne dr. Widw. Gill near Brighouse mar. Sep. 23

Abram Kirshaw and —— dr. Mr James Haslam of Rochdale mar. Oct. 23

Mr. James Tetlaw and —— dr. Mr. Charles Radcliffe of Eland mar. Nov. 27

Richd. Hardacre of Crag and Alice dr. Solomon Holdsworth of Northourum mar. Dec. 20

Mr. John Holdsworth Curate at Coley Chapel and Mary dr. Widw. Lister of Halifax Free School mar. Jan. 27

Mr. Stern of Woodhouse near Halifax and Widw. Swaine of Bradford mar Febr. 21. May

Mr. Tho : Rigg of Savil-Green near Halifax and Widw. Taylor of Norland mar. Febr. 21

Mr. — Hays — and Jane dr. Mr. John Whitaker Minr. at Manchester mar. Febr. 21

Richard Tattersall and Dorothy —— mar. Febr. 25. They hath both been Servts. at Winteredge

Abel Aykroyd and Mary dr. John Best of Godley mar. Febr. 26

William Charles Henry, Prince of Orange and Princess Anne eldest dr. of King George the 2d mar. Mar. 14

John Sutliffe and Mary Scott of Northourum mar. Apr. 15

MARRIAGES.

Jeremy Ellenthorp & Martha Laycock of Northourum mar. Apr. 15

Caleb Ashworth of Northourum & Mary Farrar mar. May. 2

Isaac Farrar of Wareley (Tho's son) mar. June 5

Martha Cordingley servt. with Mr. Huthwait mar. June 6

James Scholefield & Mary Bairstow of Northourum mar. July 20

Joseph Dean of Hud-hill in Northourum & — Firth mar. Aug. 31

Thomas Ramsden & Abigail Flather of Hipperholm mar. Sept. 12

John Hartley & Mary Low of Northourum mar. Sept. 16

Tho. Kitson of Clack-Heaton & Dinah Tattersall of Onlyhouse in Northourum mar. Oct. 14

Mr — Showers of Sheffield & Mrs Diggles of Manchester mar. at Horbury Church Oct. 16

Mr Hugh Marshall & Mrs Eliz. Oates of Leeds mar. Oct. 17

Sr Ralph Assheton of Middleton & Mrs Egerton eldest dr. of the late Lady Egerton of Heaton mar. Oct. 3

Obadiah Scholefield of Southourum & Widw. Bolton mar. Nov. 7

Joshua Sowden & Hannah Wood of Thornhill Briggs mar. Nov. 28

Mr John Farrar of Wareley & Mrs — Robinson, mar. at Bolton, Dec. 10

Theophilus Wood of Thornhill Briggs & Widow Low of Northourum mar. Jan. 13

My Son John Dickenson & Brilliana Wall mar. in London Nov. 7

John Wilkinson of Northourum & Sarah d. Robt. Forness of Maningham mar. at Bradford Jan. 22

John Wakefield of Southourum & Sarah d. John Ramsden of Park Nook mar. Apr. 7

Mr John Daniel of Leeds & Mrs Sarah Priestley of Northourum mar. Apr. 10

Mr. Tho. Whitaker minr. in Leeds & Mrs Elizabeth Darling mar. May 12

Benjamin Souwood Clark at Northourum & Hannah Higson mar. May 26

Mr John Burton of Leeds & Mrs Sarah Revely mar. at Chapel ith' Briers June 12, 1735, 100,000li left him lately by an uncle

John Pollard of Lee in Northourum & Jane Gledhill mar. at

MARRIAGES.

Illingworth June 13
Sam Sheppard of Northourum & Patience Baraclough mar.
   Aug. 4
— Higgins of Southourum & Sarah Bromit mar. Aug. 4
Nathanll. Vicars of Halifax & — Scholefield of Southourum mar.
   Aug.
Mr. Robt. Hill & Mrs. — Barnard of Leeds mar. Sep. 18
Tho. Thorp of Dumb Mill & Judeth Haigh of Marsh mar at
   Batley Sept. 21
Mr Chorley minr. near Eccles & Mrs Jane Dukinfield dr. of the
   late Sr Robert Dukinfield mar. Oct. 2
Elkanah Worrall & Grace Crosley Oct. 8
— Scott and Mary Ramsden of Northourum mar. Nov. 6
Jonathan Benn of Northourum & Susan. Hemingway mar.
   Nov. 24
Joseph Wood of Bramley & Miss Dobson mar. Dec.
Joshua Hardcastle of Great Woodhouse & Eliz. Wood of Bramley
   mar.
Thomas Wallis & Mary Mallison of Northourum married
   Feb. 11
John Woodhead of Shelf mar. Feb. 19
Mr — Brookshaw near Stockport in Chesbire and Susanna d. Mr
   Joshua Lea of Sowerby married Feb. 26
Joshua Souwood and Mary Scholfield of Southourum married
   Mar. 9
Frederick Prince of Wales and Augusta Princess of Saxe-Gotha
   mar. at London Apr.
Robt Butterfield and — dr Mr James Alderson mar. at
   Halifax May 6
Tho. Oldfield of Stocklane in Warley and — Akill of High
   Sunderland mar. May 2
David Clark of Alverthorp and M— Adkinson of Bradford mar.
   May 4
Thomas Dickenson my son and Mrs Sarah Sykes mar. in Coley
   Chapel by Dr Legh the Vicar of Halifax May 27. 1736.
Timothy Speight of Hipperholm and Anne Pierson of Northourum
   mar. June 13
John Sheppard and Elizabeth Fletcher of Northourum mar.
   July 22
John Binns and Susan Bairstow of Blackmyrs in Northourum

MARRIAGES.

mar. Sep. 26
Mr — Fisher of Amsterdam in Holland and Mrs Rachel Revely of Leeds mar at York Sep. 30. 1736.

Thomas Drake & Esther Scott of Northourum mar Oct. 10

Henry Ibbetson of Leeds Esqre. was mar. to Miss Foljamba dr. Francis Foljamba near Rotheram Esqr Dec. 23 ; a young Lady of great Beauty merit & Fortune (tis said)

Mr John Martin & Miss Chamberlaine mar. Jan. 6 & Ephraim Winne & Miss Prescot mar. Jan. 12. at Halifax

William Sheppard of Northourum & Ellen Sargisson near Skipton mar. May

John Scholefield & Sarah Scholefield mar. May. 30

Benjamin Jaggar & Sarah Bateman

— Walton of Heckinwyke & Abigail Akeroyd of Northourum mar. June. 2

— dr. Timothy Dixon of Green-lane in Northourum mar. June

Abel Wadsworth of Northourum and Martha Firth mar. June. 27

Sr. Henry Houghton of Houghton Tower Bart. and Miss Butterworth of Manchester mar. in London July. 11. 8000 li. Fortune

James Piccles near Leeds and Mary Moor of Northourum married July 29

William Wilkinson and Susanna Roust married July 28

Mr Smith Curate of Wibsey and Mrs Beaumont of Whitley Hall mar. abt. middle. July

Daniel Sharp and Mary Hird of Northourum married Aug. 17

Joseph Drake and Esther Oddy mar. Aug. 30

Mr Thomas Farrar Minr in Wareley and Hannah Wilkinson mar. Nov. 1

— Bramley and Mary Saml. Hall's dr. of Halifax mar. Dec. 1

John Bower near Bradford and Mary d. Mr Saml. Hulme of Horton mar. Jan 2

Mr John Milnes of Wakefield and Miss Shower of Sheffield mar. Feb. 8

Mr John Ramsden of Southourum and Mrs Helliwoll of Pykehouse near Littlebrook mar. Febr. 14

Jeremy Rookes of Shelf and Widow Brook of Wibsey mar. Mar. 22

Joseph Hollings of Cottingley and Miss Marshall near Rawden mar.

John Askew Junr of Northourum and Sarah d. Widw Learoyd of

MARRIAGES.

Lenthrop Mill near Thornton mar. Apr 30

Willm. Firth and Sarah Carlton of Northourum mar. May 22

Edmund Woan and Hannah Worrall of Northourum mar. June 15

Mr Willm. Lupton of Wakefield and Mary Crowther his maid Servt. mar.

Mr Tho. Gream of London and Miss Lucy Hodshon of Wandsworth in Surrey mar. Aug. 10

Dr Dearden and Miss Stead d. of Mr Valentine Stead of Halifax mar. Oct. 25

John Hobson near Coley and Sarah d. John Mortimer of Shelf , mar. Nov. 9

— Ainesley and Rachel Conder of Leeds mar. Dec. 19

Nathl Longbottom and Susanna Brierley mar. Dec. 25

John Jewet and Martha Peel of Northourum mar. Dec. 26

Mr Bawdin an Excise Man and — dr of John Taylor of Gummersall mar. Jan. 7

Mr Thomas Jackson of London & my dr. Elizabeth Dickenson mar. Apr. 16

Mr William Clay of Northourum & Mrs Eliza Conder mar. at Hunslet near Leeds May 30

Mary Wilkinson of Holdsworth, widow mar. her servant John Mitchel June 17

— Robinson & Deborah Ingham of Northourum mar. July 1

John Holdsworth & Rebecca Peel of Northourum married Aug. 23

Mr Edmund Brigg of Halifax & — Haworth mar. Aug. 16

James Scholefield & Mary d. John Askew of Northourum married Dec. 25

Mr Walker of Crow Nest in Lightcliffe & Miss Wainhouse of Pye Nest near Halifax mar. abt Dec. 25

—— Bingley & Elizabeth Moss mar. Jan. 28

John s. of Danl. Sharp of Barnshill & Sarah d. John Drake of Wall Close, Northourum, married Apr. 7. 1740

Samuel Holdsworth & Mary Scholefield mar. Apr, 30

George Farrar & Mary Moor mar. Apr. 30

Mr John Aldred minr. in Wakefield & Miss Mary Naylor mar. May 15.

Mr Robt Lumb of Silkcotes & Mrs Hannah Foster of Flanshaw mar. June 5.

Mr John Lea of Sowerby & Mary d. Mr Milnes of Salford mar. July 3. 1740

MARRIAGES.

David Maun near Hipperholm & —. Mr John Jackson of London (my Son in Law Bro.) and Miss Arrowsmith mar. abt middle of Sept.

Joseph Moor of Ovenden & — dr widw Stansfield of Sowerby mar. Oct 8.

Nathl Sowod & Sarah Medley near Northourum mar. Oct. 9

Mr. Nathl. Denison of Leeds & Miss Huis of Nottingham mar abt Nov. 1

Mr. Abram Milner & Mary dr. of the Late Martin Fielding, a bookseller in Halifax mar. Jan. 13

Willm. Chetham & —— mar. Jan. 13

Mr. John Smith Minr. at Mixenden & —— dr. Mr. — Fox of Prestwich Parish in Lancre. mar. Dec.

Edward Rookes of Rodes Hall Esqre. & Miss Leeds of Milford near Tadcaster mar. Mar. 10

John Marshall of Idle & Miss Jobson of Hull mar. at Sowerby Apr. 6. 1741

Mr. — Gibson of Slede Hall & —— dr. Mr. Thompson of Stancliffe mar. Apr.

Mr. Evan Stock Minr. at Clackheaton & Miss Mary Kitson of Syke mar. May. 5

Joshua Hardcastle of Great Woodhouse near Leeds & Miss Jane Roades near Bradford mar. June

Mr. Henry Ibbetson & Miss —— of Durham mar. abt. Sept. 20

Mr. John Milnes near Bolton & Miss Davenport of Little Lever. mar. Sept.

Mr. Thomas Oates of Leeds & Miss — Watson of Hull mar. Oct. 13

Mr. Benjamin Ingham of Ossett, a noted Methodist & Lady Margaret Hastings were married Nov. 12

Mr George Oates of Leeds & Miss — Jollie of Manchester mar. Feb.

Mr Willm. Naylor of Wakefield & Miss Mary Marsh of Bilbrough married March 25

Mr. — Dawson of Morley & Miss —— Gainsbro' mar. June 5

Joshua Ryley & Martha Worrall of Northourum mar. June. 9

Mr. Wm. Ferguson & Miss. Green of Leeds mar June 10

Mr. John Grimshaw & Miss Elizabeth Jepson dr. of my Sister in Law Mrs. Hanson of Gorton mar. June. 10. 1742

Mr. Joseph Mottershead Minr. at New Chapel in Manchester &

MARRIAGES.

Mrs. Blackmoor of Worchester mar. June

Mr. Tho. Wright Curate at Halifax & Miss Hartley mar. Aug. 10

Mr. Freeman Flower of Gainsbro' & Miss Anne Dawson of Leeds mar. at Armley Chapel Sept 22. 1742

Mr. — Seddon Minr. in Manchester & Miss —— dr. Mr. Mottershead Minr. in Manchester mar. Febr

Mr Robinson of Lincoln & Miss Cornwell of Hull mar. at London

Mr Isaac Hanson of Halifax & Miss Kay of Radcliffe Parish in Lancashire mar. Mar. 22

Sarah d. Danll. Sharp mar. at Halifax Apr. 28. 1743

Mr Tho. Lee of Leeds & Miss Margret Markham mar. abt. Apr. 12. 1743

Mr Richd. Foster of London my wife's Nephew and Miss —— mar.

Mr Farrar of Ewood & Miss — dr. of Sr. Saml. Armitage of Kirkleys married Oct. 15

Mr John Edwards of Northourum & Mrs. Hargreaves of Craven married Oct. 12. 1743

Mr Richd Whitaker & Mrs Hodgson of Bradford mar. Nov. 22. 1743 a widow wth. 5 Children

Mr R. Welch & Miss Han. Dickenson of London mar. Aug. 27. 1746 at Botofs near Bishops Gate, London

Jas. Harriott & Mary Dickenson of London mar. Sep. 29. 1747

Benjamin Dickenson and An Pendlebury mar. 26 Febr. 1744-5 at Leeds p. Vickar Cookeson

Joseph Wilkinson and Sarah Ingham of N. Ourum mar. at Coley 27 Feb. 1750

James Waddington and Mary Ramsden at Illingworth March 27th, 1750· [He died 19th Sept. 1784]

Joseph Walker and my servt. maid Hannah Peel mar. 5 Apr. 1790   B. D—.

Revd John Houghton of Norwich married Augt. 3d, 1790 to Mrs Eliz Reddy at Yarmouth.   He 60, she abt. 40 yrs old

Benj. Dickenson and Hannah Howorth of Halifax married there 6th Augt, 1792, by the Rev. Mr. Frank, Curate, He 73, and she 45

Wm. Dickenson and Nelly Pollard were married at Worcester the 19 Jan. 1796

BURIALLS.

Dr Richardson of North Bierly buried his wife abt Oct 25. 1702. She was only child of Mr. Crosley of Kirshaw-house died in Child bed, aged abt 19, the child surviv'd her but 27 days. Her name, Sarah : the child Richard

Simon Stern Esq (Justice of Peace) buried at Halifax Apr 17. 1703 having undergone a severe Salivation for a cancer in the mouth

Daughter of James Stansfield bur. at Sowerby 1702

Alice Holt (mother to Timothy Holt) bur. ffebr 1702

Old Josia Stansfield of the Breck in Sowerby bur. at Sowerby Mar. 23. 1702

Mr Robert Gledhill of Woodkirk bur. at the burying place near Tingley July 21, 1703

Wm. Cotton Esq, of Haigh Hall died May 6

Old Mrs Gaskell of Clifton buried out of Salford

Mr John Crompton minr at Cockey buried

Anthony Lea of High Bently bur. at Halifax, Sep 28 1703

Alice wife of Saml. Holdsworth bur. at Halifax Sep. 29. 1703

Robert Walker of Bingley died Sept. 30. 1703

Mrs. Gaukroger the minr of Hawarths widow. bur. at Halifax, Oct 14. 1703

Wm. Snowden Oct 15, (called Brass.)

John Bland of Norwoodgreen bur. at Halifax Nov. 20. 1703

Old Mrs. Gartside of Prestwich bur. there Nov 8

Wife of Timothy Stansfield bur Nov. 24 1703

Mr. Rich Wainhouse of the Pye Nest buried his wife Jan. 10. 1703

Mr John Allison of Ovenden bur. his little dr. Judith from Mr. Langleys of Hipperholm, Dec 22, 1703

Mr John Haliwel Curate & Schoolmaster at Middleton buried

Mary wife of Nathan Tilson buried Jan. 26, 1703

Mr John Hind, ffellow of Manchester, bur.

Saml Robuck bur. his wife at Lightcliffe Jan 31. 1703

Robt Snowden of Hanging Royd bur. Febr. 11, 1703, died at Dr. Threaplands

Mr. Ellison of Toxteth Park near Liverpool died of the Small

BURIALS.

Pox was bur. ffebr 25. a young man of abt. 200 li p. ann.

Mr. Butler of Bradford (Attorney) bur. Mar. 2

Mr Jones (landlord at ye Cock in Halifax) bur. Mar. 10

Mr Joshua Lacock the Quaker near Halifax bur. his wife Mar. 13

Mr John Ardern of Redish near Gorton (my faithfull ffriend and hearer) died in Stockport, buried April 2. 1704

Mrs Valentine of Salford widow bur Apr 4. 1704

Thomas Dickenson Esq of Salford (had bin Justice of Peace) buried Apr. 10. 1704

Richard Bold of Bold Esq, being Parliament-man for Lancashire bur. Apr.

Mr Hamor Junr. near Rochdale died at Liverpool. bur. Apr. 12. 1704

John Northen near Northourum bur Apr 19, 1704

Wife of Saml Shepard of Green lane near Northourum bur. Apr. 22

Mrs Esther dr. to Mr Byron Vicar of Bradford died suddenly of a Palsie fitt, May 6. 1704

George ffarrar Landlord of the Common house in Halifax, bur. May 10 1704

John Radcliffe of Haugh End near Sowerby Bridge bur. May 15. 1704

Widow Snowden of Hanging Royd died in Southourum May 16, 1704

Mr Naylor of Halifax bur May 17

Susanna d. to Mr Joshua Crompton near Stand of Pilkington died May 7. 1704 was at chappel twice yt day & writ Sermon

Mr. John Bowker a mercer in Manchester (my kinsman) died May 21. 1704

Joseph s. John Lairod in North-ourum died May 25, 1704

Mr Hurst, Alderman of Stockport bur. May 22, 1704

Richard Lister the Carrier of Harshod Moor died May 29

Wife of John Marshall buried at Coley Chappel June 2. 1704

Mr. George Birch of Birch Hall, near Manchester, High Sheriffe of Lancashire buried June 3. 1704

Jeremiah Swift of Northourum bur. June 17. 1704

Mr. Thomas Dixon Minister near Durham died May 29, 1704

Mr Beaumont of Whitley Hall died June 27, 1704, aged 27, left an Estate of 1500li p. an.

Benjamin Stocks school master at Northourum died suddenly in an Epileptic fit July 1. 1704, a young man

BURIALS.

Mrs Assheton wife to Parson Assheton of Prestwich died in child-
bed July 20. 1704, aged about 20, this being the 3d child
Mrs Kitchingman of Skircote green (wife to Mr. Wm. Kitching-
man) my kinswoman died of a Pluresie July 28, 1704, abt half
hour after ffive in the morning being ffriday, aged abt 58
Mrs Crompton (widow to Mr John Crompton Minr at Cockey
Chappel bur. July 21
Mrs Mary Wroe, a young woman, near Oldham bur. July 26.
1704
Robt Priestley near Halifax, an old man, bur there Aug. 21, 1704
Mary wife of John Simpson died in child bed Aug. 23. 1704 aged
abt 20, this the first child
Mr JohnDickenson of Gildersom bur Aug. 22. 1704
Mr Bentey near Brighouse bur. his wife Aug.
Mr John Heywood minister at Pontefract died at Mr Stacy's of
Dalifield near Sheffield, was buried at Hansworth Sept 6.
1704 aged 48 years & abt 20 weeks
Mrs Cagill died in childbed (her Husband being at Sturbridge
ffair) bur. at Halifax Sept 10. 1704
John Holdsworth of Northourum died Sept. 13
Mr Cotes Minr at Mansfield died Sept. 12 aged 47 & a little more
Mrs Heald (Mr.Heald of Huthersfield mother) bur. Nov. 1. 1704
Mrs Hall near Halifax bur Oct 31. 1704
Mr. Nathl Heywood minr at Ormskirk died Oct 26. 1704
Mrs Hannah Chorlton (wife to Mr John Chorlton Minr at Man-
chester) died Nov. 3. 1704
Mr Henry Finch Minr near Manchester bur. Nov. 16. 1704 aged
abt 71
Jonathan Threapland died Nov 22, 1704, aged near 82
Susanna Dickenson (my own cousin) bur. Dec 6 1704
[Michl Scholefield] The Cardmaker's wife of Norwood green
died Dec. 8
Richard Mason of Ratcliffe Bridge died, an old disciple, aged abt
91
Mrs Mitchel (sister to Mr Rich. Wainhouse of Pye Nest) bur
Dec. 19
Mr. Baraclough near Halifax Dec. 20
Grace Bentley of Lightcliffe Dec. 27
Nathan Wood near Baitings bur. Dec 25. aged 108
Mary Kirshaw near Oldham bur. Jan. 1

BURIALS.

Mr Wilkinson Minr at Illingworth died Jan. 4, aged 64 had bin Minr there 40 years

Tho. Gledhill near Coley Chapl died Jan 5

Dr John Sharp of little Horton died Jan 10. bur Jan 15. aged abt 30

Thomas Rhodes of Horton d. Jan. 12

Mr. Ash an Attorney in Manchester bur Jan 20

Hannah Dickenson (my dear & onely sister) died Jan 20, was buried Jan. 24, 1704, abt 36 and half

Mr Peter Heywood of Manchester died Jan. 27

William Clay of Northourum died Jan. 28, aged 71

Lieutenant Sharp of little Horton was buried ffebr 8, aged abt 92

Samuel Crowther of Dam Head in Northourum died ffebr 25; was seized in the chapel ffebr 18 aged 50

— Surridge near Coley Chap died ffebr. 24

Jane wife of   Ainsworth in Hipperholm died in Child-bed March 4

Grace (late wife to the aforesd Saml) Crowther died Mar. 5. was seized ffebr 26, as her husband was with a pain in the side, both died that day sevenight after

Mrs Prescot wife to Dr Prescot of Halifax died Mar. 10. 1704

Mr Dean Curate at Huthersfield, Mar.

Mr Dickson of Leeds died Mar 28. 1705 (Mrs Ray's Father)

Mr Midgeley of Halifax bur. at Luddington Apr. 6. aged abt 25

Thomas Whitley of Lane Ends near Hipperholm died Apr 8

Mr John Hough near Leeds bur. his wife Apr 14, bur. a child Apr. 12

Mr Tho. Wainman bur. his little daughter Apr 17

Mr Joseph Yates of Manchester Lawyer, had bin Justice of Peace died

Mr Roger Anderton minr at New-Castle upon Tyne died : born in Lancashire near Bolton, had bin sevl years at White Haven remov'd to N. C. scarse half a year before Death

George Oldfield near Shipden Head buried his wife May 4

Widow Whitley of Lane Ends in Hipperholm died May 4

Leopold the Emperor of Germany died May 5, aged 65

Mr Hen. Ramsden near Eland died suddenly coming to Halifax M. 12

Hannah (wife to John) Bentley of Bradford died May 16

Mr John Chorlton minr at Manchester buried May 19 ; an unspeakable loss to that Town & to the Church of God

Old Mrs Fournes died May 24

Mr Robt Miln of Rochdale, Shopkeeper buried June 2. 1705

Mr John Totty of Leeds Shopkeeper buried June 6, left a young widow big of the 2nd child

Mr John Wainhouse, Shopkeeper in Halifax died June 7

Mr Saml Atkinson, White Smith, in Leeds died June 11

John Ambler of Shipden head buried his little son Abraham June 19

Mr Davis of Salford died July

Mr Humphrey Marler of Manchester died July

Mr Lister of little Horton July

Mr Saml Wareing of Bury buried his wife abt July 20

Mr Jonathan Priestley of Westercroft died July 27 aged 71 years and 7 months, a solid Christian of considerable Piety & usefulness

Mr Tho. Ledgard of Idle died July

John Bentley of Leeds, Tanner, died Aug. 2

Elizabeth wife of John Stansfeld of Horton died of the first child Aug. 24

Mr Peter Peters Minr at Mill Hill Chappel in Leeds died Sept 4. 1705 A Choice young man of excellent parts & usefulness buried at New Church there, Sept. 7

Mr Fenton of Hunslet bur. same day

—— Curate of Huthersfield buried the same week being hurt by a fall from his Horse the week before near Halifax

Esther Whitley of Lane Ends in Hipperholm died suddenly Sep. 10

Mrs Swallow near Heckmondwike died Sept 11, had been ffrighted by seeing something in a Tree near the House on Lords day Sept. 9. was struck dumb and distracted upon it

Anthony Proctors child died Sept 16

James Stansfeld of Bowood in Sowerby buried his wife Nov. 12. 1705

John Heron of Gorton my old ffriend and constant Hearer, & Hannah Oldham near Gorton my dear ffriend and Hearer also died abt Xmas

Catherine Queen Dowager died abt Xmas

Mr Worral of Halifax bur Dec 29. Mrs. Holdens Father

Mr Joseph Clegg of Newtonheath, near Manchester died

BURIALS.

Mrs Greaves (Matthews wife) died

Mrs Holdroyd of Halifax bur. Jan 6

Mrs Leach of Manchester, Mr Greaves Daughter, died

Mr Eaton Parson of Darfield

Mr Philipson Parson of Almanbury both died first week in ye new year

Old widw. Jagger near Coley buried Jan. 29

Mr Byron, Vicar of Bradford died Febr. 1. bur. Febr. 6

Henry Hardman of Droylsden in Manchr parish died

John Lee near Coley bur. ffebr 13, aged abt 75

Mr Joseph Jackson of London, uncle to my mother Foster died Febr.

Mrs Holdsworth near Bradford buried Febr. 26, aged abt 18, abt 60 li. p. an. fell to her kinsman, a sadler in Bradford

Mr Abraham Langley of Priestley Green died Mar. 6. buried at Halifax Mar 11. a vast estate left to his brother

Tho Pool of Landimer in Shelf buried his little son Mar. 13. abt 2 years old

Mr James Ward, Curate at Thornton Chapel near Bradford died Mar. 14, at night.

Susanna Bentley who liv'd wth. Mr. Ward died Mar. 19. was seized that night Mr Ward was buried, died the night after

Thomas Gellibrand of Droylsden in Manchester Parish an old Disciple aged near 90 years buried abt March 19

Mr William Mitchel the Antinomian Preacher near Bradford died

John Dickenson my own dear Father died Mar. 28. 1706 aged 80 years and abt Ten weeks

Widow Harrison of Wakefield bur Apr 5.

Mr James Owen Minr at Salop died Apr 8. aged 51 & half abt.

John Bland of Halifax bur Apr. 12

Joseph Greaves, Taylor, in Northourum bur. Apr. 15

Mr Abraham Bentley near Brighouse bur. at Eland Apr. 25

Esther Mitchel widow, (of Katherine Slack) in Northourum buried Apr. 18, aged (its said) 100d or more.

John Scholefield in Warley, bur Apr. 19

Elias Woodhead of Shelf bur. May 6

Arthur Hey near Northourum bur May 8

Mr. Willm. Midgley the Minister at Sowerby died May 7. 1706, aged abt 30, of a palsie

Hannah d. of Mr Willm Lupton of Westgate end in Wakefield

BURIALS.

died May 8 having long lien in a languishing condition, scarse able to move hand, foot or Tongue

Mr. James Lawton minr at Liverpool died May 7. 1706, buried May 10. 1706, A young man, had preacht about 5 years, and was married May 10. 1705

Richard Heywood of Heaton in Prestwich Parish died May 24

Mary Priestley of Westercroft widow, went out of Bed from her daughter Mary, May 19, about one a Clock in the morning being Lords Day was found May 31 in the River Calder, buried June 1, had bin melancholy above a year

John Sugden of Oxheys near Norwood-Green died June 12, of not a hours sickness

Mr. Eyre of Howley Hall died June 21

Mr Tho. Whaley, Minr at Hinley in Lancashire died abt Midsumer

Mrs Chadwick, widw. in Manchester died June 28

John Ben in Shelf died July 13, 1706

Susanna Marsden in Shelf died July 23

John Taylor of Cleck Heaton in Burstall Parish died July 25

Mr Geo. Ogden, ffellow of Manchester & Vicar of Ribchester died abt July

Mrs Sergeant of Stand Hall in Prestwich Parish died Aug 2. was bur. Aug 8., a choice Gentlewoman, Eminent for Piety & usefulness

Sr John Kay of Woodsome Knight for the County of York, died Aug 8

Mr John Cowper of Leeds buried a child Aug 9. & his wife Aug 11

John Waterhouse of Shelf buried at Halifax Sept. 3. aged abt 92

Mary wife of Jonas Northen of Northourum buried at Bradford Sept 5. aged abt 80, had bin married abt 56 years

Mrs Byrom wife to Mr Byrom minr near Hulm Firth was bur Sep. 9. 1706

Richard Reiner of Mill Bridge near Heckinwyke bur. Oct 2

Jeremy Brooksbank (son of Widw. Sugden of Oxheys) died Oct 1.

Grace Best, daughter to Tho. Pool's wife of Landimer died Oct 16. aged abt 15.

Mr. James Hilton of Manchester died abt Dec 16, aged abt 78

BURIALS.

Edward Brook in Lightcliffe was in Halifax on Sat Nov. 2, died next morning

Jonathan s. of John Priestley of Westercroft died Nov. 8

Thomas s. of Mr Joseph Dawson minr at Rochdale bur. at Morley, Nov. 5

Mrs. Percivall of Manchester bur abt Nov 8

Phebe d of Mrs Ambler of Leeds died Nov. Was well when her sister was married to Mr. Green, and died a few days after

Mrs Bentley d. to old Mr. Gream buried at Halifax Nov. 20, had bin long at Caitif. Her husband is Butler at Mr. Holts of Castleton.

John s. of Mr Nathaniel Priestley of Ovenden bur. Nov. 27

John Wadsworth of Holdsworth buried a Daughter ye same day.

Mr Atkinson a Schoolmaster died in Heckinwyke Nov 29. aged 83 ; an old disciple, was grown poor, cast o'th' Town some months before, had 20s. from our people a few weeks before his death.

Mrs Sarah Scot of Leeds died Dec. 18. was well in the morning and dead at night, a young woman, 1706.

John Ramsden near Shipdenhead was seized with a violent fit of the collick Dec. 28 abt one a clock and died Dec. 29, 11 at night, a good man, a great loss, buried Jan. 1. at Halifax.

John Rushworths wife buried the same day at Coley Chappel had bin ill 17 weeks.

Matthew Holdsworth found dead in Shelf near Cockill Jan 4. aged abt 89.

John Ben of High Bentley buried at Coley Jan 5, aged 95.

Mr John Eaton (who married Mrs Jane Bird) of Warrington burd abt Jan 15

Daniel Netherwood near Southourum bur Jan. 19

Mr John Cowper of Leeds, mercht, buried Jan. 22.

Mr Holroyd call'd Esquire bur. Jan 23

Mr Tounley of Tounley & Mr Lister of Westby Hall in Lancashire died abt Candlemas.

Mr Eli Dyson & Mr John Hanson near Eland died abt Candlemas also

—— Wife of Tho Bentley in Northourum died Febr. 12

Mrs Frankland of Rawthmel died at York a little before Christmas

The mother of Martin Longbothom died near Illingworth, buried

BURIALS.

Febr. 18, aged 85
Mr. Benlows the Lawyer near Borough Briggs died Febr 23
Joseph Thorne of Osset died Feb. 23. aged 72
Mr Richard Wainhouse of Pye Nest near Halifax died Mar 13
Dame Walker died Mar. 20. at Allerton (with her son Hollings)
aged abt 83
William Buckley a carrier at Little Brongh near Rochdale died
Apr. 1. 1707, was hurt (its said) by a violent vomit a while
before: was a strong man. between 40 & 50 year old
Wilow Batterfield near Halifax buried her only daughter Apr.
4. had bur. her husband but abt a month before
Henry Blakebrough's onely son died Apr. 7. abt day break, of
a few days sickness, aged near 16
Mr John Lister minister at Tingley died Apr. 11. of a very
short sickness, buried in their Burying Place
Mrs Higson of Leeds died Apr. 11
Mr. Kirshaw minr. in Craven died at London, was bur.
Apr 18
Mrs Brooksbank of Eland died at Birks near Halifax Apr 16,
abt 4 aclock in the morning. having had a cancer cut out of
her Breast a few weeks before by Dr Threapland who also
died himself the same day at 11 aclock at night. She was
buried Apr 19 at Woodkirk & he at Wibsey the same day;
she aged abt 46, & he abt 63
Daniel s. of Daniel Hemingway of So'wood House died Apr 19
aged abt 21
Mr Hall of Booths Town buried his eldest dr. of Small Pox
Apr. 20
Daniel Hemingway of Sowood House died Apr. 23. The
ffather and son in four days
Mr Saml Lister died at Mytham (with his daughter Kitson) Apr
25. 1707 aged abt 74
Jonathan Hollings of Burstall May 10
Mr John Gawkroger ye Clark at Halifax Church was buried
May 9
Mr Clark ye Vicar of Kirk Heaton was buried May 13
Michl. Medley was kill'd at Shelf Cole pit May 19
Mrs Dixon of Hunslet lane, near Leeds died May 17
Widow Scholefield died at Closes, was buried May 20, had not
bin able to lye in bed or move hand or foot scarse for sevl

BURIALS.

months

Lord Eure died at London abt May day (Apr. 29)

Elizabeth wife of Jeremy Thorp in Shelf bur. at Coley May 27

Mr Tho. Doolittle of London died May 24, N.C. minr aged 77

Mr. Nevel of Cheet Hall died June 5

Mr. Batts of Burstall bur. June 11

Mr Hutton of Pudsey burried his daughter Dorothy June 18

Mrs Abigail Heywood of Northourum died June 12. 1707, buried June 16, aged 75

Mercy Woodhead (wife of Michl) died June 20

Sarah Stocks (Widw Stocks daughter) near Landimer died June 21

John Heywood of Heaton in Prestwich Parish died June 17

Edmund Pendleton of Crumpsall near Manchester died abt Midsum.

Mr. Wm. Walker of Crow Nest in Lightcliffe buried his little daughter (abt 6 years & half old) June 25

Mrs Mosley of Aucotes near Manchester was buried June 28, a very old gentlewoman, abt 90

Martha Heywood of Manchester was buried abt that time, my own Cousin

John Ramsden of Siddal Hall near Halifax died July 6

Abraham Hilton had bin Clark at Prestwich abt 30 years bur July 14

John s. John Ambler of Shibdenhead died July 14, aged ten years, & Mary d. of John Ambler died July 28 aged 4 years & half, both of Smallpox

Mr Tho. Johnson of Painthorp died July, An ancient Dissenting minr

Mr Baker of Ealand buried Aug. 22, left a rich young widow

Mr James Harrison of Wakefield buried his wife Aug 30

Mr. Edward Greaves Apothecary in Manchester bur. Sept 5

Widw Oldham in Crumpsall near Manchester bur. Sept 8

Mr Matthew Hallowes of Ashworth Hall near Rochdale buried Sept 12

Mr Fielding Dunne son of Mr Tho Dunne of Halifax bur. Sept. 25. a very little man abt 24 years old, an attorney

Mrs Freeman of Leeds Mother to Mrs Thomas of Chesterfield died there Sept. 27

Jonas Northen of Northourum died Sept 27. aged near 80

BURIALS.

Christopher Dade buried his son John Sept 30, aged 11 months

Mr Wm Bond minr at Plumpton near Preston died abt Michlmas

William Hollings of Wade house in Shelf ye Quaker buried his wife at their meeting place at Bradford Oct. 13

Mary wife of Martin Longbothom in Northourum died Oct 31

Widw Sutcliffe of Shibden head bur. at Bradford Nov 3, aged (its said) above 100d

John Robinson of Lim'edhouse in Northourum bur. Nov. 15

Joshua Milnes Inkeeper in Bradford bur. his wife Nov 13

Bezaleel son of Mr Saml Eaton of Manchester died abt begining of Dec.

Timothy Smith (who had long bin servt with my ffather Foster at Osset was buried Nov 22

Elkanah Wirrall of Halifax buried his little child Nov 23

John Boocock of Begrington bur. the same day aged 27 & half, left wife and 3 children

Mary wife of Abraham Kendall of Leeds (our maids sister) buried Dec. 23

Mr Atherton of Busy near Warrington died aged abt 30

Mr. C. Clark of Manchester near the Cross buried Dec 27. 1707

Mr Joseph Foolowe a Dissenting Minr near Chesterfield died Dec 8. 1707, aged about 31

Thomas Lacock of Shelf buried his wife Jan 7. of the first child having bin married abt 45 weeks

Mr Joseph Hill minr at Rotterdam who writ Notes on Schrevelius' Lexicon died abt Christmas aged 82

Mr John Gaskel of Manchester buried abt middle of Jan aged abt 30

Mr. Saml. Wadsworth of fflanshaw near Wakefield buried his wife Jan 13

Mr Spademan Justice of Peace in Darbyshire abt Alfreton died abt middle of Jan.

James son of Joseph Wilkinson in Shelf bur. Jan 14, about half a year old

Abraham Farrar near Mixenden bur. Jan. 19

Dr. Richardson bur. his child, Jan. 19

Ellen Heywood of Heaton in Prestwich Parish buried Jan. 20 .

Saml Wood near Coley buried his wife Jan. 22

Widow Hartley of Northourum died ffebr 4, 1707 aged abt 80

Widow Patrick buried at Leeds Febr. 4

BURIALS.

Francis Bentley, the Bookseller in Halifax buried Febr. 15. 1707
Mr John Simpson's stepmother bur. Feb. 16
John Strengfellow of Halifax bur. a son Feb. 22
Martha d. of Jeremiah Learoyd near Bare-Head in Northourum
bur. ffebr. 26, aged abt 12
Mr Benyon Minr at Shrewsbury died March 4, aged abt 35. A
man of rare parts. He was Doctor of Physick
Mr Richard Assheton (onely son of Sr Raphe Assheton of
Middleton) died at London, was buried at Middleton Febr 26
Mr Hook an Attorney in Halifax bur Mar. 15
Mr John Wroe of Leeds wife died Mar. 14
Isabel Swift of Halifax sister to John Priestleys wife died Mar. 22
Mr Nathl Wainhouse Parson of Silkstone died abt Mar 25, 1708,
he had bin minr at Bradford
Mr Cawcroft an Attorney in Bradford bur. his wife Mar. 28. was
Justice ffarrands dautr.
Mr David Noble Minr at Heckmondwyke bur. his wife Mar 31.
Timothy Oldfield of Northourum buried a son that was still born,
Apr. 2
Mr Assheton-Richard Greenhalgh of Brandlesome near Bury in,
Lancr. was well when he went to bed & found dead next
morning abt the latter end of March 1708, aged abt 32
Mr Francis Tallents, Minr. in Shrewsbury died Apr. 11, aged 89
The author of Chronological Tables
John Greenwoods wife Inkeeper at Norwood Green had bin in
Travel 3 days, had 3 or 4 midwives, could not be deliver'd,
till the Pangs of Death parted her & the child Apr. 12
Mr Wm. Maude near Wakefield bur. Apr. 14.
Saml Holdsworth of Northourum died Apr. 16
Mr Prime of Sheffield died April, later end, an Ancient Non Conf.
Minr.
Widow Bairstow (Mr Bairstows mother) died Apr. 16. aged 75
Tho. Whitaker of Lightcliffe bur. Apr. 25
Mr. Eli Fenton's wife died at New Castle abt later end of April,
of the 3d child p. him
Mr. John Truman of Broad Yates near Halifax bur. his wife
May 17
Mary Dickenson my own dear Mother died May 19, about 2
Clock in the morning 1708, aged abt 80
Ralph Wardleworth of Blakeley in Manchester Parish, buried

BURIALS.

May 22, aged abt 73

James Hardmans wife of Broadfield in Middleton Parish bur.
May 26, aged abt 83

Mr Thomas Waterhouse of Gorton died May 30, aged abt 40, had bin Schoolmaster there

Garvis Ingham of Osset buried May 31

Mr John Hall died at London June 6

Mrs Milne of Rochdale (widow of Mr Robt Milne) buried June 3

Mr Midgley (call'd Doctor) of Midgley fell into the water, when ffishing & was drown'd near Luddenden June 18, supposed to be a Palsie

Anne Birtinshaw an ancient widow in Gorton bur. June 23

Jeremiah Batley's wife in Lightcliffe died June 2

James Scholfield of Binns, near Southourum buried June 30

John Smith of Soper Lane in Shelf buried July 16, 1708

Widw Scholey a Papist in Osset was bur. July 17

Mr Hutton of Pudsey died July 26

Timothy s. of Widw Hemingway of So'wood House buried July 21

Mr James Naylor a minr in London died July 23, aged abt 30

Mrs Spencer died at her Son in Laws Mr Jere. Gills in Hull abt the same time

James Tetlaw of Norwood Green died Aug. 4 a useful member of our Society at Northourum aged abt 63

Widw Hemingway of So'wood House died the same day: her husband & two sons having bin buried in abt a year & four months

Tho. Noble Innkeeper in Halifax bur. Aug. 1

Jeremiah Bairstow of Halifax bur. Aug 8 a young man was abt to marry Th. Bretcliffe dr.

Mr John Wadsworth of Horbury died Aug. 14. bur Aug 15. 1708

Mr Rawson the Attorney in Bradford bur. his wife abt Aug. 8

Mr Robt Scott a mercer in Leeds buried Aug. 21

Mrs Martha Midgley (an old virgin) died at Thornton, was bur. at Halifax, Sept 11

Mr John Spademan a N. C. Minr in London died Sept 3, bur. Sep. 10

Mrs Drake of York widw bur. Sep 24

Mr Jonas Blamires Minr at Durham bur. Oct 3

Mrs Richardson of Bierley (ye Doctors mother died Oct 6, bur

BURIALS.

Oct 11

Obadiah Day of Henging Heaton buried his wife Oct 9. the same · day yt she died

Richd Wade (son to John Nalsons wife of Pump near Shibden Hall) died Oct 23

Timothy Halliday, Jeremy Baxters sisters son died at Morley with Mrs Waller Oct 24

John s. Abraham Bairstow of High Bentley died Oct 30, abt 7 weeks old

Mr James Gream near Halifax buried his son Henry Oct 31

Mr George Green of Leeds buried his son Nov. 3

George Prince of Denmark (ye Queens Husband) died Oct 28, 1708, aged 55

Widow Blamires near Rivy Beacon bur. Nov. 6

James Brooksbank of Shelf (my dear ffriend & neighbour there) a member of our Society at Northourum died No 10, aged abt 76

Mrs Eliz Mosley of Ancotes near Manchester died abt middle of November

Mr Willm Bowkers son of Bull's Head in Manchester buried Nov. 25

— Tempest of Cockill Clough buried Nov. 30

Rachel Veritie a poor silly woman buried Dec 1

Peter Ambler of Shelf died Dec 3. aged its sd 100 & upwards. Some say 108

Abraham Hanson of Green Lane in Northourum died Dec. 13

John Sowden near Bramley buried Dec. 14

Mr Joshua Horton of Chadderton, a Justice of Peace, a worthy useful man, buried at Oldham Dec. 18. His wife bur. Dec. 29.

Mr Dade, Parson of Otley died Dec. 25

Mr Francis Maude of Wakefield buried his young wife Dec. 26

Mr Saml Roberts minr at Barnesley died Lords Day morning just after 12 a clock Jan 2, had Preach't Lords day before, buried at Darton Jan 4, a brisk active young man, had preacht but abt 6 or 7 years, died of a Pluretic Fever

Nathan Baxter of Southourum buried Jan 4. a member of the Society at Kipping aged abt 80

Mr Edward Langley of Hipperholm died Jan. 14

Jeremy Walker of Norwood Green died Jan. 24

Mr Radcliffe Scholefield ye Lawyer near Rochdale died abt middle of Jan

BURIALS.

Mrs Beatrix Hutton of Pudsey buried abt Jan. 17. a young woman

Mr Timothy Jollie of Attercliffe buried his wife Jan 20

Mr Jeremiah Gill minr at Hull died at York abt Jan 23

Anne Broadley bur. at Coley Feb. 9

William Hardman of Heaton in Prestwich Parish buried his wife Febr. 15

Mary wife of Joshua Robertshaw died Febr 15 of a child-bed Fever

Martha wife of Edward Lacock bur Feb 22

Mr Accepted Lister Minr at Kipping preacht twice & administred Lds. Supper Febr. 20. died Febr 25. An excellent Preacher, a little helpless body, but a great and sound soul

Mr Joseph Lister of Kipping The Minrs Father died Mar. 11. aged abt 80, an Eminent Christian, but a fortnight between his and his son's death. both buried at Thornton Chappel

Robert Coulin a Quaker in Northouram died Mar. 7. bur. Mar. 10. Aged 80 & upwards

Widw. Stocks near Northoarum died Mar. 14

Mr Oates of Danby died abt middle of March

Mr. Ash minr at Manchester Church died abt middle of March

Mr Peter Sergeant of Stand in Prestwich Parish died March 19. bur. 23, aged abt 40

James Milne near Milneroe buried at Rochdale Mar. 28. 1709, aged abt 23

Mr Sugdens Son in Law buried Mar. 27

Anne wife of John Hill of Beggrington died of a Dropsie, bur. Apr. 7

Mary Benn, of Shelf, died Apr. 7, poor

James Bentom of Westgate End at Wakefield buried his wife Apr. 7, a spotted Fever

Mr Crosley near Sowerby bur. his wife Apr. 17

Mr. Saml Low minr at Knutsford in Cheshire, died Apr. 19. of a ffever aged abt 40, A man of good parts & usefulness. Cease Lord

Sarah Spencer of Halifax died Apr. 22. had bin lame & confin'd to th' House many years. A serious Christian, never married

Mrs Stern of Woodhouse near Halifax bur. Apr. 28. 1709

Mr Swinton Minr at Newton Chappel near Manchester buried his wife Apr. 29

BURIALS.

Mr Nathl Gaskels wife of Manchester died May 1, buried May 4

Mr Henry Naylor near Wareley bar. his wife May 4

Wm. H t o' Osset ur. his wife May 7

Mr Hall on Board Town near Halifax died May 8

— Hemingway of S w'd House died M y 7

J nas Cotes w fe in Hipperholm died M ty 9

John Bairstows wife died May 11

M Coningham Minr at Manchester bur. his youngest child May 22, abt half a year old

John Walton near Illingworth bnr. May 25

Joshua Ambler bu . his dr. May 23. abt 8 year old, near Holdsworth

Mr John Bretcliffe of Halifax bur. his wife, June 1

Mr Midgley's wife of Headley buried June 1

Dr Hall of Kipping died June 6. A sold Judicious Christian & a useful Physician aged abt 78

Mr Joseph Sykes of Leeds died June 9

M Holdsworth of Astia near Southouram died June 23

M Jeffry Lodge, near Halifax, bur June 25

Mr John Brookesbank of Eland (a young man aged abt 23) died Lords day morning Ju e 26, 1709

Mr Joseph Dawson minr at Moreley died Lords Day night June 26, 1709 aged abt 73, a precious Heavenly man

John Hyde near Manchester bur. his wife July 1

Mrs Mary Priestley (Mr Jonathan P iestleys wife of Winter Edge died Lords Day morning abt half an hour past 3 a clock July 3, aged abt 53

Mr Mailer Eaton son of Mr Saml Eaton of Manchester bur. at London July 14

Mrs Mary Firth (wife of Dr Firth of Kipping was deliver'd of a daughter July 18, died July 20, about half hour after 12 in the morning, bur in Thornton Chappel July 28

Richd Town near Halifax bur. his wife July 28

Mrs Hutton of Pudsey bur. Aug 2

Benjamin Nicholson near Luddenden bur. his wife Aug. 2

James Hannar died in Halifax Aug 16, had lived at Winter Edge

George Rickerd of Osset died Aug 17. aged 85

Isaac Longbothom of Halifax died Aug. 19

Isaac Broadley of Bradford bur. his wife Sept 1. She died of Smallpox, had bin mar. but abt 9 weeks aged abt 20

BURIALS.

Mr John Byrom minr near Hulmfirth died Sep 9. buried Sep. 12

Mr Dickson Miur at the New Church in Leeds died Sept 12

Mr Benson, Lecturer at the old Chu ch in Leeds died Sept. 15

Abigail wife of Wm Hatfie died at London Sep 15, was deliver'd of a dr. Sept 10, abt 5 weeks before her time. She was Wm Fentons dr. of Pudsay

William Corlase, (son of Mrs Wright of Lightcliffe by her former husband) died at Loudon Sept. 16

Mr Joshua Dunne, a young Physitian lately come to Halifax died of the Small Pox. Sept 13, bur. Sept. 15

Mr Henry Dickenson of Salford bur. abt middle of Sept.

Mr John Maude an Attorney in Halifax bur. Oct. 7. aged abt. 32

Mr John Clayton Chaplain at Manchester church died Oct 9, had preacht twice & administred Sacrament at Salford Lords Day before, Oct 2

Benjamin Jagger near High Cross died Oct. 11 aged abt 80

Mrs Holdsworth of Astie bur. Oct 15

Mrs Heginbothom of Salford (the Captains wife) bur Oct. 15

Joshua Bentley of Oxbeys, died Oct 14, bur. 17

Mr. Peter ffinch of Shellington near Wigan went to London to be cut for the Stone, died there before he was cut Oct 12, well skill'd in the Law, Sober & useful

Mr John Bretcliffe Apothecary in Halifax died Oct 20

Edward Thorp of Blakely bur his wife Oct. 19

Willm Buttlers wife, Northourum died Oct 20.

Martha wife of John Askew of Northourum Green buried Oct 29, 1709

Saml Whitleys wife of Shelf died suddenly Oct. 28

— Robinson of Osset died abt Nov 2

Mrs Craven of Leeds died Nov. 7. Mr Whitakers Landlady

Thomas Slack near Halifax bank top bur. his wife Nov. 15

Mr David Noble Miur at Heckmondwike bur. at Dewsbury Nov. 30

Mr Thomas Kitson of over Briar in Northourum bur. Dec 1. A very big fat man

Joseph Woodhead of Shelf bur. Dec. 9. aged 64

Mr John Lever of Market Street Lane end in Manchester died abt beginning of Dec.

Mr Edward Scott a grocer at Smithy door in Manchester died also abt same time

BURIALS.

— son of Willm Ramsden of Coley Mill bur. Dec. 7

John son of Joseph Eccles of Coley Hall died of Small Pox buried Dec. 12

Mrs Dawson of Leeds (Mr Saml Scotts wifes mother buried Dec. 14

Matthew Croyser of Green lane in Northourum bur. Dec. 19. an old man

Mr Vinion a Dutch Man, an only son, to a rich merchant had bin sometime at Mr. Milns in Wakefield, went to London, was seiz'd with a Fever, died there Dec. 26

John Ingham near Warley bur. his wife Dec. 26. She died in childbed of the first child

Joshua Milnes Inkeeper in Bradford bur. Jan. 4, 1709

Anthony Hartley near the Comon Wood bur. his wife Jan. 1

Willm Thomas near Heptinstall bur abt Jan 8.

Mr John Cheney a Shopkeeper in Warrington died Jan.

Widw Ambler of Shelf bur. Jan.

Eliezer Tetlaw of Rooks near Norwood green died Jan 14 aged 33 and abt 4 months, a good man, very useful, much lamented, left his wife great of the third child

Mary Tillotson of Northourum died Jan 19, aged abt 85 never married, sister to old Susan Mr Heywoods old Maid

Willm Walker of Stand in Prestwich Parish bur Jan 25 aged abt 90, an old Disciple

— of Norland died Jan. 27. eat his dinner well

Robert Coulin of Northourum died Jan 27. a young man

Diana wife of Saml Riddlesden of Rooks died of a Fever in Child bed Jan 30

Jeremiah Thorp of Shelf died Febr 2, a poor old man

Dame Foster of Osset my wife's grandmother died Feb 2, 1709, aged abt 95

Mr Henry Gream near Halifax died Feb 5. aged 86

John Frost the carrier in Lightcliffe buried his wife Febr. 8

Anne d. Mr Joshua Crompton bur Feb. 11

Jonas Heaton of Norwood Green died Feb 12

Widow Sowden near Scout Hall died Feb. 19

Widow Ramsden of Siddall Hall died Febr. 19

Mr Godfrey Rodes of Long Haughton Hall bur. Mar. 1. abt 22 years of age, Heir to a great estate

John Waddington of Southouru a Quaker, bur. Mar. 6. an ancient

man
Thomas Mitchell of Northourum was at Halifax Mar 4, died Mar.
8. aged abt 70 .
John Wright Inkeeper of Baily Brig was found dead in the Lane
near Home, its sd he was sadly drunk. Mar. 10
Mr Lichfield's wife of Blakely in Manchester Parish died Mar 9
Abraham Threapland School-Master at Booth Town bur. his wife
Mar. 17
James Haigh of Crumblebottom died abt Mar. 20
Jeremiah Crosley near Sowerby bur. Mar. 19
Mr Wordsworth of Water Hall near Peniston & his son Mr Words-
worth of Burton Grange near Barnesley, both buried Mar. 23
Mr King of Calico Hall bur Mar. 30. 1710
John Elsworth's wife died in child bed bur Mar. 31
Mr Joshua Sager Minr at New Chappel, at Wakefield died Mar 28
buried at a Burying Place near Woodkirk Mar 31. aged abt 44.
A worthy usefull man, a very great loss
Mr Thomas Elston Minr at Chesterfield was seized in the Pulpit
in Prayer upon the ffast Day Mar. 15. with some disorder in
his head Mar. 31. bur Apr. 3. aged —. A serious good man,
had bin a Pastor several years to a small congregation at Top-
liff & but lately remov'd from 'em
Mr James Naylor, Minr at St Hellens in Lancashire died abt Apr
8, left 13 children and his wife with child
David Hamond near Bradford Moor aged abt 90, buried Apr. 5
Robert Goodall of Norwood Green died Apr. 5
Mr. Ravald of Kestaw near Manchester bur his wife
Richard Tattersal near Sowerby Bridge bur his wife Apr. 15
Mr. Pierson Schoolmaster at Batley bur Apr 15
Thomas Bentley Inkeeper in Halifax bur. Apr. 28
Mr John Cagill near Halifax bur. a child same day
Martha d. of Mr Joshua Wright of Hipperholm died Apr. 27. a
little after 11 a clock in the fforenoon, bur. May 1. 1710, aged
10 years & abt 8 months, a Hopefull child, much lamented
Samuel Drake near Northourum died Apr. 28. bur May 1. 1710,
aged abt 76
Widow Wright the Land lady at Baily brigg died May 1
Mr Brodgate Ferrand Vicar of Bradford died May 4, buried May
6 : a young man
Mrs Susanna d. Mr Willm Richardson of High Fearneley bur.

BURIALS.

May 11, aged abt 18
Daniel Gill of Eland Hall bur May 18
Mrs Faith Sharp of little Horton bur. June 5
Mr Bryan Dixon of Hunslet Lane near Leeds died June 13
Mr Joseph Swallow of Heckmondwyke buried at Burstall June 24
Joseph Priestley of Northourum buried June 27
Benjamin Nicholson near Luddenden bur. June 28
Mr Joseph Beevors of New Miller Dam, buried his wife June 29
Edward Hodgson of Holdsworth bur. July 3, 1710
John Hanson of Lightcliffe died July 4 of a very short sickness,
    aged abt 67
Ashton Jones the Bellman in Halifax died July 4. well & dead
    in a few hours
Mr John Greenwood (call'd Lawyer) Brother to Mrs Langley died
    at Shipley buried at Bradford July 2, and Mr Hollings of Ship-
    ley buried his little daughter the same day
Eliezer s. Widw. Tetlaw of Rooks died suddenly July 6
Widow Homes of Northourum died July 24
Robert Lever Esquire of Alkrington in Prestwich parish died July
    23, bur. at Middleton July 27, aged near 87
Mr Tho. Oldham who liv'd with Sr Robt Dukinfeild bur. Aug. 7
Mr Loggau minr at Fishlake near Doncaster buried Aug. 2, aged
    abt 30
Martha Robinson of Northourum buried Aug. 17, aged 80 & abt
    5 months
Lady Hewley of York died Aug. 23
Mr Saml Eaton of Manchester minr at Stand in Prestwich Parish
    died Sep 5, aged abt. 53.   A man of unknown learning greatly
    respected & much lamented, a very great loss
Abraham Heywood of Heaton in Prestwich Parish buried Sept 16
Sarah Fenton wife of Wm Fenton of Pudsay died Sept. 10
Isaac Brear of Holdsworth died Sept 16
Joseph Marsh, Inkeeper in Halifax, bur Sep. 19
Mr Richard Foster of Osset (my wifes Grand-Father) died Sept
    20, aged abt 88, 1710
Mr Tho. Baxter minr at York died Sept 27
Lawyer Thornton of Leeds bur. Oct 11
Hannah Hodgson who lived with Madm. Kirk of Wakefield died
    Oct. 9.   A manlike woman
Sarah wife of John Glover d. of Widw. Bradbury of Wakefield

died Oct 13

Elizabeth Nicolson (a young woman) died at her Uncle Stansfeld's at Haugh End, buried Oct 30

Mr. Tho. Newhouse of Leeds died Oct 30

Alderman Rooks of Leeds died Oct 31

Timothy Crowther died at Daniel Scotts at Athersgate in Northourum Nov. 2

Robt Bairstow (Mr Bairstow's Brother) died Nov. 2

George Stocks of Hipperholm lane Ends died Nov. 5

John Robinson of Norwood Green died Nov. 5

Mr Daniel Maude near Wakefield died suddenly Nov. 13

Mrs Pendlebury of Leeds died Nov. 12.

John Hurd of Shelf bur. his wife Nov 18.

James Oates of Norwood Green died Nov. 18

Justice Stanhope near Calverley died abt Nov. 26

Mr Tho. Whitaker Minr in Leeds near 35 years died Nov. 19. bur. Nov. 21. A man of admirable parts, great Learning Piety & Usefullness. Aged abt. 60

Mr Joseph Swallow of Heckinwyke bur Nov 23. 1710

Tho Settle of Dumb Mills near Hipperholm bur. his wife **Dec.** 3

William Charnock near Halifax bur Dec 6

Mrs. Lever of Alkrington, in Prestwich died Dec.

Widow Hemingway near Shipden Hall bur Dec. 11

Widow Hanson near Eland bur. a dr. Dec. 12

Widow Sunderland of Shelf bur Dec. 17

John Drakes wife of Crosshill near Halifax bare one child **Dec.** 15, another Dec. 16, died Dec. 17, bur. Dec. 18

Saml Pollard of Marsh near Halifax died Dec. 22

John Fergusons wife of Halifax died Dec. 23

Joseph s. Mr Robt Milnes of Wakefield bur Dec 25

Richd Brown of Northourum bur. his wife, Dec. 25

Richd Empsall near Snathe bur. Dec 29. A Quaker. He married Robt Coulin's dr. of Northourum

John Metcalfe bur his d. Lydia Jan. 1

Saml Appleyard of Shelf bur. his dr. Susan Jan. 8

John Bamford of Scout bur. abt Jan. 5

Timothy Bancroft of Wareley died Jan. 16

Eliza wife of John Strengfellow of Halifax died Jan. 16

—— wife of Joseph Eccles of Coley Hall died Jan. 16

Judith d. John Priestley of Westercroft died Jan. 21

BURIALS.

Mr Lichfield of Blakely near Manchester died Jan 16, left a vast estate

Mr Matthew Pinkerton of Manchester died Jan.

Anna d. Dr Nettleton of Halifax died Jan 24, aged a year & quarter

Mr Briggs an Attorney in Halifax died Jan. 25

Abraham Jackson, Prestwich Parish bur. Jan. 27

Mr. Saml Hulme, Parson of Macclesfield buried Jan. 29

John Marshall buried at Coley Feb 1. 1710

Mary d. John Priestley of Westercroft died Feb. 4

Timothy Holt of Upper Shibden Hall died Feb. 6

Mrs Hollings of Crosley Hall bur. Feb 12

Richard Crawshaw of Horton bur. Feb. 13

Widow Brooksbank (late wife of James Brooksbank of Shelf) died Febr. 13

Mr Allison, Parson of Thornton in Craven buried his wife Feb. 16. She had born 4 children in less than a year, died in child bed : Mr Langleys Dautr.

William Hirst of Osset died Febr. 16

Joseph Croft of Shelf died Feb. 21, aged abt 80

Hannah d. John Priestley of Westercroft died Feb. 22

Isaac Spencer a Carrier in Wyke, well & dead in a few hours. Feb 21

Saml Liversidge of Priestley Green bur. his wife March 5

—— dr of Joseph Priestley of White-Windows near Sowerby Bridge bur Mar. 6

Mr. Lodge a Merchant in Leeds died Mar 6

Mr Willm Walker's wife of Lightcliffe died Mar. 7

Mr Joshua Rayner of Long Haughton Hall died Mar. 5. buried Mar. 8. at Selby

Widow Northend of Brian Scholes in Northourum buried Mar. 13

Mr — Whitaker at Mr Joshua Dawsons in Leeds died Mar. 12

Mr. Saml Taylor, Linen Draper in Manchester buried abt Lady Day

Thomas Ellcock of Gorton buried abt the same time, a serious good man, an old Disciple

Widw. Rudman of Shelf mother to Saml Appleyard died Mar. 26

Widw. Wooler near Northourum bur. Mar. 26, 1711

Daniel Sharp Father to Mr Sharp of Hipperholm bur. Mar. 31

John Sharp of ffold was kil'd at Bank Top Apr. 3. by the Fall of

BURIALS.

part of the House they were pulling down there

The Dauphine of France died Apr 6 of Small Pox

Joseph Emperour of Germany died Apr 7 of Small Pox

Jane wife of Tho Pool of Landimer died Apr. 7

Wife of John Holdsworth of Whinniroyd died Apr 15

Sarah wife of Joshua Knight junr of Cockill died Apr. 16

Mr Henry Ellis near Leeds bur. his wife Apr. 21

Mr Saml Cookson of Leeds bur. Apr. 22. A Merchant

James Wilson near Beg'rington died Apr. 22

Mary Booth of Begrington (Lady Cope's sister) bur. Apr. 30

John Siddal of Whitefield in Prestwich Parish bur. Apr. 24

Mr Robert Gartside near Prestwich Church bur. his wife Apr. 28

Wriotheseley Russel Duke of Bedford died of Small Pox May 26, aged 30

Ld Viscount Strathallan of North Brittain died of a consumption at Kensington the same day

Widw Hey of Barnshill, Northourum bur. May 7

The dr. of James Wallis, Northourum May 7

Mrs Gledhill of Eland bur. at Tingley Yate May 7

Mary Town of Barnshill bur. May 11

Wife of John Nalson junr near Shibden Hall was found dead in bed May 19 in the morning She was but married Dec. last

John Strickland of Rodley died May 27

Sarah d. Mrs Sager of Wakefield died May 28

James s. Ebenezer Naylor of Wakefield died of the Small Pox June 2, 1711, abt 11 months old

—— Daughter of Mr Abraham Dawson died at Morley June 3

Mr Shaw of Bradford bur. his wife June 9

Mary Croft of Shelf, wid. was at Northourum New Chappel June 10. writ sermon both ends, recd. the sacramt, fell sick that night, died Tuesday morning about 2 a clock June 12

Mr Henry Dodwell died abt middle of June aged abt 70. He was Head of the Non Juring party, had singular opinions in Divinity & Politicks tho' a man famous for Piety & Learning

Charles Sheffield of Clifton bur. June 19

Mr John Wildman Apothecary in Sheffield died June

Lord Fairfax of Gillim in Yorkshire, died at London July 6

Mr Peregrine Bertie (Bro. to the Marquess of Lindsey) died suddenly of an Apoplexy July 10. A Teller of the Exchequer

Mr Moult Minr at Call Lane in Leeds bur. his father in Darby-

BURIALS.

shire July 2

Mr Greaves near Rochdale bur. July 6

Mr John Sugden of Shelf bur July 14, aged 69

—— dr. John Fearnsile of Northouium bur. July 15

John Holles who was Lord Privy Seal ——

The Duke of New Castle died July 15 had an Estate of abt 60000 li. p. an. the Richest man in ye Nation

James Douglas was principal Secretary of State

The Duke of Queensborough & Dover, died July 6

Mr George Travis Minr at Hall died suddenly July 22, abt 25 years of age, his wife scarse 20, great of the 31 child

Mrs Scott of Leeds died suddenly July 23, her dautr. Mrs Read was deliver'd of a dr. about an hour after which died Aug. 3. Mrs Read bur. Aug. 13

Richard Farrar of Pudsay bur. Aug. 18

Mrs Lodge of Savil Green near Halifax died Sept. 3, 1711 mother to Mr Joseph Brooksbanks wife

Mary Town d. of Mrs Brear of Eland died Sept. 5, aged abt 11

Abraham s. of Martin Fielding, Halifax bur. Sep. 14

Mr Willm Walker bur. at Halifax Sep. 12. an ancient man, had bin melancholy some time

Mr. Shaw of Ardsley near Wakefield Junr. bur. Sep. 25. His Fathers only son, heir to a vast estate, its said 1700 p. ann.

Mr Hinley of Rochdale died abt Sept. 19 A young man, vastly rich

Mrs Hollings (mother to Justice Smith) bur. at Bradford Sept. 23

Mr Joseph Hollings of Allerton died Sep. 25 had been long under Weakness, a serious Christian. An Israelite indeed

Mr Danl Walker of Manchester bur. Sep. 29. A considerable Tradesman

John Beurdsell of Blakely bur. his wife Oct 1. My brothers wife's mother

Jude Scott of Atherton bur Oct. 9

Mr. Shaw of Ardsley near Wakefield died abt Oct. 5. had bur. his only son a fortnight

Mr Willm Sutcliffe near Heptonstall bur Oct. 12. had driven a great Trade & very rich

Jonas Blamires of Halifax bur. his wife Oct 12. aged 73

John Long near Northourum bur. his wife Oct 26

John Beurdsell of Blakely (my brothers wife's Father) bur. Nov 4

BURIALS.

John Farrar of Wareley bur. his dr. Nov. 5

Mr Joseph Crowther of Northowrum died Nov. 7 bur. Nov. 10, aged abt 74 left a great Estate

Thomas Oldfield of Wareley bur. his wife Nov. 14. Mother to Timothy Oldfield of Northourum

Mary wife of Nathan Tilson of Northourum deliver'd of a dead child Nov 18. She died presently after there was another child (or two) but she was not deliver'd of it, all bur. together Nov. 20

Jeremiah Wilkinson, Shopkeeper in Halifax, & —— Bateman's wife near Hipperholm Lane Ends & Mary d. of Thomas Clark of Scout Hall all buried at Halifax Nov. 28. (all in church together.)

John Wells of Hudd hill in Northourum bur Dec. 5

—— dr. of Mr Thorp of Hopton bur Dec. 8

Richard Musgrave Esq. bur. Dec. 11

Mr John Holdsworth Minr at Clack Heaton died Dec. 15. bur. at Burstall Dec. 18

Mr Joseph Wilkinson Vicar of Halifax died Dec. 28. bur. Dec. 31. Had bin Vicar about 20 years & a half

Robt Ferrand Esq. Justice of Peace near Bingley died Jan. 1. 1711-12

Widw. Higson (Mother to John Priestley's wife) bur. Jan. 3

The Earl of Ranelaugh died Jan. 5

Ruth wife of Danl Tempest of Northourum died Jan 8. bur. Jan. 10

Martha wife of Joshua Burnet of Wakefield bur. Jan. 11

Collonel Stanhope died Jan. 23. Mortally wounded in a late Action

William Oxley of Northourum died Jan. 21

The Dauphine & Dauphiness of France died Feb.

Mr John Heywood Minr at Blakely bur. his son John ffebr. 2

Joseph Robertshaw of Shelf bur. at Coley ffebr. 9

John Burnley Junr, Shelf, bur. Feb. 15

Grace d. Joshua Knight of Cockill in Shelf died Feb. 20. aged 31 & a half

Mr Watson's wife of Wakefield stay'd in the Lodging Room a little after her Husband was gone to bed Feb. 15. She fell upon the fire burnt one breast, one Arm off, & her Head almost to Ashes, the noisomness of the Smell was felt by some

BURIALS.

of the neighbours, at last her Husband awakt & found her in this dismal condition, an amazing Spectacle, She was buried ffeb. 17

Mr Tho. Danson died at York latter end of Febr.

Mrs Dawson of Morley died Mar 6, aged abt 74 had bin of great use in her Place

Margaret wife of Charles Hughs of Northourum died Mar. 9

Mrs Wordsworth of Burton Grange near Barnesley died Mar. 15. bur Mar. 16

Mr Wood who liv'd with old Mr Jonas Waterhouse at Bradford died Apr 17, bur. Apr. 20, aged 70, had been Schoolmaster there at the free School

Mr Town Minr at Heptinstall died May 3, had bin minr. there many years, aged 80

John Fearnside's wife bur. May 5

Jonas Atkinson of Bradford bur. May 9

Widw. Wilkinson of Hipperholm Lane Ends buried May 27

Joshua Dixon of Cliffton in Eccles Parish bur. abt. middle of May

Willm Linney of Heaton in Prestwich Parish bur. abt middle of May

Mr Edmd Ogden of Macclesfield bur. May 29

James s. James Greaves near Halifax bur June 5

John Fearnside bur. June 17

John s. Jere. Learoyd died June 22

Widw. Garnet bur July 4.

Josiah Normanton of Sowerby bur. July 6

Isaac Smith near High Cross buried his daughter Elizabeth July 10

John Crowther of Dam Head in Northourum bur. July 11

Hugh Lord Willoughby bur. July 0

Mr Richd. Stretton died at London July, a very eminent ancient Minr.

Mr Pendlebury of Leeds bur. his son Henry July 17, was begining in Small Pox

Mrs Green of Bramley struck dead with Thunder & Lightning July 21

John Terry's wife near Wibsey Slack bur. July 30

Sr John Middleton near New Castle buried his Lady

Joshua s. Mr. Robt Milnes of Wakefield bur Aug. 15

Saml Midgley's wife of Coley Hall, died Aug.

BURIALS.

Mr Joseph Sutton Minr at Hull died Aug. 25, a young man of rare Parts a great loss to the congregation, his wife & children. Cease Lord, help Lord !

Michael Doughty of Holdsworth died of the Small Pox Sep. 14

Widw. Robertshaw of Blakchill End in Northourum died Sep. 16, aged 71

Benjamin Benn of Shelf bur. Sep. 20

Mrs Hall of Booth Town widw, Sep. 21

Mr Francis Meadowcroft of Manchester bur. Sept. 10

Widw. Halliday of Morley bur. Nov. 1

Mr Anthony Markham senr of Leeds died Nov. 4

Mr Otho Holland near Manchester died Nov. 5

Mr James Mitchel Minr abt Rossendale died aged near 40

James Duke Hamilton and Lord Mohun kill'd each other in a Duel abt middle of November at London

Mrs Marsden of Manchester bur. her son, an only child, of the Small Pox Dec. 6, 1712

Katherine Bins of Halifax, an old Mid-wife, died Dec. 9

Mrs Mary Sugden Widow, late of Shelf, sicken'd at Bingley Dec. 15, died Dec. 16

Mrs Rachel d. of Madm Kirk of Wakefield sicken'd Dec. 19. between 12 & one a Clock in the morning & died between 12 & one tho same day

Widow Boyle died at Cinderhills near Coley Chappel Jan 5. aged abt 88.

Mr Willm Benson Minr at Wakefield died Jan. 12

Mr Holt of Castleton, Justice of Peace, died

Mr. Gartside of Rochdale died.

John Waterhouse of Barneshill bur. his wife Jan 24

Mr John Truman near Sowerby Brigg died Jan. 24

Mr John Stock of Salford buried two children together of Small Pox

John Eckroyd near High Cross bur. Jan. 27, 1712

Mr Richard Thorp of Hopton bur. Jan. 30

Joshua Brooksbank of Oxheys bur. his son Jan. 30, aged 22 weeks

Tempest Cordingley near Bradford bur. his wife Jan 29. His Servt had bin to invite to the ffuneral & was found dead in a field near the House Jan. 27

Widow Stocks of Hipperholm-lane-ends died Jan. 29

BURIALS.

Mr Daniel Burgess of London, Plain but Powerfull Preacher, died Jan 26, aged abt. 67

John Driver of Northourum Junior, died Febr. 9

Joseph Dean near Coley bur. Feb. 14

Jeremiah Smith of Ovenden bur. Feb 17

Josiah s. Joshua Stansfeld of Horton bur Feb. 18. aged abt 20

Henry Blakebrough of Shelf bur. his wife Febr. 20

Jennet wife of John Gill bur. at Coley, 25

Martha Wooller of Northourum died Feb. 27

James Farrar of Lands Head died Mar. 2

John Waterhouse of Barnshill died Mar. 2

Mary wife John Watkins of Northm. died 9

Mr Willm Issot bur. at Horbury Mar. 10

Mrs Pinkerton of Manchr. died abt ffeb. 16

Mr John Bretcliffe of Stony Royd died Mar. 14

Dautr. of Mrs Benson of Wakefield died Mar. 23

Charles Hughs of Northourum died Mar. 30. aged abt. 65

John Tillotson of Cockhill died Mar. 31

Willm Priestley at Baily brig died suddenly Mar. 26

—— call'd old Captain died suddenly Apr. 3

Willm. Pollard of Wyke bur. Mar. 26

Mr Ebenezer Naylor of Wakefield bur. his son Ebenezer Apr. 8

Mrs Elizabeth Ferguson of Halifax died Apr. 14, buried Apr. 17

John Pighells of Norwood Green bur. Ap. 18

Edward Haigh near Halifax, a Quaker, bur. his wife Apr. 29

Doctor Grundey of Bolton bur. May 2

Mary wife Richard Robinson of Norwood Green bur May 1. aged abt. 70

Simeon Jackson near Northourum died May 2

John Hanson's wife of Bingley bur. May 5

Mr. Savill of Medley a young gentleman, heir to a vast estate fell into a Draw Well at Whitebear in Wakefield May 8, at night. Mr Watson, of Cunsbrough went down by the Rope Imediately after him, helpt him up, got into the Buckett, both of 'em, but the Rope breaks as some were winding 'em up, they plunge down into the well & were both drown'd. They and many others had bin at a Cocking there 2 or 3 days that week

Mr Witton of Wakefield bur his son May 10.

Mrs Baron fell ill in her journey at Little brook May 2, died there

BURIALS.

May 12, bur. at Bradford by her Husband lately Vicar there

Mr Wm. Bagshaw, Minr at Stanington in Derbyshire bur. May 16

Doctor Yarbrough of Manchester bur. at New Church May 12. The first that was buried there

Mr Martin Hotham of York died suddenly May 23

Susanna Tillotson of Northourum died May 21. Had bin servant with Mr & Mrs. Heywood abt 26 years, aged abt 73

Mrs Heald of Huthersfield died suddenly May 24. being Lords Day had bin at Church & heard her Husband preach both ends of the Day

John Rooks of Royds Hall, Esq. died suddenly May 31

Mr John Andrews of Little Lever near Bolton died abt latter end of May

Mr Henry Newcome Parson of Middleton died abt middle of June

Willm Middlebrough of Osset died June 15

Mr Thomas Sargeant of Stand in Prestwich Parish bur. June 22

Widow Jagger of Lands Head in Northourum bur. July 7. an old woman

Abraham Ashworth of Wareley bur. his wife July 8, the fourth wife

Michael Woodhead of Shay in Northourum bur. July 9, aged 80

―――― Hardcastle near Leeds bur. July 21, Father to the Minister

Robert Clayton of Shelf died July 24 of a few days Sickness

Widow Bentley of Sowerby Dean bur. July 28 aged abt 98

William Scott near Wakefield bur. his son William Aug. 4, 1713

Joshua Thornes of Osset bur. Aug. 3

Mr Richard Holden of Manchester bur. his wife Aug. 16

Mrs Finney of Wakefield bur. Aug. 17

Abraham Scott of Halifax bur. Aug. 24

Mr Eliezer Heywood of Dronfield bur. his wife abt. Aug 26, having buried his eldest dr. abt 5 weeks before

Mrs Phebe Sutton died at Leeds Sep. 7

Mr Saml Smith of York bur. his wife Sep. 22. She was Mr Frankland's dautr. of Rauthmell

Mr Tho. Johnson of Leeds bur. Sep. 22

Alderman Tho. Kitchingman of Leeds bur. Sep. 24. with great Pomp

Joseph Firth of Shutt died Oct. 2. suddenly

John s. Michael Ingham of Wareley died Oct. 2

Mr John Hollings (late of Crosley Hall) died at Bradford, bur.

Oct. 3

John s. John Burton of Ossett bur. Oct. 14. abt 2 year old

Abraham Frank of lower Willow Hall near Wareley was at Rochdale Oct 26, came home abt 8 a clock at night died abt 3
a clock next morning Oct 27, its supposed that he Poyson'd
himself, having his maid servant with child

Jonas Woodhead of Shay in Northourum bur. Nov. 7

Mrs Wadsworth (late) of Horbury bur. Nov. 11

Mr. Saml Angier Minr at Dukinfield died Nov. 8. had bin almost
blind for many years, 1713

Mr Saml Harrison of Wakefield died Nov. 13, aged abt. 21, design'd for the Ministry

Mary Bland of Norwood Green, wid. died Nov. 15

Mr Barret, Minr in Nottingham died abt middle of Novr.

Widw Pendlebury near Turton in Lancr. mother to Mr. P. of
Leeds, died Nov. 18

John Wood of Barnshill bur. Nov. 26

John Frost the Carrier of Lightcliffe died Dec. 1

Madm. Beaumont died in Halifax buried Nov. 30

Thomas s. John Bentley of Northourum bur. Dec. 23

Mr Titus Alred of Bradford died Dec. 19   Design'd for the Ministry

John Cunliffe of Halifax died Jan. 11

John Jewet near Bradford died Jan. 22, an old Disciple, one of
the Kipping Society abt 90 years of age

John Harrison servt with Mr John Maude near Wakefield died of
the Small Pox bur. Jan. 20

Mr Robert Town of Eland died Jan 25 of a consumption aged
abt. 17

Eliz. wife of Tho. Gott of Bingley bur. Feb. 2, 171¾

John Hall of ffield in Northourum bur. Feb. 7

Gabriel Learoyd of Halifax bur Feb. 8

Robert Butterfield of Halifax died Feb. 11

Abraham Milner of lower Brear in Northourum died Feb. 9. aged
67

Dr John Sharp Arch-Bishop of York died Febr. 3. aged abt 68

Mr Willm Midgley near Bradford bur. Feb. 17

Mr John Lister of Horton bur. his son, F. 20

—— son of John Holdsworth of Clayton had bin running a Race
with another Boy, said I've won if it was for 100 li. fell down

BURIALS.

and died forthwith aged abt 7, Febr. 20

Mr Edward Wainhouse of Willow Hall near Halifax died Feb. 24

Mr John Martyn of Durham died Feb. 8, a very pious Usefull man

Abigail d. John Priestley of Westercroft died March 3, bur Mch 5. aged 9

Mrs Sarah Birron of Bradford died Mar. 8

Widw Thackeray of Wakefield bur. Mch. 15

James Naylor of Northourum bur. his wife Mar. 15

Widw. Waddington near Brighouse bur. Mar. 18

Old Squire of Shelf (a poor old man) bur. Mar. 18

Anne Day (our maids Aunt) bur. at Dewsbury Mar. 25. 1714

Mr. Tho Anby Parson of Thornhill and Justice of Peace died Mar. 27. 1714

John Heald (lately) of Ossett Leets bur. Mar 31

Mr Timothy Jollie Minr in Sheffield died Mar. 28, bur Mar. 31. A worthy useful man

James Cordingley of Bierley bur. Apr. 10

John Roades of Thornton bur. Apr. 15

Mr Tho. Rigg near Halifax bur. his wife Apr. 20

Michl Ramsden near Halifax d. Ap. 23

Timothy Kirshaw of Wyke bur Apr. 29

Mr Dinely of Bramhup died Apr.

Mrs Dixon of Leeds (the old Alderman's widw.) late of little Woodhouse d. Apr.

Joseph Sutton of Woodhouse bur. his wife Apr.

Richd Riddlesden of Norwood Green died Apr.

Mr Kitchingman of Hunslet died Apr. (well & dead in abt. 3 days)

James Mitchel of Norwood Green & Robt Wilson of Norwood Green died abt. May 1, both old men

Joshua Benn of Northourum died May 25, aged abt 60

Richd Bentley of Bradford died May 29, aged abt 30

Timothy Wade of Northourum died May 30

Lord Irvin of Temple Newzam, near Leeds died of the Small Pox at London May 18, bur at Whitchurch May 29, 1714, aged abt 22

Duke of Beauford died of the Gripes May 22

The Princess Sophia of Hannover died May 29 aged 84

Saml Stocks died at Landimer in Shelf June 3

Mr Boswell a Justice of Peace near Penistone died sudden only

BURIALS.

Lords Day Evening with a purse of money in his hand June 13
Mr Matthew Henry had bin Minr at Chester many years, was re-
mov'd to Hackney about 3 years ago, died at Nan'twich in
Cheshire June 22, its tho't of an Apoplexy tho' had got a fall
from his Horse day before, an eminent Minr, 57
Thomas Oldfield of Wareley died June 22, aged 80
Bryan —— servt. with Mr Brooksbank of Eland was drown'd
bathing him in the River June 25
Mr Benjn. Naylor of Manchr. bur. his wife June
John Wilson of Bradshaw bathing him in a River near Kighley on
Lords Day Evening June 27 was drown'd
Mary Mallison, widw. in Lightcliffe fell into a well in her own
cellar, taken up dead June 28
Daniel Wilkinson of Holdsworth bur. July 27
Jeremy s. Joshua Brooksbank of Oxheys bur. July 29 .
Abraham s. Mr Saml Crompton of Darby died in the Small Pox
July 18
Sr Lionel Pilkington, near Wakefield, bur. July
Queen Anne died Lords-day Morning Aug. 1. 1714. Aged 49
years & a half
Bathshua d. Mr Clough of Eland bur. Aug. 7. A week short of
a year old
Willm Holdsworth of Allerthorp near Wakefield bur. his wife
Aug. 12
Josiah Mitchel of Priestley Green bur. Aug. 22
Richard Robinson of Norwood Green died Aug. 23, aged abt 80
Mr Francis Wheatley of Wakefield bur. Aug. 27
Mr. Cass of Wakefield bur. his wife Aug. 28
Mr. Joshua Dawson, of Leeds bur. his wife Sep. 2
Margaret Pierson of Wibsey bur. Sep. 2
Anne wife of Abraham Rodes near Bradford buried
Mrs Mary Corlas died at Leeds Sep. 6. bur. at New Church Sep. 8
Mr Josiah Stansfeld of Haugh End near Sowerby Brigg died Sep. 7
Jeremiah Clay of Northourum died Sep. 11
Tim. Stocks of Northourum bur. his dr. Hannah Sep. 21, a little
Drawf [dwarf] abt 13 year old, of Small Pox
Mr Cass of Wakefield bur Oct 7
Dr Radcliffe one of the late Queen's Physitians died at London
Nov. 2
Saml Jackson of Alverthorpe bur Nov. 9

Madm Elizabeth Rodes of Wakefield bur. Nov. 11
Mr Banks Parson of High church in Hull died Nov 3. 1714
Mr Richardson Curate at Bradford bur. Nov. 19
Mr Willm Walker of Crow Nest in Lightcliffe died Nov. 26
Mr Matthew Blyford of Norwich died of Small Pox. Nov.
John Ambler of Haslehirst in Northourum bur Dec 17. aged
    near 80
Mary d. John Strengfellew died Dec 20
George Oldfield of Beggrington bur. Dec. 23
Titus Greenwood died at Staups of Sm. Pox. Dec. 27
Thomas Foster of Alverthorp bur. Dec. 18
Mrs Mary Judgkins of London died abt Xmas
Adam Taylor of Harley Green bur. his son Er, Dec 11
Mrs Lucy of Halifax died Jan 15. She was a midwife & had
    laid a wife day before
Widw Sheffield of Clifton burd. Jan. 17
Lydia d. John Priestley of Westercroft bur. Jan. 19 died of
    Small Pox
John Sonier son of Wid. S. bur. Jan. 20. of Small Pox
James Alderson of Halifax bur. a child of Small Pox. Jan. 24
Jonathan Longbothom of Booth Town bur. a child of Small Pox
    Jan. 26
Willm Dyson the Bookseller bur. two children both of a day,
    of the Small Pox being all they had Jan.
Jere. Harper of Halifax bur. his wife Feb. 3
Adam Taylor of Hally Green bur. three children of the Small
    Pox Feb. 5. one aged abt 16, another 12, another 9, full of
    Purples, another was buried Feb. 10. And he bur. a fifth child
    Feb. 12. aged 6: Thamar, Zora, Abia, Tera, Tirza
James Royds bur. at Coley Feb. 9. 1714-5
Joshua Ashworth of Wareley bur. his wife Feb. 24
Mr Benjamin Baxter a young Minr. in Nottingham died
    Feb. 19
Widw. Lord near Northourum died Feb. 27
John Holroide of Hipperholm died Feb. 27
Joshua Scholfields dr. Susan bur Feb. 27
John Askew bur. his son Joseph Mar. 3
Mr Midgley at Swan in Halifax bur. mar. 10
Anne wife of Moses Holdsworth died in Childbed March 15   ·
Dr Gilbert Burnet Bishop of Salisbury died Mar. 17. aged 73

BURIALS.

Jonath. Rigg of Wareley bur. Mar. 23

Thomas s. Saml Bentley of Shelf died in the Small Pox Mar. 23

George s. Tho. Fearnley of Holdsworth bur Mar 20

Mr Tho. Hall, Cheshire, died Mar. 25

Mr Kitchingman of Medow Lane bur. Mar. 26. 1715

Martin Longbothom of Northourum died Mar. 26

John Bamforth (my Clark at Northourum) died Mar. 27. Buried at Halifax Mar. 30. aged abt. 34

Mary d. of Jeremiah Baxter of Northourum died Apr. 5. aged 9 years & 4 Months

Martha Pighells of Salter-lee bur. Apr. 14

Joseph s. of Jeremiah Baxter of Northourum died Apr. 17. in the 17th year of his Age

Joseph Philips near Booth Town bur. Apr. 20

Mr Joshua Dutton Minr. at New Castle in Shropshire died at Nantwich in Cheshire was bur. Apr. 30

Mr John Wadsworth of Holdsworth died May. 7

Mary Lea Widw. (late wife of Anthony Lea of High Bentley) died May 11

—— Hargreaves (a young man, came from Haslinden died suddenly at the Raus near Halifax bur. May 14

Nathan Bates near Halifax died suddenly May 14

Richard Brown died May 29. at Blakehill 61

Mr John Steere Minr. at Beverley bur. June 20

Mr James Bretcliffe of Halifax bur. June 29. a young man

Lydia wife of Joseph Gargrave of Bradford died July 9

Marg'ret wife of John Milnes of Northourum died July 11

Grace Ramsden of Northourum (near Shipden head) had taken horse for Bradford July 14. Rode but a few Roods from her own house, the Horse Struck to th' Gallop she could not hold him : (thinking to save herself) Slipt off, broke her leg, whereof she died July 19. A very Pious, discreet, useful woman

Joseph s. Mrs Dunnel of Leeds bur. July 27

Mr. Lepton (th' Attorneys Father) bur. at Huuslett August 3

Mr Joshua Dun bur. at Halifax Aug 9. aged abt 80

Susanna d. Saml. Pollard of upper Shipden Hall bur. Aug 10. aged 21

Mrs. Susan Danson died at Brierley near Ludenden Aug. 17

BURIALS.

Jeremiah Ryley near Sowerby bur. Aug. 16

Samuel Day near Dewsbury died Aug 19

Mr Abraham Dawson's wife of Cottingham died Aug. 7

Justice Heber of Marton was at Church Aug. 21. died the next day

John Holdsworth was at Northourum Chappel Aug 21.died Aug 25.

Timothy Stocks of Northourum died Aug. 28

Lewis ye 14th King of France died Aug. 1. aged 77, in the 72 year of his Reign

Nathan Pighells bur. his wife Sep. 11

Mr Tho Kitson of Cliff in Lightcliffe died Sep. 11.

Mr. John Brooksbank of Eland (my worthy ffriend) died Sept.23. A man of Extraordinary Piety and Usefulness

Nathan Pighells bur. Oct. 6.

Mr. Wilson Minr at Rotheram died of a ffever Oct. 8. bur. Oct. 10

Mr. Blades of Leeds died abt. Oct. 24.

Joshua s. Joshua Robertshaw died Oct 19

John Dixon's wife of Bradford died Oct. 15

Tho. Harrison's wife of Onelyhouse in Northourum died Oct. 30.

Widw. Moorhouse died at her Son's at Norwood-Green Nov. 2. bur. at Kildwik in Craven.—Nov. 5. 1715

Mr. — Empson of Wyke (ye Attorney), died Nov 17

Mr. John Murgatroyd near Dewsbury died Nov. 7

Mr Askew an Alderman of Leeds bur. Nov. 15

Mrs Dunnel of Leeds bur. Nov. 19

Mr Richd Boys born in Halifax, Educated in both University's, afterwards wth Mr Ambrose, Mr Angier, Mr Hill, and Mr Waterhouse, was Minr. at Horbury at Drax &c fell into decay, had a monthly Allowance and went abroad for Several years, had bin marrying a Couple near Thornton Mills on Lds Day Nov. 20. in his Return late at night (missing the Brigg) was drown'd at North-Brigg near Halifax, aged 80 and abt 6 weeks

Mary Rishworth Widw. bur. at Coley Nov. 29

Mrs Anne Priestley of York (d. of Widw Priestley) died of a ffever, in 3 days, Nov. 28

Mr Thomas Whalley of Winterburn in Craven died Nov. abt. 30

Mr Joseph Lepton (late of Pudsey) died at Great Gumersal, Dec. 10. left an Estate of abt 200 p ann his wife great of first

BURIALS.

Dr Thomas Tenison A : Bp. of Canterbury died Dec : 14. aged 8 had bin A. Bp. there 21. years A worthy man, fit for the place

Thomas Shack near Harley Green died Dec. 14

John s. of Joseph Brooksbank of Eland died suddenly Dec. 22. bur Dec. 24. aged a Year & Quarter

Rached d. of John Berry died at Lee in Northourum Dec. 23

Mr John Kilvington of Leeds went to York——died there Jan. 6. of the Stone

Mr Richd. Thorp of Horton was in Wakefield Jan. 2. in Huthers-fied Jan. 3. fell sick Jan 4. and died Jan. 6. at Leezhall near Thornhill having lately purchased it for abt 1800 li, and had liv'd there a few months onely

Mr Margerison Minr. at Mirfield Church having bin out at Diner at one place & at supper at another Jan 6, came home about 12 aClock in the night died abt 3 hours after, Jan 7. Said to be an Impost Both buried at Mirfield Jan. 10

Dinah d. of Widow Jackson of Northourum bur. Jan. 11

Mr John Turner Merchant in Leverpool (Bro. Benjn's Master) died Jan. 8

James Wallis near Collier Syke bur. Jan. 19

John Hodgshons wife of Holdsworth buried the same day an. 19. both old

Widow Bradley near Batley bur. Jan. 23

Elkanah Wirral of Halifax bur. his son James Jan. 25

Mr Norfolk of Horbury bur. his onely daughter, Edith, Jan. 28

Jonas Parker of Wakefield bur Feb. 1. at Westgate-end chappel, to which he left — p. ann. for the Minister

Mr Anthony Naylor of Wareley bur. his wife ffeb. 9

Nathan Holdsworth an Inkeeper on the Heights in Northourum bur. ffebr. 10

Widw. Strickland of Rodley bur ffebr. 14

Widw Tetlaw of Norwood Green bur Feb. 15, aged abt 90

Robert Porter's wife near Halifax bur Feb. 16

Mr John Killingbeck Vicar of Leeds died Feb 13

Mr — Diggles of Leverpool died Febr. abt. 16

Mr Horton of Barkisland died Febr. 19

John Murgatroyd of the Heights near high by. died Feb. 21, aged abt. 87

Mr Tho. Butterworth of Manchester died

Mrs Crompton of Old Hall in Prestwich Parish (Mr Joseph Cromp.

BURIALS.

tons wife) died abt Apr. 4
Sr William Thornton of York Bart. bur. Febr. 27
Mr. Jackson Vicar of Dewsbury died Feb. 28
Susan Hurd of Northourum died Mar. 3
Sarah wife of Willm Clayton of Lee Lane Mar. 2
Benjn s. Mr. Ebenezer Naylor of Wakefield died Mar. 3.
Mr Joseph Holroyd of Sowerby Dean call'd Esq was Ryding from
    Halifax Mar. 25. abt one a Clock on Lds. day morning, fell off
    his Horse below Kin Cross and was taken up Dead, bur. Mar.
    27, 1716
Mr Tho. Rigg was in Halifax on Saturday Mar. 31. died the next
    morning Apr. 1
Ellen d. Tho Clark of Scout Hall died Apr. 8
Mrs Moor (only Child of Mrs Bark of Wakefield bare her first
    child Apr. 6. died soon after, aged abt. 16
Mr Byron near Leeds bur. his dr. Apr. 12. abt. 3 quarters old
Dr Adam Holland Minr at Macclesfield in Cheshire died
Mr Alexander Pollett of Heaton Yate in Prestwich Parish died
Stephen Hurd bur. at Coley Apr. 21
Mrs Lever of Market Street Lane End in Manchester died May 1
Mr. Ralph Ainsworth Minr. at Rivington in Lancashire died
James Dickenson died at Lee in Northourum bur. May. 11. aged
    abt. 88
John Hardiste near Scout Hall died May 10
Sr. Raphe Assheton of Middleton in Lanc Bart. bur. May. 10
Mr. Benjn. Wade of New Grange near Kirkstall Abbey, Justice of
    Peace, bur. May. 19
Mr. Teatam Vicar of Almanbury bur. May 18
Dinah Drake of Northourum Green Widw. died May. 20. had
    bin helpless a long time
Mr. Copley of Batley bur. May 23
Mr. — Dunne of Halifax bur. abt. June 4
Danl Bates of Halifax bur. his wife June
John Whiteley a poor man died suddenly June 21
Michael Bentley of Leeds bur. his wife June abt middle
Mr. — Simpson of York bur. June 24
Elizabeth d. of Charles Hughes of Northourum bur. July 17
Samuel Spencer of Shelf Hall bur. Aug 21
Widw. Sharp (Mothr. to Mr. Sharp of Coley bur. Aug. 22
Isaac Hollings s. of John Hollings of Cottingley near Bingley

BURIALS.

bur. Aug. 10. 1716. A Hopefull young man design'd for the ministry
Mr Nathl Holden of Halifax bur. Sep. 7
Mr James Coningham Minr in London, died Sept. 1
Mr Thomas Freke another London minr. died abt the same time viz. Sept. 7
Martha Ramsden of Park Nook bur. Sep. 20
Robt Cotton of Halifax bur. Oct 7
James Pye near Horton bur Oct. 12. of a short Sickness
Martha a wife of Saml Appleyard of Shelf died Oct. 15, bur Oct. 21
Elizabeth wife of John Ramsden of Park Nook in Southourum died Oct. 20
Thomas Hutchinson of Hunslet died Oct.
Thomas s. Mr. Christopher Dade. of Sutcliffe Wood bur. Nov. 5
Widw. Priestley near Lands Head in Northourum bur. Nov. 6
Mr Richd Brear of Eland died Nov. 8. aged 63
Bridget Doughty of Holdsworth died Nov. 11
Mrs Jackson (the late Vicar of Dewsbury's widw. bur. Nov. 14
Mrs Ramsden of Clay House near Eland bur. Dec. 22
Mrs Rawson of Bradford (wife of Mr Rawson the Attorney) bur. Dec. 22
Mr Nathanl Gaskell of Manchester died Nov. 21
Richd Town of Eland died of Small Pox at Leeds bur. at Eland Dec. 7. aged 14
Benjamin Day of Heckmondwyke bur Dec. 17. Father to Mary Day our late maid
Mary d. Mr. Gamaliel Brear of Eland & Elizabeth d. Mr. David Brear of Eland died of the Small Pox Dec. 16 bur. both in one grave Dec. 18
Ester d. John Sutcliffe, Houskeeper to Moses Holdsworth in the Green Lane in Northourum died Dec. 24 of a very short sickness
Mr. Willm Richardson of High Fearnley died Jan. 2. 1716-7
James Naylor of Lim'd House in Northourum died Jan 3
Widw Baxter near Southourum bur. Jan. 11
Mr. John Wrightson of Leeds bur. his little dr. Mary Jan. 24
Phebe dr. Mr. Wood of ffold died Feb. 1, burd. ye 6th.
Mr. Telford an Attorney at Leeds bur. Feb. 10
Mr Jonas Waterhouse of Bradford an ancient N. C. Minr died Feb. 13, in the 90th year of his age

BURIALS.

Robt. Mercer drown'd near Bradford Feb. 20
Lydia wife of John Beamont bur. Mar. 4 : of Alverthorp
Mrs. Elizabeth Holden (wife of Mr. Tho. Holden of Halifax) died
Mar. 5, burd. 8
Henry Tassey of Halifax died Mar. 8
Mrs. — Walker of Crow Nest bur. Mar. 25. 1717
Mary Longbothom of Northourum died Mar. 30
Dorothy wife of Geo. Bothomley died Apr. 3
John s. Doctr Nettleton of Halifax died Apr. 6 aged a year, 15
weeks & 4 days. 1717
Widw Hollings of Allerton died Apr. 22. bur Apr. 26. at Bradford
Mr Field Sylvester of Sheffield died May 10. bur. May 12. a
usefull man, much lamented
Mr Eliezer Birch, Minr at Manchester New Chappel died May
12, bur. May 15. A man of Eminent ministerial Abilities :
The loss is very great. Cease Lord ! Help Lord !
Isabel — of Halifax, dr of James Gregson of Northourum died
May 17
Mr Atkinson of Call-lane in Leeds Alderman & Attorney bur.
May 21
Mr. George Low a Dissenting Minr. died in Chappel le Frith in
April 1717
Mrs Crowther of Northourum died May 29. 1717, aged abt. 78
left a great estate
Mr Joseph Wood of Hold in Northourum was left Executor & a
considerable part of her Estate was left to him he fell sick
next morning & died abt 11 a Clock at night May 30. abt 27
hours after her death—his son Willm Wood was joined with
his Father in the Executorship, & is now the only surviving
Executor, being a boy about 14 years of age. O how vain is
this world, & how vain is the Hope of man
John Parkinson of Horton died May 31 of 2 or 3 days sickness
Mrs Langley of Bradford (lately wife of Mr Abra. Langley of
Priestley Green bur. June 13
Mrs. Fenton of Hunslet bur. June 19. She died of a Cancer
Mr. John Blakey of Coln in Lancr. died of a palsie bur. June 20
Martha d. John Terry of High Bentley died of 3 or 4 days illness
June 23
John Bancroft's wife of Wareley bur. June 24
Joseph Moor Junr. of Ovenden bur June 18

BURIALS.

Eli s. Elkanah Wirrall bur. June 28 abt a year old

Mr Saml Wareing of Bury in Lancr. died abt. June 1

Richard Warburton's servt maid died June 25 of a few hours sickness

Mr Benja Pollard Curate of Wibsey died June 30. bur. July 3. 1717

—— wife of Isaac Baum near Bradford bur. July 3

John s. of Mr John Wrightson of Leeds bur. July 3, aged 2 yrs 2 mths.

Willm Ellis of Halifax bur. July 12

— dr Danl Bateman of Shelf bur July 13

Mrs Hannah Bretcliffe of Halifax bur. July 17. a young woman

—— wife of John Illingworth of Ossett fell down & dyed suddenly July 29

—— dr of Ebenezer Holdsworth of Alverthorp bur. July 30 of Small Pox

Mr John Batley of Halifax bur. July 31

Mr Gamaliel Jones Minr. at Chadkirk near Stockport died June

John Stocks of Halifax fell of his horse & died suddenly in Lincolnshire where he was going to buy wool, Aug., abt the middle

Nathl. Chadwick of Halifax bur. his wife Aug. 27

Dr. Bezaleel Angier died in London abt Aug. 1   He was son of Mr Saml Angier lately minr. at Dukinfield in Cheshire

Thomas Reyner of Walter-Clough bur. his wife Aug. 29

Mr. Shaw of Leeds Junr. died at York Sept. 1

Mr. Dean Minr. at Osset bur Sept

Mr. — Sunderland Curate at Sowerby Brigg died of a few hours Sickness Sept. 15

Mr. James Alderson near Halifax bur. his eldest dr. of Small Pox Sept. 20

John Sutcliffe of Clayton-Heights died Sept. 22

Hannah Kitchin of Leeds bur. Sep. 23

Andrew Hartley of Common woodbottom, bur. Oct. 8

Michael Bentley of Lightcliffe died of Small Pox, left a wife & Child—bur Oct. 9

John Gledhill of Pule Top bur. Oct. 9

Mr — Haigh near Huthersfield bur. Oct. 3. died drunk

Tho. Broadley of Holdsworth died Oct. 12

Abigail dr. of Mr Smith of Mixenden died of the Small Pox Oct. 13

— dr. of John Midgley of Illingworth died of Small Pox. Oct 15

BURIALS.

Edward Hanson of Eland Hall found dead in his bed, Oct. 16.

Sr John Middleton of Northumberland died of a high Fever at Holbarn in London Oct. 17

Mr. Theophilus Shelton Clerk of Peace Keeper of Register at Wakefield died at Nottingham Nov.

Mr. Asaph Gledhill of Wakefield bur. his wife Oct. 28

Mr. Thomas Leach near Bingley bur. Nov. 7

Mr. Hodgshon N. C. Minr. in York died Dec.

Capt. John Fourness of Halifax died Nov. 10. bur. Nov. 12

Elizabeth wife of Robert Kitson of Upper-Brear bur. Nov. 15

Mrs. Mary Kirk of Alverthorp died Nov. 19 bur. at Woodkirk Nov. 23. aged 96

Mr. John Shaw of Bradford bur. his 2nd Wife Nov. 23

John Bancroft of Warley bur. Dec. 7

Mr. John Shaw of Bradford bur. Dec. 14

Mr. Isaac Sharp of Horton bur. his Wife Dec. 12

Widw. Elizabeth Heaton of Soperhouse near Coley Chappel bur. Dec. 16

James Pierson's wife of Landshead in Northourum Sick'ned Dec 14. died 15

John s. of Jeremy Baxter of Northourum died Dec. 18. aged 22 & a half

Michael Wainhouse of Broad Yates near Halifax fell off his Horse near Kin-Cross & was taken up dead Dec 21

Tho. s. John Morhouse near Norwood-Green bur. Dec. 24

Sr Nicholas Sherburn of Standish in Lancr. died at his son in laws house the Duke of Norfolks at Worksop in Nottingham-shire abt Dec. 19

Joshua Brearley of Hagstocks died of a very short sickness Dec 30

Dr. Wroe the Warden of Manchr. died

—— a servt of Elkanah Farrars in Ovenden Wood died of Smal Pox, bur Jan. 5

—— dr of John Bradley miller at Mill near Holdsworth died of the bite of a mad Dog, bur. Jan. 5

Benjn. Wade, of Peel House near Luddenden was in Halifax Jan. 4. fell sick, stay'd at Mount Pellon, died next Morning Jan. 5. bur. Jan. 8

Mrs Dorothy Waller of Morley bur. Jan 22

Mr Abraham Langley of Hipperholm died Jan. 24

R

BURIALS.

Mr Joseph Jackson of Leeds died at my house in Northourum Jan. 24. bur. in Halifax Church Jan. 28

Mr Carr Curate at Honley bur. Jan. 25

Mr Joshua Wright of Hipperholm my dear & faithfull ffriend died Jan. 26. between 4 & 5 a Clock in the afternoon being Lds Day aged 60 years but 5 months. A great Loss. bur. in Halifax Church Jan. 29. 1717-18

Mr Lodge Minr at Leeds New Church died Jan 31

Mr. Green bur. at Bradford, Feb. 2

Jere s. Jere Northen of Northourum bur. Feb 2. died of Small Pox

Willm Hopkinson Servt wth Anthony Practor of Cinderhills died of Small Pox, very full of purples bur. Feb. 6

Elizabeth d. Mr. Tho Holden of Halifax died Febr. 4. bur Feb. 7

Charles Talbot Duke of Shrewsbury died Feb. 1

George William s. of the Prince of Wales died Feb. 6

Elizabeth wife of Mr. John Farrar of Wareley died Feb. 25. bur. at Luddenden, 28

Mr Richd Holt minr in Leverpool died Mar.

Mary d. Mr. Sharpe Curate at Coley died Mar. 1

Caleb Scholefield of Staups in Northourum died Mar. 4. bur at Halifax Mch 7

Mr Elkana Rich s. of Mr Rich of Bullouse died of Small Pox Mar. 3

Thomas Pool of Halifax bur. his wife Mar. 13

Richd Holroide of Ribbenden bur. his wife Mar. 14

Widw Kirshaw of Holdsworth bur Mar. 20. aged abt 88

Elizabeth d. Mr. John Heywood late Minr at Pontefract bur Mar 23

John Rous of Alverthorp bur Mar, abt 18

Elizabeth wife of John Haliday at Scout Hall died Mar. 22 bur Mar. 26

Samuel Crowther of Lands-head in Northourum died Mar. 25

Doctor Colton of York bur. his wife April 3. died Mar. 31

Mr Josias Oates of Chickenley bur. Mar.

Saml Nicols of Halifax died suddenly Apr. 7

Widow Kitson late wife of Tho Kitson of Upper Brear bur. Apr. 13

Mr Francis Maude of Wakefield bur. Apr 12

John Wirral of Halifax bur. his wife Apr. 15

Mrs Susanna Nettleton sister to Dr N. died Apr. 12

Mr Richd Witton a Lawyer in Wakefield died Apr. 16

Stephen s. of my Bro. in Law Mr Stephen Foster of London died

BURIALS.

Apr. 18 aged abt 4 years & 8 mths

Anthony Fountain near Mirfield May 10

Mr John Noble of Angel in Halifax died abt. May 11

Saml Bentley's wife of Shelf bur June 3

Mr John Allison of Priestley Green died May 21

John Futhergill of Ossett died June 10. a Serious ancient Christian

Widw. Stocks of Shelf bur. at Coley June 21

John Lever Esq of Alkrington near Middleton in Lancr died June 22. bur June 27, 1718, aged abt. 42

Joseph Naylor of Ossett bur. June 3

Widw. Scholefield of Bins bur. June 2

James Grimshaw of Droylsden in Manchester Parish (having run a nail into his hand wch shortly Gangren'd) died June 27

Wm s. Mrs Langley of Hipperholm bur. July 6

Mrs Lydia Flower of Gainsbrough died at Chesterfield wth her mother

Mrs Thomas July 4. (dr of Mr Robt. Ledgard late of Leeds

Mr Tho. Clapham Vicar of Bradford died July 22

Mr Peter Ashton Curate at Milnroe near Rochdale died at Eland abt Aug. 4

Mary wife of John Hobson of Cinderhills bur. Aug 24, died of 2 or 3 days sickness

Mr Jere. Ryley of Kib-royd in Sowerby Dean died at Norwich Aug. 24

John Stringfellow of Halifax died Sep. 1. of 2 or 3 days sickness

Mrs Mary Drake of Manchester bur. Sep. 5

Willm Pullen of Bradford bur. his wife Sep. 2. (Bessy Wheater's sister.)

Tho. Smith of Bradford bur his wife Sep. 16

Mrs. Hartley wife to Mr Hartley Curate at Armley died Aug.

James Hall of Horton died Sept. 25

Judith wife of Richard Clapham of Halifax died in Child-bed Sept. 26. first Child

George Morhouse near in Hulme Firth bur. his Wife Sept. 25

Mr Timothy Heywood of Sheffield (Son to Mr John Heywood late Minr. at Pontefract) died Sept. 24. having bin mar. the 18th of the same month

Mr Anthony Allison of Priestley-Green died Oct. 2. bur. Oct. 3

Zipporah Boocock of Northourum Green died Oct. 3

BURIALS.

Mr. Joseph Whitaker, brot. up wth his Uncle Mr. Whitaker of Leeds mar. a clergyman's dr. Confined prech't at — was found dead in a draw well near his House his throat cut Sept. abt. 26

Hannah dr. of Mr James Stansfield of Bowood, bur. at Sowerby Oct. 7. 1718

John Scholefield bur. at Halifax Oct. 7, he died with his Uncle at Trimingham

Susanna wife of Jeremiah Baxter of Northourum died Oct. 10

Widw Hanson of Backall bur. at Eland Oct. 14

John Wilkinson's wife of Illingworth died Oct. 13

Mr. Mottershead Minr at Manchester bur. 1 is wife Oct. 9

Mr. Dean vicar of Batley bur. abt. Oct. 24

John Scott of Halifax bur. his wife Oct. 22

Mr. Saml. Wadsworth of fflanshaw died Oct. 26. bur Oct. 27. in Wakefield Chappel

Hannah dr. of Mr Rotheram of Dronfield died Nov. 1. aged 15 weeks

Richd. Kirshaw's wife of Wyke hang'd her Self Nov. 1

John Medley of Ash Tree in Shelf bur. Nov. 1

Mr. Elkanah Hoile of Ribbenden died Nov. 3

John Gill near Coley died suddenly Nov. 15

David s. of Caleb Ashworth of Northourum died Nov. 16. 3 quarters old

Mr. Benjamin Gill of London died Nov. 17

Susana dr. of Mr Jno Wrightson of Leeds died N. 2

Mary Rhoads near Halifax (widw.) died Nov. 21

Joseph Stocks of Kin Cross lane bur. Nov. 22

Willm Day of Childswell (our Maid's Father) died Nov. 28

Willm. Bamforth of Oats-royd bur. Dec. 6

Willm. Hodgshon of Holdsworth bur. his wife Dec. 8

Sara Scholefield of Halifax was bur. Nov. 28

Mr James Farrar of th' Ewood died suddenly Dec. 18

Timothy Stansfeld of Sowerby Dean died Dec. 19

—— d. Mr. John Gream near Halifax bur. Dec. 24

Esther Kirshaw of Wyke bur. Dec. 25

Mr — Midgley late of Headly died in Halifax, bur. Dec. 24

John Holdsworth of Clayton died Dec. 24

Joshua Burnet of Wakefield died Dec.

John s. Mr **Thomas** Holden of Halifax bur. Dec. 30

BURIALS.

Edmund s. Tho. Swaine of Shelf, bur. Dec. 30

Richard Dickenson my Sixth Child died Dec. 29. abt half hour after 6 in the Morning, was bur in the New Chappel in Northourum Dec 31 aged 3 years & near 5 weeks. His days were few and full of Trouble

Mr. Calverley of Leeds bur. Jan 20

John Walker of Lightcliffe died Jan 28 of a few hours Sickness, bur. Jan. 30. aged 88

Mr. Joseph Haigh of Honley (comonly call'd Chapman Haigh) died Feb. 2

John Jewet a Quaker died at Newel-Hall Feb. 8

Mr John Maude of Wakefield bur. his dr Frances ffebr. 13

Mrs Diggles of Manchester a Young Widow bur. by her late husband at Liverpool ffebr. 17

Mr John Greaves near Leeds bur. Feb. 3. he left 10li p. an. to Hunslet Chappel 9li 10s. to the Charity School having given a 100li to it in his life time besides other gifts &c.

Mr Mitchel Alderman of Leeds bur. Feb. 17. left a considerable Estate to three bad sons

Mr Isaac Hollings of Crosley Hall bur. at Bradford ffebr. 20. aged abt. 28 left his Estate of abt 120 p. an. to his wife & three sisters.

Mr Danl Thorp of Hopton died suddenly bur. at Mirfield Mar. 11

Mr. Parker of Carlton in Craven bur. Mar.

Mrs Empson late of Wyke bur. Mar. 22

Mary Smith near Coley Chappel bur. Mar 22

—— s. Mr Clough of Eland bur. Mar. 24

Elizabeth wife of Joseph Hainworth near Thornton bur. Mar. 27. 1719

John Askew died at Barushill Apr. 7

Joseph Hirst of Ossett died of a few hours Sickness Apr. 4

Widw Whiteley bur. at Dewsbury Apr. 8. Tho. Whiteley her husband lived near Coley Hall & at Mytham some years ago.

Ruth Mitchel d. of Wid Hartley died Ap. 9

Wid Martha Benn of Northourum Green died Apr. 9. bur. Apr. 11

Martha d. John Halliwell of Northourum bur. Apr. 19

Joseph Scott of Alverthorp bur. Apr. 21

Mr Dixon Minr at Ringley Chappel in Prestwich Parish in Lancr. bur. abt. Apr 2

BURIALS.

John Laycock of Lusburn Moor in Craven, Father to Tho Swaine's wife of Shelf bur. Apr. 23

—— wife of Ebenezer Holdsworth of Alverthorp died in child-bed, bur. Apr. 2

Mrs Mary Hollings wife of Mr Saml Hollings of Hipperholm died May 20. bur. at Halifax May 23

—— wife of George Boocock died of Small Pox in Northourum-back-lane June 1

Mr Willm Kitchingman of Skircote died June 6, very rich ; aged abt. 79

Mary 3d wife of Nathan Tilson bur. June 6

Mr John Holroide of Halifax bur. June 17

Daniel Scott of Addersgate in Northourum died June 16

Frances d. Dr Nettleton of Halifax died June 19, bur. 21

Mr Saml Wakefield of Halifax an Attorney died June 28

Francis Bentley of Halifax died July 5

Mr John Holbrook of Manchester bur his wife June 23

Saml s. Benjamin Sowood of Godley died of Small Pox July 12

Mrs Wainhouse of Halifax late of Willow Hall, widow, died Aug. 12

Judith wife of Mr Tho. Ferrand of Bradford died suddenly Aug. 19. bur. in the New Chappel there Aug. 21

Mr. John Lumb of Silk Coats died Aug. 17. bur. in the New Chappel at Wakefield Aug. 19

Mary Heron of Gorton bur. Aug. 20

James Low of Manchester bur. his wife Aug. 24

John Burton of Osset bur. Aug. 26

Willm. s. Saml Appleyard of Shelf bur. Aug. 27

Mary Scott of Athersgate in Northourum bur. Sep. 3

Mrs Judith d. Mr. Joseph Brooksbank of London died Aug. 24

Joseph Ashworth of Wakefield died Sep. 8

—— wife of Kighley of Heckinwyke bur. Sep. 8

Mr Wm Tottey of Leeds bur. Sep. 8

Mr John Millington of Manchester died at Scarbro'

Tempest Cordingley of Wibsey bur. Sept.

Mr. Tho. Holdsworth's wife of Asty died in Halifax Sep. 19

Joseph Milner died of Small Pox at Landimer Syke. Sep. 28

Mr Joseph Sutton near Leeds bur. Sept. 29

Mr King Parson at Ratcliffe in Lancr kill'd by a fall from his horse Sept.

James Hall near Southouram hang'd himself, Sep. 30

Joshua Knight of Cockill died Oct. 6

Mrs. Shaw bur. at Halifax Oct. 16. She was sister to the late Mr. Farrar of th' Ewood

Daniel Tempest of Comon house in Halifax died Oct. 24

My dear Bro. in Law Mr. Stephen Foster of London died Oct. 23

Rebecca wife of Willm Mann of Lightcliffe died suddenly Oct. 23

Mary wife of Andrew Hodgshon died Nov. 3. bur. at Dewsbury Nov 5

John Haliday died at Jere Baxters in Northourum Nov. 6

Charles Hughes of Northourum was drown'd in an old Cole Pit near Horton Nov. 6. found Nov. 8

Joshua Wilkinson bur. Nov.

Mrs Elston of Wakefield died Nov. 14

Mrs Elizabeth Nicolls of Eland married one Mr Pease near Doncaster abt. Oct. 21 abt. 5 weeks after Nov. 25, went to see her Aunt Chamberlayn of Skipton and hang'd herself there Nov. 28. her husband and her had only bin 10 days together, her Aunt died Nov. 30

John Baum's wife of Boulin bur. Dec 13.

Mrs. Gill died at Nottingham Dec. 4

James s. Tho. Clark of Scout Hall died Dec. 13

Richd s. Mr. Alexander Clough of Eland bur. Dec. 24. aged 2 y. 3 m.

Mr John Thomas minr in Chesterfield bur. Dec. 26

Jeremiah Batley of Lightcliffe died abt Dec 20

Mrs Dorothy wife of Mr. Jonath. Wright of Lightcliffe died Jan. 3. bur. Jan. 6

Judith d. Mr. Alex. Clough of Eland bur. Jan. 25. aged 5 years

Josiah Hepworth of Ossett bur. his wife Jan. 30

Andrew Hodgson's child br. Jan. 30

Mrs Anne Gream wife of Mr James Gream of Heath near Halifax died Feb 13. bur. at Halifax Feb. 16

Mr Daniel Gaskell of Clifton Hall near Manchester died Febr. 7. buried at Prestwich Feb. 10

Isaac Smith near High Cross in Northourum died Febr. 18

Joshua s. Mr Rotheram of Dronfield in Darbyshire died Feb. 11

Joseph s. Mr. Clough of Eland died Feb 20

Saml Sugden of Reavy died Mar. 6

John Hollings of Cottingley bur his wife at Bingley. Mar. 2

Wid. Martha Smith near Coley died Mar. 5

Richd Flother of Lightcliffe died Mar. 4
Mr Laycock Curate at Luddenden died Feb. 26
Mr Maude of Wakefield bur his dr. Mar 1
Mr Hawkins bur. his son John Mar 4
John Burkitt of Heckinwyke died Mar. 8. bur. at Birstall Mar 12
Joseph Drake of Northourum bur. his son Joseph Mar. 12
Mr Saml Bourn Minr. at Bolton in Lancr. bur. Mar. 8
Mr David Hartley Curate at Armley near Leeds bur. Mar. 15
Mr. Tho. Hill Minr in Derby died abt Mar. 8. or 10
Mr James Beck of Manchr bur Apr. 1
Richard s. Robt Porter near Halifax bur. Apr. 21. 1720
John Dixon of Bradford died Apr. 21
Mr James Gream of Heath near Halifax died Apr. 26
Mr. James Gream (his son) died May 2
Mr. Rook minr, at —— died abt latter end of Apr.
Mr John Benson minr at Bridlington bur. May 2
Mr John Gorwood of Hull, a Minr.
Tho. Bentley of Northourum bur. May 3
Mr Richd Richardson of High Fearncley bur June 7. A young man
Joseph Holroyd of Stump Cross in Northourum died June 15
Joshua Kitson of High Sunderland hall was well at diner went out with his man abt some work complain'd of a pain in his side, went into an Alehouse wch was near, died immediately June 16. 1720
Mr Sunderland Curate at Ribbenden died June 20 aged abt 80
Tho. Smith of Bradford died June 22
Wm. Thorp at Barnshill bur. his only child July 14. he being kill'd with a Cupboard falling on him
Edward Townend of Coley died July 10. 1720
Jane d. Mrs Furness of Halifax bur. July 28
Mr Francis Allison died in Halifax July 28
Mr Marshall Vicar of Calverley died July 23
Mr George Town died at Bryan Royd near Eland July 31, aged near 21 years
Jeremiah Holroyd of Wibsey cut his throat Aug. 21. died Aug. 25
Richd Taylor of Norland died Aug. 27
John Nettleton of Ossett bur his Wife Aug. 31
Richd Speigth of Hipperholm-lane-ends bur. Sept. 6

BURIALS.

Saml Bentley of Shelf died Sept. 1. bur. Sept 5
Joshua Stead of Bradford bur Aug. 31
Mr — Deykins of Barnsley died Sept. 11
Mr — Ashton Chaplain at Manchester church died Sept.
Mr John Priestley of Westercroft (my very dear ffriend was seiz'd
with some Illness on ffryday Sept. 9. was better next morning,
went to Halifax, was at Northourum Chapel on Lord's Day,
went to Rochdale on Monday was very ill that Evening,
return'd Home on Tuesday, died on ffryday abt 11 a Clock at
night.
John Dean at Hall-houses in Northourum was binding Corn till
8 a Clock on Saturday night Sept. 17. died abt 5 at night
next day
Mr John Rotheram of Dronfield in Derbyshire died Sept. 25
Mr Tho. Scholey a Popish Priest in Ossett died Oct 2, bur. in
Dewsbury Church, Oct. 4. without Reading
Mrs — Jackson of London (my mother Foster's Aunt) died abt
Oct.
Mr James Smith of Manningham died Oct. 8
Mr Milnes, of Kettering died Oct. 19
Mr Nathan Denton of Bolton near Haughton aged above 87 bur.
Oct. 13. being the last (that Ive heard off) of the Dissenting
Minrs ejected in 1662.
Mr — Hill Minr at Knaresborough died abt Oct. 1
Hannah wife of John Clark of Wakefield died abt Oct. 8
Mr Nevill of Cheet Hall near Wakefield died suddenly Oct 10
Mrs Esther Stern wife of Mr Stern of Woodhouse near Halifax
died at London Oct abt 18th
Mrs Fothergill of Wakefield bur. Oct. 22
Dame Buxton of Wakefield bur. Nov. 3
James s. Joshua Robertshaw of Lee in Northourum bur Nov. 16
Willm Rooks of Tanhouse died Nov. 27
Richard Hunter, of Scout died Nov. 27
Timothy s. John Sharp of Blakehill died Dec. 4
John Ramsden of Wellhead near Halifax bur. his wife Dec. 6.
she died in child bed
Mr Richd Clough an Apothecary in Stockport bur. Dec. 6. a
very useful man
Mrs Mary Clough (his wife) died Dec. 10. bur. Dec. 13
Joshua Smith of Northourum bur. his wife Dec. 20

282 *Dickenson's*

BURIALS.

Mr Haigh Curate at Horbury bur. his wife Dec.
Elizabeth Lee of Northourum bur. Dec. 27
Tho. s. Dr Nettleton of Halifax died Dec 28
Jonathan Viccars of Inghead in Northourum bur Jan 2
Joseph Oates of Mythom in Northourum bur. Jan. 6
Eliza. wife of Jere. Northend of Northourum bur. Jan. 11
Mr Watson Schoolmaster at Stand in Prestwich Parish died Jan.
Abraham Whitaker of Topliffe bur. Jan. 26
Jonathan Rawson near Halifax bur. his wife Jan. 28
Mrs Elenar Taylor wife of Mr Richard T. of Manchester died
  Feb. 10. bur. at Gorton Feb. 14, a pompous Funeral. 400d
    [&c., 2 lines in short hand]
Mr Richard Rodes of Great Haughton died ffebr 14,
    (1 line short hand)
Mr Daniel Denton Chaplain to Mr Rich of Bullouse died ffebr. 18
Mr John Dunnel of Leeds bur. ffebr. 22
Mr Wm Walker of Crow Nest in Lightcliffe bur. ffeb. 22
Michael Oldfield of Wareley died ffeb 21
Widw Jan Pickerd of Ossett. ffeb.
Mr — Rontre of Hunslet lane near Leeds bur. Feb. 10. 17 20
Mr Newson an Attorney in Lightcliffe died a Papist March 2
Henry Tomlinson of Alverthorp near Wakefield bur Feb. 21
Widw Cordingley near North Bierley bur Febr. 21
Major Bedford of Thornhill Briggs bur. Mar. 4
Saml Garnet of Tanhouse in Northourum died Mar. 8
Willm Holdsworth of Alverthorp bur. Mar. 1
George Shepley of Dewsbury bur Mar. 21
Mrs Eaton of Manchester Wid. of the late Mr Saml Eaton a
  N.C. Minr died there Febr. 19
Mr Joseph Beevers of New Miller dam near Cheet Hall bur. his
  second wife Apr. 1
Mrs Tilson of Wakefield died Mar. 25. 1721
Tho. Clark's wife of Ossett died in child-bed Mar. 27
Mr Breara the Mayor of Leeds bur his wife Mar. 31
    (line of short hand)
Michael Parker of Dewsbury an old Baylife bur. Apr. 1
Mr Marmaduke Rooks of Dewsbury bur. his wife Apr. 11. died
  in childbed
Mr Abraham Beevers of Wakefield died Apr. 18, very rich
Mr — Richardson of High Fearnley died May 8. bur May 8

Mrs Elizabeth Scholey of Ossett bur May 8. a Papist
John Crowther of Landshead bur. May 15
Mrs Heywood (Mr John Heywoods Widw) died at Balifield near
Sheffield Apr. 20
Mr Warren Curate at Honley bur May 13
Mr Joshua Laycock of Shay Hill near Halifax died May 16 a
Quaker, very rich
John Sonyer, of Harley green near Halifax bank died May 20. a
serious good man
Madm Richardson of Wakefield died June 6, 1721, having broke
her ankle bones by a fall from her Pad, May 31
Judith d. Mr Brooksbank of Eland bur. June 14
Tho Kitson of Halifax bur. June 15
Sarah d. Tho. Clark of Scout Hall died June 17 aged abt 1 & ¼
Mr Peter Peak of Manchester died abt. June 9
Lady Assheton of Middleton died at Kensington abt June 16
Ambrose Ingham near Beggrington bur. June 22, an old school-
master
Madam Cotton of Haigh Hall my dear and worthy ffriend died at
Sturbridge in Worcestershire July 8, bur. at Darton July 13
John Ramsden of Southourum bur at Halifax July 14. very rich
(tho' call'd poor John)
Mr John Simpson of Hipperholm died July 15. having languisht
sev. months
Mr Elkanah Berry Minr at Hopton died at his Fathers July 15
Mr Tho. Dunne of Halifax died July 31
Richd Nathrop of Mirfield bur. his wife Aug 2
Mr Coupe of Wakefield an Apothecary & Surgeon bur. Aug 11
Joseph Phillips of Osset near the Chappell bur. Aug 11
Mrs Sleadhill of Clayton near Thornton bur. Aug. 20
Tho. Haumond near Bradford bur. Aug 24
Mr Warner — (who married Mr. Brooksbanks dr, of London)
died Aug. 27
Mr Hall Vicar of Eccles near Manchester died Sep. 11. bur.
Sep. 13
John Wood of Greenlane in Northourum died Sept 26
John Hill of Northourum died Oct. 28
Joshua Sugden of Halifax bur Nov. 9
John Roberts of Hipperholm died Nov. 19, aged its said 114
wanting a month

BURIALS.

Hannah Oates Widw, near Norwood Green died Nov. 5

Sarah wife of William Wiggleworth of Hunslet near Leeds died Nov. 24. bur. Nov. 25

[short hand 3 lines]

Mr Stephen Langley of Hipperholm, died at Thornhill-briggs Dec. 9

Widw Gargrave of Burnet-field in Horton died Dec 3

James Alred of Bradford died Dec. 3

Mr Richd. Crowther at the Royal Oak in Wakefield bur. his wife

Tho. Harrison of Halifax bur. his wife Dec 14

Joshua Smith's wife at Priestley-green bur. Dec. 21

Mr Nathan Arderne of Redish in Manchester Parish (a Heaver of mine at Gorton died Dec. 26. had bin at Manchester the day before

Mrs. Catherine Hayhurst of Parkhead near Whaley died Nov. 16

James Binns of Ossett died Jan. 1

Mr. — Darling of Thorne died Jan. 3. bur. Jan. 6. Father to Mrs. Moults first Husband

Edward Hanson of Wood-Side near High-Fearneley died Jan. 8

Jeremiah Roads of Little Horton died Jan. bur. Jan. 12. aged. near. 80

Martha Hardistie Widw. bur. Jan. 19 from Landshead in Northourum, 1721

—— Brigg near Northourum Jan. 18

Jeremiah Holdsworth died at Whichwell in Shelf Jan

Mr Richard Walker of Walter Clough rid out Jan. 17. & was found drown'd in the River Calder Jan. 18, near Crumblebottom

(4 lines shorthand)

Doctor Gale a London Minr. died

Mr Pomfret of London died Jan.

Mr Hocker his Assistant died

Mr. Skipp another London Minr. died Jan Cease Lord !

Mr Francis Pitts of Wakefield bur. Jan. 29

Mr Piggot ye Lawyer died at Manchester Jan. 30

Mrs French of London (half line shorthand) hanged herself Jan. 30

Joseph Milner of Leeds died Febr 3, aged 83

Saml Riddlesden of Rooks near Norwood Green died Febr. 6

Mrs Hall of Hermitage near Holm Chapel in Cheshire died Febr. 3

BURIALS.

Richd Warburton of Clayton bur. Feb. 3

David Dean of Eland bur Feb. 22

Sr. Rowland Wynnes Lady of Nosthall near Wakefield died of Small Pox at Bristall abt. fteb. the middle

Sr. Rowland Wynne died of a diabetes at Bristall a few days after his Lady

Mr Isaac Wilkinson Minr at Warley died ffeb. 28, bur. at Bradford New Chappel Mar. 2. well fitted with gifts & graces as a christian & minr. A very great loss to his ffamily & congregation aged 36 years & 8

Isaac Ingham servt wth. Wm. Bentley of Shelf died Mar. 5

Nathan s. John Halliwell of Northourum died Mar. 5

Mr Norfolk of Hunslet bur. Mar. 12

Mrs Totty of Leeds widw. bur. Mar. 13

Mr Joseph Ainesley of Leeds bur. Mar. 13

Martha Pickerd of Ossett died Mar. 21

Mrs Law of Eland bur. Apr. 15

Mary wife of Joseph Crosley of Hough in Northourum died Mar. 25. 1722, aged abt. 85

Mr. Tho. Holden of Halifax died Mar. 28, bur. Mar. 30, died of a palsie

Wm. Coningham of Osset bur. his wife Apr. 11

George Addison of Halifax bur. his wife Apr. 12

Mr — Piggot vicar of Rochdale bur. Apr. 14. 1722. Aged 95. had bin vicar there almost 60. years

Widw. Isabel Longbothom of Halifax died Apr. 22

Abraham Mellen died at Fold in Northourum Apr. 28

Sarah dr. of Mr. Isaac Sharp of Little-Horton bur. Apr. 30

John his only s. bur. May. 1

Mrs. Scholefield near Ratcliffe bridge died May 3

Samuel s. of Tho. Clark of Scout Hall died May. 10. bur. May. 14

Nathl. s. of Elkanah Wirral of Halifax bur. May 20

Thomas s. of Mr. Priestley of Ovenden died at Inverness in Scotland May 13. had listed himself some time ago to be a soldier leaving his master & his Parents

Mrs. Rotheram late wife of John Rotheram of Dronfield in Derbyshire died

Hannah wife of Tho. Bland of Halifax died June 10

Mary wife of John Longbothom of Spigg in Northourum June 10

BURIALS.

John Medley near Hipperholme died June 11
Mr. Tho. Bilton of Okey Hall near Birstall bur. his wife June 13
John Heywood of Cambishaw in Prestwich Parish bur. June 15
Susan dr. of Wm. Stevenson of Ossett bur. July 19
Mr. Withington Minr. at Bolton died at Scarbro' abt. June 26
Mr. John Earnshaw of Hulm-Firth bur. July 21. being killd. in
    falling from his Horse
Mrs. Fornace of Halifax bur. her only little dr. July 22
Saml. s. Benjn. Sowood died July 21
Jonas Thornton of Bramley died at Mr. Isaac Sharps in Horton
    July. 23
David s. Charles Best of Wood End in Hipperholm died July 25
Widw. Rawson (late wife of Jonath. Rawson of Ranns near
    Halifax) died Aug. 6
Mrs. Holland of Chesterfield Widw. (Sister to Mr. Rotheram of
    Dronfield) died Aug. abt. 1
Abraham Rodes of Bradfordmoor bur his — Aug. 8
John Craven near Kipping bur. Aug. 30
Mr. Saml. Crook of Crook in Lancre. was kill'd by one Mr. Buck-
    ley in the Road near Hoghton Tower Aug. 9. Falling out about
    the way.   The Coroners Inquest brot. in Wilful Murder
Mr. Abraham Walker of Lightcliffe died Sept. 7
Sara. dr. of Elkanah Wirrall of Halifax bur. Sept. 16
Abraham Naylor of Northourum died Sept. 22
Madm. Stansfield wife of Mr. Robert Stansfield of Bradford died
    Oct. 3. bur. Oct. 6. 1722.   A very valuable useful woman
David Knight of Shelf died Oct. 9
John Ainsworth of Hipperholm died of Small Pox Oct. 14
John I [n] gham's wife of Ossett bur Oct. 18
Richd. s. Bro. Richd. Foster of Alverthorp died of the Small
    Pox Oct. 2
Abraham Ashworth of Wareley bur. his Fifth Wife Oct.
John Nicolls of Brighouse bur. his wife at Eland Nov. 13
Widow Hutcheson of Hunslet near Leeds died Nov. 13
William Kellett of Northourum died Nov. 13 aged 88
Mr. Jonathan Priestley of Winter-Edge died Nov. 17.   A Serious
    Solid Christian & of great usefulness
John s. Joseph North-end of High-Bentley bur. Nov. 22
Robt. Kitson of Upper Brear in Northourum died. Nov. 21
Mrs. Hannah Rotheram wife of Mr. Saml. Rotheram of Dronfield

BURIALS.

in Derbyshire was delivered of a son Nov. 24. abt. 12 a Clock died abt 10 a Clock at night. a good Woman a great Loss to the Family

George Oddy bur. at Coley Dec. 17. 1722

Joseph Firth died at Norcliffe Dec. 17

Mrs Gibson wife of Mr Michl. Gibson of Slead Hall in Lightcliffe bur. Dec. 24

Mrs Rawson of Shipley near Bradford bur. his wife Dec. 25

Jonath Ramsden died at Leeds Dec.

Mr John Ferguson of Halifax bur. his 3d wife Dec. 28

Mr John Brooksbank of London bur. his wife Dec.

Mr Daniel Cotton near Holmes Chappel died Jan. 1   .

Esther d. John Kellett of Northourum died Jan. 11

John Oates of Greenlane in Northourum Jan. 17

Abraham Naylor died Jan. 26, at Harley Green

Mr Richd. Wood of ffield in Northourum bur. Jan. 30

Jonathan Tattersall of Halifax bur. Jan. 30

Mrs. Rich of Bulhouse in Peniston Parish died Feb. 1. bur. abt. Febr. 5

Mrs. Clark of Attercliffe died Feb. 3

Susanna d. Dr. Colton of York died Feb. 14

Mrs Susanna d. Sr Robt Dukinfield died Jan

Mr John Cotton died at Dr. Nettletons in Halifax Mar. 8

Mr Timothy Wadsworth bur. at Luddenden Mar. 18

Mr John Farrar of Ewood died Mar. 22

Mr. Whitlock Minr in Nottingham bur. Mar. 20 in St Mary's Church where his Father was ejected for Nonconformity

Sarah d. John Terry of High Bentley bur. at Coley Apr. 12. 1723

Mr Clifford of Shelf bur. his wife Apr. 14

Mr. Griffith Minr at Darwen near Blackbourn bur. Apr. 19

Mr Holland Egerton of Heaton Hall in Prestwich Parish bur. his eldest son of small pox Apr. 21, he dy'd at Rinehill in Staffordshire

Mrs More of Halifax died May 1

John Metcalf by Norwood Green bur. May 6

Mr Richd Halstead Parson of Hutton Pannel buried

Luke Wilson (son to Mrs Aldred of Morley) died of Small Pox at his Grand Fathers (George Morhouse's) near Hulm Firth abt May 1. an Estate of abt. 200 li. p. annum thereby fell amongst

his own Fathers 3 Sisters
Charles Best died June 2 at Comon Wood End near Coley
Widw Grace Dean of Eland bur. June 4
Francis Brook bur. at Coley Ch. June 10
Mr Thomas Farrar of West ffield in Wareley bur. his wife June
21
Willm Hibbard of Manchester bur. abt June 26
Sarah d. Mr Joseph Brooksbank of Eland bur. July 3
David s. John Coulborn died July 4
Mr Tho. Sledhill of Clayton bur. abt June 26
Mr George Green of Leeds bur. his wife June 28
Mr John Turnbull minr near New Castle upon Tyne died abt
Midsumer
Mrs Elizabeth Hill died at Hackney at her sisters,Mrs Le-Blands,
abt. Middle of July
Mary wife of John Jackson of Hipperholm bur. July 30
Mr Nathanl Booth Schoolmaster at Batley died June
Susanna wife Saml Pollard of Upper Shibden Hall died Aug. 9.
bur. 11. at Halifax
Anne wife of Solomon Holdsworth of Saltinstall died Aug. 10.
bur. the 13th at Luddenden
Luke Hoile of Ovenden died of a very short sickness Aug. 18
Mr John Crompton of Chorley's wife bur. abt. Aug. 20
Mr Daniel Bentley Curate at Illingworth bur. his little dr. Aug.
19
John Jackson of Hipperholm bur. Aug. 20
Mr John Armitage of Wakefield died Aug. 28. He was the
Coroner
Joseph Lumb of Silk Cotes near Wakefield bur. Sep. 3
Wid. Farrar of Ovenden wood bur. Sep. 3
Mr Tho. Ibbison Minr at Bolsover between Mansfield & Chester-
field died Aug. 9
Mr Jeremiah Smith minr in Silver Street in London died
Mr. Skea died at York Sep. 3, had preacht a while at Scarbro'
Mrs Sarah Morton bur. at New Chapel at Wakefield Sep. 9
John Hartley of long-Shay-foot in Shelf died Sept. 12
Richd Ramsden of Siddallhall near Halifax bur. Sep. 12
Mr John Scholey of Leeds bur Sep. 17
Mr Alexander Harrison of York died Sept. 19
Elizabeth Hadfield of Wakefield

Thomas s. Jeremiah Baxter of Northourum died of Small Pox at London Sept. 19

Mr Nathl Holden of Halifax died Sept 25

Robt Wilson of Black Mires in Northourum died Oct. 2

Richd Whitaker bur. at a New Chapel at Platt in Manchester Parish where his son is Minister Oct. 22

Mr. Foxton Minr at Girdler's Hall in London died Oct. 26

George Travis of Blakeley in Manchester Parish had bin at a Race at Ashton, fell of his Horse in a Small Brook near Newton Heath & was taken up dead Oct. 31

Mrs Martha d. Sr. Robert Dukinfield (by his first Lady) died of a Cancer in her breast, abt Michaelmas Mr Scholey, Sr Robt. Dukinfield's Clerk, died near the same time

Mr — Holroide of Halifax bur. his wife Nov. 12. 1723. She died in Booth Town

James Dickenson near Southourum bank Top, died Nov 11. bur. 14 at Halifax

Mary d. Wid. Walker of Bingley bur. Nov. 15

Nathan s. Danl Sharp of Northourum died Nov. 17

John s. Mr. Joseph Brooksbank of Eland died Nov. 17

Mr Beaumont of Whitley Hall bur Nov. 18

Mr. Wilson the Parson of Hutton Pannel bur at Wakefield Nov. 21. had bin but abt half a year there since the death of his Predecessor, Mr Halstead

Jeremiah s. Jeremiah Baxter of Northourum died Nov. 24. of a Fever

Mrs Anne Colton (Dr C.'s wife & Dr. Sr. Robt Dukinfield) died of Small Pox

Roger Stocks died at Widw Sonyers at Harley Green Dec. 6. a hopeful young man

John Crosley s. of Wid. C. in Halifax bur. at London Dec 23

Mr John Delarose Minr at Sheffield died Dec. 31

Madm Hutton of Pudsay bur. at Calverley Dec. 24, a very useful woman

Benjamin Ferrand s. of Mr Tho. F. of Bradford bur. at London abt Dec. 27

James Gregson of Northourum bur Dec. 31, aged above 80

Laurence Ingham of Wareley bur. Jan. 3. aged 75

Joseph Eccles near Coley died Jan 1

Widw Elizabeth Wood of Norwood Green bur Jan. 8, had not bin

able to lye in bed for 15 years
George Bothomley near Shibden Mill bur. at Halifax Jan. 12
Mr Saml Wood Minr at Norton died
Mrs Batley of Halifax died of a very short sickness Jan. 15. 1723
Joseph Priestleys wife of White Windows in Sowerby bur. Jan. 19
Susan wife of John Bentley of Northourum died Jan. 22
Mrs Hotham of York Widw. died Feb. 1
Grace wife of Abraham Whitwham of Northourum died Febr 23
Mr. George Rooks (Bro. of Mr. Rooks of Rodes Hall) bur. Febr. 22
Mr John Nettleton (Father to Doctor Nettleton of Halifax) died
    Feb. 25. bur. at Dewsbury Mar. 2
Grace d. John Hanson of Wyke died Mar. 3. an only child
Martha d. Robt Naylor near Blake hill-end in Northourum died
    Mar. 4
Arthur Robinson died at Lee in Northourum Mar. 5
John Burnley died at Cockhill in Shelf Mar. 6
Mr Richd. Petty Curate at Eland died Mar. 7
Easter Farrar died at Landshead in Northourum Mar 9
Jeremiah Learoyd in Northourum died Mar. 17. at Wood-cock-
    hall
Sarah Wilson, Wid., died at Black Mires in Northourum Mar. 17
Mary Bradbury of Wakefield (Mother of Mr B. of London) died
    abt Febr. 18
Sr. Charles Dalston near Wakefield & Mr Savil of Medley (he
    died at London) & Mr Green of Bank near Barnsley all bur.
    in a week abt Mar. 10 or 12
Mr Waddington an apothecary in Wakefield bur. Mar. 18
William Ingham of Ossett bur. Mar. 18
Jonas Blaymires of Halifax bur. Mar. 23
Mr Tho. Butterworth of Manchester bur his son Thomas Mar. 19
    aged near 16. was Reading Divinity with Mr. Dixon Minr at
    Bolton
Mrs Mary Hyde who had kept a Boarding School in Manchester
    several years died Mar. 25, 1724
Mr Ralph Spencer of Hunslet near Leeds bur. Apr. 7
Charles Holdsworth of Hipperholm bur. Apr. 10
Mr James Taylor of Manchester died Mar. 28
Mr Richd. Walker of Lightcliffe died Apr 14
Nathl. s. Saml Midgley died at Landshead Apr. 13. short sickness
Mr Jonath. Stead's wife of Halifax died Apr. 15 left eleven

BURIALS.

motherless children
John Hanson of Bingley died of a few days sickness Apr. 25, a
young man unmarried
John Williamson of Mythom died of a ling'ring weakness Apr.
18. bur 21. at the White Chapel near Clack Heaton
Widw Ellen Vicars of Inghead in Northourum bur. May 2
Mrs Lumley who had kept a Boarding School at the Mannour in
York many years died Ap. 30
Sr. William Daws Arch-Bishop of York died at London Apr.
Sarah wife of Edwd. Gravelly near Leeds, dr. of John Baum
near Bradford, died of the 2nd child May 14, bur. at Whit-
church May 15
Joseph Batley of Lightcliffe bur. May 10
Mrs Anne Crompton (wife of Mr Saml Crompton of London) died
May 16. She was dr. of late Esqre Rodes of long Haughton
Dr Henry Sacheverel died June 5. Rectr of Holbourn
Mr Benjamin Ambler of Manchester died May 13
Mr James Lee of Leeds bur. June 6
Martha wife of Mr James Kitson of Halifax died June 7
Mr Waterhouse Minr at Ringhay in Cheshire died June 6
Thomas s. Thomas Birch of Heaton in Prestwich Parish bur.
June 10
Mary Grimshaw of Rooden lane in Prestwich Parish, wid.
(mother to Mr Grimshaw, Minr at Lancaster) died abt. Apr.
aged near 92
Israel Crabtree in Northourum died June 14
Isaac Hanson, a Grocer in Halifax, begun to be out of order abt
5 a clock at night June 17, died very soon next morning just
after 12 a clock, supposed to be an Impost or a Palsee
Mr Stockdale a mercer in Bradford bur. abt. June 8
James Holroide of Shelf bur. his wife June 26
Tho. Illingworth near Ossett bur June 30
Mr Henry Ellis near Leeds bur. July 3
Mrs Alexander of Manchester near the New Chapel hang'd herself
June 18
Mr Thomas Ferrand a Grocer &c in Bradford died July 4. bur at
New Chapel July 7
Mrs Blakely of Colne bur June 29
Mr Rich of Bullhouse in Peniston Parish bur. July 24. a worthy
usefull gentleman

BURIALS.

Mr Jackson of Gainsbro' died abt Midsummer
Mr Collins Parson of Dronfield died abt same time
Mr Saml Scholes an Apothecary Surgeon in Sheffield died Aug 11, bur. there 13
Christopher Hartley of Halifax died suddenly Aug. 18
Edward Haigh of Woodhouse near Halifax bur. Aug. 18. an Ancient Quaker
Timothy Netherwood of Harley Green near Halifax bur. Aug. 30
Mr Marmaduke Rookes of Dews'ury, Bro to Mr Rookes of Rodes Hall, bur. Aug. 31
Hannah d. Widw. Williamson of Mythom bur. Aug. 31
Wid. Susan Walker of Bingley bur. Sep. 8
Elizabeth Wheater of Westercroft died Sept. 14
Mr. Greaves the Dancing Master & Inkeeper at Royal Oak in Briggate in Leeds died of a Lethargy bur. Sept. 26, 1724
Mary d. Mr. Robt. Stansfield of Bradford died Sep. 26
John Barns of Thorns near Wakefield bur. Sep. 30
Mrs Rich, wife of Mr. Aymor Rich of Bullhouse, bur. Oct. 3, died of a consumption, left a son, had not bin married 2 years
Mrs Hannah Foster of Ossett, my wife's mother, died Oct. 4. abt 5 a clock in the evening bur. 7
Lady Hawksworth, wife of Sr. Walter, bur Oct 4
Mary Lister of Scholemoor near Bradford bur. Oct. 7
John Driver of Landshead in Northourum bur. Oct 12
Mr Robert Ravald of Kersall died suddenly in Manchester at his Inn Oct.
William Ogden of Heaton died suddenly at an Inn at Middleton, Oct.
John Hyde of Heaton died Nov. abt. 1
Mr Henry Coulborn near Radcliffe Bridge died abt. Nov. 11
John Stancliffe died in Halifax, Nov. 11
Mr William Perkins Minr at Newton near Manchester died Nov.
Mr Danl Clark of Attercliff another Dissenting Minr. died Nov. 11. bur. Nov. 16
Mr Isaac Hawkins minr at Wakefield died Nov. 24. Cease Lord! Help Lord!
David Baum of Horton bur. Nov. 23. an ancient member of Kipping Society
John Sugden died at Landimer Dec. 8
Sarah Brook of Coley died Dec. 9

Mr Joshua Stansfield of Horton bur. his wife Dec. 16

Obadiah Day near Dewsbury bur. Dec 20

Abraham Firth of Horton bur Jan

Susanna wife of Joseph Gott, Schoolmaster at Bolton Briggs bur. Jan. 12, died in childbed

Phebe wife of Isaac Farrar of Warley bur at Luddenden Jan. 15

John Wilkinson of Illingworth died Jan 27 had bin unfit for any-thing sometime

Mr John Percivall of Leverpool bur. Jan. 2

Margaret wife of Willm Hardy, bur. at Coley Chapel, Febr. 8

Mr Saml Hollings of Allerton Minr. at Pudsay bur. in Bradford Church Febr 19

Mr Jeremy Dickson of Heaton Royds bur at Bradford New Cha-pel Feb 26

Mr Abraham Crompton of Derby died Feb. 13

Wid. Brogden of North Bierley bur Ap. 9

John Drake of Croshill near Halifax bur. Apr. 14

Mr Thomas Fallows of Flanshaw died at his mothers near Bolton Briggs very suddenly, bur. Apr. 15

Mr Joseph Beevers of New Miller Dam in Sandall died Apr. 9. Very rich, made of will of Ten Thousand Pound

Bathshua d. Mr Joseph Brooksbank of Eland, bur Apr. 24

Madm Thorp of Hopton died at her son in Law's Mr Huttons at Pudsay May 8, bur. at Mirfield May 12

Mary Stocks of Shelf died May 13

Mr Henry Heginbothom of Salford Junr Entred upon his new office of receiving the Toll at the Bar between Manchester & Stockport. May 1. went out to a Pit to wash him May 5. in the morning fell in, Stick'd in the mud, and was found dead

Philemon Ellis of Alverthorp died May 28

Elizabeth wife of John Settle of Northourum died of the Measles June 15

James Kitson of Halifax bur. June 23

Mr Rossinton of Dronfield in Derbyshire bur. his wife July

Joshua Ashworth of Warley bur his Second wife July 17

Mr John Jollie Minr at Sparth near Whalley in Lancre died

Mrs. — Lister of Bradford bur. July

Mrs Batley (wife of Mr Jere. Batley of London) died July 28. She was Dr Staughton's Granddr.

Mr Abraham Walker of Lightcliffe bur Aug. 2

BURIALS..

Mrs Sylvester of Sheffield bur. July 30

John Jepson of Dewsbury (my Bro. in Law by marriage of my wife's sister) died Aug. 6. having languisht some time

Saml. Whiteley near Beggrinton in Northourum bur. Aug. 15

John Murgatroyd of Hipperholm bur. his wife Aug. 20. died in Child-bed o'th' first Child

Mary wife of William Hollings of Bowling died of a Cancer in the Throat Aug. 19. bur. Aug. 22. at th' Quaker's Chappel at Bradford

Joshua s. Joshua Robertshaw of Lee in Northourum bur. Aug 23

Mr Richd Holden of Manchester bur. his second wife Aug. 27

Ellen wife of Barzillai Hemingway near Halifax bur Aug. 28 died when lying in of the first child

Mr — Holroide near Ribbenden died Sep. 2

Mr — Wainhouse of Broad Yates near Halifax died Sep 4

Widw Anne Philips of Osset bur. Sep. 5

Willm Butler of Northourum died Sep 10

Sarah Ryley died in Northourum Sep. 15

Ruth d. John Gray of Beggrington bur. Oct. 3

Grace wife John Haliwell of Northourum died Oct. 7

Mr Baggot Chaplain at Sr Robt Dukinfields bur. Oct. 10

Mr Entwisle an ancient Justice o' th' Peace near Rochdale bur Oct. 11

Mr Bell Parson o' th' New Church in Leverpool & Vicar of Eccles died Oct. 12

Joseph Makant of Halifax died Oct. 12 both of very short sickness

Mr Walmsley of Bolton bur. Oct. 16

Jeremy Whiteley of Northourum bur Oct. 17

Joseph s. Mr Lister of Shibden Hall died of Small Pox, bur. Nov. 6

John Hirst Inkeepr. in Osset bur.

Anne dr. of John Archer of Ossett died Nov. 9. a year & a half old

Dr. Gastrell Bishop of Chester died Nov.

—— s. of Mr. Richd. Milnes of Stockport died

Mr. Nathl. Denison near Leeds bur. his wife Nov.

Mr. John Cagill near Halifax bur. his dr. Dec. 2. of Small Pox

Mr. — Fausett near Halifax bur. his — Nov. 29 of Small Pox

Mr. Brook the Parson of Hoyland o'th' Hill bur. Dec. 2

Elizabeth wife of Abram Foster near Bradford bur. Dec. 12

BURIALS.

Elizabeth dr. of Widw. Spencer of Shelf Hall bur. Dec. 14.

Joshua Brigg of Norwoodgreen bur. Dec. 14

John Dawson of Water Yate near Dewsbury bur. Jan. 6

Mary dr. of Widw. Wood of green-lane in Northourum died of Small Pox Jan. 5. aged abt. 18

Mr Kennet, Vicar of Bradford bur. his wife o'th' Small Pox Jan. 15

Christiana wife of Nathan Fearnside (dr. of Mr. Clifford of Shelf) bur. Jan. 10

Joshua Thornes of Ossett was in Wakefield Jan. 7. died next day Jan. 8. bur. Jan. 11

Widw. Curtis of Ossett was bur Jan. 20

Martha Bland died in my house June 17. bur. at Coley Jan. 18

Sarah dr. Bro. Clapham died at Nathl. Lea's Jan. 20. bur. at Halifax Jan. 21

Edmund Tattersall of onlyhouse in Northourum died Jan. 27

Mr. Valentine Stead of Halifax bur. his little son William Jan. 25

James Kighley near Kipping bur. Jan. 24

John s. Mr. Eli Dawson of Horton bur. Feb. 3

Joseph Pollard of Wibsey bur. Feb 16

Mr James Sill of Wakefield died Feb. 20

Mr. Richd. Holden a Grocer in Manchester born in Halifax bur. Febr. 27

Ellen Holt Widw. bur. Mar. 2. died at Upper-Shipden-Hall in Northourum

Esther wife of Jonas Hemingway of Shelf bur. Mar. 3

Mr. Garfot of York bur. his wife Feb. 27

Widw. Whitaker mother of Mr. John Whitaker Minr. at Platt near Manchester bur. Mar. 1

Willm. Proctor Innkeeper at Baitings bur.

Anne Kent bur. from Heath near Halifax Febr. 23

Mrs Marrow of Leeds died Mar 12

James Berry of Lee in Northourum bur. Mar. 14

Thomas Watmough Keeper of the Jail at Halifax bur. Mar.

— Scott of Alverthorp bur. Mar. 7

Mr William Maud of Alverthorp bur. his wife (She was Mr Partridge's dr. the Almanack Maker, 20000 li fortune

Mr John Brooksbank of London died Mar. 11

Tho. Holdsworth of Alverthorp died

BURIALS.

Mr. Joseph Taylor died at Dr. Nettleton's in Halifax Apr. 1. bur. Apr. 5. in Halifax Church.

— Sellers died at Joseph Milnes bur. Apr. 11.

Mr. Roger Bolton, Fellow at Manchester Church bur. his wife Apr. 12.

Thomas s. Richd. Roust Apr. 14 (4 Months old)

Elizabeth dr. of Joseph Wilkinson of Lower Brear bur. Apr. 21. abt. 18 weeks old found dead in bed

William Hird of West Scholes a rich Quaker bur. Apr. 22.

Mr John Pigot Minr. at Bolsover bur. his wife Apr.

Mrs Walker of Manchr. widw. bur. May 5

Mrs Busfield of Rishforth Hall bur. Apr. 28

Richard Dickenson my Eleventh Child died May 5. about 7 a'clock at Night, was bur. in the New Chapel in Northourum May 7. aged one year and 26 days

Sarah dr. Mr Gamaliel Breara of Bryan Royd near Elland bur. May 1

Mrs Baker of Eland bur. May 2

Judith wife of John Watkinson bur. at Illingworth May 11

Mary dr. Richd. Gray bur. at Coley Chapel May 28 abt. a quartr. old. found dead in bed

Judith Dickenson near Southourum bank top died May 28. bur. at Halifax May 31

Mrs Blaymires of Halifax bur. June 16

Mr Joseph Brooksbank of London died June 11 very rich, Religious & Usefull, a very great loss

Joseph Jepson of Dewsbury died of a few hours sickness June 21 (Father in Law to my Wife's Sister.)

Mr Francis Parrot Curate at Chapel-Thorp was seized with a Palsie, in the Pulpit, just after the Text July 17. died in a few hours, bur. July 19

Mr Jonath. Stead of Halifax bur. his dr. — July 20, 1726, She died at Leeds, having bin but a few weeks at School there

Sr Arthur Kay Bart, Knight for Yorkshire died at London, bur. at Almanbury Church July 23

Madam Rayner of Great Houghton died at Rhodes Hall July 22 bur. at Wibsey chapel July 26 A person of great Knowledge, Piety, Worth and Usefulness. Having bin about a month under a Palsie

Christopher Wrightson of Leeds was buried July 27

BURIALS.

Mary wife of Willm Jackson of Northourum died of a few days sickness July 28

Widw. Mary Crowther of Green lane in Northourum died Aug. 6

Joseph Milnes of Greenlane in Northourum died Aug. 6

Joshua eldest son of Joseph Armitage of Hunslet bur. Aug. 11

Mrs Crompton, wife of Mr C. minr. in Doncaster, died Aug. 13

Mr James Wood minr at Chowbent in Lancashire bur. his wife Aug. 20

Willm. Sharp of Godley died Aug. 29. bur in Northourum Chapel yard Sept. A plain upright hearted Christian

Mr Slater, Parson of Almanbury bur. abt Sep. 8

Widw Kellett of Northourum bur. Sep. 10

Mr John Taylor of York (Widw. Taylor's son of Clackheaton died Sept

Mr James Ingham of Halifax bur. his wife Sep. 26

Widw Sarah Ingham of Ossett bur. Oct. 1

Robt Low of Northourum bur. Oct. 2

Mr Buckley late of Whitfield near Shay Chapel in Oldham Parish died abt. May 1

Mr Robert Fern a Dissenting Minr died at Wirksworth June 6, 1727, aged 75

King George died at Osnaburg with his Brother the Bishop of that place June the 11th in the 67 year of his age & in the 13 year of his Reign over Great Britain

Mr Tho. Ramsden of High Fearneley died July 29, aged 28, bur. at Eland Aug. 1. a young son of his that was bur. at Wibsey Febr. 1. taken up and bur. with him

Mr Jonath. Wright minr in Lightcliffe died June 25, aged abt. 67 & half, bur. in Halifax Church June 28. [bap. Dec. 1659]

Jeremiah Chadwick of Dewsbury bur. July 14

John Armstead of Wakefield bur. July 25 aged abt 78, A serious useful christian

Hannah wife of John Firth of Wheatley bur. July 24

Mr Jackson Curate at Armley bur. July 28

Timothy Kirshaw of Wyke bur. July 29

— Outhwaite Inkeeper in Bradford bur. July 28

Mary — servt maid at Dr Nettletons died of a few days sickness, Aug. 5, bur. Aug. 6

Saml Threapland of Lightcliffe bur. Aug. 20

Phebe wife of John Hird of Shelf bur. Aug. 20

BURIALS.

John Bradley of Batley bur. Aug. 17
Mr John Riley minr at Topliffe died Aug. 19
Mr. Boys, a French Man, bur. at Halifax Sep. 12
Mr Samll. Stansfield of Bradford died Sep. 1
Mrs Gream of Shay Hill died Sep. 13. of a few hours sickness.
Mr Willm Moult minr. at Call Lane Chappell in Leeds died Sep.
    15 a very great loss to that congregation and the Church of
    God.   Cease Lord.   Help Lord
Susan wife of John Rodes of ffold in Northourum died Oct. 4
Sarah wife of Joshua Brooksbank of Landimer in Shelf died in
    child bed Oct. 16. & the Child Richard the day after. She was
    bur. Oct. 19. abt 5 at night
Sarah wife of James Priestley of Shelf died Oct. 18
Joseph s. Samll. Holdsworth of Greenlane in Northourum died of
    Small Pox Oct. 31
Squire Benn of Northourum Green died Nov. 5
— dr Mr Robt Stansfield of Bradford bur Nov. 16, died o'th'
    Small Pox
John Bentley of Upper lane in Northourum died Nov. 18
Moses Hepworth of Mythom bur. Nov. 21
Mr Sylvester of —— in Darton Parish bur. Nov. 24
— son Mr Robt Stansfield of Bradford died o'th' Small Pox Dec. 1
Doctr. Swaine of Bradford bur. his wife Dec. 15
Tho. Wright an Innkeeper at Bradford bur. Dec. 18
Mrs Fleetcroft of Manchester bur Oct. 11. 1726
Mrs Bella dr. of Mr Garfat of York died Oct. 6
Widw Thornton of Bramley bur. Oct. 21
Mr James Harison of Wakefield bur. Oct. 30
Mr Richd. Milnes of Chesterfield bur. his wife Oct. 28. She
    died o'th' 2d child
Mr Richd Percivall of Manchester a very ancient Tradesman died
    suddenly Nov.
Mr John Farrar of Warley died Dec. 15
Widw. Phebe Gregson of Northourum bur. Dec. 19
Isabel Woodhead died at Wid. Sonyers Dec. 24
Widw Wilkinson of Shelf bur. Dec. 27
John Sharp of Blakehill junr. bur. his wife Dec. 29
Phebe Scott, Widw., bur. Dec. 31. aged 88 ; she died with her
    dr. at Athersgate in Northourum
John Turner of Green Lane Northourum died suddenly Dec. 30

BURIALS.

James Longbottom of Booth Town in Northourum died suddenly Jan. 4

Widw. Mary Greenwood of Southourum bank top. died Jan 9. bur. at Halifax Jan. 12

Mr Tho Hodgson of Bradford bur. Jan. 26

Jane d. Mr Lepton of Leeds died (of a few days sickness) at Okey hall, bur. at Birstall Jan 29 [3 lines shorthand.]

— son of John Popplewell of Heckinwyke died 'oth' Small Pox Feb. 3. bur. Feb. 4

John s. Joseph Hanson of Oxheys bur at Coley Chapel Febr. 16.

Saml Whitchead of Street near Atherton bur Feb. 17

Joshua Stocks of Northourum died Feb. 22

Benjamin s. John Askew of Northourum died Febr. 27

— son Mr Henry Wadsworth of Holdsworth bur. Mar. 2

Sarah wife of Tho. Fozard of Ossett, died Mar. 6, Languisht long

Mr Wm. Lepton an Attorney near Leeds died Mar.

Mrs Hannah Coulborn (wife of Capt. Coulborn) died in Salford, bur. Mar. 1

Widw Ramsden of Quarles in Northourum died Mar. 17

Mrs Wilson of Leeds (mother to the Lawyer) bur. Mar. 30

Mrs Eliza Fallons of Wakefield died Mar. 31. a young widow

Mr Wm Tong minr at Salters Hall in London died Mar. 21

Mr Henry Heginbothom of Salford bur Mar.

Nathanl Booth of Wyke bur. his wife Apr. 5

Mr Haigh Curate at Horbury bur Apr. 10

George s. Wm Jackson of Northourum died Apr 22

Farrer Best s. Wid. Best of Wareley bur. May 6

Elizabeth Day of Henging Heaton Wid. bur. May 16

Mr Richd Taylor of Bin Royd in Norland bur. his wife Dec. 25. His child Jan 15

Mr Samll Nicoll near Eland died Dec. 25

Mary Ashworth of Wakefield Widw. bur. Dec. 30

William Clayton of Lee lane in Northourum bur. Jan. 3

John s. Wid. Ingham died Jan. 12

William Mann of Lightcliffe died Jan. 14

Mr Robert Richmond had bin Minr. at Clack Heaton, died at Toph, near Wisket Hill Jan. 21. bur at New Chapel by Bradford Jan. 25 had bin unfit for his work by melancholy for several years

Samuel — died at Mr Brooksbanks of Eland Jan 20 a good

old man near a 100d had bin many years taken care of in that ffamily according to th' order of old Mr Brookbank before his death

Samuel s. of Mr. Rotheram of Droufield died of a few hours sickness Jan. 20. abt 5 years & 2 months old

Mrs Langley of Hipperholm died in Leverpool Febr. 11. bur. Feb. 14

Mrs Langley her dr. in Law (her eldest son's Widw.) died in Hipperholm the same day Feb. 11. bur. Feb. 15

Elkanah Baxter of Leeds s. of Jeremy Baxter of Northourum died Feb. 16

Widw Spencer of Shelf Hall bur Febr. 22

Mr. George Lodge near Halifax bur. his wife Febr. 24

Mr Wilkinson of Green Head near Huthersfield (A Justice a'Peace) buried Mar. 4

Mr Wheatley bur. at Halifax Mar. 7. A Young man, came from abt. Pontefract

Mrs Frances Vernon of Warmingam in Cheshire died Mar. 5

John Craven of Westercroft in Northourum was sowing Corn in a Field call'd Chesiwells near the Chapel fell down with the Hopper on his Arm & the seed in his Hand, & died upon the Place Mar. 7

Mr James Grimshaw died in Manchester—had bin Minr. in Lancaster, but of late discompos'd in mind, and unfitt for his Work

Mr. Samll. Delarose minr. in Stockport died Feb.

Mr. Sharp of Hipperholm bur. his wife Mar. 22

Joshua Sonyer died at London Mar. 13

Mrs Hannah Priestley of Wintcredge died at her Fathers, Mr Milnes of Wakefield Mar. 26. bur. at New chapell there Mar. 28. 1728

Grace d. Mr. Gaunt of Halifax died suddenly Apr. 8. 1728. (2 lines shorthand)

Mr James Milnes of Chesterfield bur. his wife Apr. 12

Mr Joseph Holmes of Lightcliffe bur. his wife Apr. 5

Mr. Kennerly the Jail-Keeper at Halifax died Apr. 17

John Watkins of Northourum died Apr. 17

Judith Story of Hough in Northourum died Apr. 23

Mr Lister Headschoolmaster at Halifax Free School died Apr. 23

Mr Joshua Crompton died at his son in Law's Mr Robt Wareings

BURIALS.

in Bury Apr. had bin useful in the Church & World

Mr Joseph Smithson near Ossett bur. Apr.

Mr. Christopher Dade died near Otley Apr.

Hannah wife of Joseph Lumby of Farnley bur. May 9

Phebe wife of William Clark died May 10 at Scout Hall in Northourum

— wife of Robt Hindle of Sculcote brow in Northourum bur. May 6

Sarah Scott of Aldersgate in Northourum died May 18

John Nalson near Shipden Hall bur. May 24

Widw. Haliday (Jere. Baxter's sister) died at London of a few days sickness May 19

Mr Lightbown minr at Lostock in Cheshire died May

Mary Broadley of Cinderhills bur. at Coley June 17

Mr. Murgatroyd near Luddenden bur. June 3

James Swaine of Norwoodgreen died June 7

Mrs Brooksbank wife of Mr Joseph B. of Eland died June 8

Mrs Hardcastle of Leeds died with her dr. Hanson in Halifax July 14 of a few hours sickness in the 80th year of her age

Mrs Hampson of Rochdale bur. abt. July 8

Mad. Parker of Carlton in Craven bur. from Rodes Hall at Wibsey July 24. 1728

John Hanson of Bingley died in York Jail bur. July 29

John Hamilton of Cross in Halifax bur. Aug. 10

Samll. Sunderland kil'd in a Coal Pit in Southourum bur. Aug. 16

—— kil'd by falling of a house in Halifax bur. Aug. 16

Benjamin Thomas near Halifax died of a few hours sickness, going to Huthersfield bur. Aug. 16

— Roper of Booth Town died suddenly bur. Aug. 16. Sevll. other sad Accidents this week

Mr Ralph Worsley of Platt near Manchester buried Aug. 14

Mr Radcliffe Scholefield near Radcliffe Bridge in Lancashire bur. Aug. 16. minr at Ringhay in Cheshire

Mr John Kenyon minr at Toxtoth Park near Leverpool bur. Aug. 19

Mr Samll. Gill of London my wife's Cousin, an only child, hopeful, his mother very rich died Aug. 24. having undergone much pain, & severe operations by a Fistula in ano.

BURIALS.

occasion'd by sliding down the Rail of a pair of Stairs hastily

Mr. Walton curate at Marsden Chappel bur. Aug. 29

Doctor Heslop of Old Hall bur. at New Chappel at Stand in Prestwich Parish in Lancashire Aug.

Mr Nathanael Priestley of Ovenden died Sept. 5. bur. Sept. 9. in Halifax Church, a worthy eminent minr., a great loss especially to the congregations at Halifax and Bradford

Mr Lupton curate at Sowerby-bridge Chappel, bur. his wife Oct. 1

Mrs Brear (Mr Gamaliel's wife) bur. at Eland, Sep. 30

William Dickson of Halifax bur. Sep. 30

Mrs Stansfield (wife of Mr John Stansfield of Sowerby Town) bur Oct. 7

Eunice wife of Joseph Brook below Winteredge died Oct. 7

Mr Robert Milnes died at Ovenden Oct. 11 .

Richard s. Willm Jackson of Northourum died Oct. 12

William Stevenson of Ossett & —. his wife both buried together Oct. 30

Job s. Charles Pollett of Heaton Yate bur. Oct. 18

Mr John Prescott of Callicoe Hall near Halifax died Nov. 11

William Hodgshon of Bradford died Dec. 6

— Kay a Farrier in Halifax died Dec. 7

Wid Laycock of Knott by Lisburn Moor (mother to Tho. Swaine's wife) bur. Dec. 16

Joseph Priestleys wife of Fieldhead near Birstall died Dec. 29

Doctr. Watkinson's wife bur. at Halifax Jan. 1

, John Tenant a Grocer in Halifax died Jan. 8

Mr. Hill Curate & Schoolmaster at Bradford died Jan. 15, bur. Jan 17

Henry Blakebrough of Shelf bur. Jan. 17

Abraham Pelling of Halifax bur. Jan 17

Widw. Driver of Northourum bur. Jan 20

Mary d. Widw Tattersalls o'th' onely House in Northourum bur Jan 20

Wid. Jennet Sharp of Northourum bur. Jan. 23

Mr Elkanah Horton of Thornton bur. at Sowerby Jan. 28

Mr. Hays of Pudsay bur. at Bradford Jan. 28

— wife of Wm Clayton of Northourum bur Febr. 5

William Tattersall near Padiham in Lancr. bur. Feb. 28

Widw Firth of Kipping bur. Feb. 15

Sr William Lowther of Swillington died at London Mar. 6
Dr Willm Prescott died at York Mar. 7
Mr Finch Lindley of Bowling near Bradford bur. Mar. 18
Mr Exley Curate at Bramley died
Moses Holdsworth of Northourum died at London Mar. 29
Mrs Dun of Halifax died Apr. 6. bur. Apr. 8. aged about 87
Mr Thompson minr in Stockton preacht on Lords Day Apr. 6. his
  Text What shall we do to be saved? Supt, went to bed in
  usual Health, awakt abt. one a Clock, was ill, died abt. two
Mr Scott vicar of Wakefield died of a few hours Sickness Apr. 15
Mrs Overing (wife of Mr John Overing of Leeds died in child bed
  Apr. 13. was buried in Mill-hill Chapel Apr 15 being the first
  that was bur. there
Mr Drake Vicar of Kirby overblow bur. Apr. 21
— s. of Mr Richd Cooke of Halifax bur. Apr. 22
John Hird of Shelf bur. Apr. 23
Willm Jackson of Cinderhills bur. Apr. 23
Wid. Dinah Woodhead of Shelf bur Ap. 25
William Harrison of Britton Moor bur. at Sandall Apr. 19. his
  wife bur. Apr. 24
John Elsworth of Rodley died in Rothwell Jail. Hannah his dr.
  a little before
Mrs Walker of Siddall near Halifax bur. May 14
Mr Chamberlain of Halifax bur. May 15, has left an Estate of
  17000 pounds (as it's said)
Thomas Fozard of Ossett bur. May 15
Mr. Huthwaite of Nottingham died May 13, 1729, (Mr. Huth-
  waites Father of Westercroft.)
Mr Jackson Schoolmaster in Northourum bur. his wife May 26
Susanna d. Timothy Sharp of Halifax died May 27
Mr Westby of Ranfield bur. his wife at London May
Mr — Issot died at Fold in Northourum June 3d of a few hours
  sickness
Widw Hickson of Hough in Northourum died June
Mr. Stancliffe Jackson of Gainesbrough died abt. June 24
Hannah Crowther of Northourum died July 14
Rebecca wife Joshua Dean of Hud Hill in Northourum died July 16
Mr Richd Hutton of Pudsay died at Mr. Markham's in Hunslet
  lane near Leeds July 20
Mrs Clemence Worsley wife of Mr Charles W. of Platt near

BURIALS.

Manchester died

Mr Dobson of Armley died at Leeds bur. Aug. 6

Jeremy Blamyres of Bradford bur. Aug.

Widw. Dawson of Hunslet bur. Aug. 12.

Dr Thomas Dixon, of Bolton, died Aug 14. Useful as Preacher, Physician & Tutor

John Crabtree near Reavy Hall died Aug. 21

Grace Crabtree, his wife, died Sep. 6

Mr Jeremiah Aldred minr near — in Lancr. died Aug. 1729

Mr Ebenezer Buxton of Wakefield died Sep. 2

Mr Tho. Baron of Leeds died suddenly Sep. 3

Jane wife of Abraham Kirshaw near Halifax died Sept. 6

Mr Richard Haigh of Ovenden a young Clergyman died Sept. 8

— Wife of Jonas White of Allerton was kill'd by the stroke of a Horse Sep. 11

Sarah d. of Bro. Richd Foster died Sep. 14

Mr. Gee, Minr in Leicester bur. Sep. 22

Mr William Pendlebury minr at Mill Hill in Leeds died at Bath in Somersetshire Sep 23. A Worthy Useful man, a great loss to his family, Congregation & the Church of God. Cease Lord! Do not proceed in Displeasure

Mr Tho. Cagill of Halifax died Oct. 4

Mr. Slaters wife of Wakefield died Oct 10

Nathl. Booth of Northourum died Oct. 11

John s. Michl Bland of Halifax died Oct. 10

Widw Wales of Leeds died Oct 22

Mr Bowman Vicar of Dewsbury bur. Oct. 22

Mr Joshua Mercer of Halifax bur. his wife Oct. 26, She died suddenly

Sr. Robt. Dukinfield of Dukinfield in Cheshire bur. Nov. 9

Mr Joseph Heywood minr. at Stand in Lancr bur. Nov. 1

Mr James Lister of Shipden Hall died Nov 1

John Berry of Lee in Northourum died Nov. 15

Samll s. Jonath. Farrar of Wareley, a hopefull young man, design'd for the ministry, died Nov. 18.

— a great loss to his large Family & to Mill Hill Congregation

Widw Nalson near Shibden Hall died Dec. 1

Mary Priestley died Dec. 5. bur. at Bradford. Dec.

William Armitage of Hunslet bur. Dec. 8

Mr John Wood of Fold in Northourum died at London Dec. 13.

BURIALS.

design'd for a Clergy-Man or a Physician

Mr John Smith near Wakefield bur. Dec. 29

Mr Robt. Hill of Leeds (my s. John's Master) bur. his wife Jan. 16. She died in Child-bed. The Child was bur. Jan. 17

Hannah Viccars of Halifax bur. Jan 18

Mary Day died at Caleb Ashworth's in Northourum Jan. 2

Jonath. Duckworth near High Cross bur. Jan 19

Saml. Sheppard of Landshead in Northourum died Jan. 20

My Bro. in Law Mr Richd Foster of Flanshaw died abt 3. a'clock on Lordsday Morn. Febr. 1

John Northend (s. to Caleb Northend of High Bentley bur. at Coley Febr. 6

Mr Jackson Curate at Sowerby bur. Febr. 11

Mehetabel wife of Caleb Ashworth of Northourum bur. Febr. 12

Abraham Ashworth of Wareley (Caleb's Father) died Febr. 13. having his Sixth wife at his death

Nathanl s. Mr Jonathan Priestley of Winter Edge died at his Grand-Father's Mr Robt Milnes in Wakefield Febr. 13. bur. Febr. 16 i'th New Chapel

Mrs. Overing of Leeds bur. Febr abt 25

Sarah wife of Michael Ingham (who lived formerly at Hipperholm) bur. at Halifax Mar 9

William Hartley bur. Mar. 7. at Bradford-New Chappel

Mrs Hawkins of Wakefield bur.

Mr Tho. Holroide an Attorney in Halifax died Mar. 15

Mr Busfield of Rishforth near Bingley a Justice of Peace died suddenly Mar. 21

Mr Lupton Curate at Sowerby Bridge Chappel bur. Mar. 25. 1730

Abraham Kirshaw of Halifax died Mar. 26. of a few days Sickness

Sarah wife of John Hargreaves of Norwood-green died in Child-bed. Apr. 9

Mr John Cooke of Halifax died Apr. 14. had bin very useful as a Tradesman & Christian

Mr Richd Smith near Wakefield died Apr. 15

John Jackson School-master in Northourum died of a few days Sickness Apr. 16

Mr Crossley of Kirshaw House bur. Apr. 22

Vidw Crosley (mother to my Bro in Law Mr. Richard Clapham)

T

BURIALS.

died with her dr. Mrs Lea at High Bentley Apr. 23. bur at Halifax Ap. 26

Widw Grace Wilkinson of Shelf bur. Apr 28

Mr James Milnes minr. near Bolton bur. May 4

Sir Holland Egerton of Heaton near Manchester died Apr. 25 buried at Madely in Staffordshire

Mr Hirst an Attorney died at Mirfield June 2

Timothy Scott of Shelf died May 21

John Nalson died suddenly May 24, in an Alehouse at Baily Hall by Halifax

Mrs Elizabeth [ ] of Mr John Maude of Wakefield died May 24

Mr Eliezer Heywood Minr in Dranfield in Derbyshire died May 20, aged 73 and abt. 6 w.

Mr Tho. Horncastle Steward of Wakefield Court died abt 10 of June

Mr John Midgley near Horton died June 24 bur. June 26

Mr Dawson his brother in law bur, June 2—

Mr John Walker Curate at Thornton in Craven bur. June 26

Joshua Knight of Northourum died June

Mr James Stansfield of Bowood in Sowerby bur. June 29

Mrs Ryder of Leeds bur. July 3

Mrs Lumley of Leeds bur July 10

Nancy d. Stephen Ambler near Clayton bur. July 19

Mr John Leach's wife near Bingley bur. July 10

Mr Cotes of Gainsbro' died July

Tho. Hodgson of Bradford died of a few hours sickness July 1—

Joshua Cordingley of Halifax died suddenly at Shibden Mill July 20

Josia Holdsworth of Sowoodhouse died July 22, bur. July 25

Mr Anthony Naylor of Wareley died July 25

Mr Tho. Cotton an ancient Dissenting minr. in London died

Mrs Banks of Hutton Pannel died

Benjamin Buckle

— son of Mr Horton of Coley Hall died of small pox, Aug. 2, bur. at Eland Aug. 3

Mrs Hampson (Dr Nettletons sister) died in childbed at Leverpool Aug. 1

George Bentley of Shelf died in Halifax Aug. 12

Jeremiah Baxter of Northourum died Aug. 17

Robert Dean of Halifax bur. Aug. 17

— son of Mr George Cotton of Wakefield died Aug. 25

BURIALS.

Abraham Milner of Skircote Green bur. Aug. 28

Joshua s. of Tho. Swaine of Shelf died Aug. 30

Mrs Kennet the Vicar of Bradford's 2d wife bur. Sept. 10

Samuel Appleyard of Shelf died at London Aug. 31

Susanna Appleyard (his dr.) died in Sowerby of the Small Pox Sept 15

Thomas Jagger of Ossett bur. Sep. 11

Mr Richard Foster of Ossett my dear and honour'd Father in Law died Sept. 17. having undergone severe strangury pains for a considerable time, had bin eminently useful as a Christian and as a Tradesman

Mrs Elizabeth Stansfield of Hough End near Sowerby Bridge, Widw of Mr Josiah Stansfield died Sept. 18, a good woman and usefull in her place

Mr Saml. Taylor of Norland died Sept. 18, had bin depriv'd of the use of his memory and unfit for business for some time

Grace wife of Elkanah Boys near Bradford died Sept. 19

Mr — Wroe Curate at Newton near Manchester died Sept. 19. 1730

Mr Tho. Bretliffe of Manchester died Sept.

Charles Pollett of Heaton Yate near Manchester died Sept. 30

Mr Nathanael Lea of High Bentley died Oct. 8

Madm Elizabeth Thomas died at Hull Oct 11, bur at St. John's Church in Leeds Oct. 16

Mrs Brooksbank died at Brearley Mill, Oct. 15, bur. Oct. 20, at Luddenden.

Robert Faucett of Halifax bur Oct. 22

Dr. Wm. Talbot Ld. Bp. of Durham died Oct 1—. the 71st Bp. of that Diocese : had bin Bishop of Oxford and Salisbury. His wife died Nov. 23

John s. Widw. Frost died at Landimer Nov. 2.

Richard s. of my Bro. in Law Mr Richard Clapham of Halifax bur. Nov. 5

Samll. s. of Samll Crowther bur. Nov.

John s. Samll. Askew bur Nov. 2—

Mr James Allison Parson of Thornton in Craven bur. at Halifax Nov. 29

Mrs Holdsworth bur. at B   Nov. 19

Jeffery Chadwick of Halifax bur. Dec. 2

Peter Ambler's wife bur. at Coley Dec.

BURIALS.

Widw. Oddy bur. at Coley Dec. 28
Joshua Wilkinson bur. at Coley Dec 28
Mr Wm Hopwood an Attorney in Halifax bur. Jan. 4
William Dean of Skircote Green bur. Jan. 15
Robt. Naylor's wife of Blakehill bur, Jan. 17
Timothy Carr an old servt at Quarles bur. Jan. 20
Mr John Heywood minr at Blakley New Chapel near Manchester
bur. there Jan. 28, a great loss to the Congregation and his
family. Lord pity & provide
Mr Nathanael Robinson senr of Gainsbrough in Lincolnshire
buried
Mr Samll. Astley Preacher at Rivington was bur. at Bolton Feb. 8
Mr Edward Rothwell Preacht at Bury Jan. 31, died Febr. 8 of
a suppression of urine, bur. in his own Chapel in Holcomb
Febr. 10
John Learoyd died in Horton bur. at the New Chapel near Brad-
ford Mar. 3. a serious christian
Widw. Deborah Knight of Northourum bur. at Halifax Mar. 3.
Mr. Isaac Hemingway Curate at Rotheram lately remov'd to
Attercliffe Chapel died Mar. 2
John Watkinson bur. at Illingworth Mar. 27
Grace (d. of the late John Learoyd) wife of John Rodes of
Horton died in child bed Apr. 2
John Milnes of Northourum died Apr. 4
John Dickenson of Heaton Yate near Manchester, my dear and
only Brother, died Apr. 6. in the 71st year of his Age. He
feared God from his youth, and above many.
Mary wife of John Coulborn died Apr. 13. after a long tedious
weakness for several years
Timothy Wood of Little Town died Apr. 1
Mr John Farrar of Ewood bur. Apr. 23
Mr George Lodge near Halifax bur Apr.
Mr Cowper minr in Hyde near Denton in Lancashire died Apr. 26
Mr Seddon minr at Cockhay in Lancashire died Apr. 27
Mr Joseph Hankinson minr at Wirksworth died Apr. 29 was
born near Altringham
Mrs Sarah Preston in Craven died May 15, Wid. She was dr
of Mr John Newhouse of Leeds
Mr John Brook the Apothecary Surgeon bur. his wife at Birstall
May 14

BURIALS.

William s. Mr Joshua Hardcastle minr at Horton Chapel bur. there May 18

Widw Drake of Halifax bur June 10

John Best of Cold Well Hill near Halifax died June 16, aged 84

Jonathan Hughes died at Wm Jackson's in Northourum June 17

Widw Kirshaw died with her son Abraham at Skircote Green bur at Halifax June 21

John Bentleys wife of Bradford bur June 22

Joseph Butterfield bur. June 22

Mr Tho. Barns minr in Newcastle died June 80

Widw Holdsworth of Sowoodhouse died June 2—

Willm Scott of Shelf died July 7

Mr Tho Burton Vicar of Halifax died July 22 bur. July 25

Joseph s. Joseph Hanson of High Fearneley was kill'd by a horse near Wadehouse in Shelf July 17

Mr Jeremiah Bairstow minr at Eland died July 28 in the 62d year of his age

Mr. Crook (had lived awhile in Halifax) bur. his wife Aug. 2. She died in child-bed of her first child with her relations near Morley, bur. at Beeston

Widw. Heald of Wakefield bur. Aug. 4

Mr Batt of Eland Aug. 6

Joseph Crosley of Northourum Aug. 24

Mr Wilkinson of Nowel Hall near Otley bur. Sept. 15

Mr Edmd. Brigg of Halifax bur. wife Sep. 19

Tho. Wharton of Booth Town bur. at Illingworth Sep. 23

Mrs Cotton wife of Mr William, Westby Cotton of Haigh Hall bur. Oct 22

William Rookes of Rodes Hall Esqr. died Oct. 25. bur. in Wibsey Chapel Oct. 27

William Robinson of Robert Town bur. Nov. 10

Mary wife of John Robinson of Green Lane in Northourum, Nov. 10

Joseph Godley bur. at Halifax Nov. 15. Father of the Curates of Ossett & Croston

Mr. Anthony Markham of Leeds a considerable merchant died Nov. 20, bur. 22

Mrs Smith, wife of Mr John Smith of Southourum died Dec. 15

Doctr. Tho. Colton of York died Dec. 15, aged 73, a worthy & eminently useful Minister

BURIALS.

Mr Joshua Cordingley minr in Wareley died Dec. 16, a very modest humble and useful Preacher

Mr Edward Farrand of St Ives near Bingley died Dec. 18

Mrs Robuck his sister a few days after

Mr. Sill Curate at Wakefield died Dec. 22

Mr Helm near Brighouse died Dec. 27. bur. at Eland Dec. 31

Mr Henry Gill near Brighouse died Dec. 27. bur. at Eland Dec. 29

Widow Mary Hodgson of Holdsworth died Dec. 29

Ellen wife of Abel Wadsworth died Jan. 2. immediately after bearing a child.

Mr. Swaine a rich tanner at Bradford bur. Jan. 6

Mr. Paley Curate at Hunslet near Leeds bur. Jan. 13

Mr — Field of Heaton near Bradford bur. Jan. 14

Nathl. Skelton near Mixendon died Feb. 22

Joseph Crowther of Plowroyd in Northourum bur. Feb. 3

William Sutliffe Inkeeper at Bayly Brigg bur. his wife

Mrs Wadsworth of Holdsworth, bur. Mar. 7

Mary wife of Benjamin Souwood bur. Mar. 7. had been helpless and useless ten years and more.

Mrs Herle of Manchester died Feb. 22, very old

Mr William Assheton Parson of Prestwich died Febr. aged near 80

—— dr. of Mr. Garforth of York died Mar. 12, an only child her Father having a vast Estate

Mrs Smith wife of Mr John Smith of Manchester died Mar.

John Ambler of Shibden Head in Northourum died Mar. 17

George Taylor of Norland bur. Mar. 22

Mary Benn of Northourum died Mar. 26, 1732

Mr. Tho. Fearnley an Attorney in Birstall died Mar. 26

Mr Roger Marrow a Leeds merchant bur. M r. 27

Ralph Egerton Esq of Harleston in Staffordshire died of a Fever at his Lodgings in Tavistock Street, London, Apr. 3. He was 4th son of Sr. John, bro. to Sr. Holland, uncle to Sr. Edward Egerton in Lancr

Mr James Diggles of Manchester bur. Apr. 10

Mrs Millington of Manchester bur. Apr. 13

John Whitcley of Ossett bur. Apr. 18

Mr Abraham Sharp, Curate of Sowerby Bridge died Apr. 15, bur. at Halifax Apr. 17

BURIALS.

Widw Susan Scott of Shelf bur. Apr. 22

Lady Hoghton mother to Sr Henry Hoghton of Hoghton Tower in Lancre. died Apr. 30

Mr Richd. Milnes formerly minr. in Stockport h ad left of Preaching many years died May 5

Mr. Mush minr. in Selby bur. May 5

John Coulborn died at Winteredge May 26

Nathanael Booth of Lightcliffe bur. there May 9

Joseph Taylor of Norland bur. June 2

Mrs Phebe Huthwait (wife of Mr. James Huthwait) died at Westercroft June 2. bur. at Halifax June 5

Mr John Banks of Hunsworth died June 8, bur. June 7

Mr Wm. Vernon of Warmingham in Cheshire died

Dr. Samll. Brook Curate of St John's Church in Leeds died June 12, bur. privately at Birstall June 14

Mr — Copley Parson of Thornhill & Fellow of Manchester bur. June

Mr. John Hulme son of Obadiah Hulme of Levensholm near Manchester, had bin there to see his Relations, got home to London July 15, died July 16

Mrs Eliz. Griffith died in Manchester July 29

James Taylor of Ardick-Green near Manchester died Aug. 4

Widw Mary Makant of Halifax died Aug. 17

Mrs Wilkinson wife of the late Vicar of Halifax bur. Aug. 25

Mr Abraham Threapland, Schoolmaster in Booth Town died Aug. 6

John Ramsden of Clayton died Aug. 8. a rich Farmer, born at Quarles in Northourum

The Honble Ld. Levisham son to the Earl of Dartmouth died of the small pox at his house in Hollis Street near Cavendish Square. He married the only dr. & heir of Sr Arthur Kay of Woodsome in Yorkshire Bart, by whom he left one son & 2 daughters

Mrs Rebecca Rigby wife of Mr Rigby bur. in Manchr. Chapel, Sept. 26

Tho. son of John Terry of High Bentley bur. Oct. 9

Richd Stern Esqre died at Bradford in his Journey to York Oct. 9. bur. at Halifax Oct. 13

Mr. Nathl Denison of Shipscar near Leeds buried Oct. 19

Mr Jonath. Stead of Halifax bur. Oct. 19

BURIALS.

Mr — Armitage (nephew & heir to Sr John Armitage of Kirkleys Bt.) died of Small Pox there Oct. 28

Mr Scoffen had bin a Conformist, turned to be a Dissenting Minr. Preacht & died at Sleeford in Lincolnshire, bur. Nov. 12

Mr. John Holland, minr. at Alfreton in Derbyshire died of 2 days sickness Nov. 19

Mr. Clark of Stanley died in Wakefield, Nov. 27. A young Lawyer, just coming into business, left a wife and son.

Sr John Armitage of Kirkleys Bart. died Dec. 2. bur. Dec. 7. aged near 80

Doctr. Wm Baker Bishop of Norwich died at the Bath Dec. 4. in the 64 year of his Age, was consecrated Bp. of Bangor, Aug. 11. 1723, translated to Norwich Dec. 19. 1727

Dr William Bradshaw, Bp. of Bristol died Dec. 16. at the Bath

Mr John Gream of Shay Hill died Jan. 15. bur. in Halifax Church Jan 17.

— son of Edward Wright of Boulshaw in Northourum bur. Jan 14

John Ramsden of Well Head near Halifax bur. his 2d wife Febr 3

Joseph Wilkinson of Whitehall in Northourum died Feb. 4, aged 65. A useful tradesman and Christian

Mrs. Sarah Cornwall of Hull (sister to Mr Joseph Brooksbank of Eland) died Febr. 1

Mr Abraham Dawson Minr at Cottingham died Febr. 5

Mr Ebenezer Naylor of Wakefield bur. his wife Febr. 14

Mr Joshua Stansfield of little Horton bur. Feb. 14, aged about 86

Joseph Gargrave of Burnet Field near Bradford died in Rothwell Jail bur. Febr. 17. 1732-3

Widw. Oxley of Landimer Syke bur. Feb. 19

Widw Townend near Coley Chapel bur. Feb. 19

Mary wife of John Woodhead of Shelf bur. Feb. 19

Joseph Wroe of Leeds bur. Febr. 19

John Fowler of Leeds bur. Feb. 19

John Hirst the Printer in Leeds died Feb. 20

Mrs Lister (Widw of Mr John Lister Minr at Topliffe) died Febr. 21

Mr Michl Hoile of Field in Northourum died Feb 22

John Waterhouse of Woshaw lane bur. Feb. 19

Wid. Judeth Clark of Morley bur. Mar. 8

Wid. Mary Learoyd of Northourum bur. Mar.

Mr. George Ibbison of Leeds bur. Mar. 19

BURIALS.

Abraham Swaine of Bradford bur. Mar. 19

Widw. Grace Burnley of Northourum bur. at Coley Chapel Mar. 25. 1733

James Kirshaw died at Scout Hall of 3 days sickness Mar. 27

Mr William Clifford died in Northourum Apr. 18. bur. at Halifax Apr. 21. He was many years Curate at Lightcliffe afterwards at Haworth, had left Preaching some years being very old

Margaret wife of Tho. Swaine of Shelf died of the 14th child May 6

John Brook of Coley died May 7

Mr. Geo. Heald of Macclesfield in Cheshire

Mr Nathan Sharp had bin Curate at Coley & Schoolmaster in Hipperholm near 30 years, died May 9. bur. May 12. in Coley Chapel aged near 59,—1733

Mr Tho. Walker of Walter Clough bur. at Halifax May 11

Obadiah Scholefield of Southourum bur. his wife May 16. having bin lame & helpless a long time

Mrs Hannah Holden died wth. her Grand-dr. (Mr Nathl Priestley's wife) in Northourum May. 15. bur. in Halifax Church May 17. aged 77. Excelling many in good temper Piety and usefulness

Mary wife of John Conney of Holdsworth died June 1. bur. at Halifax June 3

Richd. Wilkinson of Illingworth bur. his wife June 25

John Bramfett and two of his Children bur. at Coley Chapel July 12. being Stifled or Smother'd to Death with Smoak and fire which broke out in the night in the house where they liv'd at the End o'th'Common Wood and burnt a great part of it &c.— How terrible is God in his doings—who shall not fear him— What a Mercy that our Houses are Safe from fire—Within 2 or 3 weeks before Several men and beasts were struck dead & Much Damage done otherways by Thunder and Lightning

Mr Alexander Clough of Eland bur. at Hackney near London Aug. 1. 1733

Mrs Susanna Wadsworth of Holdsworth died Aug 16. bur. Aug. 18

Mrs — Lockwood of Black-house near Hulm-firth bur. Aug. 25

Sarah dr. Robt Pickard of Ossett (wife of Francis Wilson of Halifax) bur. Sept. 4

Mr James Gream of Py-nest near Halifax bur. Oct. 5

Mr Saml Brook died at Crow-Nest in Lightcliffe Oct. 15. left a young Widw. dr Widw Walker there

Sr John Stapylton fell off his Horse near Aberforth and died
presently, was making Interest to be a Knight for the County
of York His Seat is Myton. Horse was frighted and threw
him. Oct.

Mrs Mary Rookes of Rodes Hall died Nov. 2. She was the Widw
of William Rooks Esq & dr. of Willm. Rodes of Great Houghton Esq a Choice, useful, Pious Woman

Mr — Slce an Attorney in Leeds was bur. Nov. 5. its said worth
29000 li

Willm Ashley of Wyke schoolmaster at Buttershaw died Nov. 11

Jeremy Northend of Brian-Scholes in Northourum bur. Nov. 22

Timothy Kirshaw of Wyke bur. Nov.

Mr. Joseph Holmes of Lightcliffe died Dec. 1

Mr. — Smith Curate at Eland died Dec. 4

Isaac Baum of Bradford bur. Nov. 30. aged. 83

Miss. Anne Rookes of Rodes Hall died Dec. 11 aged 9 years
& 6 weeks

John Fozard was drown'd in the Brook near his house at Batley
Carr, Dec. 14. Coming from Wakefield Market

Widw. Grace Milner died at Hipperholm lane Ends Dec. 31.
bur. Jan. 4 aged near 96

Mrs. Bentley (Mr. Danl Bentley's wife Curate at Illingworth)
died Jan. 5

Benja. Wilkinson's wife near Halifax bur. Jan. 10

Peter s. Mr. Eli Stansfield of Sowerby bur. Jan. 16. had bin
some time with Dr. Nettleton being designed for a Physician

Joseph Priestley of White Windows near Sowerby Brigg died
Jan. 15

Mrs. Walker of Walterclough died Jan. 15

Castor Brook of Wibsey Coach Man at Rodes Hall died Suddenly
Jan. 15

Dr Leech of Manchester died Jan 18

Mrs. Walker of Hipperholm bur. Jan. 22

Abraham Haigh of Marsh bur. Jan. 23

Mr. Isaac Naylor of Halifax bur. his wife Jan. 24

Mr. John Crompton Minr. in Doncaster bur. Jan.

Mrs. Moody his dr. died Febr.

Mr Willm. Rawson Attorney at Law in Bradford died Feb. 2

Widw. Nicolls. of Halifax died Febr. — was bur. Febr. 8

Widw. Holmes of Lightcliffe bur. Febr.

Mr. Richd Reyner of Mill Brigg near Heckmondwyke bur his wife Mar. 14

Mary dr. Mr. Isaac Sharp of Horton bur. Mar. 13

Widw. Sugden of Oxheys in Shelf died at Scout Hall in Northourum Mar. 17

Richard Pollard of Reavy bur. Mar.

Widow Mary Sager of Wibsey bur. Mar. 25

Mr Ely Stansfield of Sowerby was at Rochdale on Monday, got home very ill on Tuesday about Noon, made his will on Wednesday Night, and died about 6 o'Clock next morning, viz. Apr. 11. 1734

Mr. Abraham Rodes of Bradford Moor died Apr. 17. 1734

Mr. Ely Dyson of Clay House near Eland bur. Apr. 18

Henry Bedford of Shelf died May 4

Mr Lindley of Bowling, a Justice of Peace, & Keeper of the Register in Wakefield died May — in Wakefield, bur. May 10. at Bradford

Mrs Martha Bairstow died in Halifax May 8, bur. there May 10, was at Northourum Chapel May 1. & at Halifax Chapel May 3d, only sick 5 days

— dr. of Mr. Wm. Wood, Pump near Shibden Hall bur. May 28

John s. Tho. Wilkinson of Halifax bur May 29

Mrs Stead wife of Mr Samll. Stead of Halifax bur. May 29, had bin married (its said) 59 years

— s. of Mrs Marsden died of 2 or 3 days sickness May 29. A Fever

Mr. Murgatroyd an old Attorney near Dewsbury bur. May 27

Wm. Walker of Halifax bur. June 3. He had long collected the vicars dues

Mr Huntington of Holbeck near Leeds bur. June 22

Widw. Kitson a midwife in Halifax died of a Palsie July 11 (seiz'd July 4th)

Mrs. Eliz. Alwood of Chesterfield died of a few days Illness July 1, 1734. She was dr. of Mr. Robinson of Gainsbrough & second wife of Mr. John Alwood

Mr. Joseph Hardcastle of Great Woodhouse near Leeds died July 18

Joseph Northend of High Bentley bur. Aug. 8

Mrs. Suttell of Leeds bur. Aug.

BURIALS.

Tho. Ramsden of Northourum bur. Aug. 15

Mrs. Buxton of Wakefield died Aug. 15

Mr. Robt Milnes of Wakefield died Aug. 23. was bur. in the
Chapel, a Pompous & Solemn Funeral

Mrs Eleanor Clows of Manchr died July 31

Christopher Marshall, Sexton at Halifax Church, died Sept. 16

Mr Nicolas Beal minr. at Idle New Chapel died Sept. 16. bur. in
the sd Chapel Sept. 19 *

Lady Bland of Hulm Hall near Manchester bur.

Lady Egerton of Heaton Hall near Manchester (wife of Mr John
Brook) formerly wife of Sr. Holland Egerton, mother to Sr.
Edward, died in child bed Sep. 25

Mr Tho. Leach of Kighley bur. Oct. 12

William Wigglesworth near Leeds died of a very short sickness,
bur. Oct. 28

Mr — Fenner of London went from Halifax to ¦Wakefield Oct.
28, died there, bur. 30

Mary wife of Abraham Hemingway near Dewsbury died Oct 30.
bur. Nov. 2

Richard Roust of Northourum died Nov. 1

Mr. Hollings of Shipley near Bradford died Oct. 31, bur Nov. 3

Widw Mary Priestley of Northourum died Nov. 5 bur. Nov. 7.
aged 65 : one of great Piety and Usefulness

Mrs Lydia Rotheram of Dranfield in Derbyshire died Oct. 1

George Holroide of Halifax died Nov. 9. came in full of drink,
laid down on his bed, was found dead.

Mr Nathll. Booth of Gildersom, a Baptist Preacher bur. Nov. 5
at Morley

Mr Ebenezer Gill Minr. in Hull died

Mary wife of Tho. Lister bur Dec. 12

Mr Samll Cotton died at Severley Dec.

Mary Robinson of Thornton bur. Dec. 9

Widw Mary Craven of Westercroft died Dec. 13

Widw Sarah Booth of Northourum died Dec. 23, and her Sister
in Law —

Widw Lydia Butler died in the same house Dec. 26

John Naylor of Ossett died Dec. 22

— dr of Dr. Firth of Kipping bur. Dec. 30

Mary wife of Tho. Thorp of Dumb Mill died Jan. 4. 1734-5

* See *Nonconformity in Idel & History of Airedale College.*

BURIALS.

Mrs Wilkinson of Illingworth died. Jan. 18, aged near 80

Timothy Viccars of Halifax bur. Jan. 29

Mr Tho. Fenton of Hunslet near Leeds remov'd lately to Houghton Tower, went to Preston Jan. 16, died there Jan. 17. bur. Jan. 21. His wife sister to Sr Henry Houghton and now left with ten children

Tho. White a rich Butcher in Ossett was drown'd near Wakefield Febr. 1. or Jan. 31. in the night time, bur. at Thornhill Febr. 3

Mrs Murgatroyd near Dewsbury bur. Febr. 8

Joseph Sunderland bur. Mar. 5. died in Eland

Mr. Walker near Dewsbury fell of his Horse at Westgate end in Wakefield into the water where he lay for sometime, died in abt. three days, Mar.

John Pollards wife of Lee in Northourum bur. Mar. 16

Tim. Chadwick's wife in Halifax bur. Mar. 18.

Sir Walter Hawksworth died at York Mar. 17

Mr John Wadsworth of Sheffield bur. his wife Mar.

William s. Joseph Hanson bur. Apr. 2, half year old.

— Whitley died in Northourum Apr. 15

John Tenant of Heddingley near Leeds died suddenly Apr. 18

William Jackson of Northourum died Apr. 20

Mr Tho Holdsworth of Astie in Southourum died Apr. 20

Widow Wilkinson of Holdsworth died May 6, aged 81

Abraham Scott of Northourum died May 7

— dr. of Mr. John Lum of Silkcotes near Wakefield bur. May 19

Abraham Broadley of Halifax bur. May 23

William Bentley Apparitor & Clark at Halifax Church being Arrested and imprison'd in London died there May

Robert Northend of Northourum died May 28, said to leave 1000 li a piece to his 2 sons and 2 dautrs

Abraham Burnley of Lightcliffe bur. June 7

Gershom Holdsworth of Alverthorp bur. at Topliffe June 17

— wife of Mr Wm. Lupton of Wakefield bur. June 17 found dead in bed by her husband

Widw Armitage of Heckmondwyke bur. June 23

Widw Fothergill of Ossett bur. at the New Chapel July 11, aged 89

Widow Sarah Rhoades died at Tanhouse in Northourum July 17. bur. at Bradford July 22

Richd Northrop of Hopton died July

Stephen Hall of Wareley was bur. Aug. 15

BURIALS.

— wife of John Holroid of Cockill bur. Aug.

Widow Lum of Silk Cotes (sister Fosters Mother) died Aug. 2— at Flanshaw, bur. Aug 2—

[—] was kill'd by falling into a coal-pit in Shelf about midnight Sept 7 or 8

— dr. of Mr. Robt. Moody of Doncaster died at Mrs Moults in Leeds Sep. 10. bur. Sep. 12

Mrs Abigail Ryley died at Breck in Sowerby of a short sickness Sep. 14

Timothy Oldfield of the Swan in Halifax died Sept. 20

— dr. of Mr. Lupton late Curate at Sowerby Bridge was kill'd at Meddle bottom Mill Sep.

Mr John Cockcroft Attorney in Bradford bur. Sep. 25

Mr. Jere. Lupton of Wakefield died Sep. 26

Mr Wm Dukinfield of Staly Hall died abt Aug. 29

Mr James Taylor had bin in Ireland some years came to his relations in Manchester was seiz'd with a Fever & died there abt July 25

Mr John Ash Minr in Derbyshire died Oct 2, aged 64

Mr Tho. Colton of York died Oct. 8. aged 12 years & 8 months heir to a considerable estate

Mr John Brook Minr in York died Oct. 22. a worthy man the loss very great to his Family & Congregation

Mr. Worthington Minr at Dean roe then about

Jonathan Laycock a Skinner lately remov'd out of Halifax to Westercroft died Oct. 25

Sarah wife of Joshua Threapland of Northourum died Oct. 31. bur. Nov. 3

Samll Threapland of Willow Hall bur. his wife Nov. 3

Widow Kitson of Brear in Northourum bur. Nov. 12

Mr Michael Gibson of Slade Hall near Brighouse bur Nov. 16

Tho. Walshaw of Ossett died abt. Nov. 15

Widow Sarah Hanson of Halifax died suddenly Nov. 20, 1735

George Stansfield of Sowerby was found dead upon a Moor Nov. 21. had bin long Melancholy

Mr. Sheffield Curate of Sowerby died Nov. 23

— Buck of Allerton, Father to Mr John Buck Minr at Bolton bur. Dec. 12

Joshua Dean of Hud-hill bur. his wife Jan. 2

Lady Asheton of Middleton died of small pox. Jan. 8. She was

BURIALS.

⌐ wife to Sr Ralph Asheton dr. of the late Sr Holland Egerton of Heaton Hall

John Hodgson of Halifax died Jan 26 bur. there Jan. 28

Mr. Holdsworth of High Town died Jan. 28

Daniel Sugden of Halifax died Febr. 5

James s. Mr Nathll. Priestley of Northourum died Febr. 6

Mr — Dean of Marshall Hall near Eland bur. his wife Febr. 9

Mr — Booth of Halifax bur. his wife Febr. 13

Sarah — of Comon-House in Halifax bur. Feb. 20

Sarah Cryer of Bradford bur. Feb 17

Mr Benjamin Foster my wifes brother died at New York in America Feb. 25

Susanna Sugden of Royal Oak in Halifax bur. Feb. 24

Mrs Armitage Governess of a Boarding School in Leeds bur. Feb. 22

Mr Whitley Heald (son to Mr Heald late Vicar of Huthersfield) fell down in the Pulpit and died abt Febr. 1

Anthony Proctor of Cinderhills near Coley Chapel bur. Mar. 25. 1736

James Dawson of Clayton Heights died Mar. 25

Anne Ambler, Widw, late of Shiben head died with her dr. (John Smith's wife) near Bingley, Mar. 26

Richd Holroide of Ribbonden died Mar. 28

Thomas Dichenson (my son John's son) died in London Mar. 30

Roger Tatham of Halifax died Apr. 2

Sr George Armitage of Kirkleys bur. Apr. 24

Grace Hartley of Northourum, Widw, aged abt 80, bur. Apr. 30

Mr Matthew Smith Minr at Mixenden died Apr. 29 bur. May 4, aged 95. as its said or thereabout Had bin very painful and Successful in his work

Sarah wife of John Walker of Shelf bur. May 11

Mary wife of John Jewet of Clayton bur. May 12

Mrs Susanna Wright of Wakefield died May 25

Sister Fosters Aunt, of Flanshaw

The Rt. Hon. Arthur Ingram Viscount Irwin in the County of Cuningham in Scotland Lord Lieutent. and Custos Rotuloru. of the East Riding of Co. of York and of the Town of Kingston upon Hull, died a Batchelor at his house in Grosvenor Square, London on Sunday May 30. is succeeded in Title and Estate by his Bro. Henry

Elizabeth d. Timothy Ramsden of Northourum died of Small Pox
in Halifax June 8
Lydia Craven bur June 13, died at Northfield Yate
Judeth Holdsworth of Barnshill in Northourum bur. June 16
Mrs Hannah Wright (late of Hipperholm) died in Halifax June
19. bur. June 22, aged 80
Miles Ingham of Northourum died June 21
Mr Tho. Lee of Leeds died June 24, had bin very Active and
useful as a Mercht, a Justice of Peace, was a member of the
Dissenting Congregation at Mill-hill died very rich
Mrs Jane Heys dr. of Mr John Whitaker Minr at Plats near
Manchester died June 26
Martha d. of Timothy Ramsden died of Small Pox July 11 bur.
at Northourum Chapel, 13th
Mrs Wainman (Wife of Mr Tho. W. of Bradford) burnt to death
in the house July 23
John s. Mr James Ingham of Halifax died of Small Pox July 31
Mr James Batley's wife of Halifax died of Small Pox Aug. 3
buried 4
Joshua Rayner of Halifax bur. Aug. 9
Mrs Midgley of Schole-Moor died Aug. 29 bur. at Bradford Sep. 1
Lady Russel wife of Sr Henry Hoghton died going from Bath
Aug.
Mrs Catherine Buckle died in London Sept. 1. My wife's 2d
cousin
Daniel Mitchel of Ovenden bur. his son design'd for the ministry
aged about 18, died of Small Pox, Sep.
— dr of Joshua Akill of Halifax died suddenly Sept. 21
Miss Rigg of Halifax died Sep 2—
John Best of Godley died Sep 2—
John Sharp died Oct 10 at Barnshill
Mrs Lapigh died at Pontefract about Sept 23
Thomas Jackson of Ossett died at Aberforth in his return from a
Fair at York Nov. 3
Mary d. of John Flather of Northourum died of Small Pox Nov. 8
Ephraim Benn of High Bentley bur. Nov. 7
Mr John Simpson of Hipperholm bur. his son Nov. 12, and his
dr. Nov. 15 both of Small Pox.
Mr. John Finch Curate at Thornton in Bradford Parish died
about Sept. 29

BURIALS.

Mrs. Mercy Whitaker of Leeds (my Wife's near Kinswoman) died Nov. 19. the same day of the Month on which her husband died 26 years before She was eminently pious & useful, aged 77
Elizabeth dr. Mr. Isaac Sharp of Horton died Nov. 24
Mr. Saml. Stead of Halifax bur. Dec. 8. aged — very rich
Mr. — Booth of Halifax died Dec. 28 aged — very rich
Mrs. Ingram of Wakefield died Dec. 29 bur. Jan. 1
Rosa. Sharp died Dec. 31. bur. at Coley Chapel Jan 3
Joseph Woodhead of Shelf Hall died Jan. 21
— wife Joshua Kitson near Halifax died Jan 21
Dr. William Wake A.B. of Canterbury died at Lambeth Jan. 24. 1736, in the 79 year of his Age, had bin Arch Bishop there 21
Widw Crowther of Plow-Royd in Northourum bur. Mar. 1
John Dixon of Scout bur. Mar. 21.
Sarah Storey bur. at Coley Mar. 8. died at Sowood-house
Mrs. Jane Ashley of Bolton died Febr. 15
Edward Ferguson a Scotchman bur. in New Chapel in Halifax Mar. 25. 1737. The first that was bur. there
Mrs. Powel of Leeds bur. Mar. 21
John Baines of Thorns near Wakefield. Mar. 18
Benjamin s. Benjamin Souwood bur. Apr. 1
John Bairstow of Northourum bur. Apr. 2
Widw Anne Jackson of Ossett Apr. 17
Mrs. Wainhouse of Broad Yates near Halifax died May bur. May 6
Mrs. Jenkinson of Lime Ditch near Manchester died Apr. 25
Joseph Brook of Crumblebottom in Southourum kill'd his Wife in a most barbarous manner, being great with Child Apr. 29
Mr. Joshua Lea of Sowerby died May 20
Hannah wife of Caleb Pierson of ffair weather-green bur. May 28
Samuel Mitchel a young man near Shibden Mill died of a few days Sickness May 29
Martha Hardcastle of Leeds bur.
John Denison of Flanshaw near Wakefield was at Church twice June 19 & dead before Morning bur. 22nd day
Widw Hannah Wood died wth. her dr. Mrs. Wainman in Pudsay bur. at Bramley June 22
Francis Romsbottom was in Halifax June 25. died abt. an hour after he came home
Robert Ramsden of Siddall Hall died June 27. had bin declining

some time

Mrs Baptista Sager died in Wakefield June 28 bur. the 29 in the
New Chapel where her husband had bin Minister 1737

Thomas Wilkinson of Halifax bur. his dr. July 8 and his dr. —
July 11

Widw Eylam of Heath near Halifax died July 13, had bin a noted
Speaker amongst the Quakers

William Wood of Halifax was at chapel July 17, died next day

Sarah Learoyd dr. of John L. late of Northourum died July 26
of a short sickness

John Bentley of Bradford bur. July 29

— wife of Benjamin Binns of Northourum died abt middle of
July

Miss Hannah Markham of Leeds went to London last Spring, died
at her. Aunt Fosters of abt. 24 hours sickness July 24

Joseph s. Joseph Stead of Northourum died of 3 or 4 days sickness Aug. 2. bur. in Northourum Chapel Aug. 4. an only child

Mr Richard Taylor of Manchester my very good & faithful Friend
& constant Hearer at Gorton died Aug. 1. bur. Aug. 3. aged
near 80, very rich in wealth and good works

Widw Jepson of Dewsbury was bur. Aug. 10. mother to my sister Hansons first Husband

William Wilkinson near High-Cross died Aug. 11. that day ffort-
night that he was married to Widw. Roust

James Kirshaw near Halifax bur. Sept. 11

Tho. Moss of Ossett died Sept. 18

Mrs Phebe Oates of Halifax bur. Sep. 16

Mrs Anne Basnet of Liverpool died Sept 13.   She was dr. of Mr
Samll Eaton of Manchester

William Woodhead of Shelf died of a few days sickness Oct. 1

George Carter of Hunslett bur. Oct. 2

Mr — Bayok of South Cave near Hull bur. Sept. 29 aged 90 or
upwards   A Dissenting Minr. supposed to be the oldest minr.
in England

Miss Sarah Walker of Walterclough died in Halifax bur. Oct. 14
abt 18 year old

Joseph Stocks of Northourum died Oct. 23

Mr Turner Minr in Knutsford died Oct.

Mr Butterworth of Manchester died Oct, aged abt 85

— Dr of Mr Reddish of Dukinfield died Oct.

BURIALS.

— Readihough of Holdsworth died Oct. 31

Mr Hilton of Hilton in Lancashire died — an old man, very rich, had lately married a young gentlewoman

— son of Mr Richd Milnes of Wakefield died of Small Pox Oct.

Rachel d. of Jonath. Oldfield near Beggrington bur. Nov. 8

Stephen s. Stephen Ambler of Shibden Head bur. Nov. 8

Joseph Nicholson of Wareley bur. Nov. 11

Jeremy Peel of Northourum died Nov. 10

Madm. Hopkinson of Gainsbrough died Oct. 25. Vory rich, pious & useful

Thomas Thorp of Slead Syke near Brighouse (a Papist) died Nov. 21

Jonathan Tattersall of only house in Northourum died Nov. 23

Thomas s. Stephen Ambler of Shibden Head died Nov. 22

Wilhelmina-Dorothea-Carolina Queen Consort of Great Britain died Lord's day night at 10-o'clock Nov. 20. of a Rupture & Mortification in the Bowels, aged 55 years 8 months & 13 days

— wife of Tho. Laycock of Shelf bur. Nov. 26

Sarah wife of Jeremy Rookes of Shelf died Nov. 30

Mr John Stansfield of Sowerby Town bur. Dec. 6

John s. Mr. Richd. Tottie of Leeds died Dec. 22

Joshua Ambler of Haselhirst in Northourum died Dec. 26

— wife of Saml. Sugden of Royal Oak in Halifax bur. Jan. 11. died in Child-bed of her first Child

Nathan Hainworth of Shugden in Northourum bur. Jan. 24 aged 84

Mr. James Milnes of Chesterfield died Jan.

Mr. Robt. Bragg an Ancient Minr. in London died Febr. 13

James Bartlett of Shelf bur. Febr. 19

Lydia dr. Willm Hird bur. at Northourum Chapel Febr. 23

Mr. Pollard Curate at Thornhill died near Huthersfield, bur. Febr. 22

Dr. Finch died at York Febr. 14

Joseph Moor of Ovenden died Febr. 8

Henry Green of Halifax died Suddenly Febr. 28

Widw. Ellen Sonier died Mar. 2. had bin long in Communion at Northourum

Widw. Sarah Naylor of Ossett died Mar. 10

Mr. — Flower of Gainsbrough died of an Apoplexy

Mrs Clegg of Manchester bur. Mar. 31. aged 85

Dr. Baldersome near Mirfield bur. About Apr. 2

BURIALS.

John Conney of Holdsworth died Apr. 15. bur. at Illingworth Apr. 18

James Greaves wife near Booth-Town Apr 25

Mr. John Ferguson of Halifax died May 1. bur in the New Chapel there May 3

Mr. — More of Kendall died Apr. 1

John Firth's wife of Priestley-green bur. May. 1

Mary d. Tho. Swaine of Shelf died May 20

Thomas Webster of Dewsbury died at Middle of May

Mr Robt. Gibson of Slead-hall near Brighouse died May 20

John Firth of Priestley-green bur. May 28

[½ line short hand.]

Henry Moorhouse (Brother to our Maid) died in London June 6. his Scull was broke by a Stroke which a Maid Servt. gave him a few days before

Mr. Tho. Drake of Halifax died June 14

Mr. Hananiah Elston Minr. at Eland died June 22. bur. June 24

Mr. — Hanson an Attorney bur. at Halifax June 24

John Waddington of Priestley-green bur. June 29

Mr. Henry Markham of Leeds died

Widw. Brook of Clack-Heaton bur. at Birstall July 1

Mr Gundy the Curate at Sowerby bur his wife July 15

Abraham Broadley bur. at Coley Chapel Aug. 2

Jonathan Wade of Northourum bur. Aug 7

Mr — Hollings of Shipley died Aug 24

Mrs Wood of Fold died Aug. 24, both bur. at Halifax Aug. 27

Mr Ramsbottom of Birks Hall died Aug. 26

Mr Samll Stansfield of Horton died Oct. 21

Mr James Alderson of Halifax bur. his wife Oct. 24

Mr Greensmith of Chesterfield died

Mr Joshua Hoile minr at Swauland died Oct.

Mr John Crompton's wife of Gainsbrough died in childbed o'th' 2nd child Oct. 31

Mrs Wainhouse of Northgate in Halifax bur. Nov. 10

Charles Haigh of Marsh in Southourum died about Nov. 6

Lady Armitage of Kirkleys died Nov. 22. 1738

Jeremy Ellenthorp of Northourum died Dec. 7

Titus Greenwood of Northourum died in London Dec. 10

John Stephenson of Ossett died Dec. 7

Mr Beaumont of Halifax bur. his wife Dec. 28

BURIALS.

Robt. Naylor of Northourum bur. Jan. 4

Rachel Hanson Widw, died in Clackheaton with her dr. Jan 11, bur. Jan. 15, aged abt. 80

— wife of Tho. Bland junr of Halifax bur. Jan. 18

Elizabeth wife of Tho. Wilkinson bur. at Coley Jan. 21

— wife of John Kellett of Shelf died Jan 27

Lydia wife of John Kellett of Northourum died Feb. 2

— Nicolson bur his wife at Luddenden Febr. 9. She died in childbed of her first child

Mrs Mary Banks wife of Mr Tho. Banks Parson of Hutton Roberts &c., Sister of My son Thomas's wife died of a short sickness Febr 1

Thomas s. Mr Tho. Whitaker of Leeds bur. Febr. 9

Thomas Wilkinson of Holdsworth died Febr. 19. bur at Halifax Febr. 21

Josia Craven of Frisenall near Bradford died abt Febr. 20

Mrs Willous of Wakefield bur. at Horton Chapel Mar. 2

John Murgatroyd of Hipperholm died at Bradford Mar. 20, bur. Mar. 23

Robert s. Mr. George Cotton of Wakefield bur. Mar. 27

Christopher Metcalf of Halifax bur. Mar. 27

John Greenwood of Norwood Green died Mar. 31

Jacob Hemingway of Boothroyd near Dewsbury died Apr. 1

John Wood of Bramley died Apr. 6

Mr. George Hopwood an Attorney in Halifax bur. Apr. 10

Edward Kay of Leeds bur. his wife Apr. 9

Mr William Gream of Heath near Halifax died Apr. 12, bur. Apr. 15

Mr Joseph Dawson Minr in Rochdale died Apr. 15, A very worthy good man, had preacht there 40 years &c.

Mrs. Wareing of Wakefield died Apr. 14, bur. the same day

Susanna d. Mr Willm Sykes of Salford died Apr. 13. A child of my son Thomas's wife's Brother's about 6 years of age

Richard Brown of Bank Top near Halifax bur. his wife Apr. 25

Dr Nicholas Saunderson Professor of Mathematicks in Cambridge died about middle of Apr. 1739 had bin blind from 2 years of Age, but by the strength of a surprising Genius & a close Application to Study, attained so great a Proficiency in his Art as to be accounted one of the greatest Mathematicians that ever lived

Peter Toulson of Leeds died Apr. 20

John Fauthrop of Collier Syke bur. his wife May 2

Dr Dearden of Halifax died May 7

Mr James Swaine (son of Tho. Swaine of Shelf,) an Attorney, died in London, May 4

James Murgatroyd of Shelf died May 21

Elizabeth wife of Joshua Hardcas'le of Woodhouse bur. May 10 or thereabts.

Mercy wife of Theophilus Wood died May 30

James Haworth's wife of Southou;um bur. at Halifax June 24

Mr Joshua Hill Curate at Lightcliffe was buried there June 11. had bin blind & unfit to preach a long time, & the chapel oft empty

Martin Fielding of Halifax bur. June 22 aged about 85

— son of Mr. Wm. Sykes of Salford fell into the River & was drown'd

Mrs Eliz. Hill (dr. of Revd Mr Frankland of Rawthmell) died at York June 20

Mr Rawson (John) a young clergyman died in Bradford July 5

Caleb Ashworth of Northourum died July 8, bur. at Halifax July 10

Mr Joshua Dawson of Leeds bur. July 10, aged 90, an old Disciple

Jacob s. of Mr Busk of Leeds died of a few days sickness in Manchester July 20, (bur. at Leeds July 24). His Father had paid 200 li. with him as an Apprentice there a few years ago

Thomas Mallison of Hipperholm bur. July 22, aged 82

Ebenezer Holdsworth of Alverthorp died abt July 12

Mrs Wright of Wakefield bur. July 28, an ancient woman unmarried

Mary d. Jonas Laycock of Shelf bur. Aug. 1

Widw Hanson of Northourum bur. Aug. 3

Nathll. Holdsworth of Norland bur. his wife Aug. 6. died in child bed

James Milner of Brackenbed died of a few hours sickness Aug. 19

William Hodgson of Bowling died with his mother in Hunslet Aug. 23

Mrs Jane Priestley of Ovenden. (Relict of the late Revd Mr. Nathanl. Priestley) died of a few hours sickness Aug. 27. aged abt. 71

BURIALS.

Lydia Oxley died in Hipperholm at Widw. Bentley's Sept. 10

Mr William Heron Steward of the Court in Wakefield died Sept. 14

Isabel Oddy of Wibsey died Oct. 3

James Ibbetson of Leeds Esqre a very rich merchant died Oct. 16

Mrs Greensmith of Chesterfield died abt. that time

Mary d. John Smith of Hungerhill in Northourum died of a few hours sickness Oct. 26, aged abt. 21

Richard Warburton died near Bradford Oct. 29

Mrs Gibson widw. of Mr. Robt. Gibson of Slead Hall died in Manchester Nov. 5

Mr Luke Hoile's wife of Ovenden died in childbed Nov. 8. a few days after she had born 2 children

Mrs. Grimshaw d. of Mr. John Lockwood of Ewood & wife of Mr Grimshaw Curate at Todmorden was bur. at Luddenden Nov. 5

Mr Henry Gream of Shay hill near Halifax bur. Nov. 22, 1739, aged 79

The Earl of Strafford died Nov. 15

Robt. Wiversley of Shelf a poor old man died Dec. 2

Mr. Joshua Rider of Leeds bur. Dec. 5

— Murgatroyd of Willow Edge near Halifax was found fall'n of his Horse & dead near his own House Dec. 6

Sarah Learoyd Widw. died at Westercroft was bur. at New Chapel near Bradford Dec. 1—. near 80 year old

Mr. — Ireton died at the Copperas house near Booth Town in Northourum Dec. 30

Mr — Deerden of Hollings near Luddenden bur. Dec. 27

Lady Elizabeth Hastings of Ledsom near Pontefract died Dec. 22. A Lady of Extraordinary Charity

John Marshall of Idle bur. his wife Dec. 25. died of 2d. child

Jonas Priestley of Field Head near Birstall bur. his wife, died of 5th child

Barbara wife of John Scott of Tanhouse died Jan. 7. after a long and sore affliction

Martha wife of Wm. Northend of Sim Carr in Northourum bur. Jan 16, aged 80. &c.

Hannah d. of Brother Clapham died at my House Jan. 20, bur. Jan. 24

Daniel Empsall of Norwood Green bur. Jan. 24

Mr Samuel Hallows a Justice of Peace near Rochdale died Jan. 21

BURIALS.

Mrs Mottershead of Manchester his sister died,'died Febr. 1

Mr James Ingham of Halifax died Febr. 5 a great loss to the Dissenting Congregation

Mary d. John Wilkinson (late of Mytham) bur. Febr. 6

Hannah wife of John Fothergill of Ossett died Febr. 2

Mrs Elizabeth Clapham (my dear Sister in Law) died in Halifax Feb. 10., greatly beloved & greatly lamented, bur. Febr, 13, 1739

Mary Sharp Widow died at Barnshill Febr 19. aged abt. 90

Isaac Farrar of Warley died Feb. 20

Tho. Oldfield died at Field in Northourum Febr. 22

Mrs Mary Walker died in Halifax Febr 27, had bin married but about 7 or 8 weeks to Mr Walker of Crow Nest in Lightcliffe

William Horton Esqre Justice of Peace died at Coley Hall Febr 27. bur. at Eland. Mar. 5

Mrs Beaumont of High Town died of a few hours sickness Mar. 3

Edin wife of Robert Booth of Hipperholm died Apr. 4

Tho Hardcastle near Leeds bur. his wife

William Rodes of Haughton Esqr died at London, bur. at Darfield near Haughton beginning of April 1740

Mr. Alwood Minr at Sutton in —— died abt. same time

Mrs Gream of Shayhill died Apr. 21 the Wid. of Mr John Gream

Mr Joseph Brooksbank curate at Luddenden bur. May 9

Edward Fletcher near Great Horton bur. May 23, died suddenly, aged 82

Richard Fletcher his Brother buried June 4. aged 79

Judeth wife of John Mortimer of Shelf died June 6

Wm Holroide of Hipperholm bur. June 30

Mrs Martin of Willow Hall died June 30

Mr Richd Scholefield Minr at —— lately remov'd from Whitworth in Rochdale Parish

Mrs. Bathshua Gill of London (my wife's kinswoman) died July 7, of 3 days sickness

Paul Greenwood of Halifax Banktop died July 10

Mrs Oldfield of Stocklane in Wareley died of a few hours illness July 22

Susanna Milner of Skircote-green died suddenly July 24

Widw Mary Tillotson died in Northourum Aug. 7

Thomas s. John Wilkinson of Northourum died Aug. 25 of Small Pox

BURIALS.

Mr Joshua Jones Minr. in Manehester died at Chester Aug. 25

Mrs Smith of Mixenden (the late Minrs. Widw.) was bur. in the Chapel there. Sept 19

Nathl. —— of Bowood in Sowerby bur. Sept. 25. The first bur in New Chapel

Susan. wife of John Smith of Hunger-hill in Northourum died Oct. 6. 1740

Mrs. Stead Mr. Valentine Stead's wife of Halifax died Oct. 8

John Askew of Northourum died Oct. 19. walkt to Halifax day before

Mrs Sarah Milnes late of Ovenden died in Halifax Oct. 20

Mr Henry Ibbetson of Leeds bur. his wife Oct. 20

Mrs Myers a Quaker died at her Brothers, Mr. Laycock at Shay-hill bur. Oct. 21

Joseph Bothomley of Dam-Head in Northourum bur. his wife Nov. 7

Widw Ingham (Mother of Saml. Starkey of Shelf) bur Nov. 15

—— s. Saml. Gargrave of Horton bur. Nov. 15

Mrs. Lee, a Widw. died wth. her Mother Widw. Cowling at Folly Hall, was bur. at the Quakers burying place at Harrodwell Nov. 20

John Kellet of Northourum Died Nov. 21

Mr. Nathl Jenkinson of Lime Ditch near Oldham bur. Nov 20. 1740

Mr Wm. Elmsall of Thornhill an Attorney died abt. Nov. 1

Robert Midgley the gail-keeper in Halifax bur. his wife Dec. 2

Mr John Town near Halifax bur. Dec. 27

John Milnes died Dec. 29 at Birstall in his journey from Leeds where he had been Apprentice, was born in Northourum but had liv'd Several years in Alchingham in Cheshire

Hannah wife of John Clayton of Brown Roide Hill bur. Jan. 11

Miss Hannah Heywood of Dronfield in Derbyshire died Jan. 11

John s. Mr Benjamin Coke of Halifax (being Inoculated) died of the Small Pox Jan. 31

John Bland s. of Tho. Bland of Halifax died Febr. 15

Dr Tho: Hadfield Minr. Physician and Tutor a Peckham died Febr.

Nathl. Holdsworth (Solomon's son) died of Small Pox in London Febr. 26

Joshua Dean of Hudhill in Northourum died Mar. 2

BURIALS.

Mr Gilbert Brooksbank of Halifax died Mar. 10

Mrs Butterworth wife of Mr Tho. Butterworth of Manchester bur Mar. 18. 1740

John Fauthrop of Collier Syke died Mar. 20

Mr Day Curate in Leeds died

Susanna dr. Saml. Askew. of Northourum bur Mar. 31. 1741

Rebecca dr. James Wells of Shelf bur Apr. 5

Widw Taylor of Clack-Heaton died Apr. 16

Mr. — s. Mr Tho. Butterworth of Manchester died abt beginning of Apr.

Dr Richd Richardson of North Bierley died Apr. 21. an Eminent Physician had bin Justice of Peace, very rich, aged 78. bur. Apr. 24. at White Chapel near Clack-Heaton

John Waddington of Ovenden Wood bur. May 13

Tho: Wilkinson a broker in Halifax bur. ·May 3

Mr Michael Angier of Manchester died May abt. Middle

Richard s. Mr John Milnes of Wakefield bur. May 1

—— wife of Mr John Farrar of Wareley bur. June 18. at Winwick in Lancre.

Mrs Rayner (Mr Joshua Rayner of Leeds Mother) bur. June 25

Mr John Dawson of Morley died Sept. 2

Susanna wife Mr Thomas Farrar of Westfield in Warley bur. Sept. 3

—— wife of Mr Jonathan Longbottom of Booth Town bur. Sept. 15

Nathanael Sutliffe of Shelf died of a few hours Sickness Sept. 15. bur Sept. 17

Knox Ward of London Esq (who Mar. Dr Nettleton's dr of Halifax) died Sept. 30

Widw. Stables died at her drs. Widw Wrights in Halifax very Old

Nath. Dickenson died in the Harbour at Carthagena abt. latter end of March 1741. as I am informed of a tedious weakness which I hope brought this my poor child to Start serious thoughtfulness

My Son Joseph Dickenson died about latter end of May or beginning of June 1741 of a Fever upon the Sea which was very fatal to many. he had been in two battels but not hurt. this ffever seiz'd him in the passage from Carthage.

Mrs Marsden in Sowerby Oct. 19

Mrs Lydia Milnes of Salford bur. Oct 31 at Stockport in Cheshire where her late Husband Mr Richard Milnes had bin minister

BURIALS.

Mary wife of John Booth of Hove Edge in Lightcliffe died Oct. 30
Mrs Wright (the Curate of Halifax wife) buried Nov. 2
Mr — Stockdale of Bradford a mercer died Nov.
Mrs Sarah Lumb wife of John Lumb of Silk cotes bur. Nov. 12
Joshua Lea near Sowerby Brigg died Dec. 1
Samll. Nicolls of Halifax bur. Dec. 18
Mr Wm Haliday minr at Bullous died in Halifax Dec. 11. of a
few hours Illness
Mr Isaac Smith Vicar of Haworth bur. Dec. 1—
Mr Francis Parrot Lecturer at Halifax — years died Dec.—
Susanna d. Joseph Hanson bur. at Northourum Chapel Jan 6.
1741-2
Mr Burrows Curate at Hunslet near Leeds and Mr. Holt Vicar of
Calverley died abt same time
Benjamin Beaumant of Hipperholm died Jan. 17
Martha wife of Saml. Appleyard of Sou'wood House bur. Jan. 17
Jonath. Milner of Northourum bur. Jan. 23
Dr Tho: Nettleton of Halifax died Jan. 9. bur. at Dewsbury Jan.
12. a very eminent and useful physician
Elizabeth dr. Mr Cordingley of Warley died Febr. 2. bur. Febr. 4
Tho. Bland of Halifax died Febr. 9. bur. Febr. 12
Mr Rawson an Apothecary in Halifax died Febr. 10
Mr — Holmes of Lightcliffe died Mar. 14. a great encourager of
the Methodists
John Turner's wife of North-brigg bank died Mar. 17
Lady Win wife of Sr Rowland Win of —— died Mar.
Sr. Charles Duckinfield died abt. Febr.
Robt. Hulme of Gorton died Mar.
John Crabtree's wife of Booth Town died Mar. 25
Richd Walton's wife of Halifax died about Mar. 17
Widw. Lister of Halifax Free School buried March 21
Miss Dearden of Hollings bur. at Luddenden Mar. 28. 1742 [4
lines Shorthand.]
Widow Mallison bur. at Lightcliffe Mar. 31. 1742
Mr Abraham Forness of Manningham bur. April 2
Mr John Milnes near Bolton bur. his wife abt the Middle of Apr.
had bin mar. but abt. seven months
Mrs Lister of Horton bur. Apr. 24
Timothy Clay Clark at Horton Chapel bur at Bradford May 19,
aged 72

BURIALS.

Mr Richd. Horton of Holroide near Barkisland died June 8

James Smith of Norland bur. June 19

John Mortimer of Shelf ffieldhead died June 22. bur. at Coley
June 25

Mr. — Thompson Eldest s. of Mr Thompson of Stancliffe a
young Clergyman died June 25. Heir to a great estate there.

Isaac Starkey s. Mr Saml Starkey of Shelf died in London June

Tho. Cordingley of Halifax died June 27

Jonadab Bentome of Halifax died June 27

Lady Dukinfield died in Salford, aged 95. bur. July 10

Jeremiah Bottomley of Northourum died July. 12

Francis Bentom of Halifax bur his wife July. 1

James s. John Swaine of Shelf died July 30

Mr Abraham Sharp of Little Horton the great Mathematician
died July. 18. bur. July 21. aged 89

Titus Stansfield of Sowerby bur. Aug 8

Sr. Darey Lever of Alkrington near Middleton in Lancre bur.
Aug. 15

Mrs Hide (wife of Mr Tho. Hide of Southwark died of a Fever in
Childbed Aug. 24

Isaac Wilkinson of Horton died Suddenly Aug. 28. aged 87. A
very Solid Serious Christian

John Appleyard of Haworth Parish bur. Sept. 1

Sarah wife of James Wilson of Upper Shibden Hall bur. Sept. 3.
dr. of John Jewet of Northourum

Elkanah Worrall Junr. of Booth Town bur. Sept. 2

Mary d. John Jewet of Northourum died Oct. 13.

Mary Greenwood Widow died at Halifax Bank Top Oct. 14

Widw Elizabeth Hodgson died at her Son in Law Joseph
Armitage's in Hunslet Oct 23

Mr Wm. Lupton of Wakefield bur. Oct. 12. an ancient christian,
very useful

Mr — Bothomley died at Baily Hall near Halifax, bur. Oct. 22

Mr John Naylor of Longbothom in Warley died Nov. 24

John Walton near Illingworth died Nov. 24

Mr Tho. Farrar of West ffield in Warley bur. Dec. 10

John Scott Junr, died in Northourum Dec. 9, having overstrain'd
himself with running

John Mann of Landshead in Northourum bur, at Coley Dec 1—

Widw Sarah Sharp of Lanshead died Dec. 18

BURIALS.

Mr George Legh of Onterton in Cheshire died in Manchester Nov.

Mr Samuel Wareing of Bury died Dec.

— dr John Wilkinson died at Manningham, was bur. at Bradford Jan. 1—

Mrs Ambler of Meadow Lane in Leeds bur. Jan 17 aged 86

Mr Wainman minr in Bingley bur. his wife Jan 20

Mrs Stansfield of Bowood in Sowerby died Jan 20 in her 70th year

[½ line short hand]

Samll. Oddey of Wibsey died Jan. 21

Widw Wilkinson of Horton bur. Febr. 5. aged 95 (as it is said)

Elizabeth only child of my Bro. in Law Mr. Richard Clapham died at Mr. Robt Ramsdens Febr. 6 in the 18th year of her age.

Samll. Starkey of Shelf bur, Feb. 21

Sarah d. Henry Stephenson of Lim'd House in Northourum died · Feb. 25

Eli Stansfield of Sowerby bur. Feb. 28

Mrs Frankland of Bramah died at York March

Mr John Dobson Minr at —— near Shrewsbury died Mar. 3

Jonathan Farrar of Wareley bur. Mar. 17

Mr Samuel Witter a young Preacher in Hull bur. Mar. 24

Dr Lancelot Blackburn A.Bishp. of York, died at London Mar. 23

Widw. Best of Coldwell bur Apr. 1

Mr Pemberton a rich Merchant in Leverpool bur. Apr. 7

Martha wife of Abraham Scholefield. of Norcliffe bur. at Light-cliffe Apr. 16

Mr Robert Wright an Eminent Dissenting Minr. in London died Apr.

Jonath. Oldfield near Beggrington bur. his second wife May 1. They had bin married but about 21 weeks

John Moorhouse of Pudsay died of a few days sickness. bur. Apr. 27

Widw. Brooksbank of Loggrams near Bradford bur. May 6

Elizabeth wife of Stephen Holdsworth bur. May. 6

Widw. Northrop near Mirfield died May 7

Abraham Baum of Bowling bur his wife May 8

Mrs Towers wife of Mr John Towers Minr. at Hopton went to Hull to see her dr. Mrs. Mell ; Mrs Towers died there May — & Mrs Mell died also May

Eliezer Dawson (Brother of Mr Eli Dawson Minr. in Halifax)
bur. at Morley aged [70] that day
John Scott of Tanhouse died May 19 Aged 68. bur. 22d
Thomas Scholefield of Northourum died of a few hours sickness
May 27 aged abt. 70
Mr Edmund Brigg, Attorney in Halifax bur May 30
Widw Elizabeth Mann bur. at Coley June 12
Jonas Dobson of Shugden Head in Northourum bur. his wife
June 27 aged abt. 84
James Gill of Southourum died July 3 ·
Abraham Whitwham of Northourum died July 4 in his 95th year
Mr John Holland chaplain at Norton with Esqre Offley was
buried July 4
Mr Jonathan Priestley of Winteredge died July 9 in the 49th
year of his age. A worthy good Christian, a great breach in
the ffamily and congregation
Hannah wife of Mr John Clay of Northourum died July 9. aged
61. bur. in the Chapel at Northourum July 13
Mr. Wm. Dodge Minr in Sowerby died July 11, bur. in the
Chapel July 14, A useful Preacher & Physician
Mary wife of John Gill of Southouram bur. at Northouram
July 24
Mr James Stansfield of ffieldhouse in Sowerby buried July
Mr Isaac Sharpe of Little Horton died July 26
Richd Witton of Lupset near Wakefield Esqre died Aug. 1,
Lawyer and Justice of Peace
Miss Pemberton of Leverpool died
Grace wife of Mr. Wm. Bentley of Shelf bur. at Coley Aug. 17
Miss —— dr. of the late Mr. Samll. Wareing of Bury in
Lancashire bur. Sep. 9
Miss —— dr. of the sd. Mr Wareing died also, Sept. 11
Sr. George Savil of Rufford in Nottinghamshire died Sept. 16
Joseph Brigg of Norwood Green bur. Sept. 18. 1743
Mr Rudsdale Minr in Gainsbro' bur. his wife Aug.
Mr Cromwel of Gainsbrough bur. Aug.
John Campbel Duke of Argyle &c, died Oct. 4, had been an
Eminent Warriour and Patriot. A great Loss
—— Beaumont of Whitley Hall Esqre died Oct.
Miss Anne Gream of Heath died Oct 18 of 24 hours sickness,
aged near 16

BURIALS.

Dr William Whitaker of Ludgate Hill, London died Nov. 10. very rich

Mr John Hollings Junr. died in Hunslet, bur. from his Fathers at Cottingley Oct. 18

Mr — Fox of Prestwich Parish bur. his wife Nov. 21

Mr. Wm. Ferguson of Halifax bur. his child Nov. 27

The Revd. Mr Thomas Dickenson minister at Northourum, Dyed 26th December 1743 aged 73 abt one in the morning. Nature being far spent, a visible decay appeared abt July or August wch encreased gradually till the time of his death. He preached at Gorton Chappel in Lancashire, ordained May 24, 1694, removed to Northourum in the year 1702, about 42 years at Northourum. He was an Eminent usefull faithfull Minister of Gods word, a meek & humble Xtian, an affectionate & tender Parent, a loving Husband. a sincere Friend & social Neighbour a chearfull companion, very temperate, had an uncommon memory, lived well, & dyed looking for the Mercy of our Lord Jesus Christ unto Eternity

Mr John Wrightson Grocer of Leeds dyed 25 March 1750, buried 28. aged 63 years, rich

Mrs Mary Lee dyed at Winteredge 26th May 1750, bur. at Leeds 28th

Mrs Hanson the wife of Mr Isaac Hanson Grocer in Halifax dyed 11th was buried the 15th May 1750

Mrs Han. Priestley wife of Mr Nathaniel Priestley dyed 6th was buryed 10th March at Halifax 1752

Mrs Sarah Hudson died 20 May 1784

Hannah d. Benj. Dickenson dyed 25th was bur. 26th of October 1751. aged 19 weeks & 1 day

Thomas s. Benj. Dickenson dyed the 9th was bur. the 10th May 1752 aged 7 weeks & 4 days

Joseph Stead died 2d was bur. 4th June 1752 aged 62 years

An d. of Benj. Dickenson dyed at Leeds Aug. 14. 1753, aged 6 years and about 46 weeks

Revd. Mr. Hesketh died 19 Jan. 1774

Tho. Kitson died 28th Decr. 1784 who had liv'd Servt wth. B. Dickenson upwards of 36 years aged abt. 60

John Ramsden died 14 March 1783 aged 65 years

Robt Lumb died 21 May 1785 bur. at Luddenden 25th, aged 71 yrs.

Mrs Ramsden of Hazlehurst died March 9th 1789 an Excellent good Christian & my old acquaintance, aged 95 years

Mrs Hannah Welch wife of Mr Richd Welch, Newgate Street, London, died 11th April 1770, in the 58th year of her age

Mrs Elizabeth Oldfield of London died 20th April 1775, aged 64. Her Husband Wm. Oldfield died 20th April 1766, both buried [Bunhill Fields, crossed out] in the ground of St Lukes Old Street [entered by T. D. Harriott who was present at both Funerals]

Rev. Wm. Pendlebury of Burythorpe died feb 22d. 1776 in the 62d year

Mrs Sarah Dickenson of Wakefield died Apr. 1st 1776. in the 79 year

Richd. Welch of London went to bed well as usuall, the 17th & found dead in his bed next morning 18 May 1786

Thomas Dickenson of Wakefield died 24 Nov. 1757 aged 51 Buried at N.Ouram the 27tb

John Dickenson dyed at Huthersfield June 25th bur. at North-ouram the 28th 1764 aged 51 years

Hannah Higgins dr. of John Dickenson of London, died Sept 13, 1764, aged 26   ,

My Dear Mother Mrs Hannah Dickenson died in London 28th July 1765 abt. 10 in the morning aged 80 bur. in Bunhill Fields, London

Thomas Dickenson Minister at Northouram in Halifax parish and Hannah Foster of Osset were married Oct 24. 1705.

Their Children.	Names.	Born.	
1	Thomas	1706	August 16th
2	Joseph	1707	Octr. 13th
3	Elizabeth	1709	Decr. 28th
4	Hannah	1712	May 5th
5	John	1713	Feb. 11th
6	Richard	1715	Nov. 26th
7	Mary	1717	Apr. 19th
8	Benjamin	1719	March 18th
9	Anne	1721	Apr. 4th
10	Nathaniel	1722	Jan. 17th
11	Richard	1725	Apr. 9th
12	Joshua	1727	Mar. 29th

John Dickenson of Heaton Gate in Lancashire died 25th Dec.

BURIALS.

1775

Margrett wife of Revd Josa Dickenson of Gloucester died the 14 Augt. 1773

Docr. Leigh Vicar of Halifax, LLD. died 6th Dec 1775 aged 82 A moderate candid Christian, served the Parish in that capacity 44 yrs with great respect from all Denominations

The Revd. Thos. Whitaker of Leeds died 4th Augt, 1778, aged 80 years

Doctr Isaac Watts died 25th Novr 1748 aged 75 years. A most heavenly minded man

Mr Nathl. Priestley late of Northouram died at Cross-hills near Halifax the 5th April 1781, in the 82nd year of his age. A worthy good man

Lady Simpson died 14 July 1784, suddenly in a garden at Greenwich

Joshua the son of Revd Josa Dickenson of Gloucester born Mar. 30. 1766, married at Halifax April 24th 1787 to Hannah Greenwood daughter of John Greenwood of Ashinghurst fould near Todmorden

Mrs Houghton died 29 March 1790 at Norwich, aged 72 last June

Wm. Oldfield of London died Apr. 20. 1766

Rev. Wm. Pendlebury died Feb. 22. 1776

Eliz. Oldfield died 20 April 1775

Ann wife of Benj. Dickenson died 2d May 1778 bur. at Northourum the 5th. in the 60th year of her age

Mr Jas. Harriott of London, aged 65, died the 18th day of Octr. 1783, abt 2 in the morning

Ann dr. of Mr. Saml Fenton died the 22d Oct, 1783, abt 8 in the morning

Betsey Welch of London died July 1783

March 2d 1792 died the Revd Titus Knight who had been a Preacher 45 years and esteemed great in all the Churches, in the 74th year of his age

Mrs Mary Rookes of High Fearnley died 30th April 1793, in 77 year of her age

Ellen the wife of Mr. S. Fenton of Leeds died 13 Sepr. 1794. on a visit at Mr Leach's West Riddlesden near Keighley. Buried at Mill Hill, Leeds, aged 70

Abt the middle of August 1794 died Thomas the eldest son of Mr Saml Fenton of Leeds aged 36 and upwards

BURIALS.

25 Dec. 1794 died suddenly Saml Fenton husband to the sd Ellen & Father to sd Thomas

Mrs Hannah Lumb died at Leeds 20th Feby. 1795 in the 79th year of her age

Elizth. the wido of Mr Sanderson near Blackburn died at Mr Leach's at Riddlesden the 27th Feby 1795, aged 78 own couzn. to Mrs Dickenson the former

The Revd John Ralph of Halifax died April 9th 1795, aged 50, had been pastor to the Meeting 28 years

The Revd George Whitfield dyed Sepr. 30. 1770. at Newbury in New England in America, in the 56th year of his age. A great, good Christian, & most Laborious Preacher of the Gospel

Hannah daughter of John Howorth of Cross Flatts in Southouram born 21st Novr 1747. Baptized 7 Decr at Briers Chappell. NB. This acct. extracted from the Register of Halifax

Decr. 10. 1796 died the Rev. Josa Dickenson of Gloucester in the 70th year of his age

Died —— Mr Abram. Balme of Bradford in the 96 year of his age. NB 'Tis sd. so. But I think not quite so old

Mar 2d 1797 died my sister Ann Dickenson of London in the 76 year of her age

April 6, 1797 died Mr. Wm Buck of London, a most humane and benevolent man indeed

Mr Hillhouse of Halifax died Apr. 23, 1797 in the 94 year of *her* [sic] age

January 26th 1796 died Mr. Wm. Pollard of Halifax aged 59 years. Manufacturer

The Revd. Mr. Dawson of Cleck Heaton died Decr. 16, 1795 aged 58 yrs. A most Excellent Christian. NB. See Acct in Magn. for Oct. 1796

The Revd. Mr. Simpson of Wareley died —— aged 75 years & his daughter Hannah died the 28 January 1796

Mr Thos. Leach of West Riddlesden died 4 May 1796

Mr Robt Parker of Callico Hall nr Halifax died 23 May 1793 aged 73 years

Mrs Morris of Halifax died 8 Mar. 1796, aged 61 years

Feb. 16. 1798 died Benj. Dickenson of Ellen Royd near Halifax aged 78 years

Oct. 29. 1801 Mr Geo. Lockwood of Honley was married to Hannah widow of the above mentioned Benj. Dickenson

Aug. 10. 1802 Mr Wm Dickenson of Ellen Royde near Halifax died, aged 54 years, bur. at Northowram Chaple

July 25. 1824 died in Bristol, Mrs Ellen Dickenson, widow of the above Wm. Dickenson aged 64. Buried at the Baptist burying ground in that City.

Finis.

INDEX OF SURNAMES.

Rogers, 114
Rontree, 210, 282
Rook, 280
Rookby, 98, 114, 156
Rooks* 45, 46, 47, 63. 69, 71, 73,
 82, 114, 171, 173, 174, 176, 178,
 180, 183, 187, 206, 213, 214,
 229, 231, 253, 261, 281, 282, 290,
 292, 309, 314 bis, 323, 337
Root, 71 bis, 76, 114
Roper, 26, 301
Rosbottom, 197
Rose, 74, 128 bis
Rossendale, 50, 68, 73, 84 bis, 201,
 202
Rossinton, 293
Rothera, 51
Rothwell, 308
Rotheram, 173, 174, 176, 209, 220,
 224, 276, 279, 281, 285, 286 bis,
 300, 316
Roubottom, 202
Roust, Rouse, 182, 183, 185, 187,
 219, 223, 229, 274, 296, 316, 322
Royds, *see Roades*, 265
Royston, 220
Rudd, 152
Rudiord, 81
Rudman, 52, 254
Rudsdale, 334
Runfit, 158
Rupert, P., 67
Rusby, 95, 165, 167, 170
Rushem, Russam, 120 bis, 131
Rushworth, 22, 24, 25, 26 bis, 27,
 31, 35, 43, 46 bis, 52 bis, 53, 63,
 79, 80, 89, 187, 225, 240
Russel, 73, 135, 255, 320
Rycroft, 73
Rylands, 95, 99
Ryley, 83, 86, 168, 186, 220, 231,
 267, 275, 294, 318
Ryther, 128, 163, (? Rider)
Sacheverel, 291
Sadler, 123
Sagar, Sager, 47, 76, 92, 96, 107,
 154, 165, 167, 251, 255, 315, 322
Sailes, 160
Sale, Sayle, 33, 35, 59, 62, 92, 103,
 114 bis, 128, 151

Saltonstall, 17, 61
Samples, 212
Sampson, 102, 129, 139
Sanderson, 57, 138, 139, 143, 147,
 338
Sandiford, 65, 214, 220, 224
Sandal, 75, 135, 144
Saptón, 161
Sargeant, 261
Sargisson, 229
Sarvant, 129, 139
Saunderson, 325
Savage, 128
Savil, 53, 65, 78, 103, 260, 290,
 334
Sawer, 135, 162
Saxe Gotha, 228
Saxton, 131, 139
Scafe, 135
Scalbert, 69
Scarbro', 46, 47, 48, 53, 62
Scarrow, 119, 125
Scholefield. 19, 33, 34, 35 bis, 38,
 39, 49, 150, 164, 166, 168, 171
 bis, 173 bis, 186, 188 bis, 189,
 190, 191 bis, 192 pass, 193 bis,
 194, 195, 196, 201, 207, 210, 213,
 214, 216, 221, 223, 227 bis, 228
 bis, 229 bis, 230 bis, 235, 238,
 241, 245, 246, 265, 274, 275, 276
 bis, 285, 301, 313, 328, 333, 334
Scholes, 292
Scholey, 121, 202, 245, 281, 283,
 288, 289
Schorey, 138
Schrevelius, 243
Scoffen, 312
Scolcroft, 55, 65½
Scott, 17, 19, 22, 36 bis, 37, 40,
 43, 48, 49, 82, 94, 99, 100, 106,
 133 bis, 140, 146, 153, 158, 160,
 165, 166, 167, 171, 176, 180, 185,
 186½bis, 187, 188 bis, 190, 191,
 193, 198 pass, 201, 205, 208, 212,
 218, 219, 221, 223 bis, 226, 228,
 229, 240, 245, 249, 250, 253, 256
 bis, 261 bis, 276, 277. 278 bis,
 295, 298, 301, 303, 306, 309,
 311, 317, 327, 332, 334
Sedall, 139 pass

* I have an Article on this family from 1300 to 1600, in *Bradford Antiquary*, Part I.

INDEX LOCURUM.

For Places in CAPITALS refer to the accompanying Map.

CORRECTIONS.

Page.

18—April, add 1645.

23—1526, read 1652.

32—Five baptisms omitted, added on page 108. The baptisms for six pages after p. 32, are copied from Mr. Heywood's Vellum Book, probably by Mr. Dickenson.

33—Insert [1684] before April 1.

42—panu, read *per annum.*

62—Mr. Robert Ferrand's *second* wife is not given in the Ferrand pedigrees.

64—After last line, add ' suddenly, July 21, 1696.'

65—The latter-half of the entries on this page are evidently for 1680, continued from p. 63,—1679. The rest on pages 63-4-5 are after-insertions, and of dates stated from the *Vellum Book.*

74—Read Tobie ff., del *mm.*

76—Lager, read Sager.

76—Galkroger. This gentleman, curate of Haworth, is omitted in my list in *Haworth Past and Present*, and in Mr. James' *Bradford.* The Rev. C. B. Norcliffe, M.A., York, had kindly supplied the omission before I met with it in Heywood's Register. He probably succeeded Mr. Moore in 1684 (p. 107); he appears as curate in 1699 and 1701.

78—Henley, read *Honley.* So given in the "Vellum Book."

80—From this page the burials profess to be numbered, but there are numerous errors, besides the gross one it commences with, 1670. On page 86 is a sudden drop of 600.

101—Wm. Garth's wife Ann. So given in Calverley Register.

108—Murgatroyd, 170 [5] ?

110—115—Mr. Marsh's list contains several errors. For Coope read *Core.* Ford read *Todd,* Hull read *Hall,* Jaile read *Sale,* Leighton read *Laughton en le Morthen.*

117—Ind. is an abbreviation for indicted.

120—Mr. Norcliffe recognises in *Michael Gawbutt* of Snaith,
Mr. Tawbutt or Talbot, whose inventory he has printed;
see *History of Snaith.*
148—Edward Jackson's *house.*
268—Thorp of Horton, read *Hopton.*
276—Confined, read *conformed.*
325—Horton Chapel (?) *Hopton.*

Names in the "Introduction" and "Corrections."

Abram	Eure	London	Sale
Aked	Fawcett	Lister	Scales
Asquith	Ferrand	Margerison	Scruton
Bartle	Galkroger	Marsh	Sewell
Barber	Garth	Milner	Simpson
Baxter	Glasgow	Mitchell	Slate
Bentley	Hall	Moore	Smith
Bingley	Halley	Murgatroyd	Speight
Bland	Hanson	Newth	Spencer
Bolton, Lanc.	Haworth	Nichol	Swaine
Bradford	Hesketh	Norcliffe	Tawbutt
Brigge	Heywood	Pearson	Tetlaw
Burkhead	Hipperholm	Pendlebury	Thorp
Calamy	Hodgson	Pickering	Thomas
Calverley	Honley	Pollard	Todd
Clark	Hopton	Prescott	Topcliffe
Clay	Horton	Priestley	Vint
Coley	Hunter	Ramsden	Walker
Core	Ingham	Robertshaw	Wawn
Dale	Irvin	Roides	Whitaker
Dickenson	Jackson	Rooks	Wilkinson
Drake	Kershaw	Rushworth	Wilson
Earnshaw	Laughton	Ryland	Woodkirk
Eastwood	Lea	Sager	Wright

J. S. JOWETT, PRINTER BRIGHOUSE.

THE

REV. OLIVER HEYWOOD, B.A.,

1630-1702;

His Autobiography, Diaries, Anecdote and Event Books;

Illustrating the General and Family History of
Yorkshire and Lancashire:

(From MS. Volumes in the possession of Isaac Heywood, Esq., S. Roberts, Esq., M.A., F.R.S., and T. Stamford Raffles, Esq., J.P.)

In Three Volumes of over 350 pages each, illustrated,
bound in cloth, Six Shillings each.

One Volume, or the Three, may be ordered.
The Volume embracing 1672 to 1690 is nearly
completed.

————▸✷◂————

A partial idea of their genealogical and historical interest
may be formed from the LIVES of Heywood by Dr. Fawcett,
Rev. R. Slate, and, particularly, Rev. Joseph Hunter, F.S.A.

REV. OLIVER HEYWOOD'S DIARIES, &C.

Please enter my name as Subscriber for [*one*] *three volumes of* **Rev. O. HEYWOOD'S DIARIES,** *&c., at 6s. per volume.*

_____

_____

_____

To J. Horsfall Turner,

Idel, Leeds.

Haworth Past and Present, 20 Illustrations, 8s.

Independency at Brighouse, 4 Illustrations, 8s.

Nonconformity in Idel, and History of Airedale College, 10 Illustrations, 8s.